VOLUME 1

A VOICE IN THE DARK
CREATED BY

LARIME TAYLOR

published by
Top Cow Productions, Inc.
Los Angeles

VOLUME 1

BY

LARIME TAYLOR

FOR THIS EDITION COVER ART BY
LARIME TAYLOR & SYLV TAYLOR

ORIGINAL EDITIONS EDITED BY
DUNCAN EAGLESON & BETSY GONIA

ORIGINAL EDITIONS PRODUCTION ASSISTANCE
AROIHKIN KAY

FOR THIS EDITION BOOK DESIGN AND LAYOUT BY ADDISON DUKE

IMAGE COMICS, INC.
Robert Kirkman – Chief Operating Officer
Erik Larsen – Chief Financial Officer
Todd McFarlane – President
Marc Silvestri – Chief Executive Officer
Jim Valentino – Vice-President

Eric Stephenson – Publisher
Ron Richards – Director of Business Development
Jennifer de Guzman – Director of Trade Book Sales
Kat Salazar – Director of PR & Marketing
Jeremy Sullivan – Director of Digital Sales
Emilio Bautista – Sales Assistant
Branwyn Bigglestone – Senior Accounts Manager
Emily Miller – Accounts Manager
Jessica Ambriz – Administrative Assistant
Tyler Shainline – Events Coordinator
David Brothers – Content Manager
Jonathan Chan – Production Manager
Drew Gill – Art Director
Meredith Wallace – Print Manager
Monica Garcia – Senior Production Artist
Jenna Savage – Production Artist
Addison Duke – Production Artist
Tricia Ramos – Production Assistant
IMAGECOMICS.COM

TOP COW PRODUCTIONS, INC.
Marc Silvestri - CEO
Matt Hawkins - President & COO
Elena Salcedo - Operations Manager
Ryan Cady - Editorial Assistant
Vincent Valentine - Production Assistant

To find the comic shop
nearest you, call:
1-888-COMICBOOK

Want more info? Check out:
www.topcow.com
for news & exclusive Top Cow merchandise!

INTRODUCTION

by

Terry Moore

In his later years, Renoir's failing eyesight and arthritic hands threatened to prevent him from doing what he loved most, paint. But artistic talent doesn't live in the eyes or hands, it lives in the mind. Renoir overcame his challenges by working on ever larger canvases and painting with the brush strapped to his forearm. The result? Beautiful, of course. It's Renoir. He would have painted with a brush in his mouth if he had to and it still would have looked like a Renoir.

Larime Taylor has to do that—paint with a brush in his mouth. The result? You're holding it in your hand. And it's stunning.

Unlike Renoir, Taylor doesn't work on a 60 inch canvas. He works on a computer where details are expected and wobbly lines are unforgivingly, accurately reproduced. The irrepressible talent that dwells in Taylor has not only overcome these challenges, it may have turned them into his biggest assets because *A Voice In The Dark* is a story told with a unique, deliberate focus. Like the art, the story is deceptively layered and demands your attention. The characters are presented in relentless close-ups that invade your space and force you to deal with their issues.

The story is Zoey's—the book is her college diary. While the other kids struggle to find themselves and their social roles, Zoey struggles with the ethics of being an 18-year old serial killer. Every minute of Zoey's days are structured around two things: the silence between kills and the psychopathic act of behaving "normal." All of which is made more challenging by the college town and its people who are not exactly normal themselves.

Of course, the irony is that each of us is the voice in the dark of this Orwellian world. We're all Zoey, counting the days between our traumas and trying to behave normal. We all mumble her inner dialogue and wonder who might be listening. We all commit our little murders in one way or another and wonder if it really makes any difference at all.

So the truth of the matter is, Larime Taylor is working on a giant canvas after all. Like Renoir, he's portraying humanity, one person at a time. This book is a compelling story from the mind of a powerful artist. It's *A Voice in The Dark*, and the voice is you.

Terry Moore
Houston, TX

a VOICE in the DARK

"BLOOD MAKES NOISE, PT. 1"

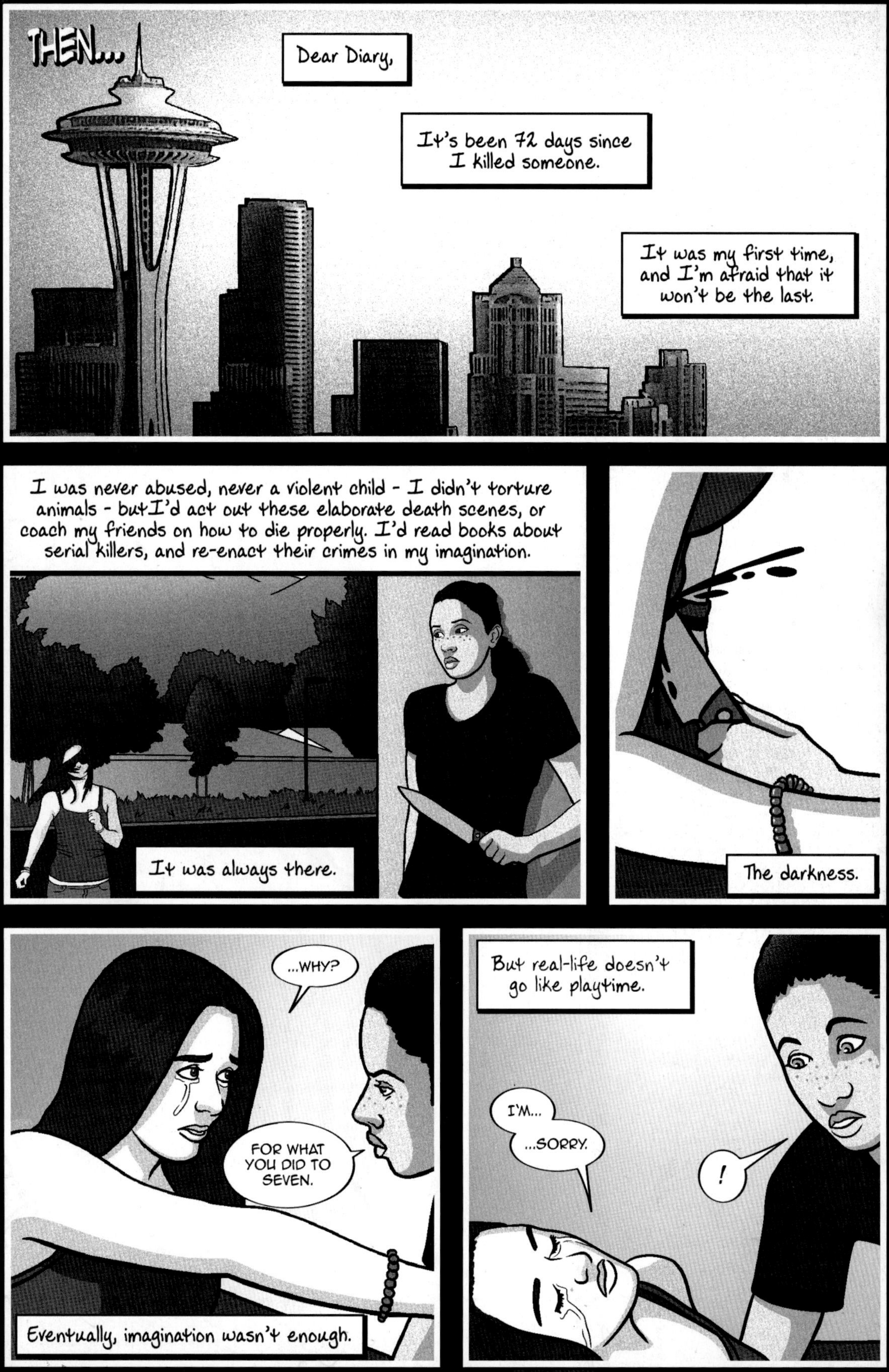
THEN...
Dear Diary,
It's been 72 days since I killed someone.
It was my first time, and I'm afraid that it won't be the last.
I was never abused, never a violent child - I didn't torture animals - but I'd act out these elaborate death scenes, or coach my friends on how to die properly. I'd read books about serial killers, and re-enact their crimes in my imagination.
It was always there.
The darkness.
...WHY?
FOR WHAT YOU DID TO SEVEN.
Eventually, imagination wasn't enough.
But real-life doesn't go like playtime.
I'M...
...SORRY.
!

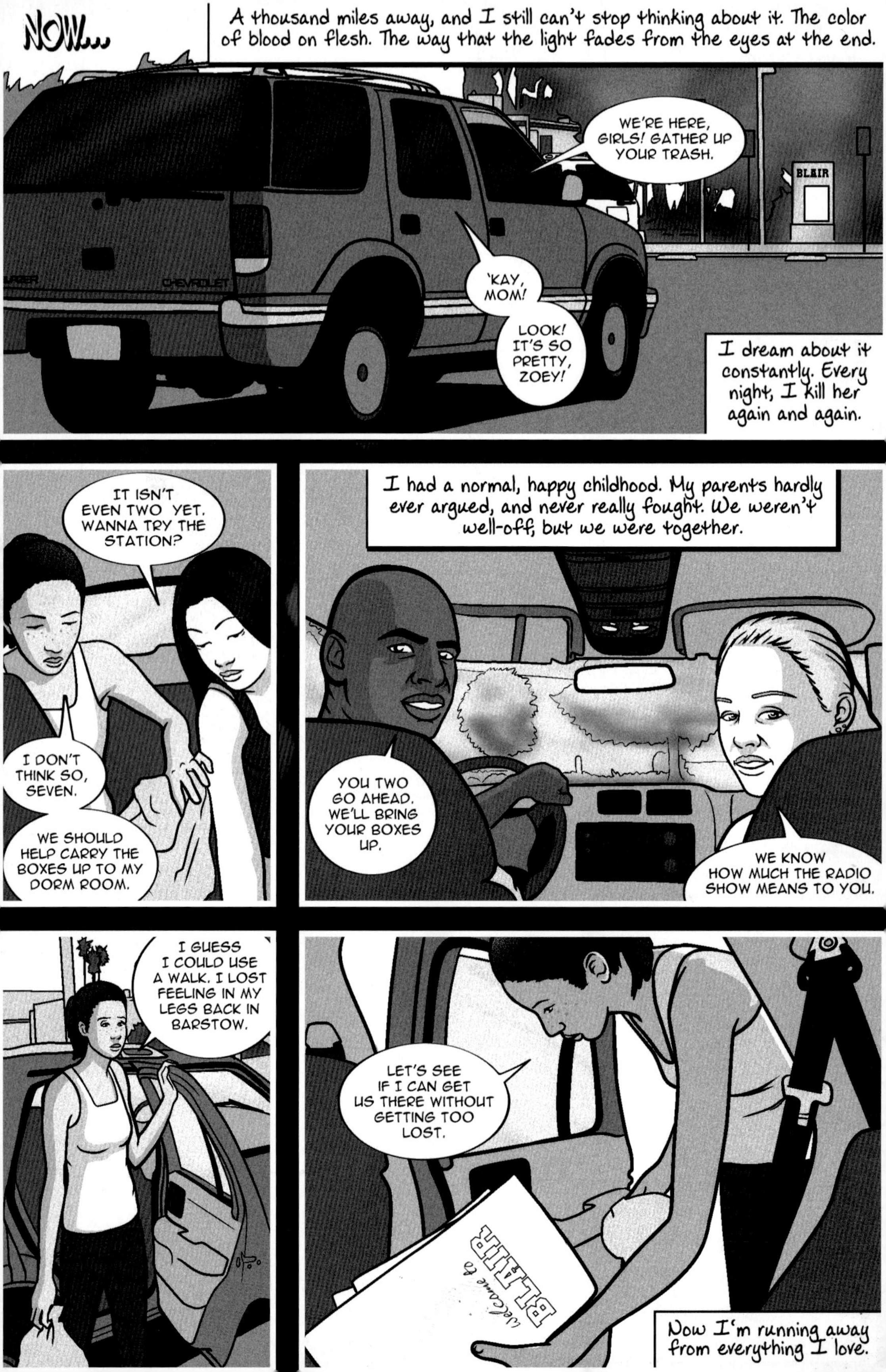
NOW...
A thousand miles away, and I still can't stop thinking about it. The color of blood on flesh. The way that the light fades from the eyes at the end.
WE'RE HERE, GIRLS! GATHER UP YOUR TRASH.
BLAIR
CHEVROLET
'KAY, MOM!
LOOK! IT'S SO PRETTY, ZOEY!
I dream about it constantly. Every night, I kill her again and again.
IT ISN'T EVEN TWO YET. WANNA TRY THE STATION?
I DON'T THINK SO, SEVEN.
WE SHOULD HELP CARRY THE BOXES UP TO MY DORM ROOM.
I had a normal, happy childhood. My parents hardly ever argued, and never really fought. We weren't well-off, but we were together.
YOU TWO GO AHEAD. WE'LL BRING YOUR BOXES UP.
WE KNOW HOW MUCH THE RADIO SHOW MEANS TO YOU.
I GUESS I COULD USE A WALK. I LOST FEELING IN MY LEGS BACK IN BARSTOW.
LET'S SEE IF I CAN GET US THERE WITHOUT GETTING TOO LOST.
Welcome to BLAIR
Now I'm running away from everything I love.

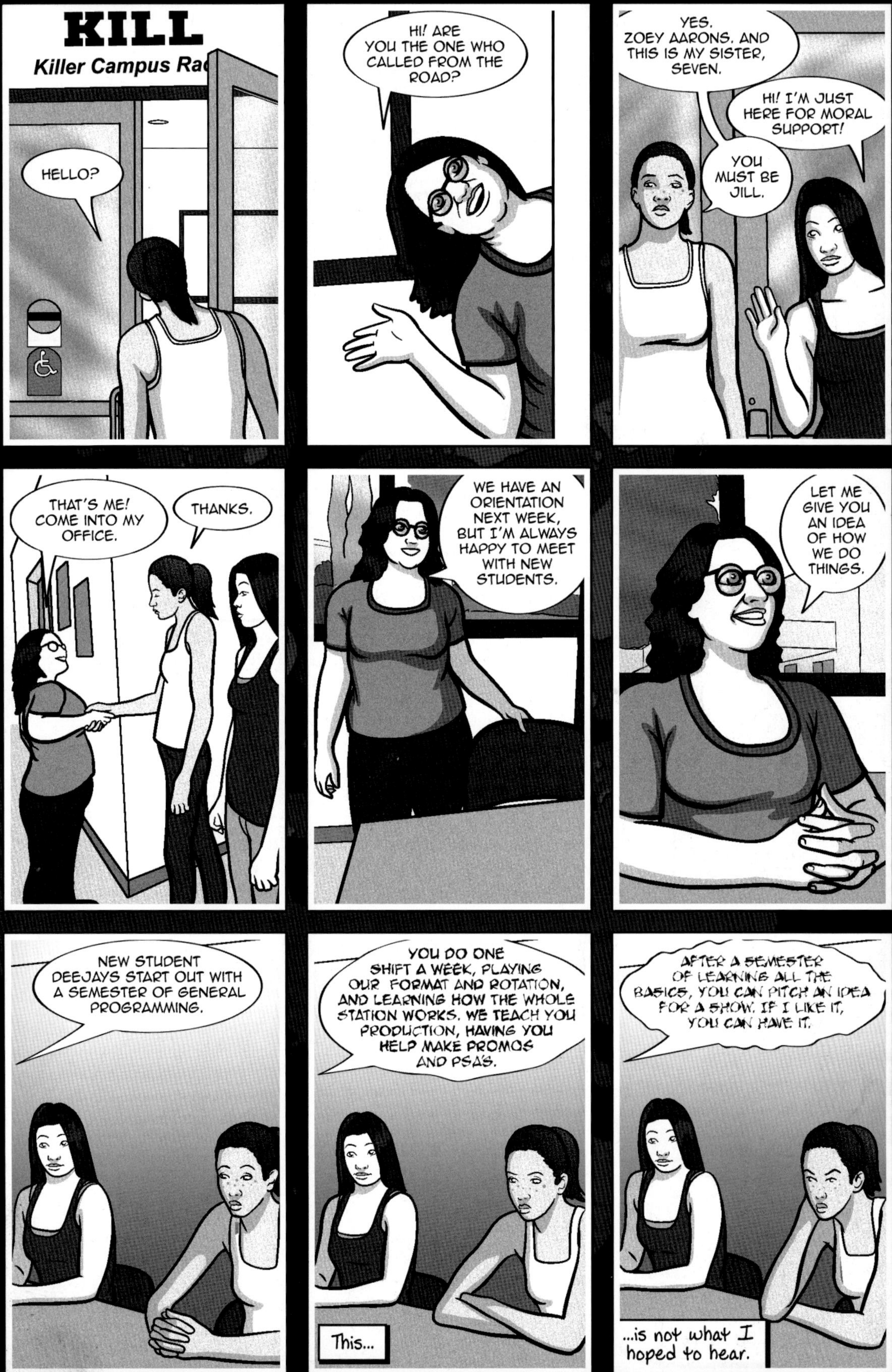
KILL
Killer Campus Ra
HELLO?
HI! ARE YOU THE ONE WHO CALLED FROM THE ROAD?
YES. ZOEY AARONS. AND THIS IS MY SISTER, SEVEN.
HI! I'M JUST HERE FOR MORAL SUPPORT!
YOU MUST BE JILL.
THAT'S ME! COME INTO MY OFFICE.
THANKS.
WE HAVE AN ORIENTATION NEXT WEEK, BUT I'M ALWAYS HAPPY TO MEET WITH NEW STUDENTS.
LET ME GIVE YOU AN IDEA OF HOW WE DO THINGS.
NEW STUDENT DEEJAYS START OUT WITH A SEMESTER OF GENERAL PROGRAMMING.
YOU DO ONE SHIFT A WEEK, PLAYING OUR FORMAT AND ROTATION, AND LEARNING HOW THE WHOLE STATION WORKS. WE TEACH YOU PRODUCTION, HAVING YOU HELP MAKE PROMOS AND PSA'S.
This...
AFTER A SEMESTER OF LEARNING ALL THE BASICS, YOU CAN PITCH AN IDEA FOR A SHOW. IF I LIKE IT, YOU CAN HAVE IT.
...is not what I hoped to hear.

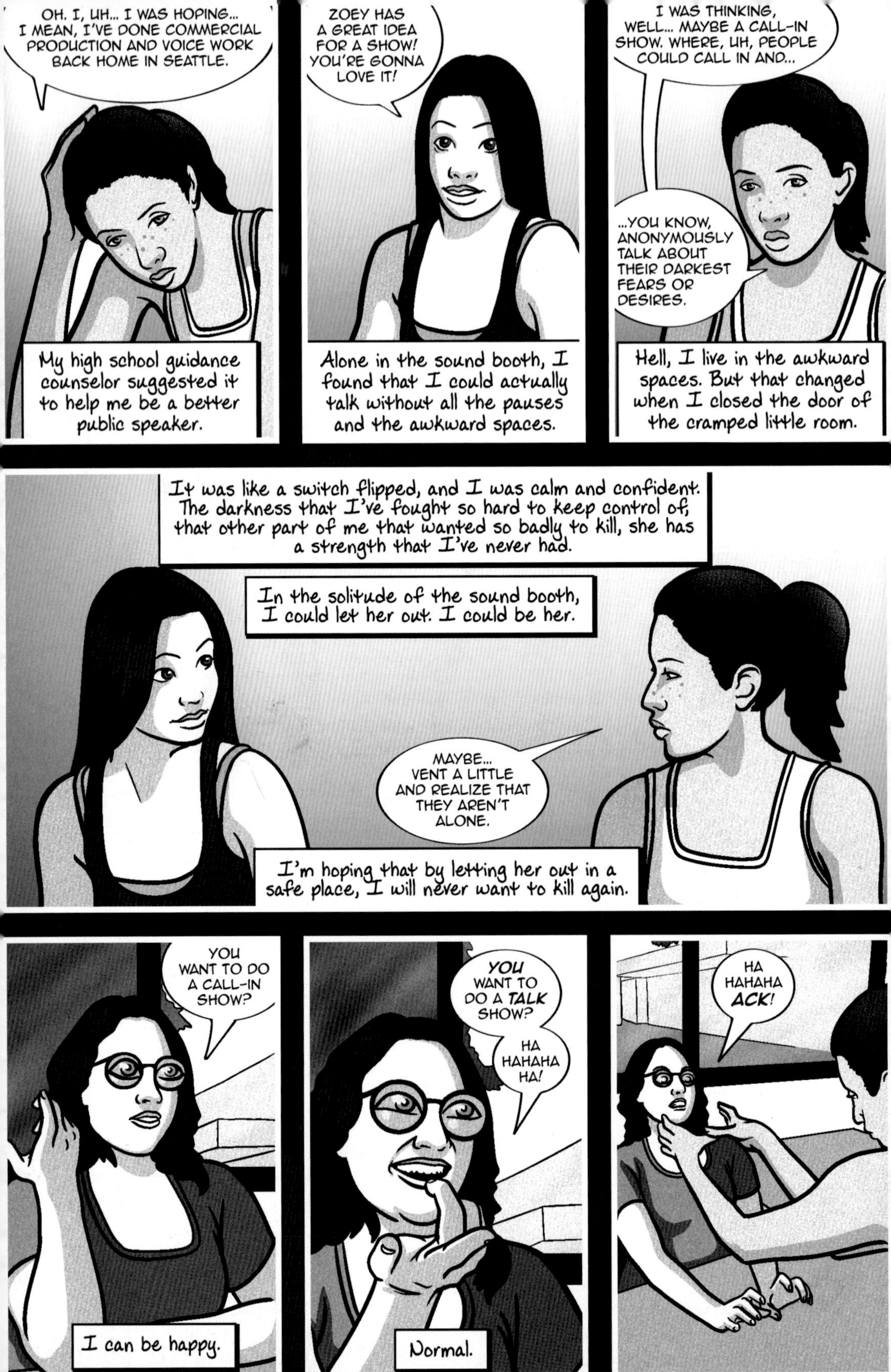
OH. I, UH... I WAS HOPING... I MEAN, I'VE DONE COMMERCIAL PRODUCTION AND VOICE WORK BACK HOME IN SEATTLE.
My high school guidance counselor suggested it to help me be a better public speaker.
ZOEY HAS A GREAT IDEA FOR A SHOW! YOU'RE GONNA LOVE IT!
Alone in the sound booth, I found that I could actually talk without all the pauses and the awkward spaces.
I WAS THINKING, WELL... MAYBE A CALL-IN SHOW. WHERE, UH, PEOPLE COULD CALL IN AND...
...YOU KNOW, ANONYMOUSLY TALK ABOUT THEIR DARKEST FEARS OR DESIRES.
Hell, I live in the awkward spaces. But that changed when I closed the door of the cramped little room.
It was like a switch flipped, and I was calm and confident. The darkness that I've fought so hard to keep control of, that other part of me that wanted so badly to kill, she has a strength that I've never had.
In the solitude of the sound booth, I could let her out. I could be her.
MAYBE... VENT A LITTLE AND REALIZE THAT THEY AREN'T ALONE.
I'm hoping that by letting her out in a safe place, I will never want to kill again.
YOU WANT TO DO A CALL-IN SHOW?
I can be happy.
YOU WANT TO DO A TALK SHOW?
HA HAHAHA HA!
Normal.
HA HAHAHA ACK!

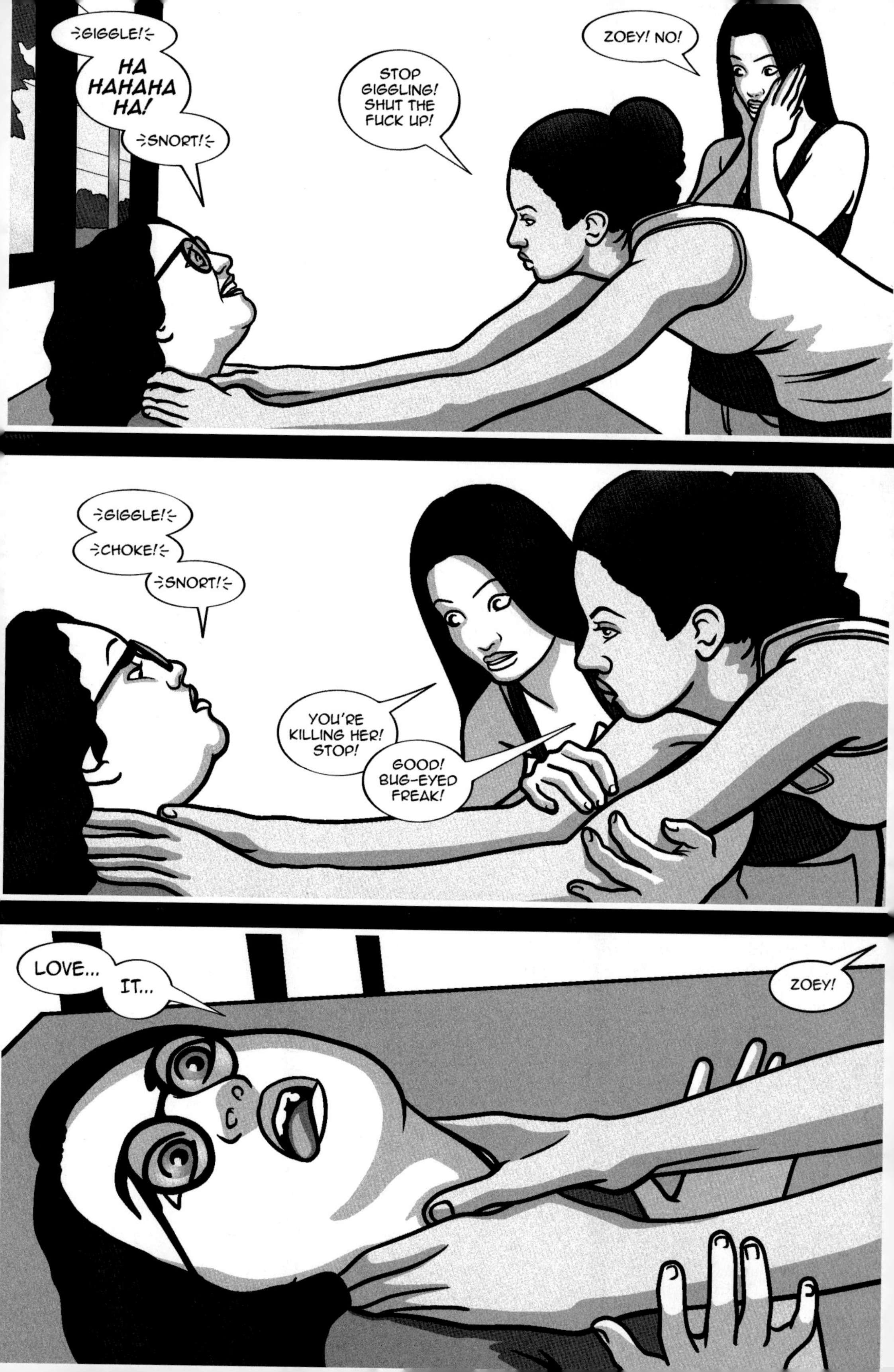
GIGGLE!
HA HAHAHA HA!
SNORT!
STOP GIGGLING! SHUT THE FUCK UP!
ZOEY! NO!
GIGGLE!
CHOKE!
SNORT!
YOU'RE KILLING HER! STOP!
GOOD! BUG-EYED FREAK!
LOVE... IT...
ZOEY!

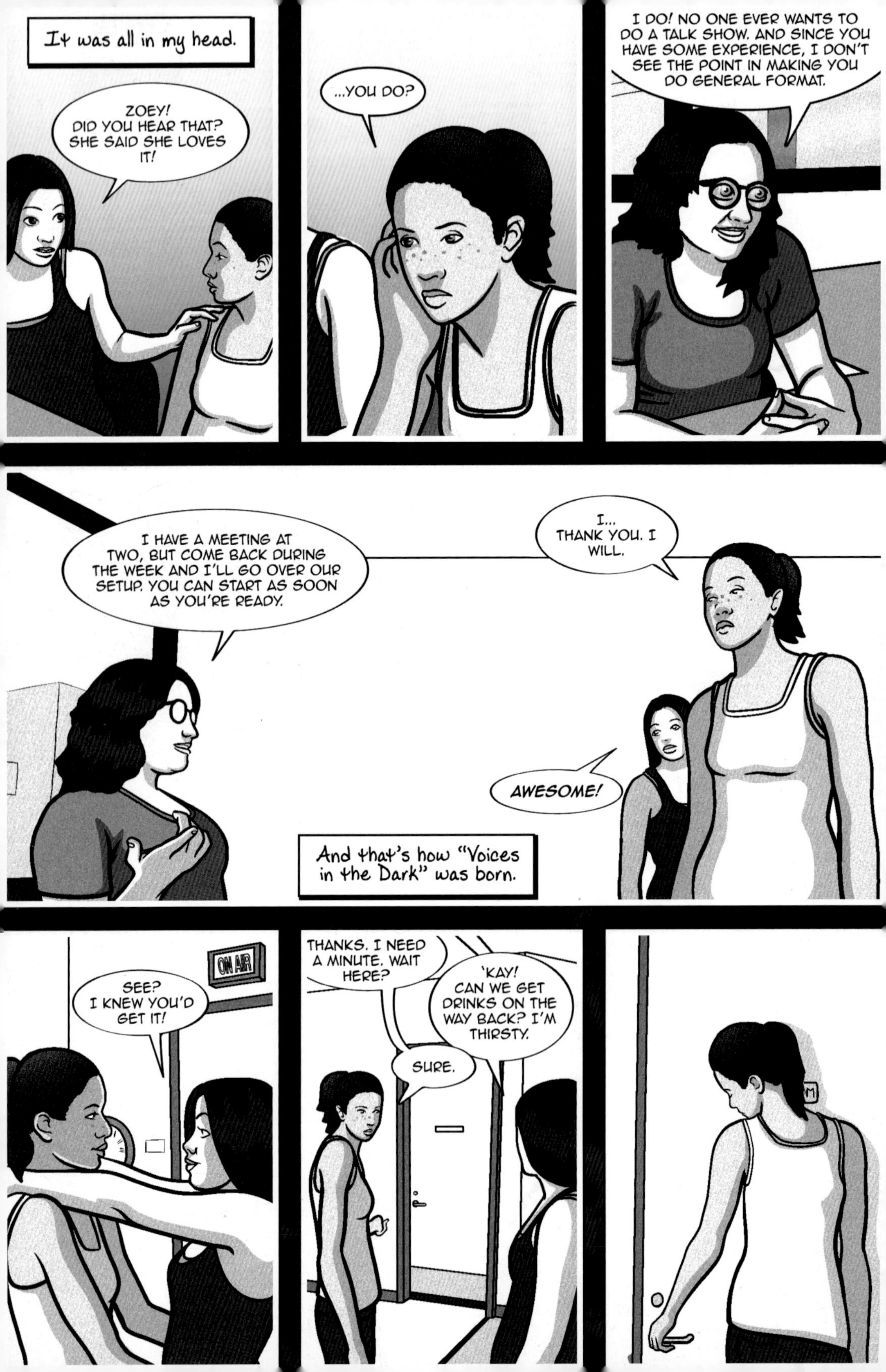

It was all in my head.
ZOEY! DID YOU HEAR THAT? SHE SAID SHE LOVES IT!
...YOU DO?
I DO! NO ONE EVER WANTS TO DO A TALK SHOW. AND SINCE YOU HAVE SOME EXPERIENCE, I DON'T SEE THE POINT IN MAKING YOU DO GENERAL FORMAT.
I HAVE A MEETING AT TWO, BUT COME BACK DURING THE WEEK AND I'LL GO OVER OUR SETUP. YOU CAN START AS SOON AS YOU'RE READY.
I... THANK YOU. I WILL.
AWESOME!
And that's how "Voices in the Dark" was born.
ON AIR
SEE? I KNEW YOU'D GET IT!
THANKS. I NEED A MINUTE. WAIT HERE?
'KAY! CAN WE GET DRINKS ON THE WAY BACK? I'M THIRSTY.
SURE.

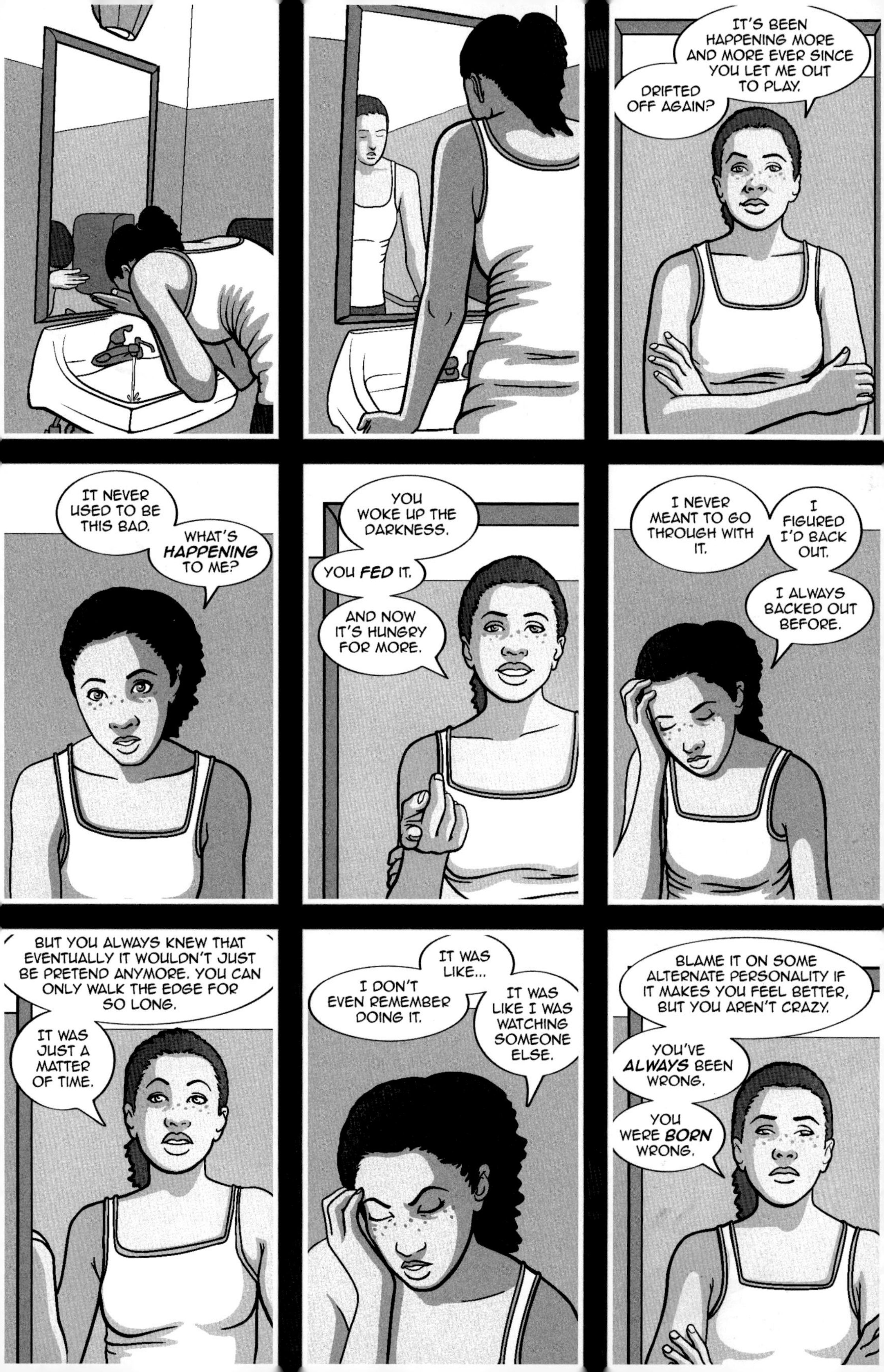
DRIFTED OFF AGAIN?
IT'S BEEN HAPPENING MORE AND MORE EVER SINCE YOU LET ME OUT TO PLAY.
IT NEVER USED TO BE THIS BAD.
WHAT'S HAPPENING TO ME?
YOU WOKE UP THE DARKNESS.
YOU FED IT.
AND NOW IT'S HUNGRY FOR MORE.
I NEVER MEANT TO GO THROUGH WITH IT.
I FIGURED I'D BACK OUT.
I ALWAYS BACKED OUT BEFORE.
BUT YOU ALWAYS KNEW THAT EVENTUALLY IT WOULDN'T JUST BE PRETEND ANYMORE. YOU CAN ONLY WALK THE EDGE FOR SO LONG.
IT WAS JUST A MATTER OF TIME.
I DON'T EVEN REMEMBER DOING IT.
IT WAS LIKE...
IT WAS LIKE I WAS WATCHING SOMEONE ELSE.
BLAME IT ON SOME ALTERNATE PERSONALITY IF IT MAKES YOU FEEL BETTER, BUT YOU AREN'T CRAZY.
YOU'VE ALWAYS BEEN WRONG.
YOU WERE BORN WRONG.

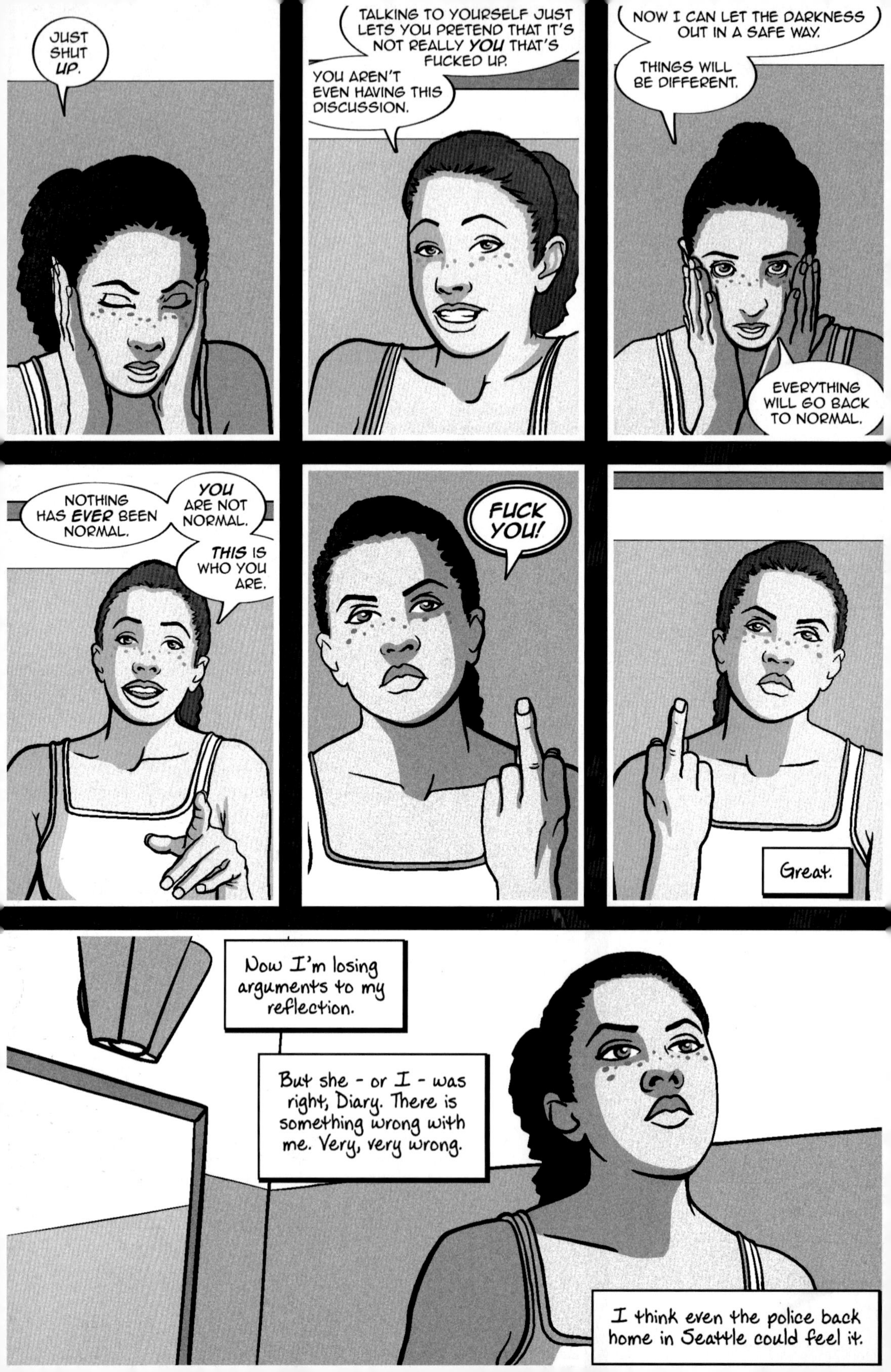

JUST SHUT *UP*.
TALKING TO YOURSELF JUST LETS YOU PRETEND THAT IT'S NOT REALLY *YOU* THAT'S FUCKED UP.
YOU AREN'T EVEN HAVING THIS DISCUSSION.
NOW I CAN LET THE DARKNESS OUT IN A SAFE WAY.
THINGS WILL BE DIFFERENT.
EVERYTHING WILL GO BACK TO NORMAL.
NOTHING HAS *EVER* BEEN NORMAL.
YOU ARE NOT NORMAL.
THIS IS WHO YOU ARE.
FUCK YOU!
Great.
Now I'm losing arguments to my reflection.
But she - or I - was right, Diary. There is something wrong with me. Very, very wrong.
I think even the police back home in Seattle could feel it.

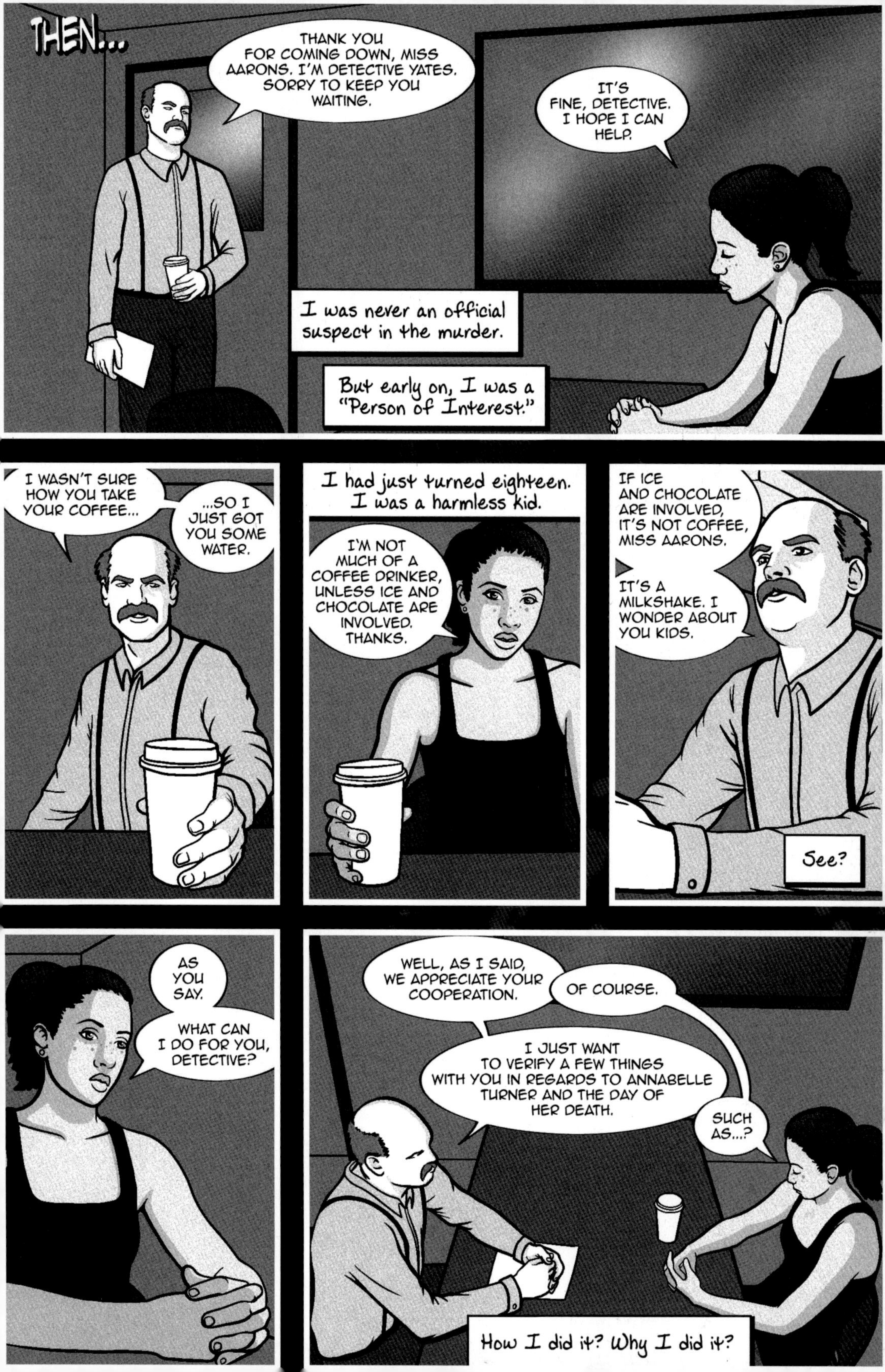
THEN...
THANK YOU FOR COMING DOWN, MISS AARONS. I'M DETECTIVE YATES. SORRY TO KEEP YOU WAITING.
IT'S FINE, DETECTIVE. I HOPE I CAN HELP.
I was never an official suspect in the murder.
But early on, I was a "Person of Interest."
I WASN'T SURE HOW YOU TAKE YOUR COFFEE...
...SO I JUST GOT YOU SOME WATER.
I had just turned eighteen. I was a harmless kid.
I'M NOT MUCH OF A COFFEE DRINKER, UNLESS ICE AND CHOCOLATE ARE INVOLVED. THANKS.
IF ICE AND CHOCOLATE ARE INVOLVED, IT'S NOT COFFEE, MISS AARONS.
IT'S A MILKSHAKE. I WONDER ABOUT YOU KIDS.
See?
AS YOU SAY.
WHAT CAN I DO FOR YOU, DETECTIVE?
WELL, AS I SAID, WE APPRECIATE YOUR COOPERATION.
OF COURSE.
I JUST WANT TO VERIFY A FEW THINGS WITH YOU IN REGARDS TO ANNABELLE TURNER AND THE DAY OF HER DEATH.
SUCH AS...?
How I did it? Why I did it?

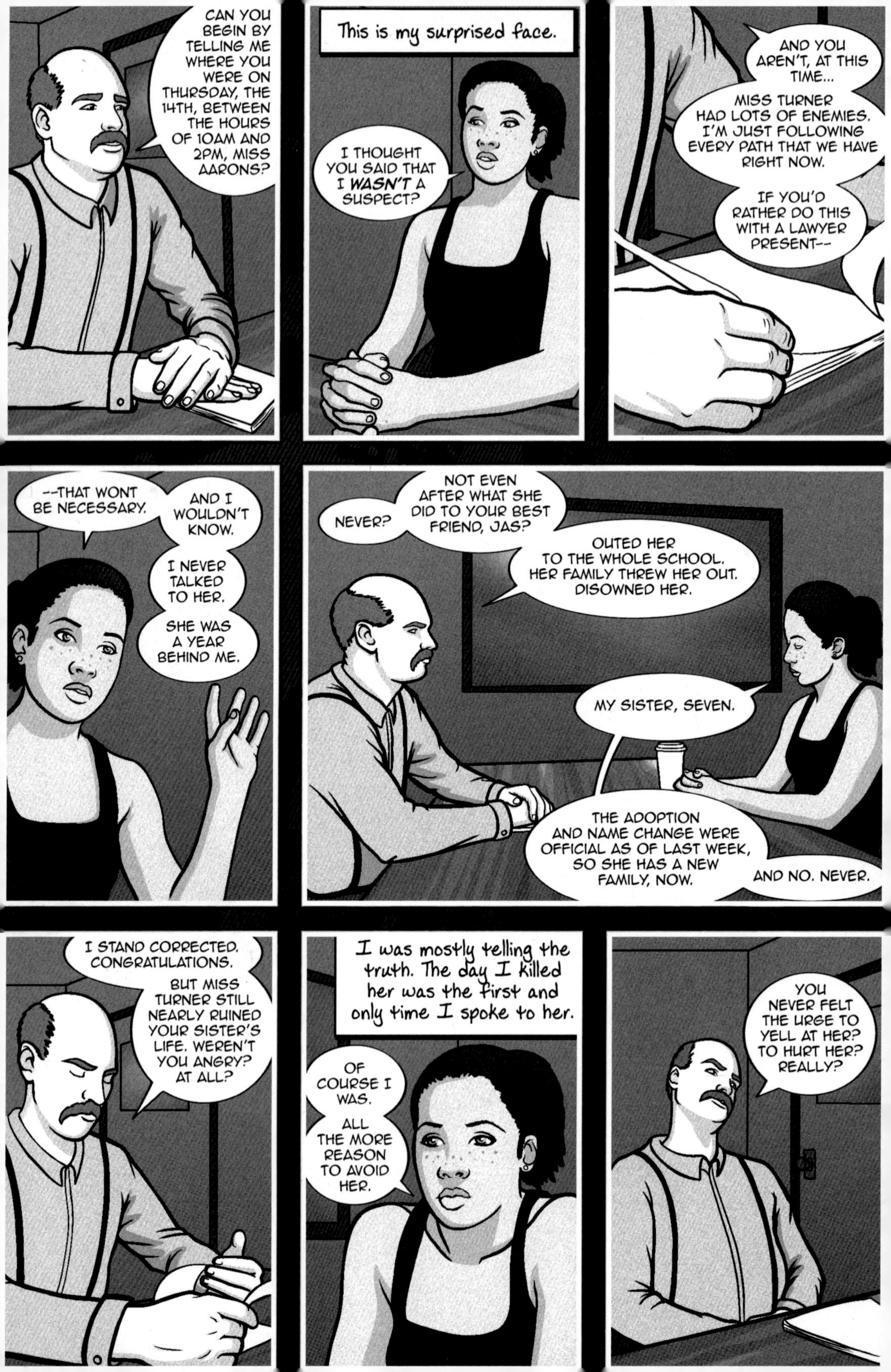
CAN YOU BEGIN BY TELLING ME WHERE YOU WERE ON THURSDAY, THE 14TH, BETWEEN THE HOURS OF 10AM AND 2PM, MISS AARONS?
This is my surprised face.
I THOUGHT YOU SAID THAT I *WASN'T* A SUSPECT?
AND YOU AREN'T, AT THIS TIME...
MISS TURNER HAD LOTS OF ENEMIES. I'M JUST FOLLOWING EVERY PATH THAT WE HAVE RIGHT NOW.
IF YOU'D RATHER DO THIS WITH A LAWYER PRESENT--
--THAT WONT BE NECESSARY.
AND I WOULDN'T KNOW.
I NEVER TALKED TO HER.
SHE WAS A YEAR BEHIND ME.
NEVER?
NOT EVEN AFTER WHAT SHE DID TO YOUR BEST FRIEND, JAS?
OUTED HER TO THE WHOLE SCHOOL. HER FAMILY THREW HER OUT. DISOWNED HER.
MY SISTER, SEVEN.
THE ADOPTION AND NAME CHANGE WERE OFFICIAL AS OF LAST WEEK, SO SHE HAS A NEW FAMILY, NOW.
AND NO. NEVER.
I STAND CORRECTED. CONGRATULATIONS.
BUT MISS TURNER STILL NEARLY RUINED YOUR SISTER'S LIFE. WEREN'T YOU ANGRY? AT ALL?
I was mostly telling the truth. The day I killed her was the first and only time I spoke to her.
OF COURSE I WAS.
ALL THE MORE REASON TO AVOID HER.
YOU NEVER FELT THE URGE TO YELL AT HER? TO HURT HER? REALLY?

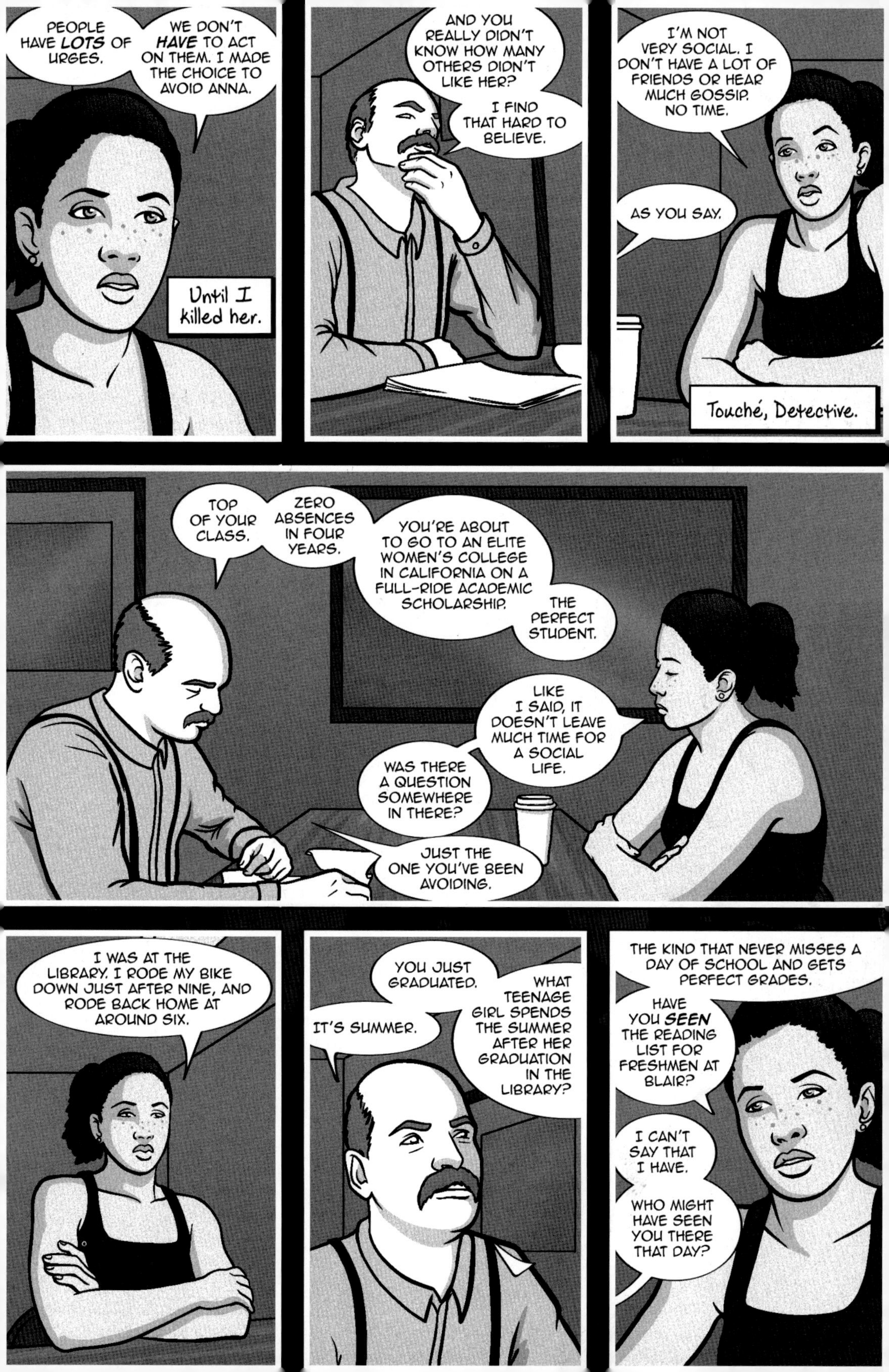
PEOPLE HAVE LOTS OF URGES.
WE DON'T HAVE TO ACT ON THEM. I MADE THE CHOICE TO AVOID ANNA.
Until I killed her.
AND YOU REALLY DIDN'T KNOW HOW MANY OTHERS DIDN'T LIKE HER?
I FIND THAT HARD TO BELIEVE.
I'M NOT VERY SOCIAL. I DON'T HAVE A LOT OF FRIENDS OR HEAR MUCH GOSSIP. NO TIME.
AS YOU SAY.
Touché, Detective.
TOP OF YOUR CLASS.
ZERO ABSENCES IN FOUR YEARS.
YOU'RE ABOUT TO GO TO AN ELITE WOMEN'S COLLEGE IN CALIFORNIA ON A FULL-RIDE ACADEMIC SCHOLARSHIP.
THE PERFECT STUDENT.
LIKE I SAID, IT DOESN'T LEAVE MUCH TIME FOR A SOCIAL LIFE.
WAS THERE A QUESTION SOMEWHERE IN THERE?
JUST THE ONE YOU'VE BEEN AVOIDING.
I WAS AT THE LIBRARY. I RODE MY BIKE DOWN JUST AFTER NINE, AND RODE BACK HOME AT AROUND SIX.
YOU JUST GRADUATED.
IT'S SUMMER.
WHAT TEENAGE GIRL SPENDS THE SUMMER AFTER HER GRADUATION IN THE LIBRARY?
THE KIND THAT NEVER MISSES A DAY OF SCHOOL AND GETS PERFECT GRADES.
HAVE YOU SEEN THE READING LIST FOR FRESHMEN AT BLAIR?
I CAN'T SAY THAT I HAVE.
WHO MIGHT HAVE SEEN YOU THERE THAT DAY?

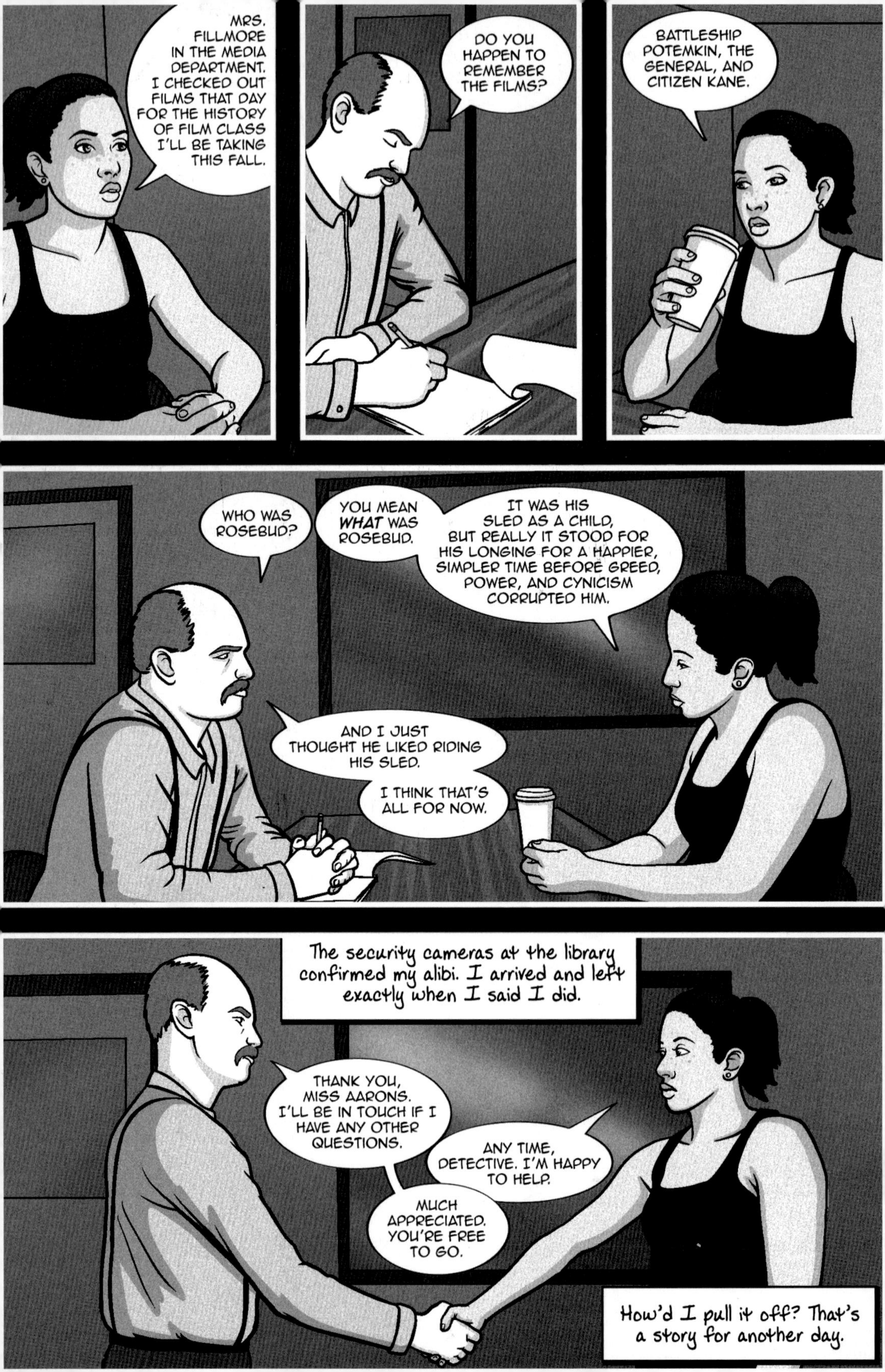
MRS. FILLMORE IN THE MEDIA DEPARTMENT. I CHECKED OUT FILMS THAT DAY FOR THE HISTORY OF FILM CLASS I'LL BE TAKING THIS FALL.
DO YOU HAPPEN TO REMEMBER THE FILMS?
BATTLESHIP POTEMKIN, THE GENERAL, AND CITIZEN KANE.
WHO WAS ROSEBUD?
YOU MEAN *WHAT* WAS ROSEBUD.
IT WAS HIS SLED AS A CHILD, BUT REALLY IT STOOD FOR HIS LONGING FOR A HAPPIER, SIMPLER TIME BEFORE GREED, POWER, AND CYNICISM CORRUPTED HIM.
AND I JUST THOUGHT HE LIKED RIDING HIS SLED.
I THINK THAT'S ALL FOR NOW.
The security cameras at the library confirmed my alibi. I arrived and left exactly when I said I did.
THANK YOU, MISS AARONS. I'LL BE IN TOUCH IF I HAVE ANY OTHER QUESTIONS.
ANY TIME, DETECTIVE. I'M HAPPY TO HELP.
MUCH APPRECIATED. YOU'RE FREE TO GO.
How'd I pull it off? That's a story for another day.

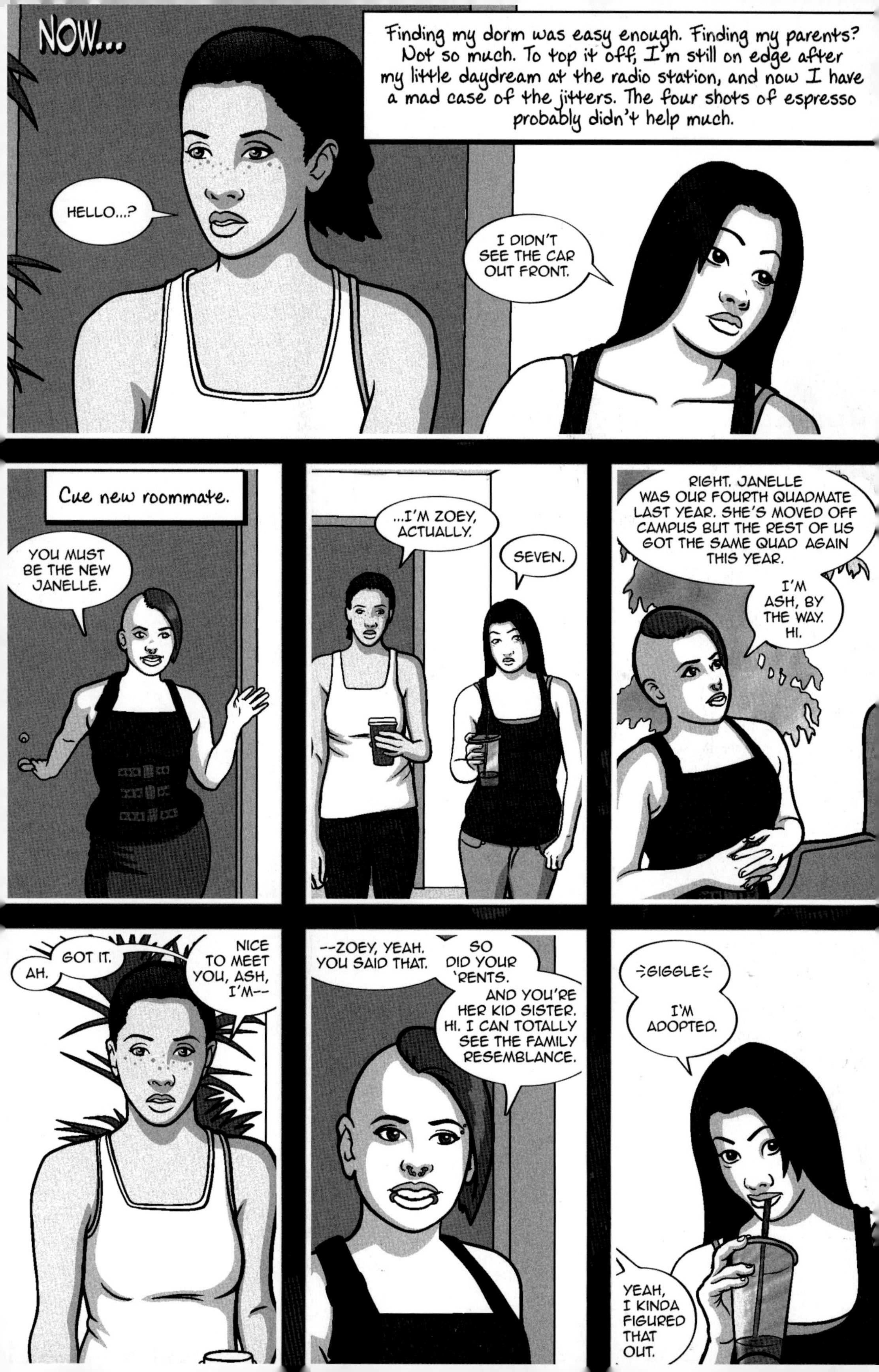
NOW...
Finding my dorm was easy enough. Finding my parents? Not so much. To top it off, I'm still on edge after my little daydream at the radio station, and now I have a mad case of the jitters. The four shots of espresso probably didn't help much.
HELLO...?
I DIDN'T SEE THE CAR OUT FRONT.
Cue new roommate.
YOU MUST BE THE NEW JANELLE.
...I'M ZOEY, ACTUALLY.
SEVEN.
RIGHT. JANELLE WAS OUR FOURTH QUADMATE LAST YEAR. SHE'S MOVED OFF CAMPUS BUT THE REST OF US GOT THE SAME QUAD AGAIN THIS YEAR.
I'M ASH, BY THE WAY. HI.
AH.
GOT IT.
NICE TO MEET YOU, ASH, I'M--
--ZOEY, YEAH. YOU SAID THAT.
SO DID YOUR 'RENTS.
AND YOU'RE HER KID SISTER. HI. I CAN TOTALLY SEE THE FAMILY RESEMBLANCE.
GIGGLE
I'M ADOPTED.
YEAH, I KINDA FIGURED THAT OUT.

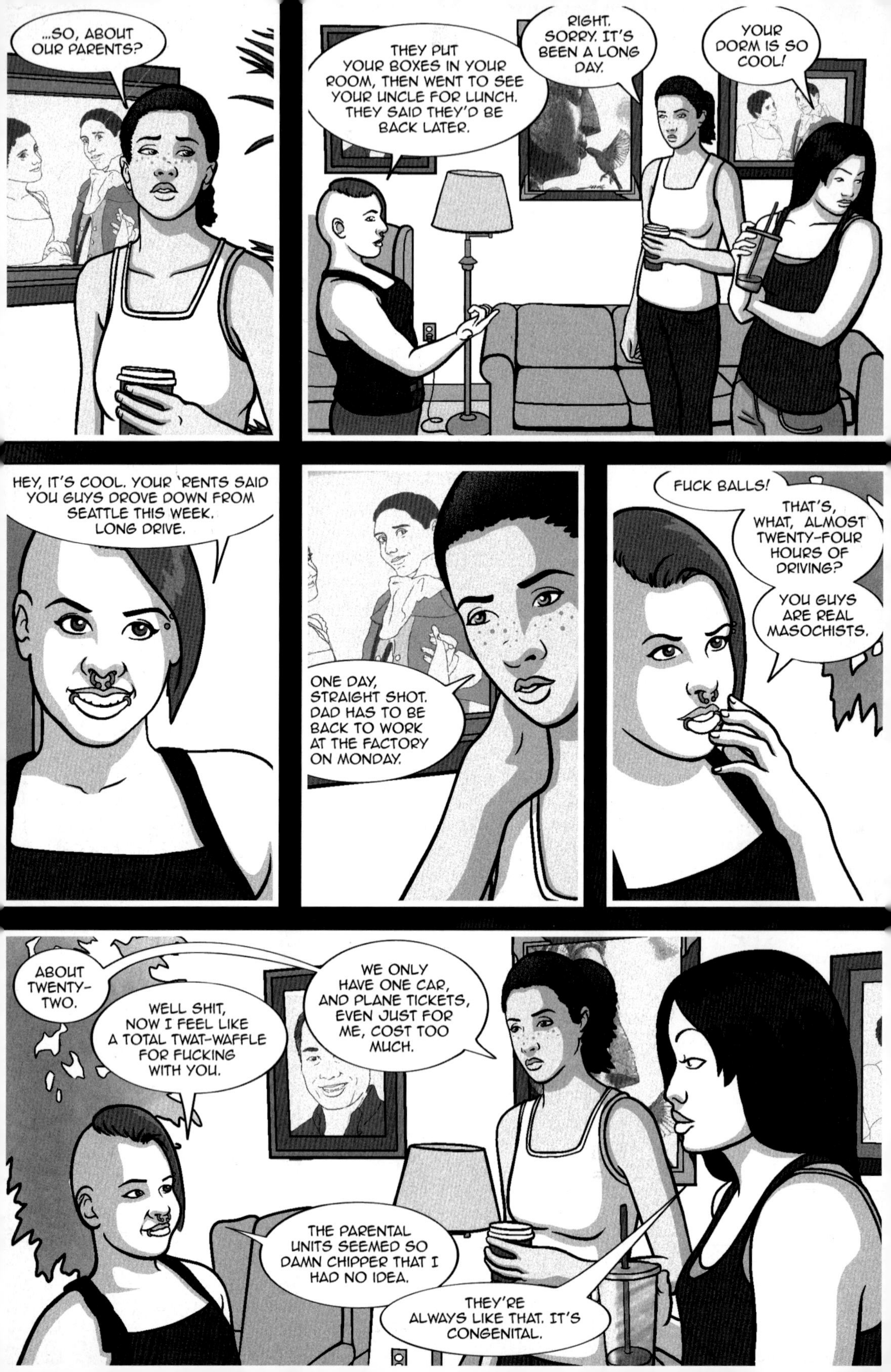
...SO, ABOUT OUR PARENTS?
THEY PUT YOUR BOXES IN YOUR ROOM, THEN WENT TO SEE YOUR UNCLE FOR LUNCH. THEY SAID THEY'D BE BACK LATER.
RIGHT. SORRY. IT'S BEEN A LONG DAY.
YOUR DORM IS SO COOL!
HEY, IT'S COOL. YOUR 'RENTS SAID YOU GUYS DROVE DOWN FROM SEATTLE THIS WEEK. LONG DRIVE.
ONE DAY, STRAIGHT SHOT. DAD HAS TO BE BACK TO WORK AT THE FACTORY ON MONDAY.
FUCK BALLS!
THAT'S, WHAT, ALMOST TWENTY-FOUR HOURS OF DRIVING?
YOU GUYS ARE REAL MASOCHISTS.
ABOUT TWENTY-TWO.
WELL SHIT, NOW I FEEL LIKE A TOTAL TWAT-WAFFLE FOR FUCKING WITH YOU.
WE ONLY HAVE ONE CAR, AND PLANE TICKETS, EVEN JUST FOR ME, COST TOO MUCH.
THE PARENTAL UNITS SEEMED SO DAMN CHIPPER THAT I HAD NO IDEA.
THEY'RE ALWAYS LIKE THAT. IT'S CONGENITAL.

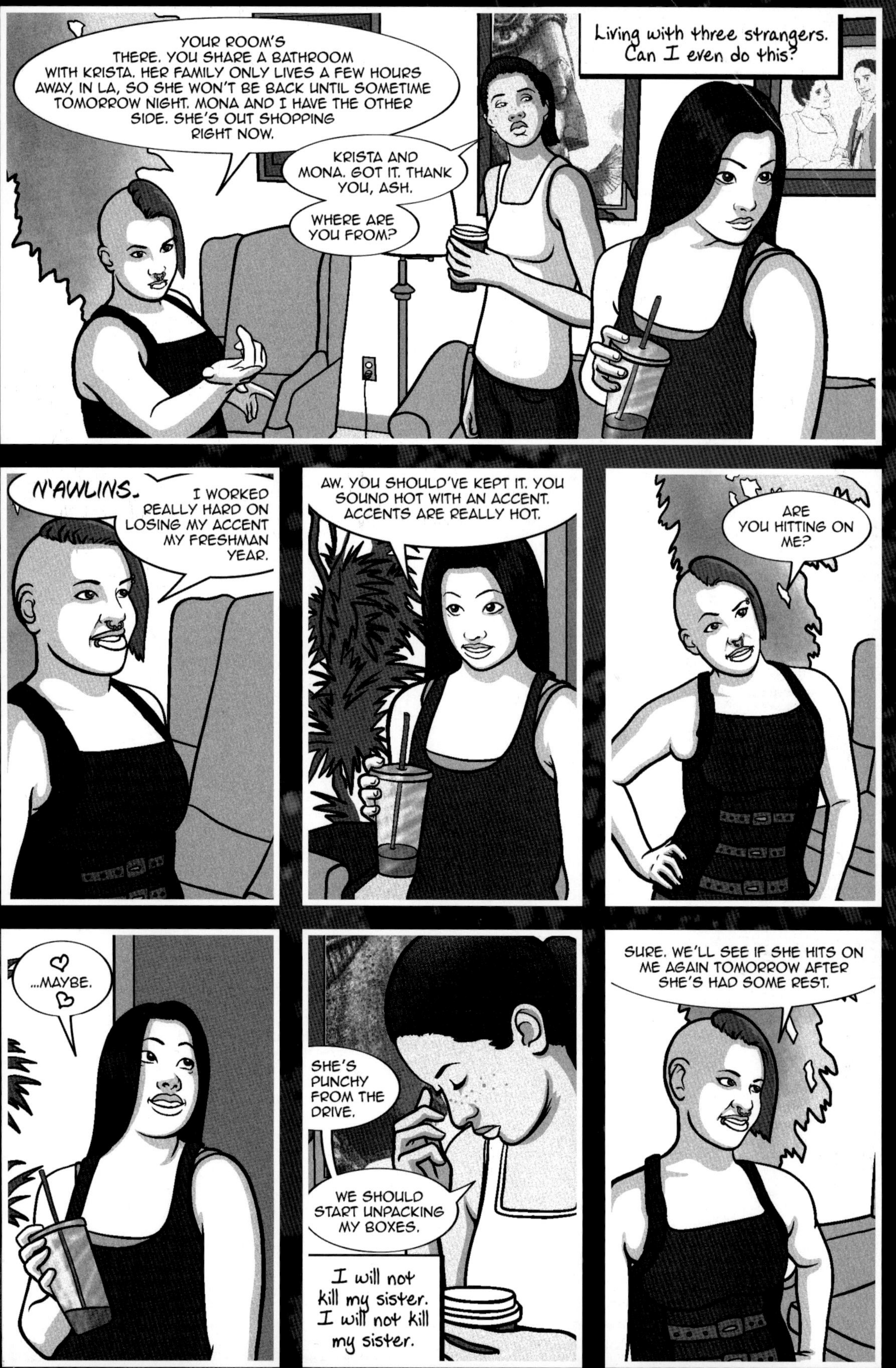

YOUR ROOM'S THERE. YOU SHARE A BATHROOM WITH KRISTA. HER FAMILY ONLY LIVES A FEW HOURS AWAY, IN LA, SO SHE WON'T BE BACK UNTIL SOMETIME TOMORROW NIGHT. MONA AND I HAVE THE OTHER SIDE. SHE'S OUT SHOPPING RIGHT NOW.
Living with three strangers. Can I even do this?
KRISTA AND MONA. GOT IT. THANK YOU, ASH.
WHERE ARE YOU FROM?
N'AWLINS.
I WORKED REALLY HARD ON LOSING MY ACCENT MY FRESHMAN YEAR.
AW. YOU SHOULD'VE KEPT IT. YOU SOUND HOT WITH AN ACCENT. ACCENTS ARE REALLY HOT.
ARE YOU HITTING ON ME?
...MAYBE.
SHE'S PUNCHY FROM THE DRIVE.
WE SHOULD START UNPACKING MY BOXES.
I will not kill my sister. I will not kill my sister.
SURE. WE'LL SEE IF SHE HITS ON ME AGAIN TOMORROW AFTER SHE'S HAD SOME REST.

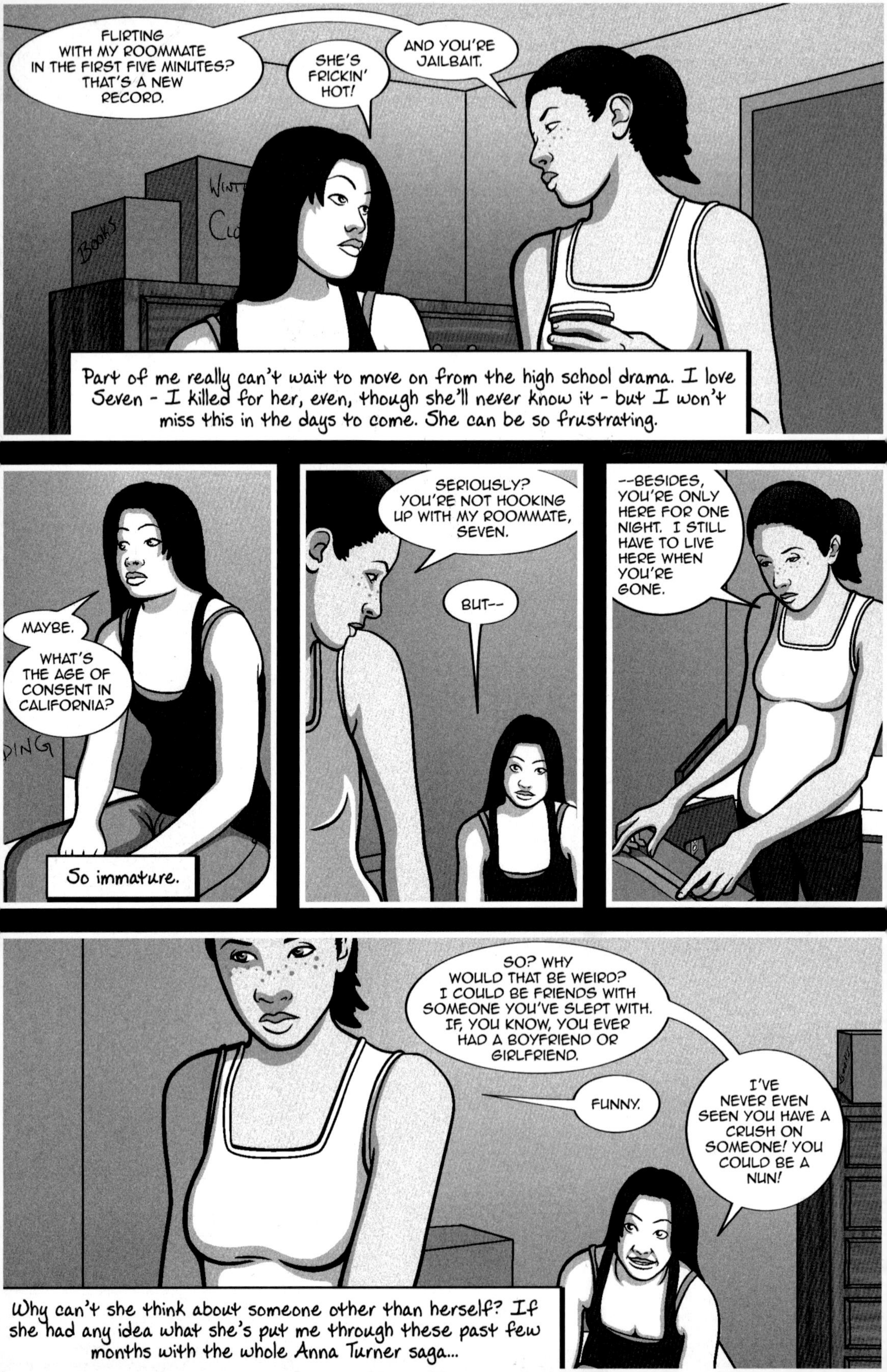
FLIRTING WITH MY ROOMMATE IN THE FIRST FIVE MINUTES? THAT'S A NEW RECORD.
SHE'S FRICKIN' HOT!
AND YOU'RE JAILBAIT.
Part of me really can't wait to move on from the high school drama. I love Seven - I killed for her, even, though she'll never know it - but I won't miss this in the days to come. She can be so frustrating.
MAYBE.
WHAT'S THE AGE OF CONSENT IN CALIFORNIA?
So immature.
SERIOUSLY? YOU'RE NOT HOOKING UP WITH MY ROOMMATE, SEVEN.
BUT--
--BESIDES, YOU'RE ONLY HERE FOR ONE NIGHT. I STILL HAVE TO LIVE HERE WHEN YOU'RE GONE.
SO? WHY WOULD THAT BE WEIRD? I COULD BE FRIENDS WITH SOMEONE YOU'VE SLEPT WITH. IF, YOU KNOW, YOU EVER HAD A BOYFRIEND OR GIRLFRIEND.
FUNNY.
I'VE NEVER EVEN SEEN YOU HAVE A CRUSH ON SOMEONE! YOU COULD BE A NUN!
Why can't she think about someone other than herself? If she had any idea what she's put me through these past few months with the whole Anna Turner saga...

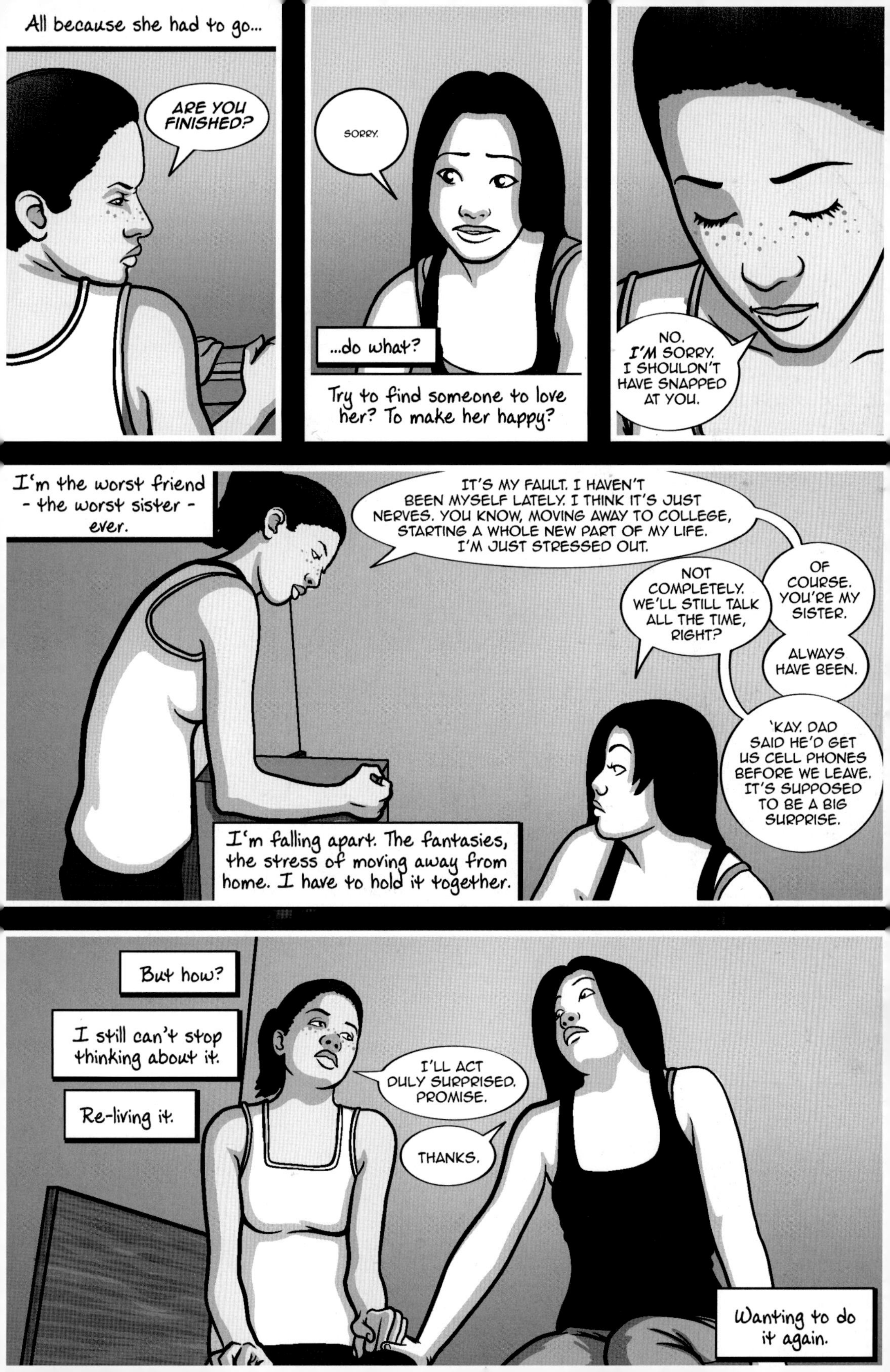
All because she had to go...
ARE YOU FINISHED?
SORRY.
...do what?
Try to find someone to love her? To make her happy?
NO. I'M SORRY. I SHOULDN'T HAVE SNAPPED AT YOU.
I'm the worst friend - the worst sister - ever.
IT'S MY FAULT. I HAVEN'T BEEN MYSELF LATELY. I THINK IT'S JUST NERVES. YOU KNOW, MOVING AWAY TO COLLEGE, STARTING A WHOLE NEW PART OF MY LIFE. I'M JUST STRESSED OUT.
OF COURSE. YOU'RE MY SISTER.
ALWAYS HAVE BEEN.
NOT COMPLETELY. WE'LL STILL TALK ALL THE TIME, RIGHT?
'KAY. DAD SAID HE'D GET US CELL PHONES BEFORE WE LEAVE. IT'S SUPPOSED TO BE A BIG SURPRISE.
I'm falling apart. The fantasies, the stress of moving away from home. I have to hold it together.
But how?
I still can't stop thinking about it.
Re-living it.
I'LL ACT DULY SURPRISED. PROMISE.
THANKS.
Wanting to do it again.

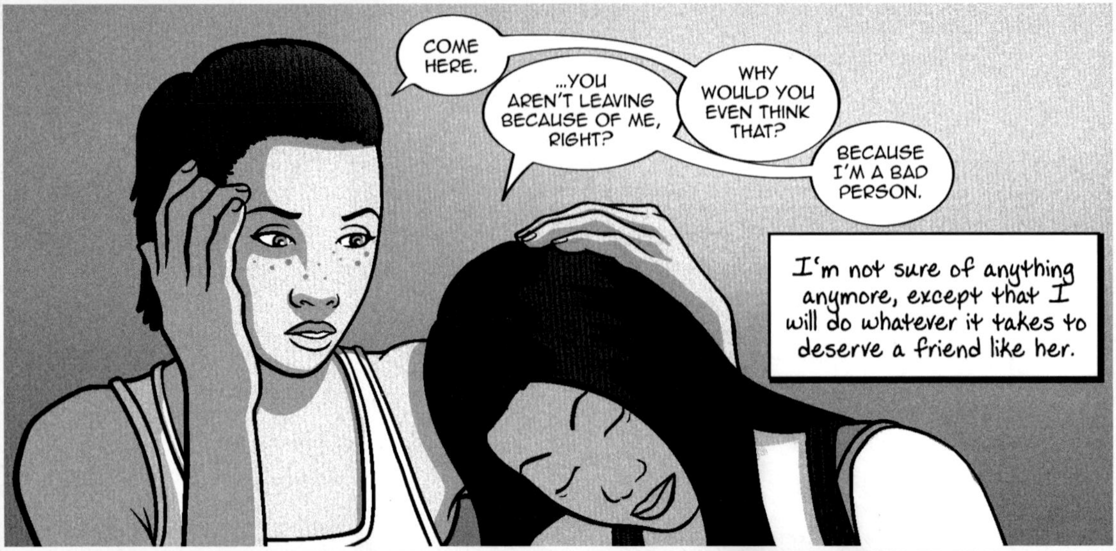
COME HERE.
...YOU AREN'T LEAVING BECAUSE OF ME, RIGHT?
WHY WOULD YOU EVEN THINK THAT?
BECAUSE I'M A BAD PERSON.
I'm not sure of anything anymore, except that I will do whatever it takes to deserve a friend like her.

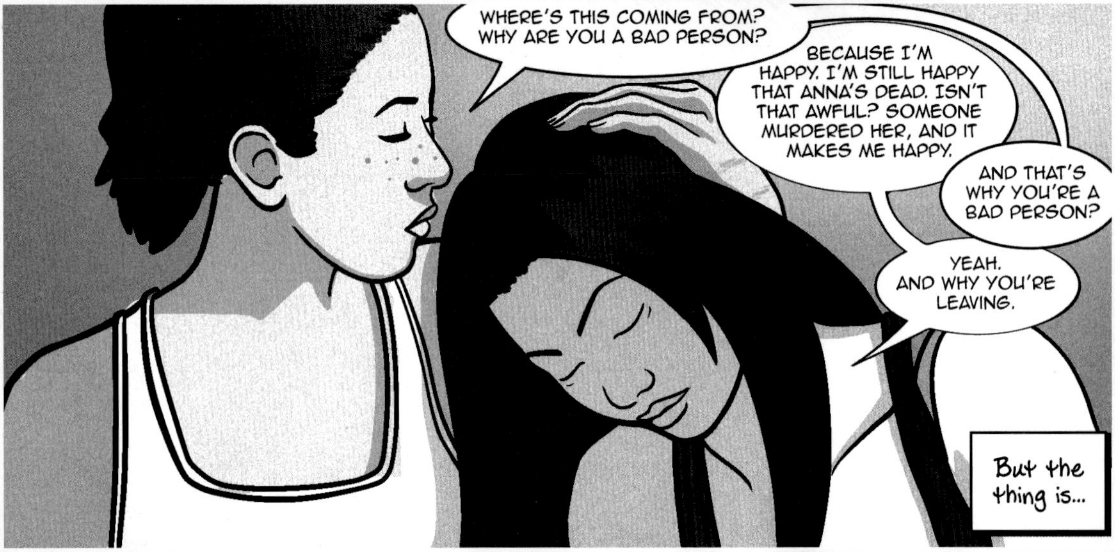
WHERE'S THIS COMING FROM? WHY ARE YOU A BAD PERSON?
BECAUSE I'M HAPPY. I'M STILL HAPPY THAT ANNA'S DEAD. ISN'T THAT AWFUL? SOMEONE MURDERED HER, AND IT MAKES ME HAPPY.
AND THAT'S WHY YOU'RE A BAD PERSON?
YEAH. AND WHY YOU'RE LEAVING.
But the thing is...

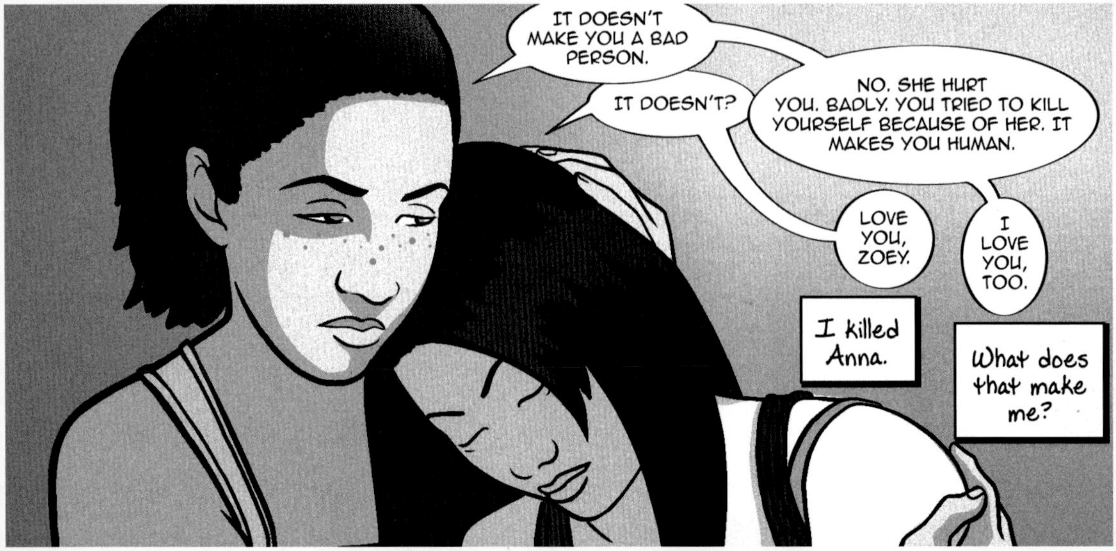
IT DOESN'T MAKE YOU A BAD PERSON.
IT DOESN'T?
NO. SHE HURT YOU. BADLY. YOU TRIED TO KILL YOURSELF BECAUSE OF HER. IT MAKES YOU HUMAN.
LOVE YOU, ZOEY.
I LOVE YOU, TOO.
I killed Anna.
What does that make me?

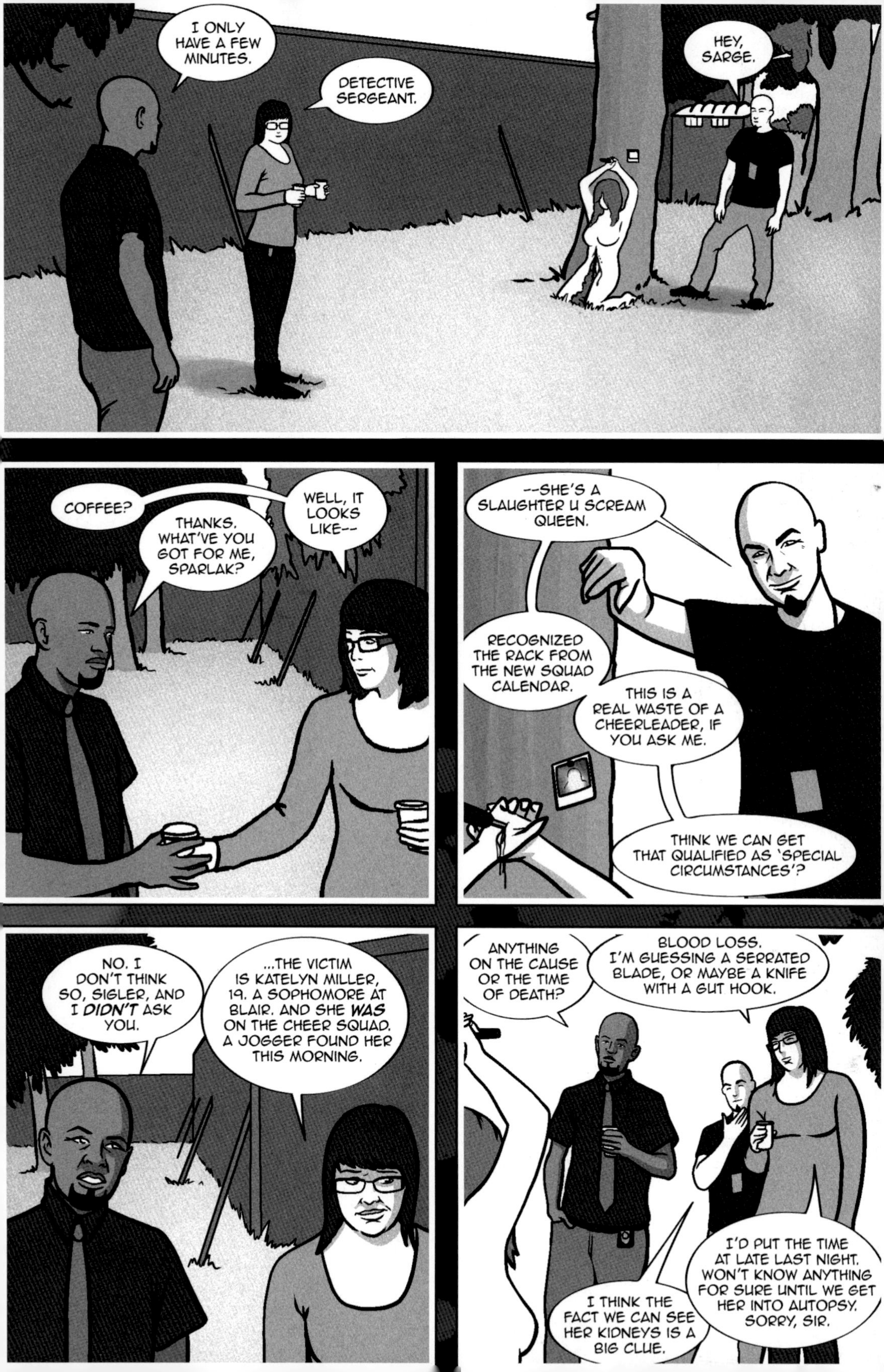
I ONLY HAVE A FEW MINUTES.
DETECTIVE SERGEANT.
HEY, SARGE.
COFFEE?
THANKS. WHAT'VE YOU GOT FOR ME, SPARLAK?
WELL, IT LOOKS LIKE--
--SHE'S A SLAUGHTER U SCREAM QUEEN.
RECOGNIZED THE RACK FROM THE NEW SQUAD CALENDAR.
THIS IS A REAL WASTE OF A CHEERLEADER, IF YOU ASK ME.
THINK WE CAN GET THAT QUALIFIED AS 'SPECIAL CIRCUMSTANCES'?
NO. I DON'T THINK SO, SIGLER, AND I *DIDN'T* ASK YOU.
...THE VICTIM IS KATELYN MILLER, 19. A SOPHOMORE AT BLAIR. AND SHE *WAS* ON THE CHEER SQUAD. A JOGGER FOUND HER THIS MORNING.
ANYTHING ON THE CAUSE OR THE TIME OF DEATH?
BLOOD LOSS. I'M GUESSING A SERRATED BLADE, OR MAYBE A KNIFE WITH A GUT HOOK.
I THINK THE FACT WE CAN SEE HER KIDNEYS IS A BIG CLUE.
I'D PUT THE TIME AT LATE LAST NIGHT. WON'T KNOW ANYTHING FOR SURE UNTIL WE GET HER INTO AUTOPSY. SORRY, SIR.

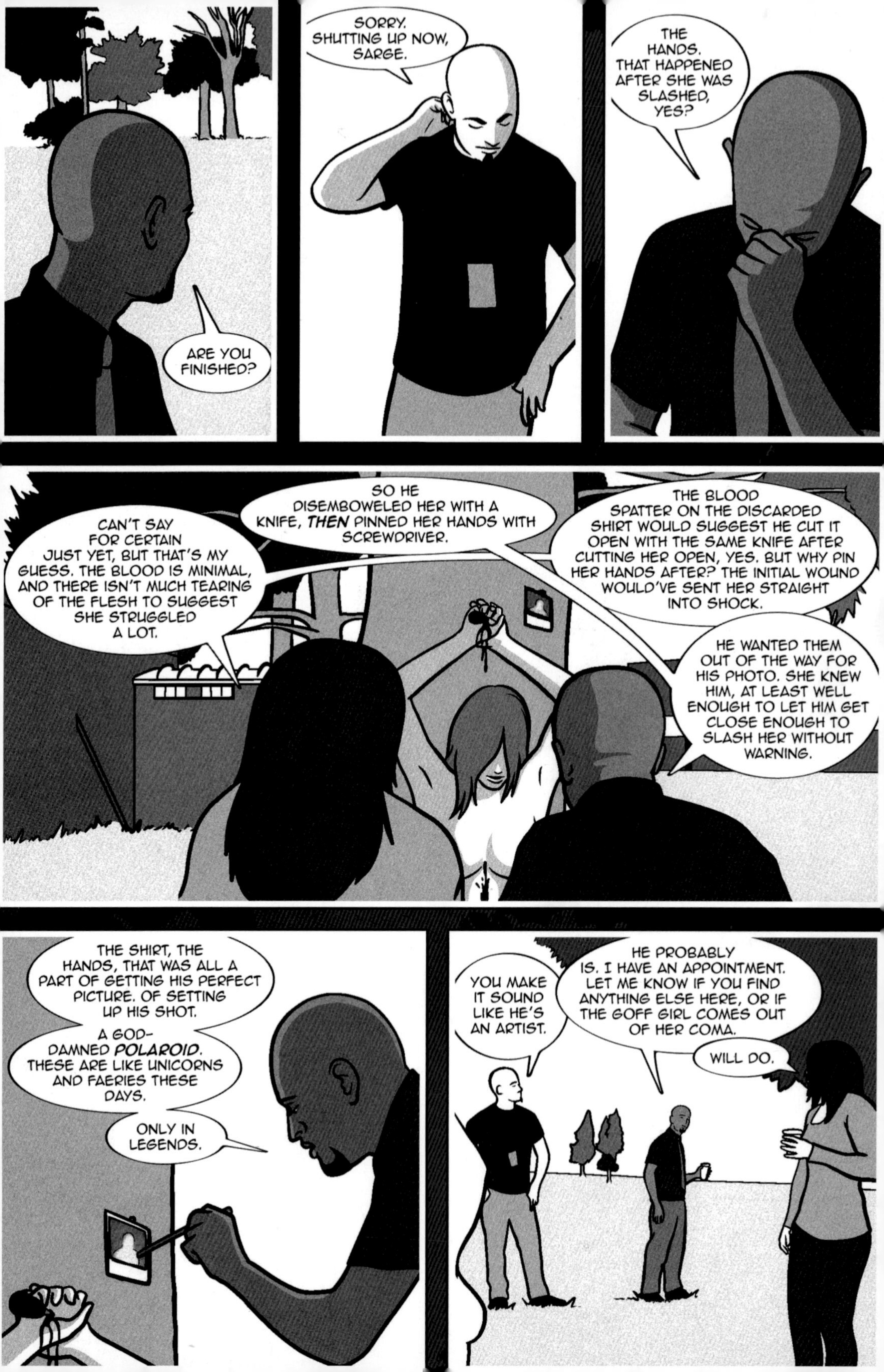
ARE YOU FINISHED?
SORRY. SHUTTING UP NOW, SARGE.
THE HANDS. THAT HAPPENED AFTER SHE WAS SLASHED, YES?
CAN'T SAY FOR CERTAIN JUST YET, BUT THAT'S MY GUESS. THE BLOOD IS MINIMAL, AND THERE ISN'T MUCH TEARING OF THE FLESH TO SUGGEST SHE STRUGGLED A LOT.
SO HE DISEMBOWELED HER WITH A KNIFE, ***THEN*** PINNED HER HANDS WITH SCREWDRIVER.
THE BLOOD SPATTER ON THE DISCARDED SHIRT WOULD SUGGEST HE CUT IT OPEN WITH THE SAME KNIFE AFTER CUTTING HER OPEN, YES. BUT WHY PIN HER HANDS AFTER? THE INITIAL WOUND WOULD'VE SENT HER STRAIGHT INTO SHOCK.
HE WANTED THEM OUT OF THE WAY FOR HIS PHOTO. SHE KNEW HIM, AT LEAST WELL ENOUGH TO LET HIM GET CLOSE ENOUGH TO SLASH HER WITHOUT WARNING.
THE SHIRT, THE HANDS, THAT WAS ALL A PART OF GETTING HIS PERFECT PICTURE. OF SETTING UP HIS SHOT.
A GOD-DAMNED ***POLAROID***. THESE ARE LIKE UNICORNS AND FAERIES THESE DAYS.
ONLY IN LEGENDS.
YOU MAKE IT SOUND LIKE HE'S AN ARTIST.
HE PROBABLY IS. I HAVE AN APPOINTMENT. LET ME KNOW IF YOU FIND ANYTHING ELSE HERE, OR IF THE GOFF GIRL COMES OUT OF HER COMA.
WILL DO.

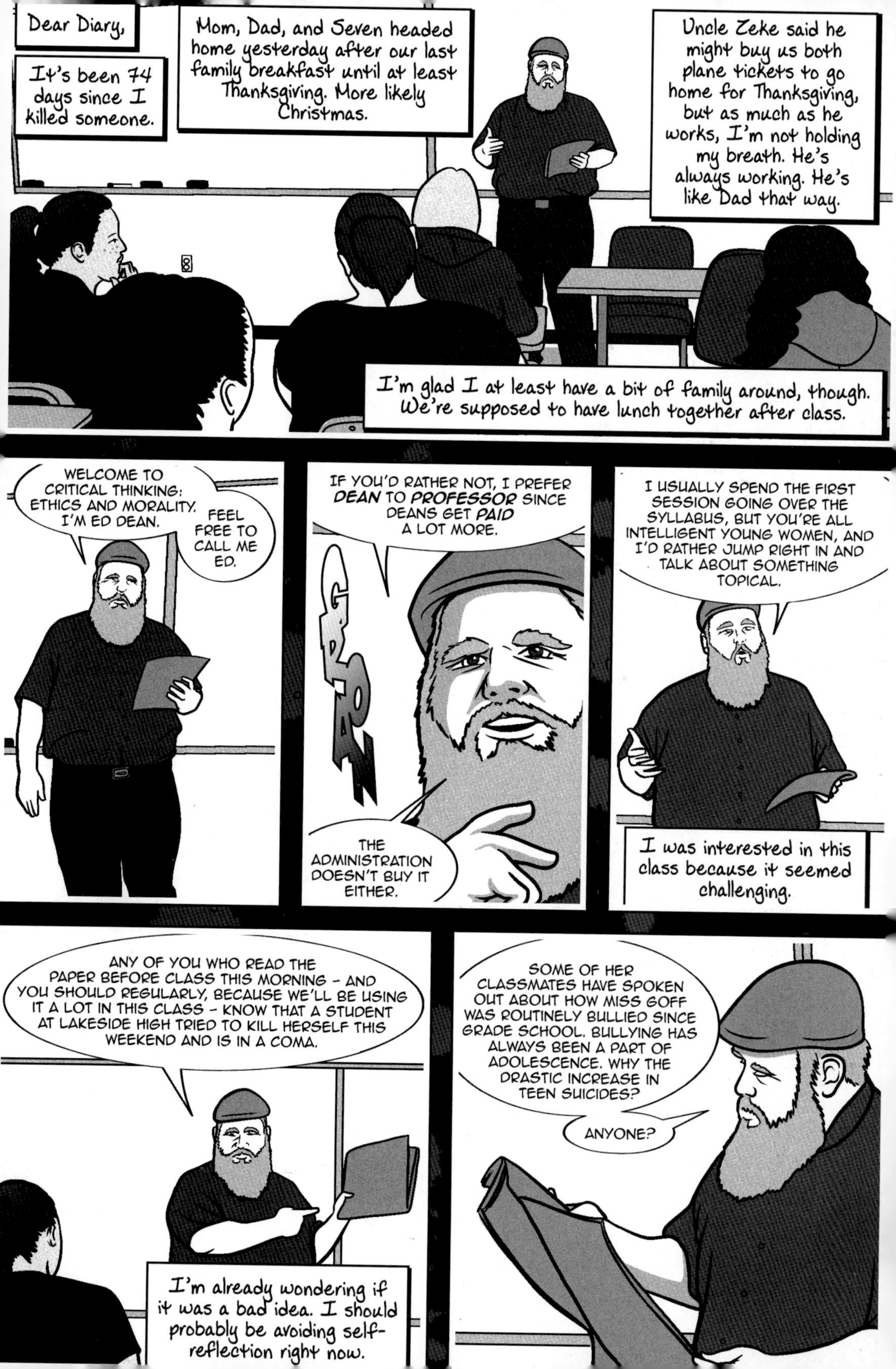

Dear Diary,
It's been 74 days since I killed someone.
Mom, Dad, and Seven headed home yesterday after our last family breakfast until at least Thanksgiving. More likely Christmas.
Uncle Zeke said he might buy us both plane tickets to go home for Thanksgiving, but as much as he works, I'm not holding my breath. He's always working. He's like Dad that way.
I'm glad I at least have a bit of family around, though. We're supposed to have lunch together after class.
WELCOME TO CRITICAL THINKING: ETHICS AND MORALITY. I'M ED DEAN.
FEEL FREE TO CALL ME ED.
IF YOU'D RATHER NOT, I PREFER *DEAN* TO *PROFESSOR* SINCE DEANS GET *PAID* A LOT MORE.
GRRRAAH
THE ADMINISTRATION DOESN'T BUY IT EITHER.
I USUALLY SPEND THE FIRST SESSION GOING OVER THE SYLLABUS, BUT YOU'RE ALL INTELLIGENT YOUNG WOMEN, AND I'D RATHER JUMP RIGHT IN AND TALK ABOUT SOMETHING TOPICAL.
I was interested in this class because it seemed challenging.
ANY OF YOU WHO READ THE PAPER BEFORE CLASS THIS MORNING - AND YOU SHOULD REGULARLY, BECAUSE WE'LL BE USING IT A LOT IN THIS CLASS - KNOW THAT A STUDENT AT LAKESIDE HIGH TRIED TO KILL HERSELF THIS WEEKEND AND IS IN A COMA.
I'm already wondering if it was a bad idea. I should probably be avoiding self-reflection right now.
SOME OF HER CLASSMATES HAVE SPOKEN OUT ABOUT HOW MISS GOFF WAS ROUTINELY BULLIED SINCE GRADE SCHOOL. BULLYING HAS ALWAYS BEEN A PART OF ADOLESCENCE. WHY THE DRASTIC INCREASE IN TEEN SUICIDES?
ANYONE?

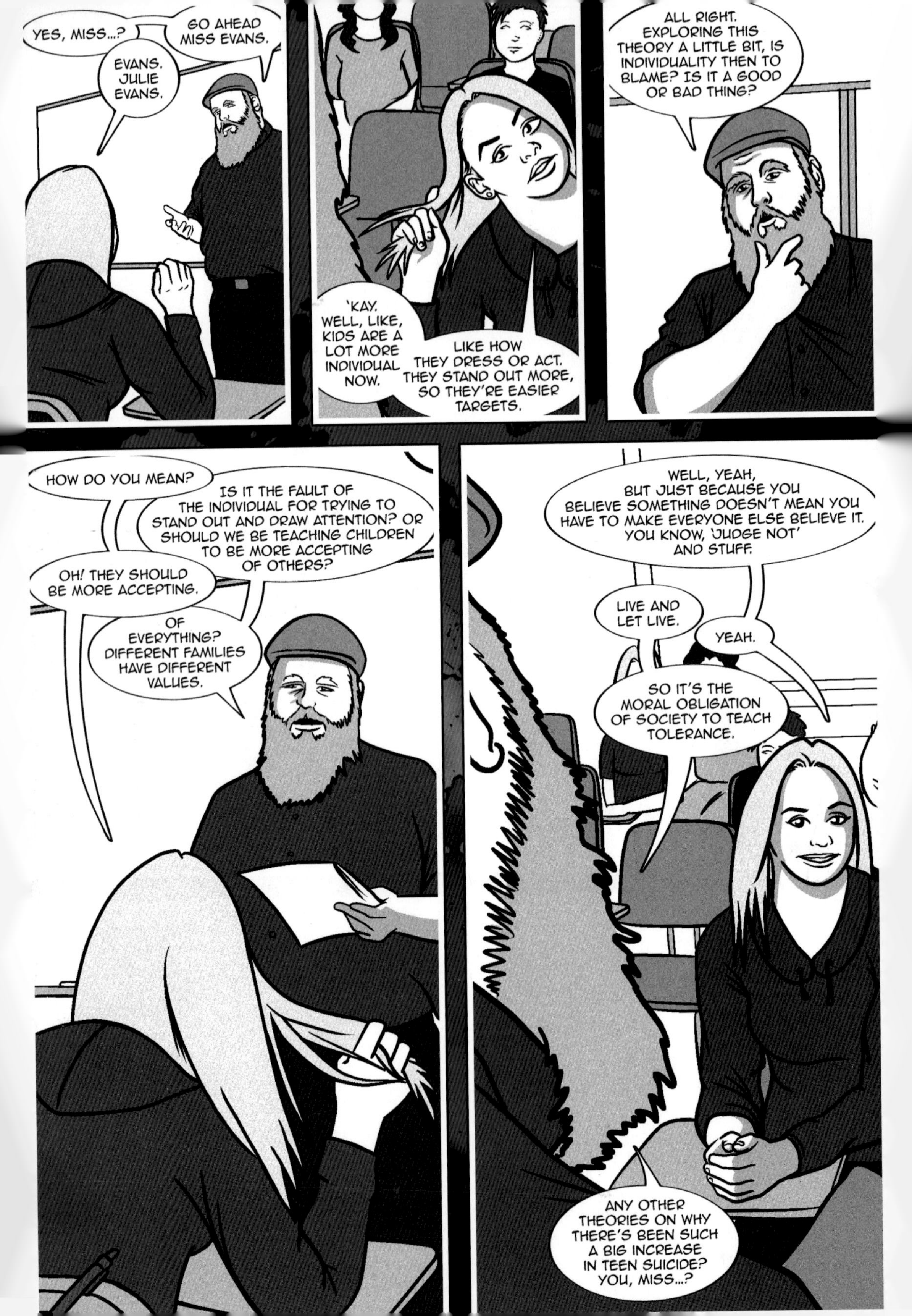
YES, MISS...?
EVANS. JULIE EVANS.
GO AHEAD MISS EVANS.
'KAY. WELL, LIKE, KIDS ARE A LOT MORE INDIVIDUAL NOW.
LIKE HOW THEY DRESS OR ACT. THEY STAND OUT MORE, SO THEY'RE EASIER TARGETS.
ALL RIGHT. EXPLORING THIS THEORY A LITTLE BIT, IS INDIVIDUALITY THEN TO BLAME? IS IT A GOOD OR BAD THING?
HOW DO YOU MEAN?
IS IT THE FAULT OF THE INDIVIDUAL FOR TRYING TO STAND OUT AND DRAW ATTENTION? OR SHOULD WE BE TEACHING CHILDREN TO BE MORE ACCEPTING OF OTHERS?
OH! THEY SHOULD BE MORE ACCEPTING.
OF EVERYTHING? DIFFERENT FAMILIES HAVE DIFFERENT VALUES.
WELL, YEAH, BUT JUST BECAUSE YOU BELIEVE SOMETHING DOESN'T MEAN YOU HAVE TO MAKE EVERYONE ELSE BELIEVE IT. YOU KNOW, 'JUDGE NOT' AND STUFF.
LIVE AND LET LIVE.
YEAH.
SO IT'S THE MORAL OBLIGATION OF SOCIETY TO TEACH TOLERANCE.
ANY OTHER THEORIES ON WHY THERE'S BEEN SUCH A BIG INCREASE IN TEEN SUICIDE? YOU, MISS...?

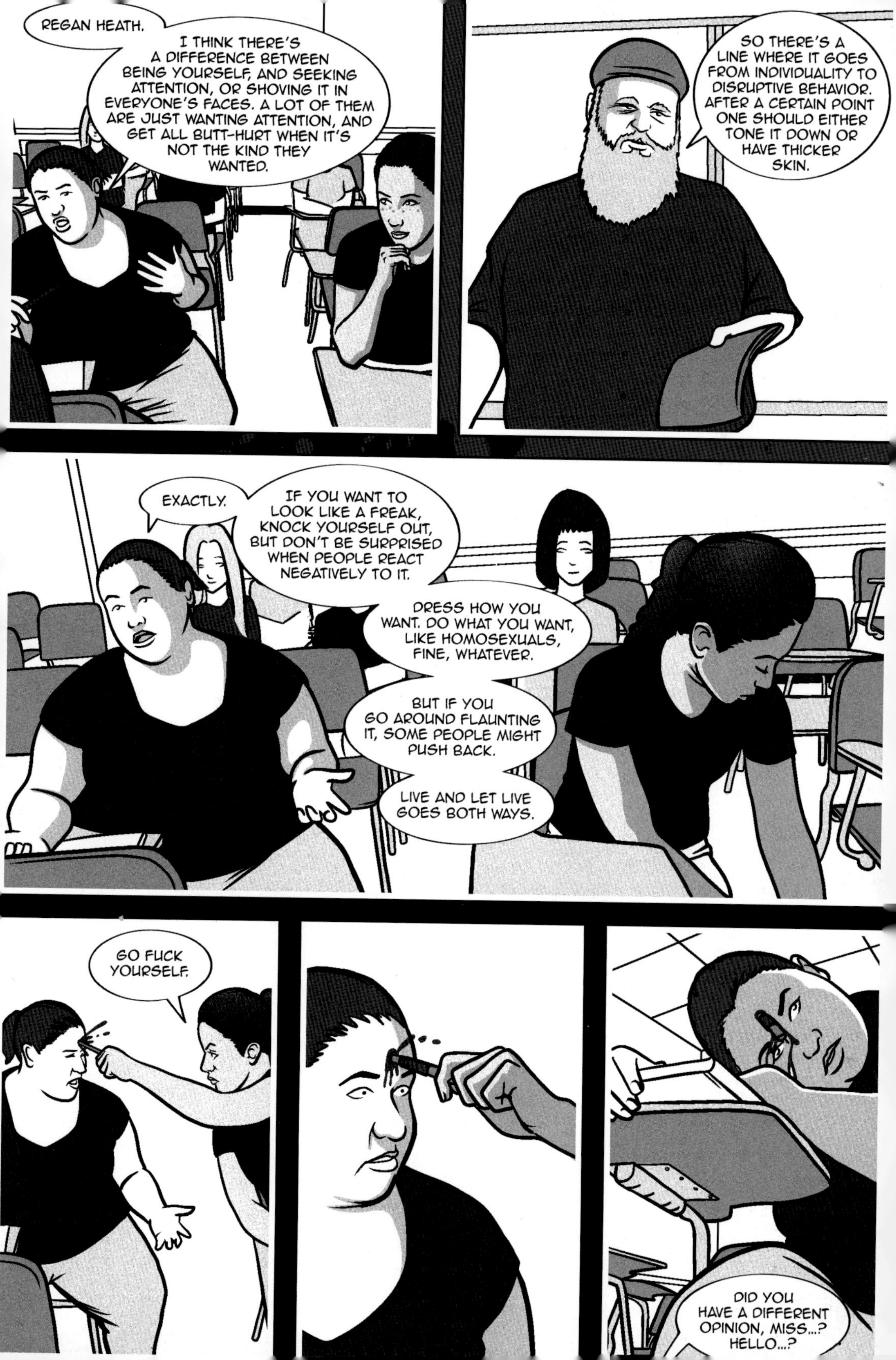
REGAN HEATH.
I THINK THERE'S A DIFFERENCE BETWEEN BEING YOURSELF, AND SEEKING ATTENTION, OR SHOVING IT IN EVERYONE'S FACES. A LOT OF THEM ARE JUST WANTING ATTENTION, AND GET ALL BUTT-HURT WHEN IT'S NOT THE KIND THEY WANTED.
SO THERE'S A LINE WHERE IT GOES FROM INDIVIDUALITY TO DISRUPTIVE BEHAVIOR. AFTER A CERTAIN POINT ONE SHOULD EITHER TONE IT DOWN OR HAVE THICKER SKIN.
EXACTLY.
IF YOU WANT TO LOOK LIKE A FREAK, KNOCK YOURSELF OUT, BUT DON'T BE SURPRISED WHEN PEOPLE REACT NEGATIVELY TO IT.
DRESS HOW YOU WANT. DO WHAT YOU WANT, LIKE HOMOSEXUALS, FINE, WHATEVER.
BUT IF YOU GO AROUND FLAUNTING IT, SOME PEOPLE MIGHT PUSH BACK.
LIVE AND LET LIVE GOES BOTH WAYS.
GO FUCK YOURSELF.
DID YOU HAVE A DIFFERENT OPINION, MISS...? HELLO...?

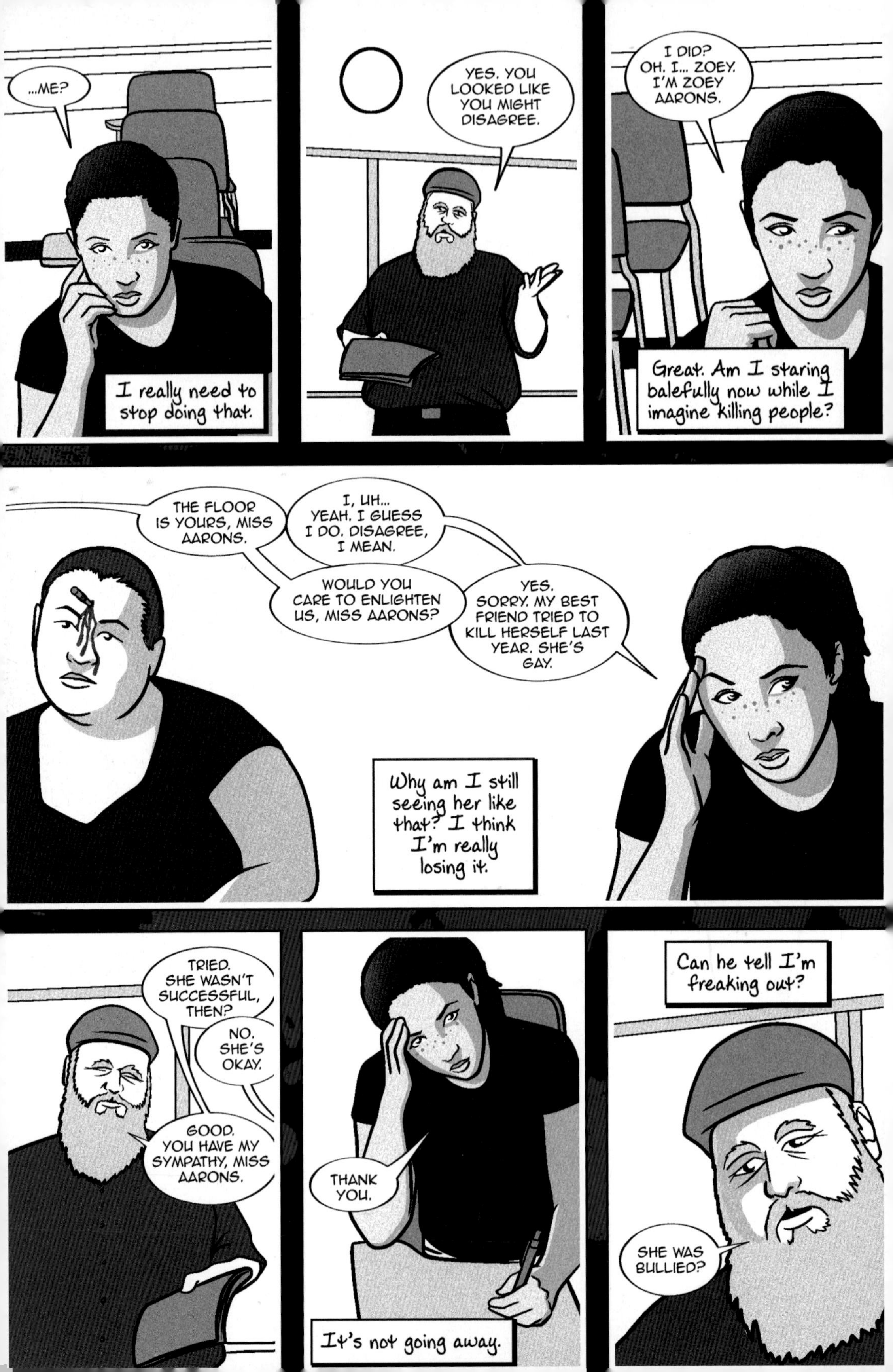
...ME?
I really need to stop doing that.
YES. YOU LOOKED LIKE YOU MIGHT DISAGREE.
I DID? OH. I... ZOEY. I'M ZOEY AARONS.
Great. Am I staring balefully now while I imagine killing people?
THE FLOOR IS YOURS, MISS AARONS.
I, UH... YEAH. I GUESS I DO. DISAGREE, I MEAN.
WOULD YOU CARE TO ENLIGHTEN US, MISS AARONS?
YES. SORRY. MY BEST FRIEND TRIED TO KILL HERSELF LAST YEAR. SHE'S GAY.
Why am I still seeing her like that? I think I'm really losing it.
TRIED. SHE WASN'T SUCCESSFUL, THEN?
NO. SHE'S OKAY.
GOOD. YOU HAVE MY SYMPATHY, MISS AARONS.
THANK YOU.
It's not going away.
Can he tell I'm freaking out?
SHE WAS BULLIED?

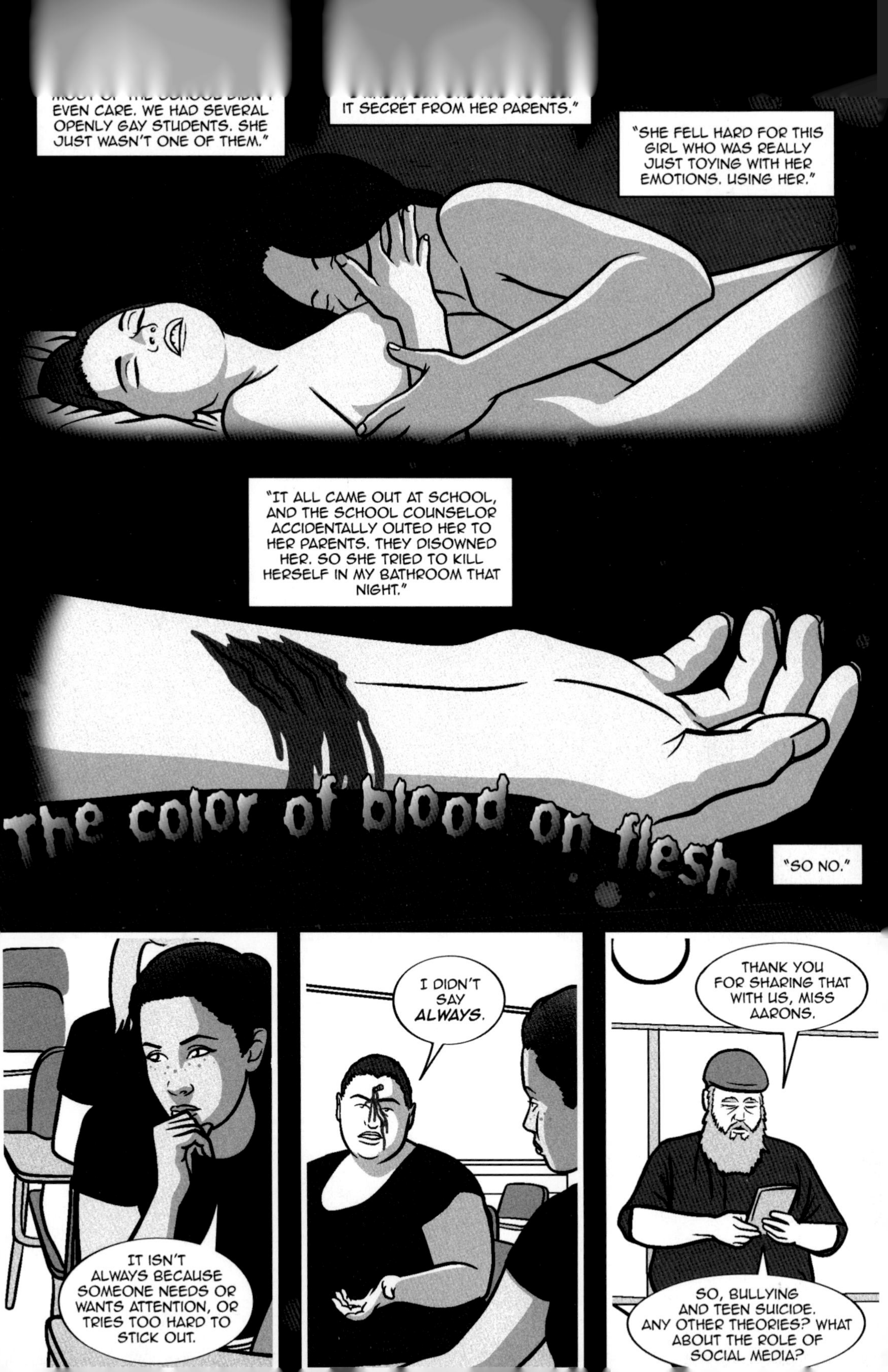
EVEN CARE. WE HAD SEVERAL OPENLY GAY STUDENTS. SHE JUST WASN'T ONE OF THEM."
IT SECRET FROM HER PARENTS."
"SHE FELL HARD FOR THIS GIRL WHO WAS REALLY JUST TOYING WITH HER EMOTIONS. USING HER."
"IT ALL CAME OUT AT SCHOOL, AND THE SCHOOL COUNSELOR ACCIDENTALLY OUTED HER TO HER PARENTS. THEY DISOWNED HER. SO SHE TRIED TO KILL HERSELF IN MY BATHROOM THAT NIGHT."
the color of blood on flesh
"SO NO."
IT ISN'T ALWAYS BECAUSE SOMEONE NEEDS OR WANTS ATTENTION, OR TRIES TOO HARD TO STICK OUT.
I DIDN'T SAY *ALWAYS*.
THANK YOU FOR SHARING THAT WITH US, MISS AARONS.
SO, BULLYING AND TEEN SUICIDE. ANY OTHER THEORIES? WHAT ABOUT THE ROLE OF SOCIAL MEDIA?

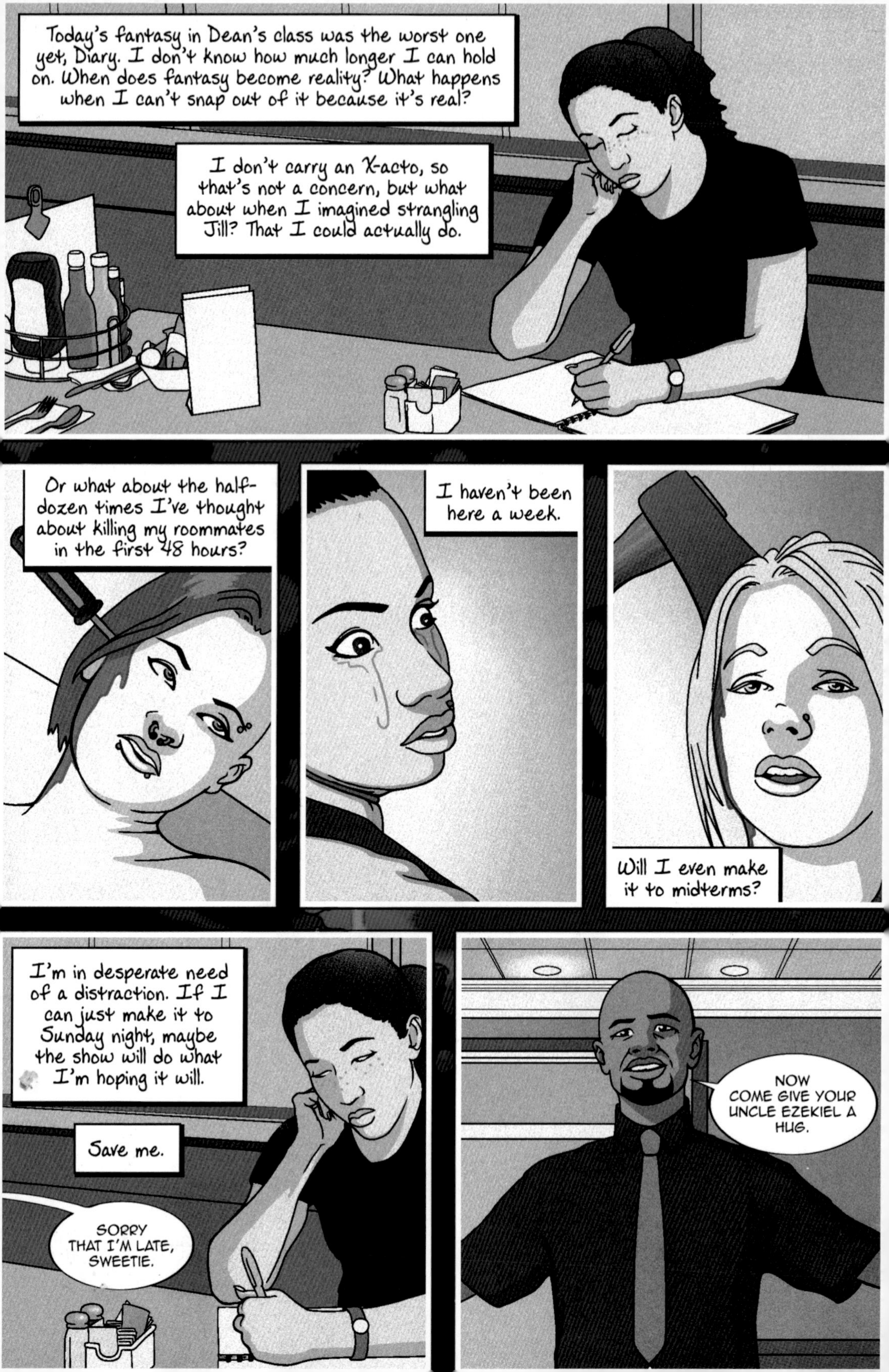

Today's fantasy in Dean's class was the worst one yet, Diary. I don't know how much longer I can hold on. When does fantasy become reality? What happens when I can't snap out of it because it's real?
I don't carry an X-acto, so that's not a concern, but what about when I imagined strangling Jill? That I could actually do.
Or what about the half-dozen times I've thought about killing my roommates in the first 48 hours?
I haven't been here a week.
Will I even make it to midterms?
I'm in desperate need of a distraction. If I can just make it to Sunday night, maybe the show will do what I'm hoping it will.
Save me.
SORRY THAT I'M LATE, SWEETIE.
NOW COME GIVE YOUR UNCLE EZEKIEL A HUG.

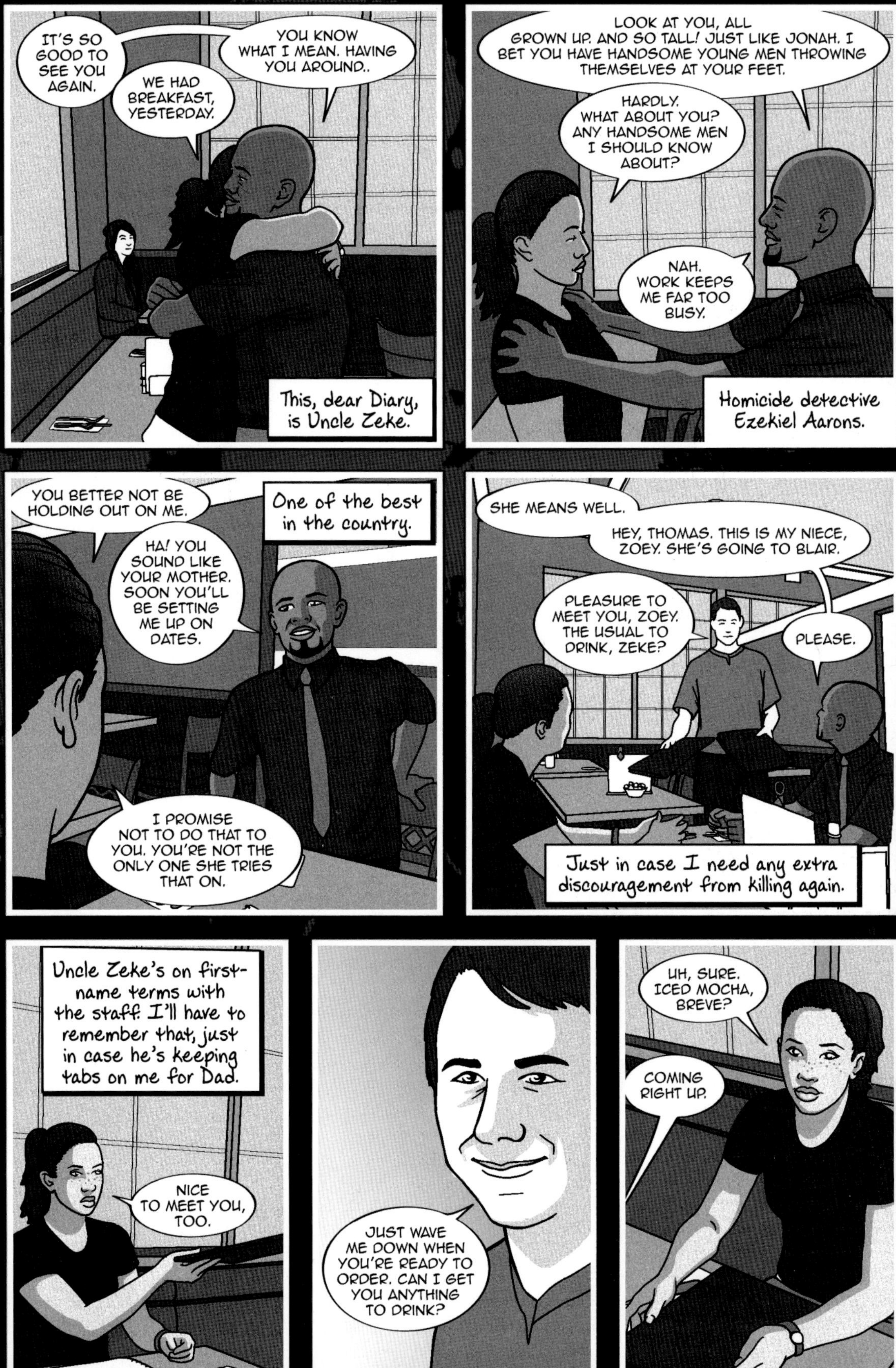
IT'S SO GOOD TO SEE YOU AGAIN.
WE HAD BREAKFAST, YESTERDAY.
YOU KNOW WHAT I MEAN. HAVING YOU AROUND..
This, dear Diary, is Uncle Zeke.
LOOK AT YOU, ALL GROWN UP. AND SO TALL! JUST LIKE JONAH. I BET YOU HAVE HANDSOME YOUNG MEN THROWING THEMSELVES AT YOUR FEET.
HARDLY. WHAT ABOUT YOU? ANY HANDSOME MEN I SHOULD KNOW ABOUT?
NAH. WORK KEEPS ME FAR TOO BUSY.
Homicide detective Ezekiel Aarons.
YOU BETTER NOT BE HOLDING OUT ON ME.
One of the best in the country.
HA! YOU SOUND LIKE YOUR MOTHER. SOON YOU'LL BE SETTING ME UP ON DATES.
I PROMISE NOT TO DO THAT TO YOU. YOU'RE NOT THE ONLY ONE SHE TRIES THAT ON.
SHE MEANS WELL.
HEY, THOMAS. THIS IS MY NIECE, ZOEY. SHE'S GOING TO BLAIR.
PLEASURE TO MEET YOU, ZOEY. THE USUAL TO DRINK, ZEKE?
PLEASE.
Just in case I need any extra discouragement from killing again.
Uncle Zeke's on first-name terms with the staff. I'll have to remember that, just in case he's keeping tabs on me for Dad.
NICE TO MEET YOU, TOO.
JUST WAVE ME DOWN WHEN YOU'RE READY TO ORDER. CAN I GET YOU ANYTHING TO DRINK?
UH, SURE. ICED MOCHA, BREVE?
COMING RIGHT UP.

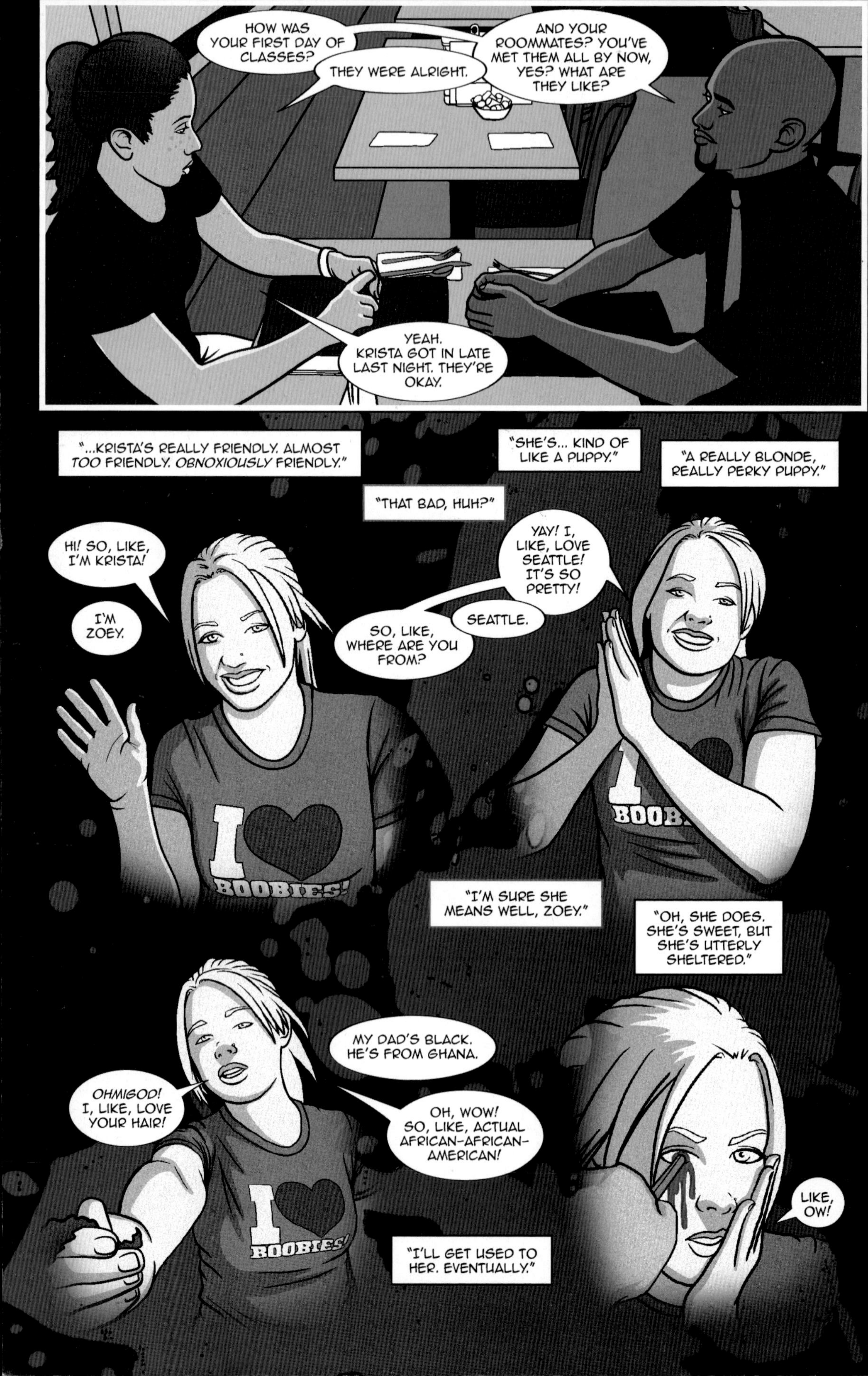
HOW WAS YOUR FIRST DAY OF CLASSES?
THEY WERE ALRIGHT.
AND YOUR ROOMMATES? YOU'VE MET THEM ALL BY NOW, YES? WHAT ARE THEY LIKE?
YEAH. KRISTA GOT IN LATE LAST NIGHT. THEY'RE OKAY.
"...KRISTA'S REALLY FRIENDLY. ALMOST *TOO* FRIENDLY. *OBNOXIOUSLY* FRIENDLY."
"SHE'S... KIND OF LIKE A PUPPY."
"A REALLY BLONDE, REALLY PERKY PUPPY."
"THAT BAD, HUH?"
HI! SO, LIKE, I'M KRISTA!
I'M ZOEY.
SO, LIKE, WHERE ARE YOU FROM?
SEATTLE.
YAY! I, LIKE, LOVE SEATTLE! IT'S SO PRETTY!
I ♥ BOOBIES!
"I'M SURE SHE MEANS WELL, ZOEY."
"OH, SHE DOES. SHE'S SWEET, BUT SHE'S UTTERLY SHELTERED."
OHMIGOD! I, LIKE, LOVE YOUR HAIR!
MY DAD'S BLACK. HE'S FROM GHANA.
OH, WOW! SO, LIKE, ACTUAL AFRICAN-AFRICAN-AMERICAN!
"I'LL GET USED TO HER. EVENTUALLY."
LIKE, OW!

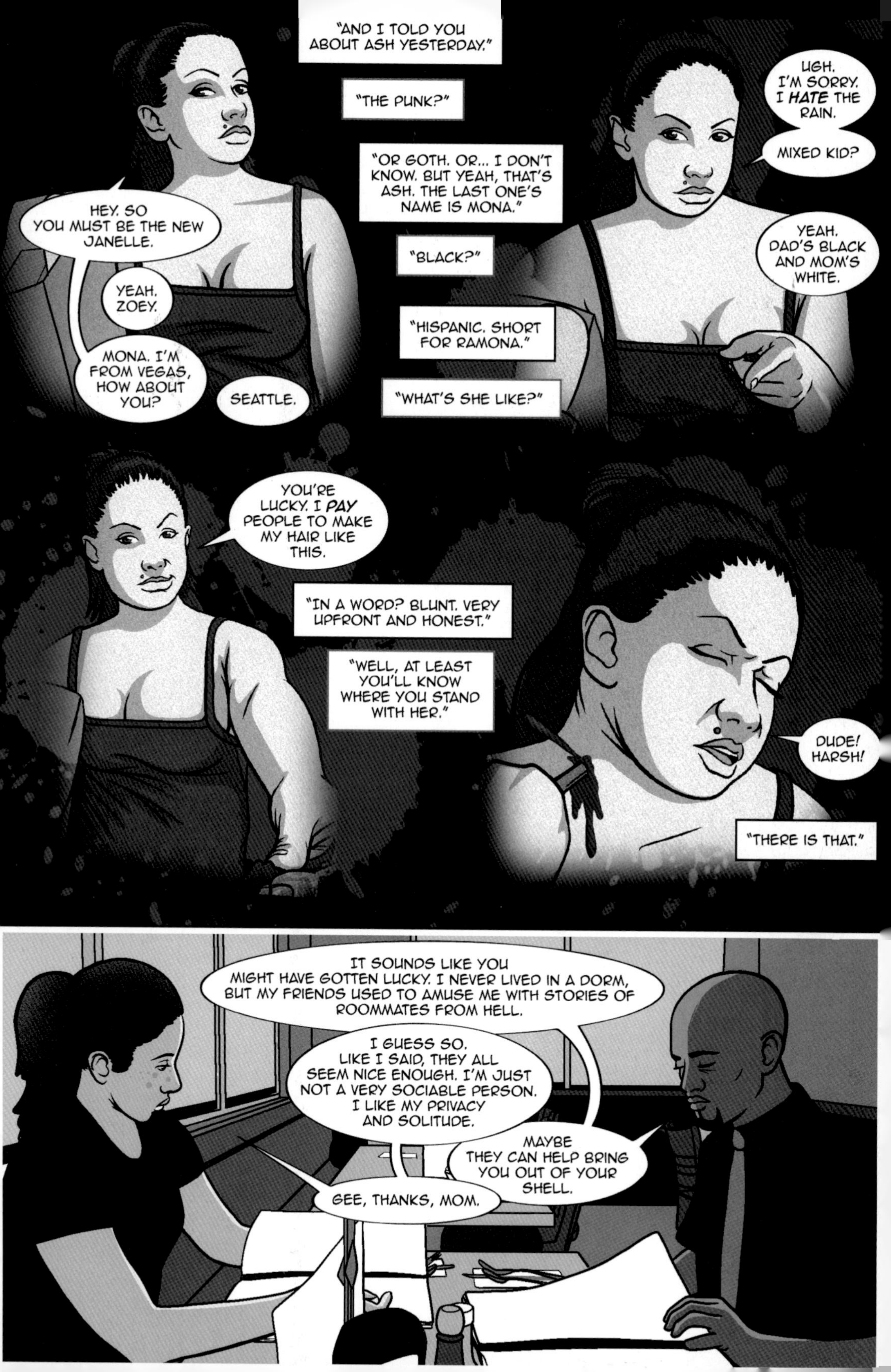
"AND I TOLD YOU ABOUT ASH YESTERDAY."
"THE PUNK?"
"OR GOTH. OR... I DON'T KNOW. BUT YEAH, THAT'S ASH. THE LAST ONE'S NAME IS MONA."
"BLACK?"
"HISPANIC. SHORT FOR RAMONA."
"WHAT'S SHE LIKE?"
HEY. SO YOU MUST BE THE NEW JANELLE.
YEAH. ZOEY.
MONA. I'M FROM VEGAS, HOW ABOUT YOU?
SEATTLE.
UGH. I'M SORRY. I *HATE* THE RAIN.
MIXED KID?
YEAH. DAD'S BLACK AND MOM'S WHITE.
YOU'RE LUCKY. I *PAY* PEOPLE TO MAKE MY HAIR LIKE THIS.
"IN A WORD? BLUNT. VERY UPFRONT AND HONEST."
"WELL, AT LEAST YOU'LL KNOW WHERE YOU STAND WITH HER."
DUDE! HARSH!
"THERE IS THAT."
IT SOUNDS LIKE YOU MIGHT HAVE GOTTEN LUCKY. I NEVER LIVED IN A DORM, BUT MY FRIENDS USED TO AMUSE ME WITH STORIES OF ROOMMATES FROM HELL.
I GUESS SO. LIKE I SAID, THEY ALL SEEM NICE ENOUGH. I'M JUST NOT A VERY SOCIABLE PERSON. I LIKE MY PRIVACY AND SOLITUDE.
MAYBE THEY CAN HELP BRING YOU OUT OF YOUR SHELL.
GEE, THANKS, MOM.

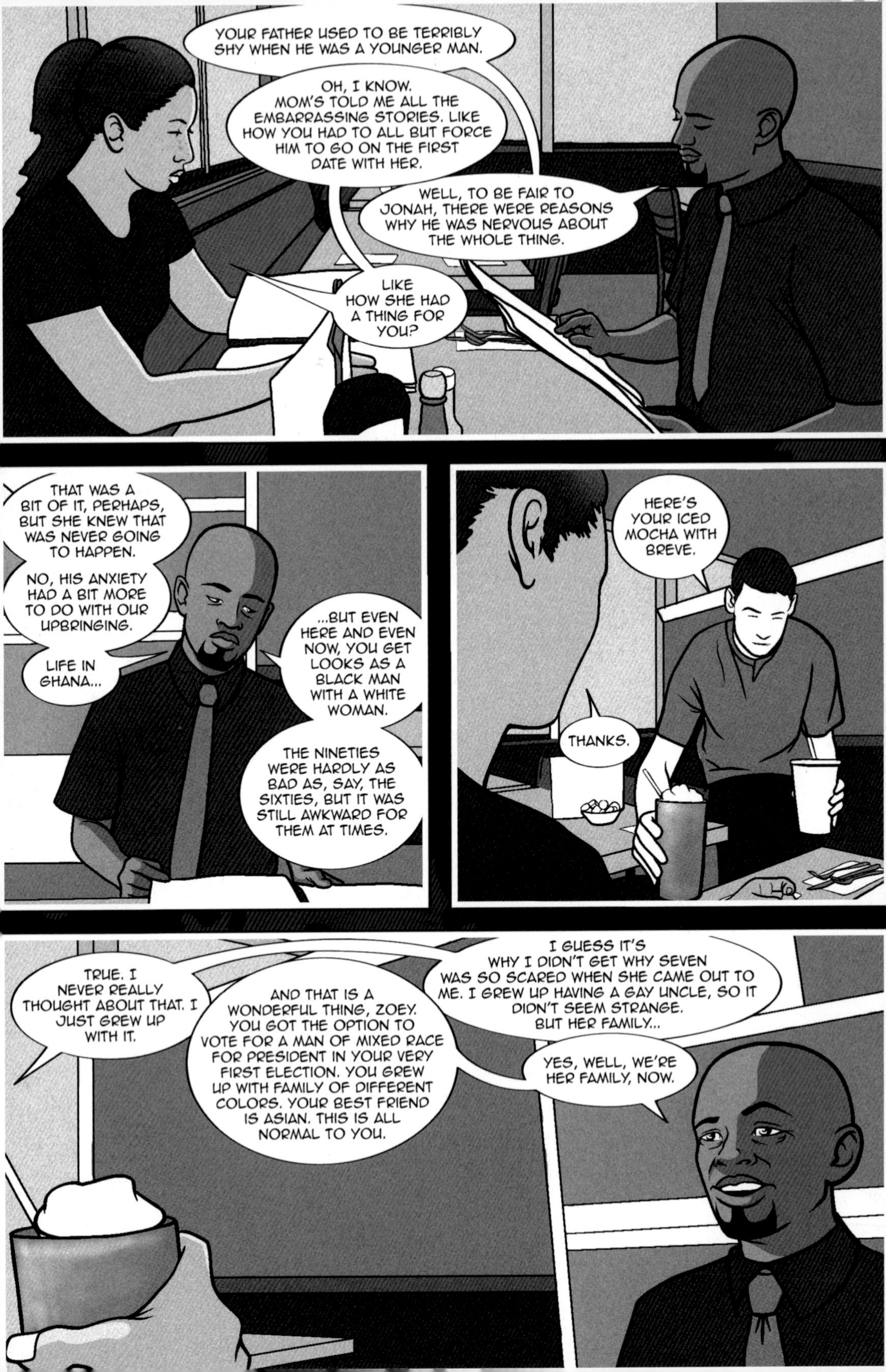
YOUR FATHER USED TO BE TERRIBLY SHY WHEN HE WAS A YOUNGER MAN.
OH, I KNOW. MOM'S TOLD ME ALL THE EMBARRASSING STORIES. LIKE HOW YOU HAD TO ALL BUT FORCE HIM TO GO ON THE FIRST DATE WITH HER.
WELL, TO BE FAIR TO JONAH, THERE WERE REASONS WHY HE WAS NERVOUS ABOUT THE WHOLE THING.
LIKE HOW SHE HAD A THING FOR YOU?
THAT WAS A BIT OF IT, PERHAPS, BUT SHE KNEW THAT WAS NEVER GOING TO HAPPEN.
NO, HIS ANXIETY HAD A BIT MORE TO DO WITH OUR UPBRINGING.
LIFE IN GHANA...
...BUT EVEN HERE AND EVEN NOW, YOU GET LOOKS AS A BLACK MAN WITH A WHITE WOMAN.
THE NINETIES WERE HARDLY AS BAD AS, SAY, THE SIXTIES, BUT IT WAS STILL AWKWARD FOR THEM AT TIMES.
HERE'S YOUR ICED MOCHA WITH BREVE.
THANKS.
TRUE. I NEVER REALLY THOUGHT ABOUT THAT. I JUST GREW UP WITH IT.
AND THAT IS A WONDERFUL THING, ZOEY. YOU GOT THE OPTION TO VOTE FOR A MAN OF MIXED RACE FOR PRESIDENT IN YOUR VERY FIRST ELECTION. YOU GREW UP WITH FAMILY OF DIFFERENT COLORS. YOUR BEST FRIEND IS ASIAN. THIS IS ALL NORMAL TO YOU.
I GUESS IT'S WHY I DIDN'T GET WHY SEVEN WAS SO SCARED WHEN SHE CAME OUT TO ME. I GREW UP HAVING A GAY UNCLE, SO IT DIDN'T SEEM STRANGE. BUT HER FAMILY...
YES, WELL, WE'RE HER FAMILY, NOW.

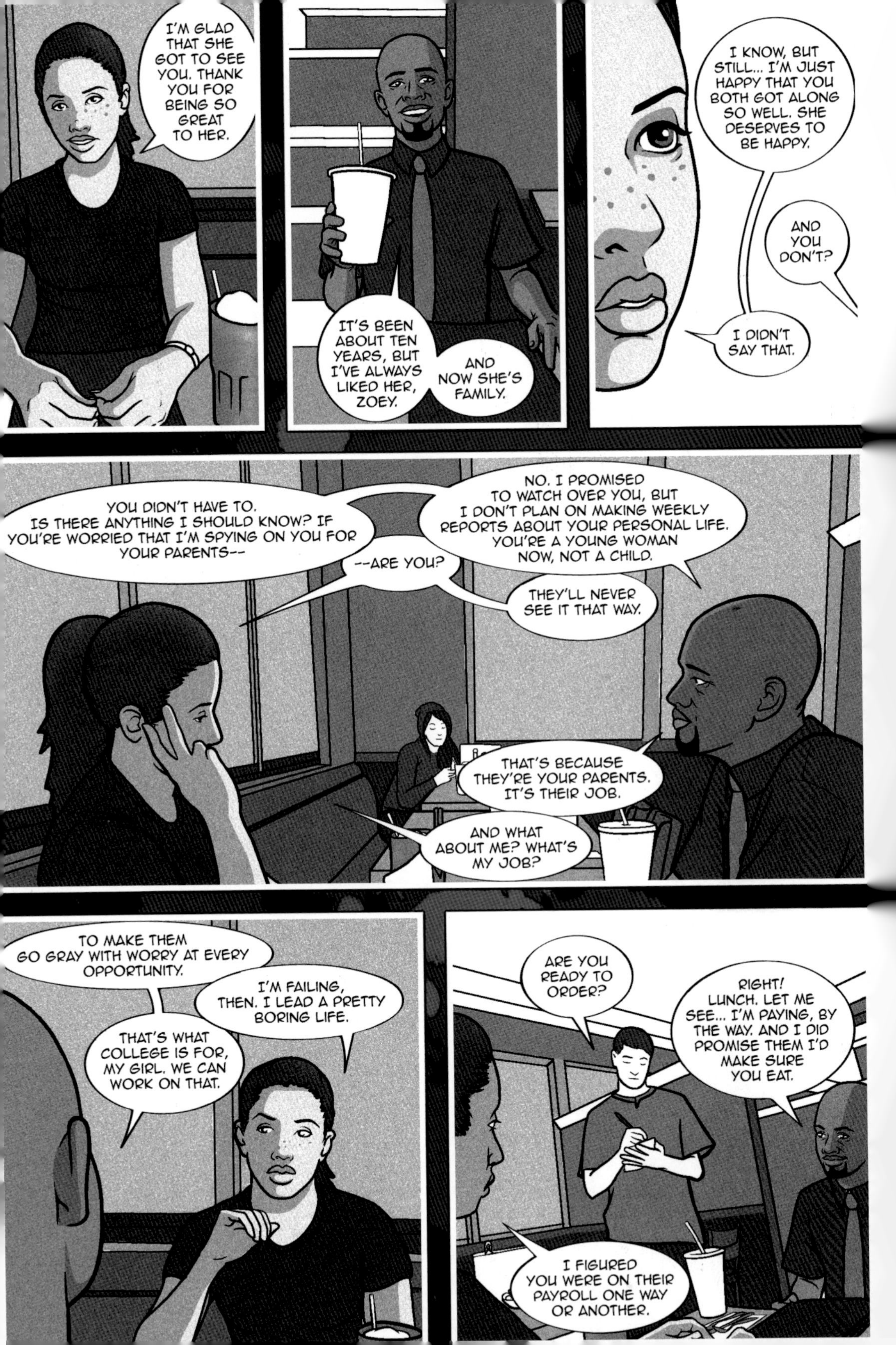

I'M GLAD THAT SHE GOT TO SEE YOU. THANK YOU FOR BEING SO GREAT TO HER.
IT'S BEEN ABOUT TEN YEARS, BUT I'VE ALWAYS LIKED HER, ZOEY.
AND NOW SHE'S FAMILY.
I KNOW, BUT STILL... I'M JUST HAPPY THAT YOU BOTH GOT ALONG SO WELL. SHE DESERVES TO BE HAPPY.
AND YOU DON'T?
I DIDN'T SAY THAT.
YOU DIDN'T HAVE TO. IS THERE ANYTHING I SHOULD KNOW? IF YOU'RE WORRIED THAT I'M SPYING ON YOU FOR YOUR PARENTS--
--ARE YOU?
NO. I PROMISED TO WATCH OVER YOU, BUT I DON'T PLAN ON MAKING WEEKLY REPORTS ABOUT YOUR PERSONAL LIFE. YOU'RE A YOUNG WOMAN NOW, NOT A CHILD.
THEY'LL NEVER SEE IT THAT WAY.
THAT'S BECAUSE THEY'RE YOUR PARENTS. IT'S THEIR JOB.
AND WHAT ABOUT ME? WHAT'S MY JOB?
TO MAKE THEM GO GRAY WITH WORRY AT EVERY OPPORTUNITY.
I'M FAILING, THEN. I LEAD A PRETTY BORING LIFE.
THAT'S WHAT COLLEGE IS FOR, MY GIRL. WE CAN WORK ON THAT.
ARE YOU READY TO ORDER?
RIGHT! LUNCH. LET ME SEE... I'M PAYING, BY THE WAY. AND I DID PROMISE THEM I'D MAKE SURE YOU EAT.
I FIGURED YOU WERE ON THEIR PAYROLL ONE WAY OR ANOTHER.

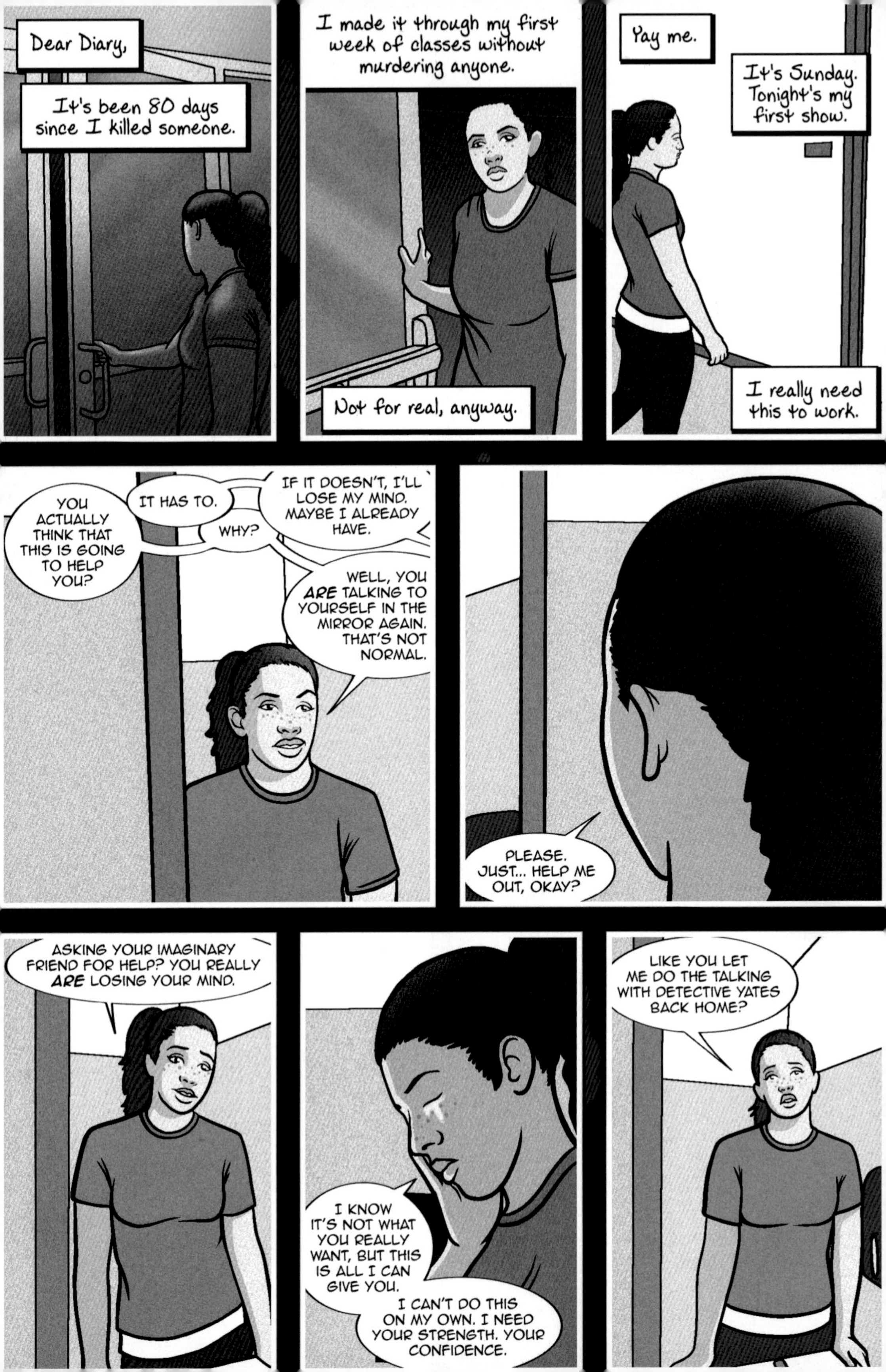

Dear Diary,
It's been 80 days since I killed someone.
I made it through my first week of classes without murdering anyone.
Not for real, anyway.
Yay me.
It's Sunday. Tonight's my first show.
I really need this to work.
YOU ACTUALLY THINK THAT THIS IS GOING TO HELP YOU?
IT HAS TO.
WHY?
IF IT DOESN'T, I'LL LOSE MY MIND. MAYBE I ALREADY HAVE.
WELL, YOU *ARE* TALKING TO YOURSELF IN THE MIRROR AGAIN. THAT'S NOT NORMAL.
PLEASE. JUST... HELP ME OUT, OKAY?
ASKING YOUR IMAGINARY FRIEND FOR HELP? YOU REALLY *ARE* LOSING YOUR MIND.
I KNOW IT'S NOT WHAT YOU REALLY WANT, BUT THIS IS ALL I CAN GIVE YOU.
I CAN'T DO THIS ON MY OWN. I NEED YOUR STRENGTH. YOUR CONFIDENCE.
LIKE YOU LET ME DO THE TALKING WITH DETECTIVE YATES BACK HOME?

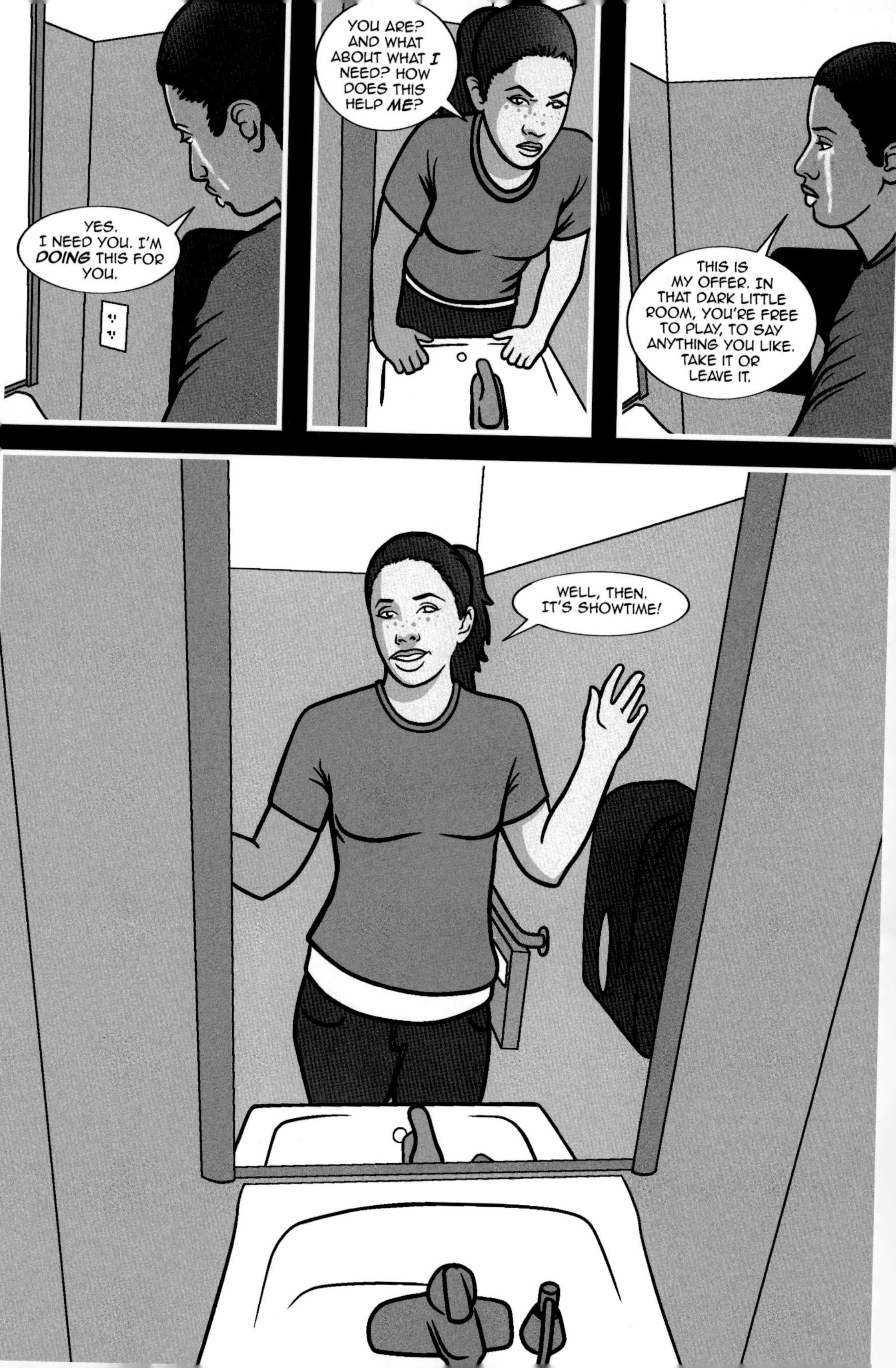
YES. I NEED YOU. I'M *DOING* THIS FOR YOU.
YOU ARE? AND WHAT ABOUT WHAT *I* NEED? HOW DOES THIS HELP *ME*?
THIS IS MY OFFER. IN THAT DARK LITTLE ROOM, YOU'RE FREE TO PLAY, TO SAY ANYTHING YOU LIKE. TAKE IT OR LEAVE IT.
WELL, THEN. IT'S SHOWTIME!

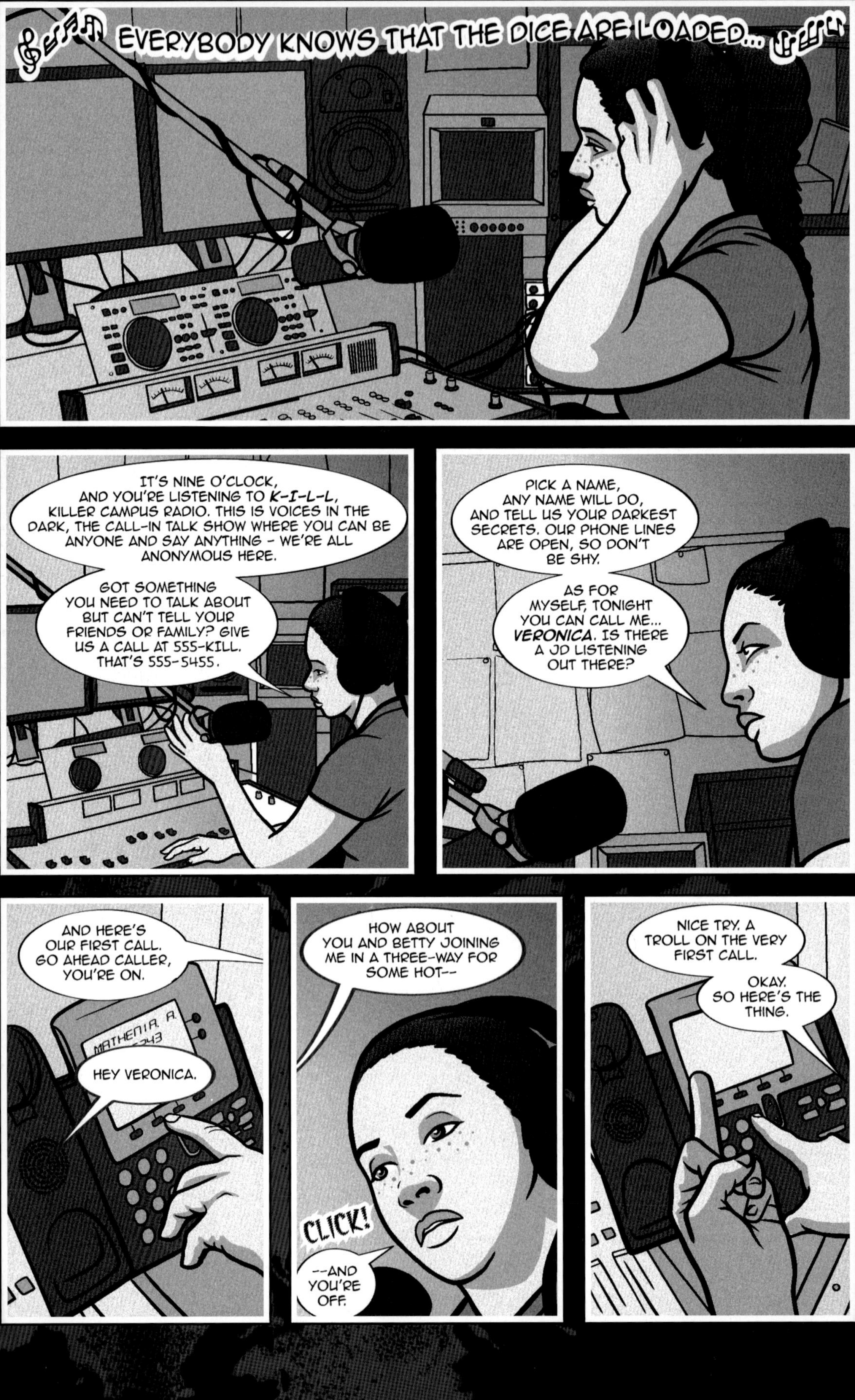
EVERYBODY KNOWS THAT THE DICE ARE LOADED...
IT'S NINE O'CLOCK, AND YOU'RE LISTENING TO K-I-L-L, KILLER CAMPUS RADIO. THIS IS VOICES IN THE DARK, THE CALL-IN TALK SHOW WHERE YOU CAN BE ANYONE AND SAY ANYTHING - WE'RE ALL ANONYMOUS HERE.
GOT SOMETHING YOU NEED TO TALK ABOUT BUT CAN'T TELL YOUR FRIENDS OR FAMILY? GIVE US A CALL AT 555-KILL. THAT'S 555-5455.
PICK A NAME, ANY NAME WILL DO, AND TELL US YOUR DARKEST SECRETS. OUR PHONE LINES ARE OPEN, SO DON'T BE SHY.
AS FOR MYSELF, TONIGHT YOU CAN CALL ME... VERONICA. IS THERE A JD LISTENING OUT THERE?
AND HERE'S OUR FIRST CALL. GO AHEAD CALLER, YOU'RE ON.
MATHENIA, A.
HEY VERONICA.
HOW ABOUT YOU AND BETTY JOINING ME IN A THREE-WAY FOR SOME HOT--
CLICK!
--AND YOU'RE OFF.
NICE TRY. A TROLL ON THE VERY FIRST CALL.
OKAY. SO HERE'S THE THING.

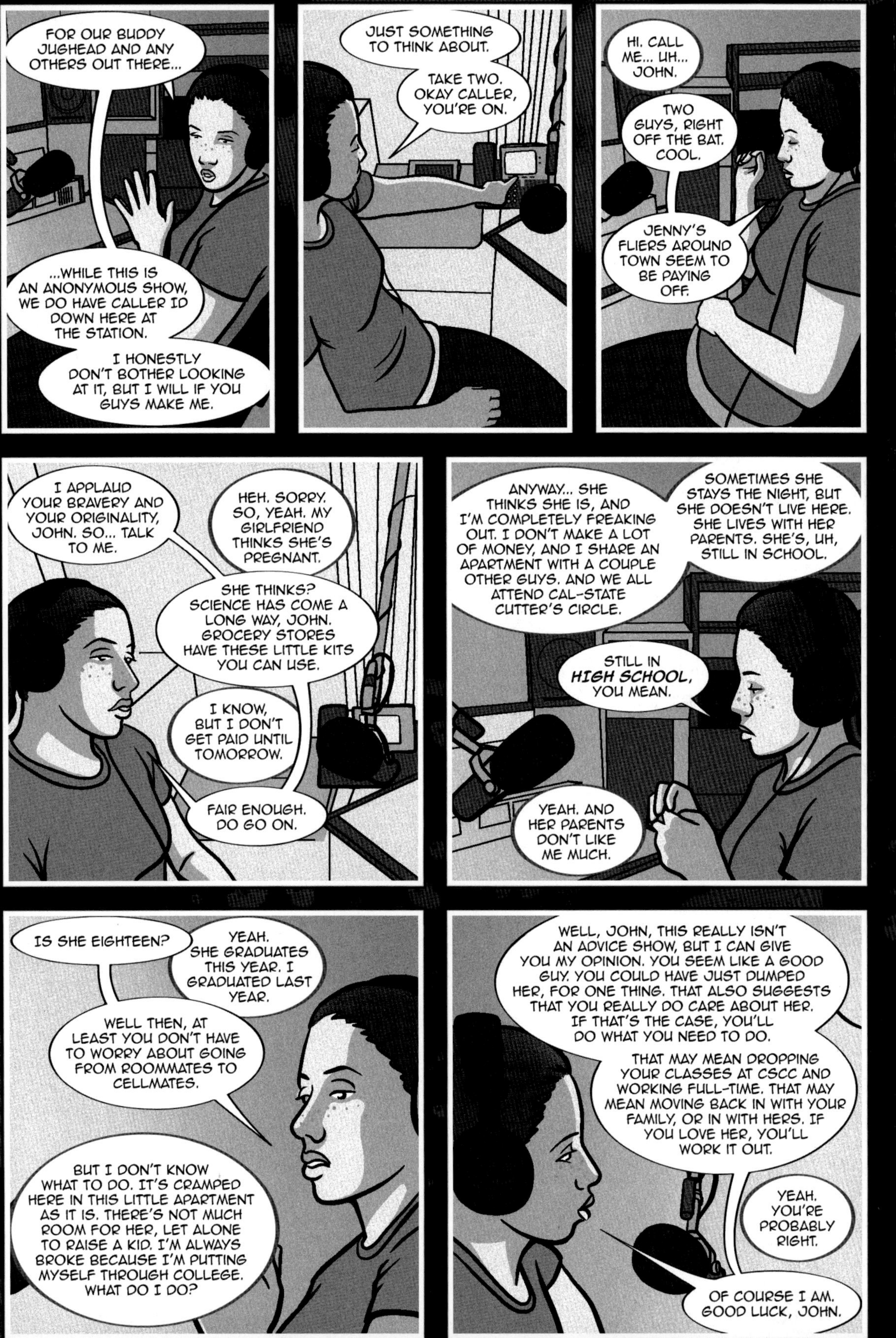
FOR OUR BUDDY JUGHEAD AND ANY OTHERS OUT THERE...
...WHILE THIS IS AN ANONYMOUS SHOW, WE DO HAVE CALLER ID DOWN HERE AT THE STATION.
I HONESTLY DON'T BOTHER LOOKING AT IT, BUT I WILL IF YOU GUYS MAKE ME.
JUST SOMETHING TO THINK ABOUT.
TAKE TWO. OKAY CALLER, YOU'RE ON.
HI. CALL ME... UH... JOHN.
TWO GUYS, RIGHT OFF THE BAT. COOL.
JENNY'S FLIERS AROUND TOWN SEEM TO BE PAYING OFF.
I APPLAUD YOUR BRAVERY AND YOUR ORIGINALITY, JOHN. SO... TALK TO ME.
HEH. SORRY. SO, YEAH. MY GIRLFRIEND THINKS SHE'S PREGNANT.
SHE THINKS? SCIENCE HAS COME A LONG WAY, JOHN. GROCERY STORES HAVE THESE LITTLE KITS YOU CAN USE.
I KNOW, BUT I DON'T GET PAID UNTIL TOMORROW.
FAIR ENOUGH. DO GO ON.
ANYWAY... SHE THINKS SHE IS, AND I'M COMPLETELY FREAKING OUT. I DON'T MAKE A LOT OF MONEY, AND I SHARE AN APARTMENT WITH A COUPLE OTHER GUYS. AND WE ALL ATTEND CAL-STATE CUTTER'S CIRCLE.
SOMETIMES SHE STAYS THE NIGHT, BUT SHE DOESN'T LIVE HERE. SHE LIVES WITH HER PARENTS. SHE'S, UH, STILL IN SCHOOL.
STILL IN ***HIGH SCHOOL,*** YOU MEAN.
YEAH. AND HER PARENTS DON'T LIKE ME MUCH.
IS SHE EIGHTEEN?
YEAH. SHE GRADUATES THIS YEAR. I GRADUATED LAST YEAR.
WELL THEN, AT LEAST YOU DON'T HAVE TO WORRY ABOUT GOING FROM ROOMMATES TO CELLMATES.
BUT I DON'T KNOW WHAT TO DO. IT'S CRAMPED HERE IN THIS LITTLE APARTMENT AS IT IS. THERE'S NOT MUCH ROOM FOR HER, LET ALONE TO RAISE A KID. I'M ALWAYS BROKE BECAUSE I'M PUTTING MYSELF THROUGH COLLEGE. WHAT DO I DO?
WELL, JOHN, THIS REALLY ISN'T AN ADVICE SHOW, BUT I CAN GIVE YOU MY OPINION. YOU SEEM LIKE A GOOD GUY. YOU COULD HAVE JUST DUMPED HER, FOR ONE THING. THAT ALSO SUGGESTS THAT YOU REALLY DO CARE ABOUT HER. IF THAT'S THE CASE, YOU'LL DO WHAT YOU NEED TO DO.
THAT MAY MEAN DROPPING YOUR CLASSES AT CSCC AND WORKING FULL-TIME. THAT MAY MEAN MOVING BACK IN WITH YOUR FAMILY, OR IN WITH HERS. IF YOU LOVE HER, YOU'LL WORK IT OUT.
YEAH. YOU'RE PROBABLY RIGHT.
OF COURSE I AM. GOOD LUCK, JOHN.

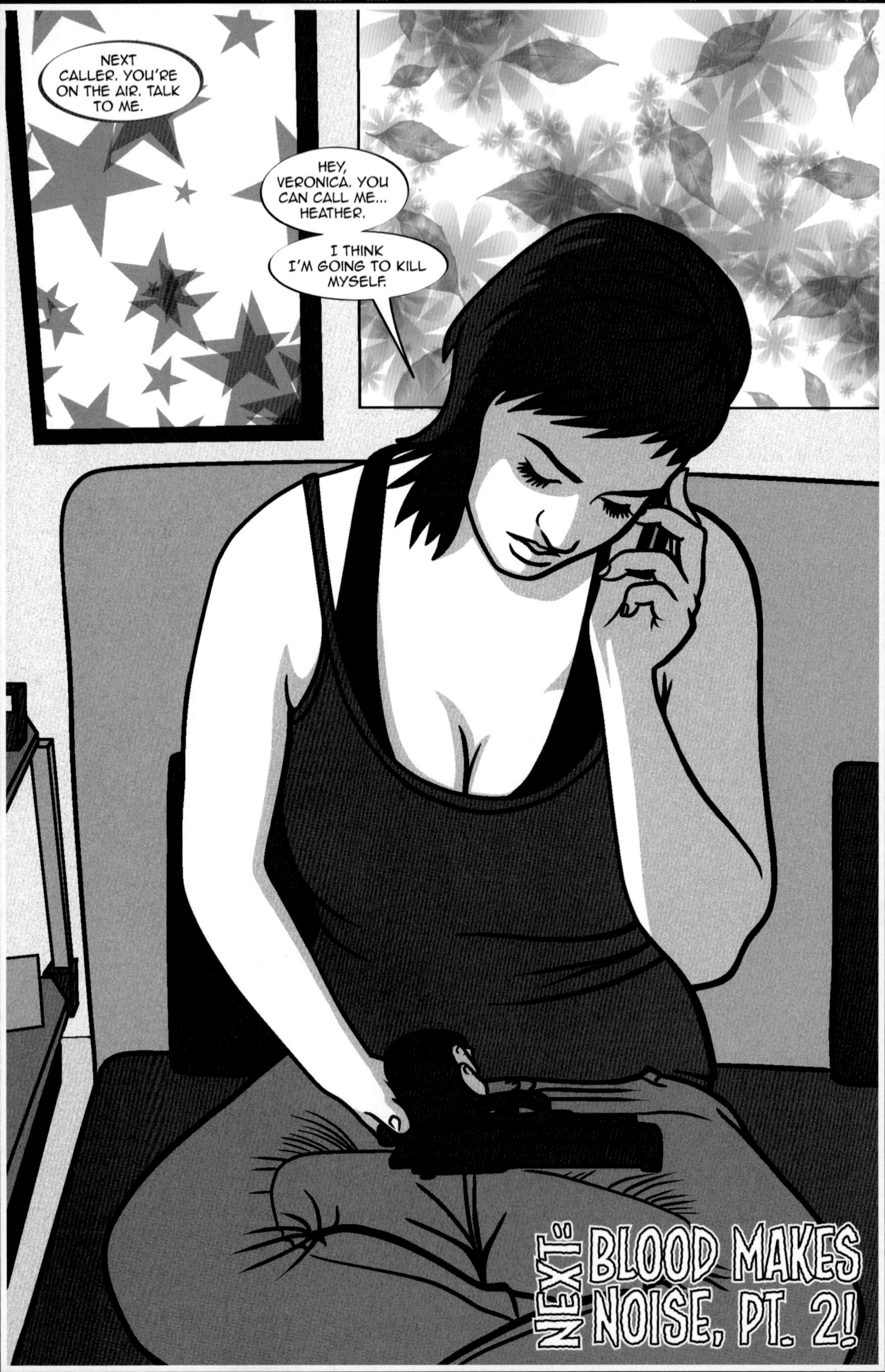
NEXT CALLER. YOU'RE ON THE AIR. TALK TO ME.
HEY, VERONICA. YOU CAN CALL ME... HEATHER.
I THINK I'M GOING TO KILL MYSELF.
NEXT: BLOOD MAKES NOISE, PT. 2!

a VOICE in the DARK

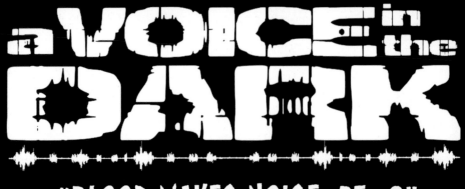

"BLOOD MAKES NOISE, PT. 2"

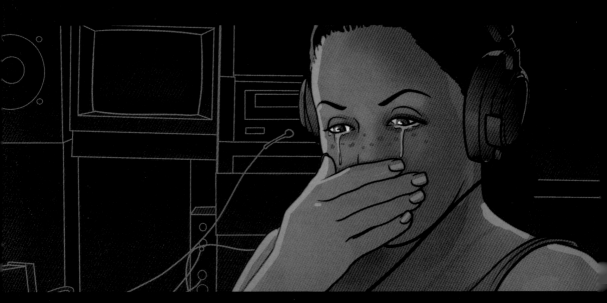

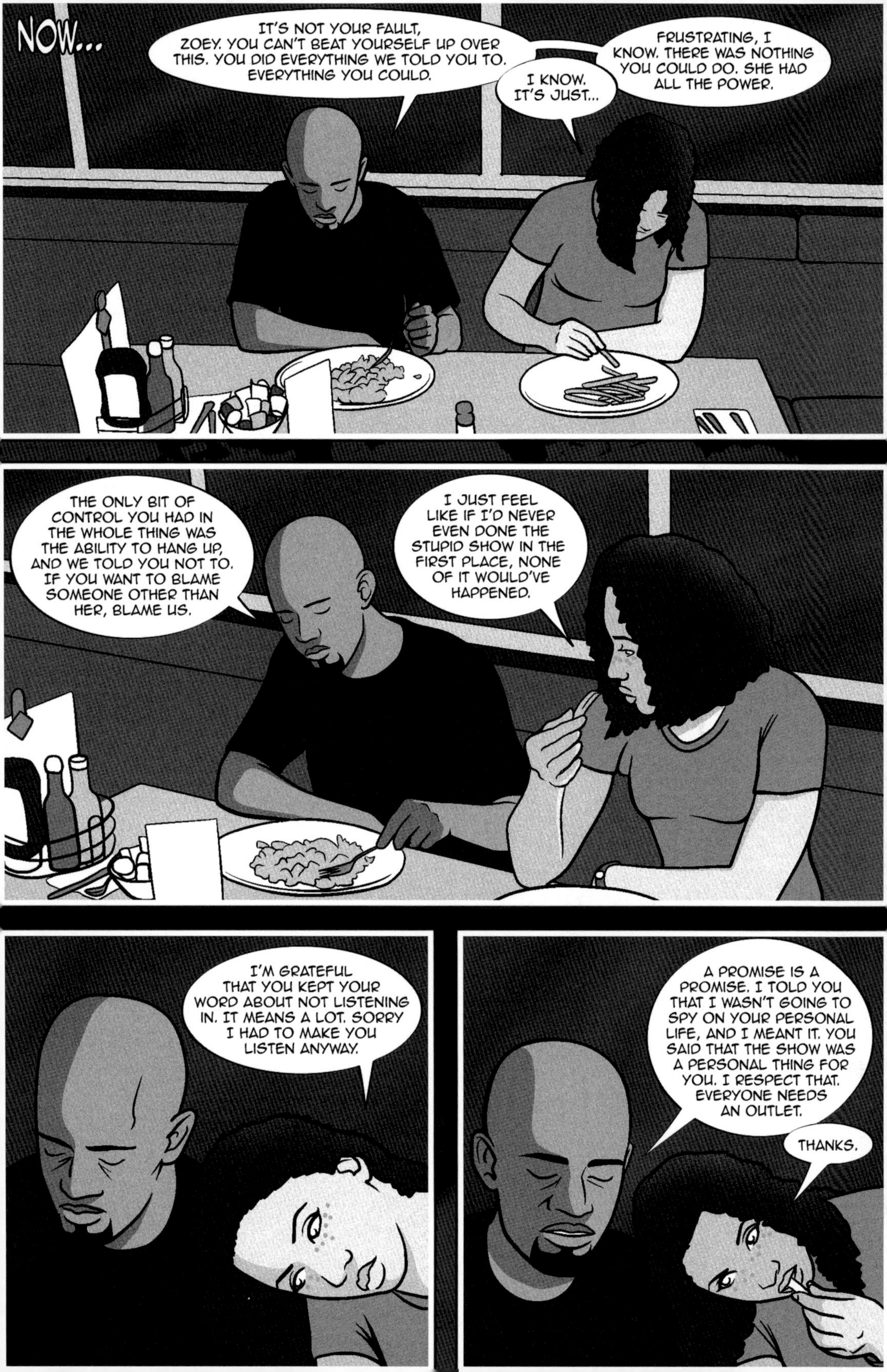
NOW...
IT'S NOT YOUR FAULT, ZOEY. YOU CAN'T BEAT YOURSELF UP OVER THIS. YOU DID EVERYTHING WE TOLD YOU TO. EVERYTHING YOU COULD.
I KNOW. IT'S JUST...
FRUSTRATING, I KNOW. THERE WAS NOTHING YOU COULD DO. SHE HAD ALL THE POWER.
THE ONLY BIT OF CONTROL YOU HAD IN THE WHOLE THING WAS THE ABILITY TO HANG UP, AND WE TOLD YOU NOT TO. IF YOU WANT TO BLAME SOMEONE OTHER THAN HER, BLAME US.
I JUST FEEL LIKE IF I'D NEVER EVEN DONE THE STUPID SHOW IN THE FIRST PLACE, NONE OF IT WOULD'VE HAPPENED.
I'M GRATEFUL THAT YOU KEPT YOUR WORD ABOUT NOT LISTENING IN. IT MEANS A LOT. SORRY I HAD TO MAKE YOU LISTEN ANYWAY.
A PROMISE IS A PROMISE. I TOLD YOU THAT I WASN'T GOING TO SPY ON YOUR PERSONAL LIFE, AND I MEANT IT. YOU SAID THAT THE SHOW WAS A PERSONAL THING FOR YOU. I RESPECT THAT. EVERYONE NEEDS AN OUTLET.
THANKS.

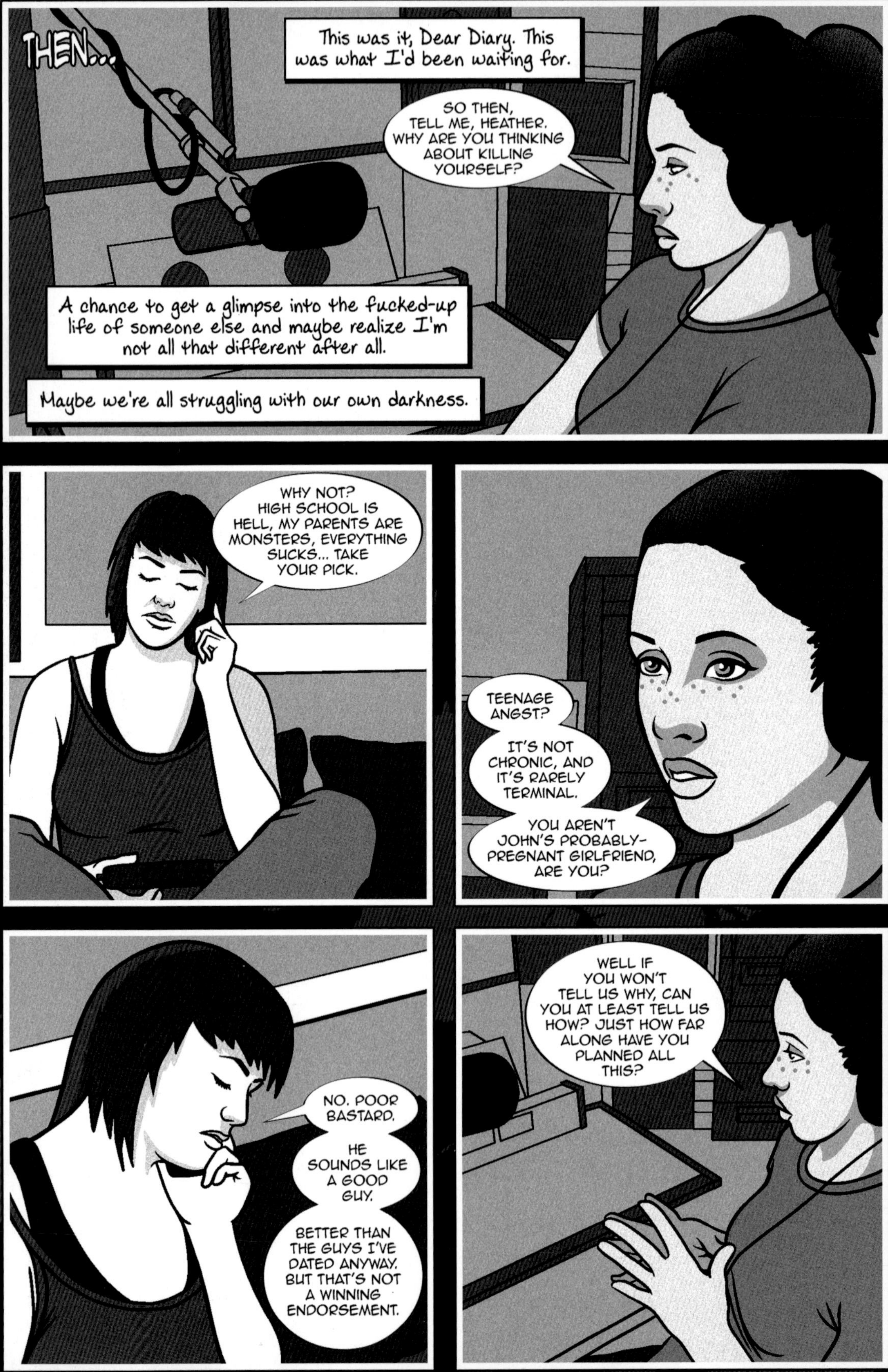
THEN...
This was it, Dear Diary. This was what I'd been waiting for.
SO THEN, TELL ME, HEATHER. WHY ARE YOU THINKING ABOUT KILLING YOURSELF?
A chance to get a glimpse into the fucked-up life of someone else and maybe realize I'm not all that different after all.
Maybe we're all struggling with our own darkness.
WHY NOT? HIGH SCHOOL IS HELL, MY PARENTS ARE MONSTERS, EVERYTHING SUCKS... TAKE YOUR PICK.
TEENAGE ANGST?
IT'S NOT CHRONIC, AND IT'S RARELY TERMINAL.
YOU AREN'T JOHN'S PROBABLY-PREGNANT GIRLFRIEND, ARE YOU?
NO. POOR BASTARD.
HE SOUNDS LIKE A GOOD GUY.
BETTER THAN THE GUYS I'VE DATED ANYWAY. BUT THAT'S NOT A WINNING ENDORSEMENT.
WELL IF YOU WON'T TELL US WHY, CAN YOU AT LEAST TELL US HOW? JUST HOW FAR ALONG HAVE YOU PLANNED ALL THIS?

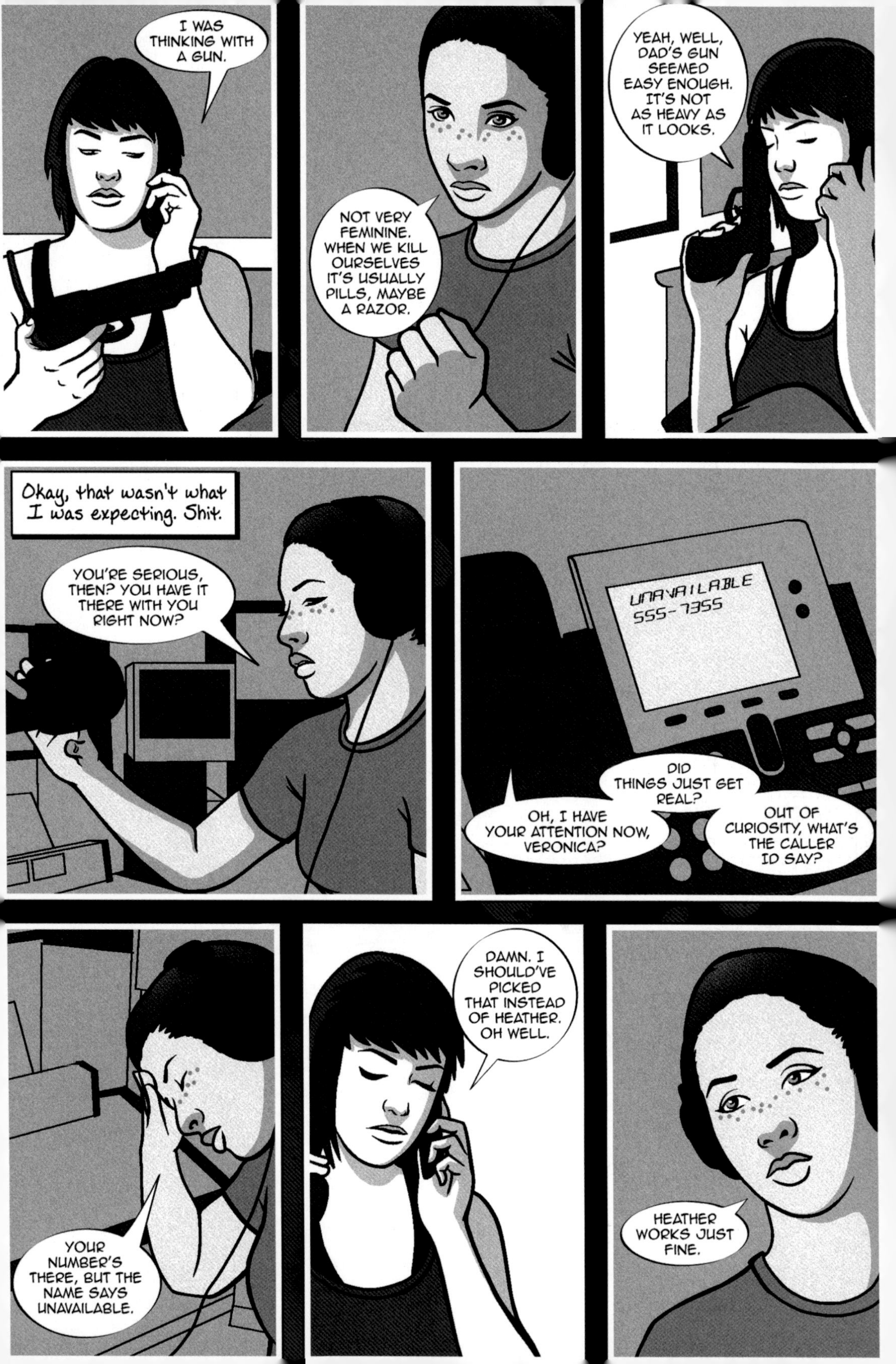
I WAS THINKING WITH A GUN.
NOT VERY FEMININE. WHEN WE KILL OURSELVES IT'S USUALLY PILLS, MAYBE A RAZOR.
YEAH, WELL, DAD'S GUN SEEMED EASY ENOUGH. IT'S NOT AS HEAVY AS IT LOOKS.
Okay, that wasn't what I was expecting. Shit.
YOU'RE SERIOUS, THEN? YOU HAVE IT THERE WITH YOU RIGHT NOW?
UNAVAILABLE
555-7355
OH, I HAVE YOUR ATTENTION NOW, VERONICA?
DID THINGS JUST GET REAL?
OUT OF CURIOSITY, WHAT'S THE CALLER ID SAY?
YOUR NUMBER'S THERE, BUT THE NAME SAYS UNAVAILABLE.
DAMN. I SHOULD'VE PICKED THAT INSTEAD OF HEATHER. OH WELL.
HEATHER WORKS JUST FINE.

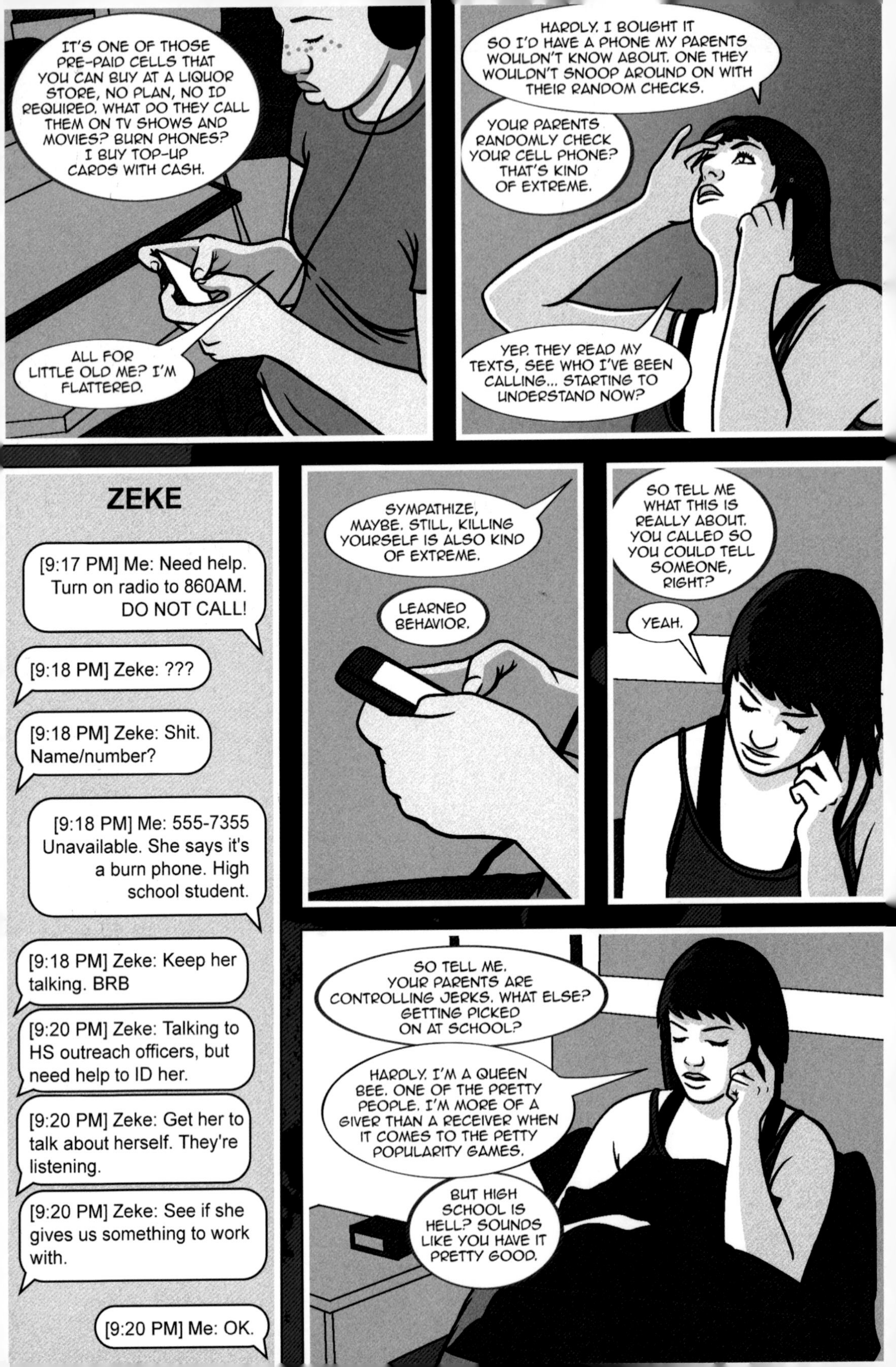
IT'S ONE OF THOSE PRE-PAID CELLS THAT YOU CAN BUY AT A LIQUOR STORE, NO PLAN, NO ID REQUIRED. WHAT DO THEY CALL THEM ON TV SHOWS AND MOVIES? BURN PHONES? I BUY TOP-UP CARDS WITH CASH.
ALL FOR LITTLE OLD ME? I'M FLATTERED.
HARDLY. I BOUGHT IT SO I'D HAVE A PHONE MY PARENTS WOULDN'T KNOW ABOUT. ONE THEY WOULDN'T SNOOP AROUND ON WITH THEIR RANDOM CHECKS.
YOUR PARENTS RANDOMLY CHECK YOUR CELL PHONE? THAT'S KIND OF EXTREME.
YEP. THEY READ MY TEXTS, SEE WHO I'VE BEEN CALLING... STARTING TO UNDERSTAND NOW?
ZEKE
[9:17 PM] Me: Need help. Turn on radio to 860AM. DO NOT CALL!
[9:18 PM] Zeke: ???
[9:18 PM] Zeke: Shit. Name/number?
[9:18 PM] Me: 555-7355 Unavailable. She says it's a burn phone. High school student.
[9:18 PM] Zeke: Keep her talking. BRB
[9:20 PM] Zeke: Talking to HS outreach officers, but need help to ID her.
[9:20 PM] Zeke: Get her to talk about herself. They're listening.
[9:20 PM] Zeke: See if she gives us something to work with.
[9:20 PM] Me: OK.
SYMPATHIZE, MAYBE. STILL, KILLING YOURSELF IS ALSO KIND OF EXTREME.
LEARNED BEHAVIOR.
SO TELL ME WHAT THIS IS REALLY ABOUT. YOU CALLED SO YOU COULD TELL SOMEONE, RIGHT?
YEAH.
SO TELL ME. YOUR PARENTS ARE CONTROLLING JERKS. WHAT ELSE? GETTING PICKED ON AT SCHOOL?
HARDLY. I'M A QUEEN BEE. ONE OF THE PRETTY PEOPLE. I'M MORE OF A GIVER THAN A RECEIVER WHEN IT COMES TO THE PETTY POPULARITY GAMES.
BUT HIGH SCHOOL IS HELL? SOUNDS LIKE YOU HAVE IT PRETTY GOOD.

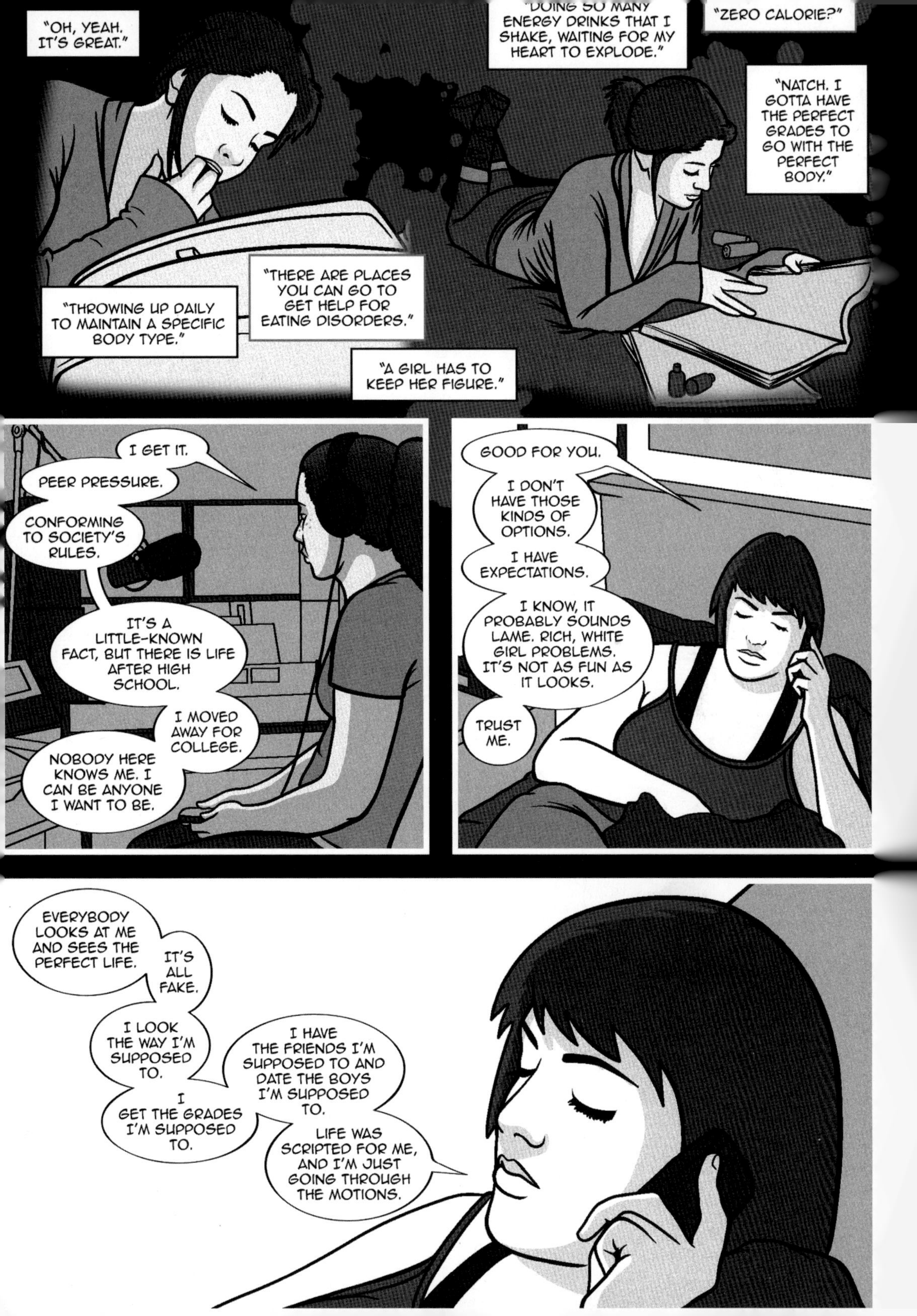
"OH, YEAH. IT'S GREAT."
"THROWING UP DAILY TO MAINTAIN A SPECIFIC BODY TYPE."
"THERE ARE PLACES YOU CAN GO TO GET HELP FOR EATING DISORDERS."
"A GIRL HAS TO KEEP HER FIGURE."
"DOING SO MANY ENERGY DRINKS THAT I SHAKE, WAITING FOR MY HEART TO EXPLODE."
"ZERO CALORIE?"
"NATCH. I GOTTA HAVE THE PERFECT GRADES TO GO WITH THE PERFECT BODY."
I GET IT.
PEER PRESSURE.
CONFORMING TO SOCIETY'S RULES.
IT'S A LITTLE-KNOWN FACT, BUT THERE IS LIFE AFTER HIGH SCHOOL.
I MOVED AWAY FOR COLLEGE.
NOBODY HERE KNOWS ME. I CAN BE ANYONE I WANT TO BE.
GOOD FOR YOU.
I DON'T HAVE THOSE KINDS OF OPTIONS.
I HAVE EXPECTATIONS.
I KNOW, IT PROBABLY SOUNDS LAME. RICH, WHITE GIRL PROBLEMS. IT'S NOT AS FUN AS IT LOOKS.
TRUST ME.
EVERYBODY LOOKS AT ME AND SEES THE PERFECT LIFE.
IT'S ALL FAKE.
I LOOK THE WAY I'M SUPPOSED TO.
I GET THE GRADES I'M SUPPOSED TO.
I HAVE THE FRIENDS I'M SUPPOSED TO AND DATE THE BOYS I'M SUPPOSED TO.
LIFE WAS SCRIPTED FOR ME, AND I'M JUST GOING THROUGH THE MOTIONS.

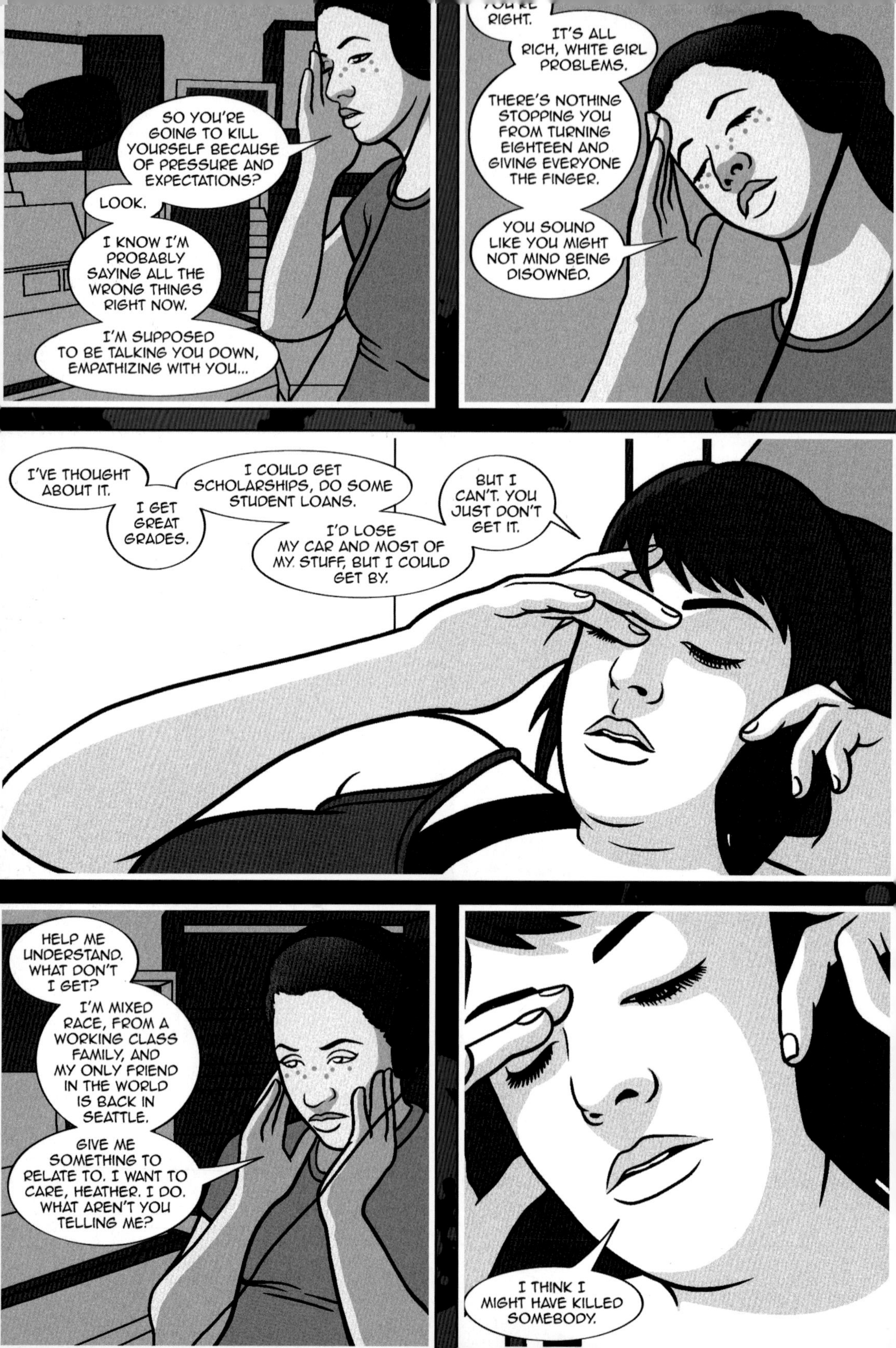
SO YOU'RE GOING TO KILL YOURSELF BECAUSE OF PRESSURE AND EXPECTATIONS?
LOOK.
I KNOW I'M PROBABLY SAYING ALL THE WRONG THINGS RIGHT NOW.
I'M SUPPOSED TO BE TALKING YOU DOWN, EMPATHIZING WITH YOU...
RIGHT.
IT'S ALL RICH, WHITE GIRL PROBLEMS.
THERE'S NOTHING STOPPING YOU FROM TURNING EIGHTEEN AND GIVING EVERYONE THE FINGER.
YOU SOUND LIKE YOU MIGHT NOT MIND BEING DISOWNED.
I'VE THOUGHT ABOUT IT.
I GET GREAT GRADES.
I COULD GET SCHOLARSHIPS, DO SOME STUDENT LOANS.
I'D LOSE MY CAR AND MOST OF MY. STUFF, BUT I COULD GET BY.
BUT I CAN'T. YOU JUST DON'T GET IT.
HELP ME UNDERSTAND. WHAT DON'T I GET?
I'M MIXED RACE, FROM A WORKING CLASS FAMILY, AND MY ONLY FRIEND IN THE WORLD IS BACK IN SEATTLE.
GIVE ME SOMETHING TO RELATE TO. I WANT TO CARE, HEATHER. I DO. WHAT AREN'T YOU TELLING ME?
I THINK I MIGHT HAVE KILLED SOMEBODY.

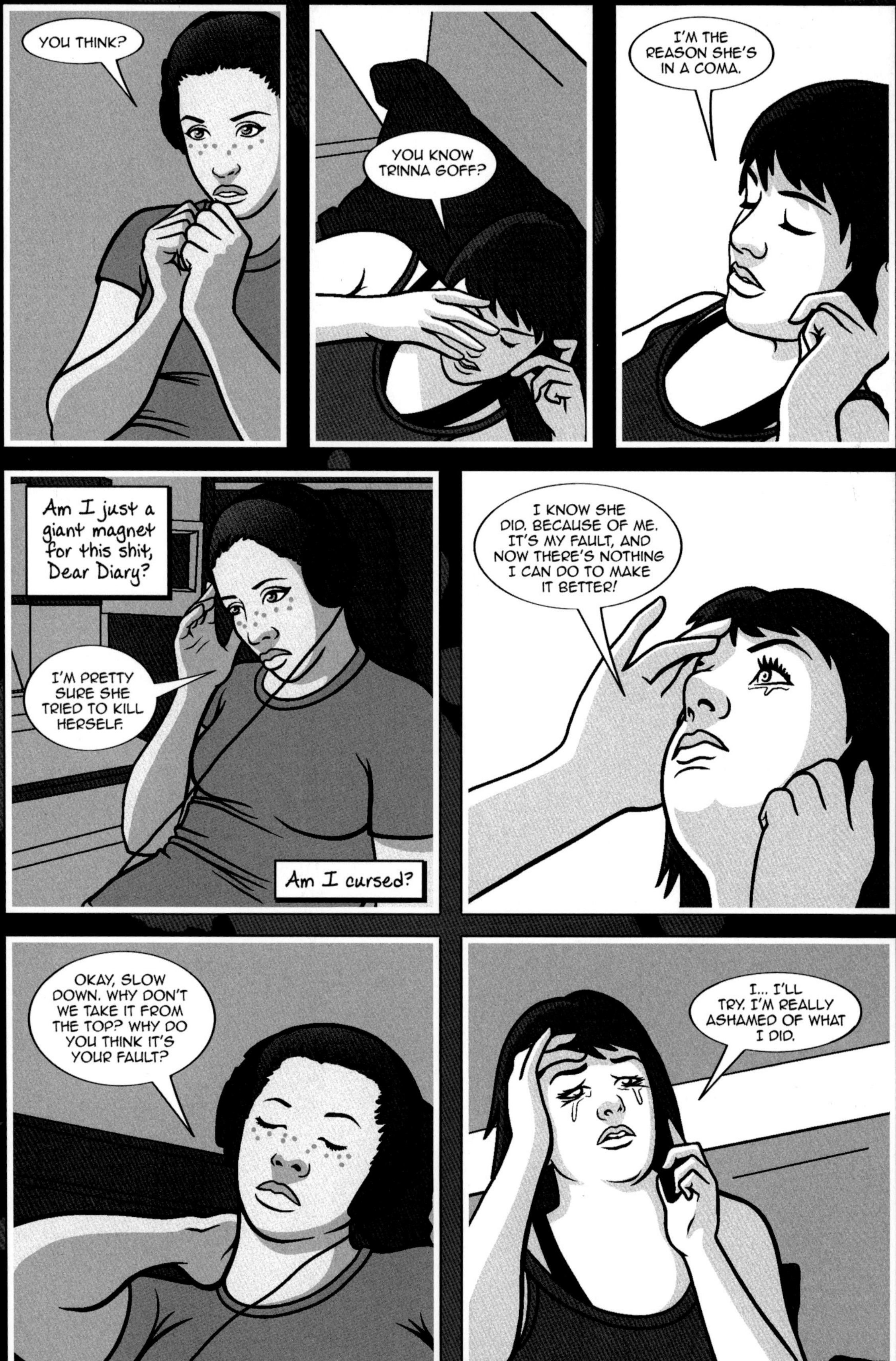
YOU THINK?
YOU KNOW TRINNA GOFF?
I'M THE REASON SHE'S IN A COMA.
Am I just a giant magnet for this shit, Dear Diary?
I'M PRETTY SURE SHE TRIED TO KILL HERSELF.
Am I cursed?
I KNOW SHE DID. BECAUSE OF ME. IT'S MY FAULT, AND NOW THERE'S NOTHING I CAN DO TO MAKE IT BETTER!
OKAY, SLOW DOWN. WHY DON'T WE TAKE IT FROM THE TOP? WHY DO YOU THINK IT'S YOUR FAULT?
I... I'LL TRY. I'M REALLY ASHAMED OF WHAT I DID.

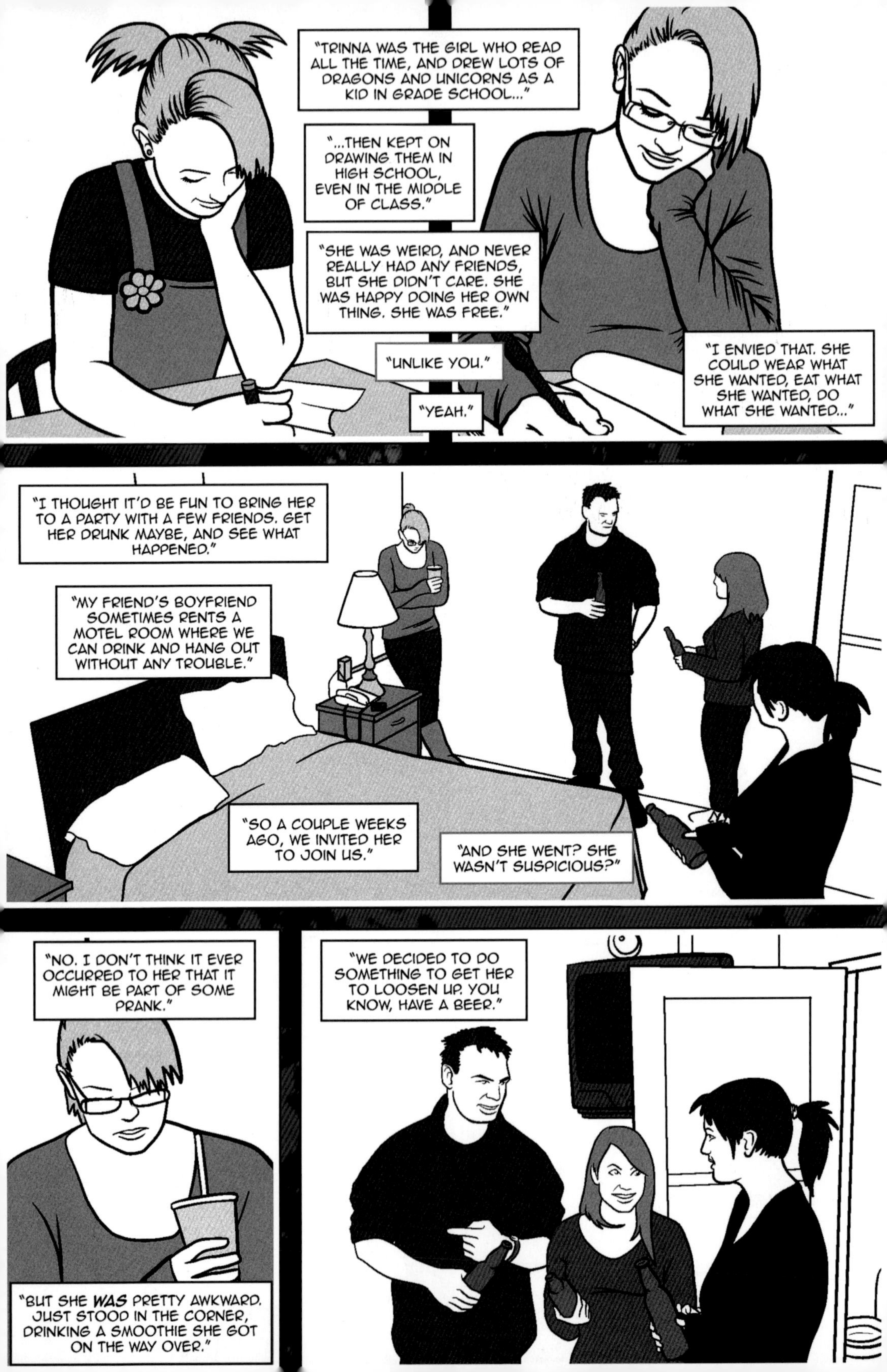
"TRINNA WAS THE GIRL WHO READ ALL THE TIME, AND DREW LOTS OF DRAGONS AND UNICORNS AS A KID IN GRADE SCHOOL..."
"...THEN KEPT ON DRAWING THEM IN HIGH SCHOOL, EVEN IN THE MIDDLE OF CLASS."
"SHE WAS WEIRD, AND NEVER REALLY HAD ANY FRIENDS, BUT SHE DIDN'T CARE. SHE WAS HAPPY DOING HER OWN THING. SHE WAS FREE."
"UNLIKE YOU."
"YEAH."
"I ENVIED THAT. SHE COULD WEAR WHAT SHE WANTED, EAT WHAT SHE WANTED, DO WHAT SHE WANTED..."
"I THOUGHT IT'D BE FUN TO BRING HER TO A PARTY WITH A FEW FRIENDS. GET HER DRUNK MAYBE, AND SEE WHAT HAPPENED."
"MY FRIEND'S BOYFRIEND SOMETIMES RENTS A MOTEL ROOM WHERE WE CAN DRINK AND HANG OUT WITHOUT ANY TROUBLE."
"SO A COUPLE WEEKS AGO, WE INVITED HER TO JOIN US."
"AND SHE WENT? SHE WASN'T SUSPICIOUS?"
"NO. I DON'T THINK IT EVER OCCURRED TO HER THAT IT MIGHT BE PART OF SOME PRANK."
"BUT SHE *WAS* PRETTY AWKWARD. JUST STOOD IN THE CORNER, DRINKING A SMOOTHIE SHE GOT ON THE WAY OVER."
"WE DECIDED TO DO SOMETHING TO GET HER TO LOOSEN UP. YOU KNOW, HAVE A BEER."

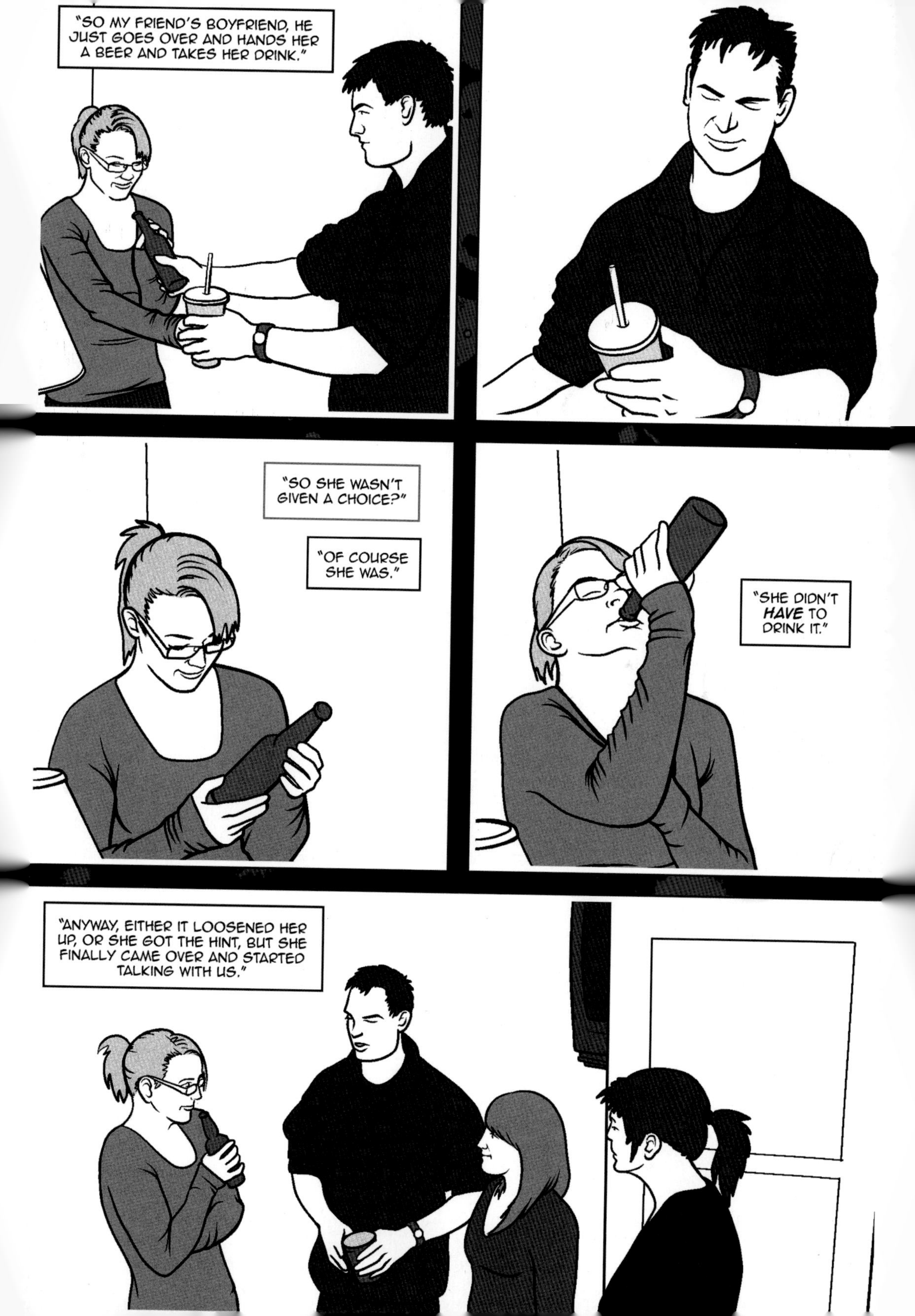
"SO MY FRIEND'S BOYFRIEND, HE JUST GOES OVER AND HANDS HER A BEER AND TAKES HER DRINK."
"SO SHE WASN'T GIVEN A CHOICE?"
"OF COURSE SHE WAS."
"SHE DIDN'T *HAVE* TO DRINK IT."
"ANYWAY, EITHER IT LOOSENED HER UP, OR SHE GOT THE HINT, BUT SHE FINALLY CAME OVER AND STARTED TALKING WITH US."

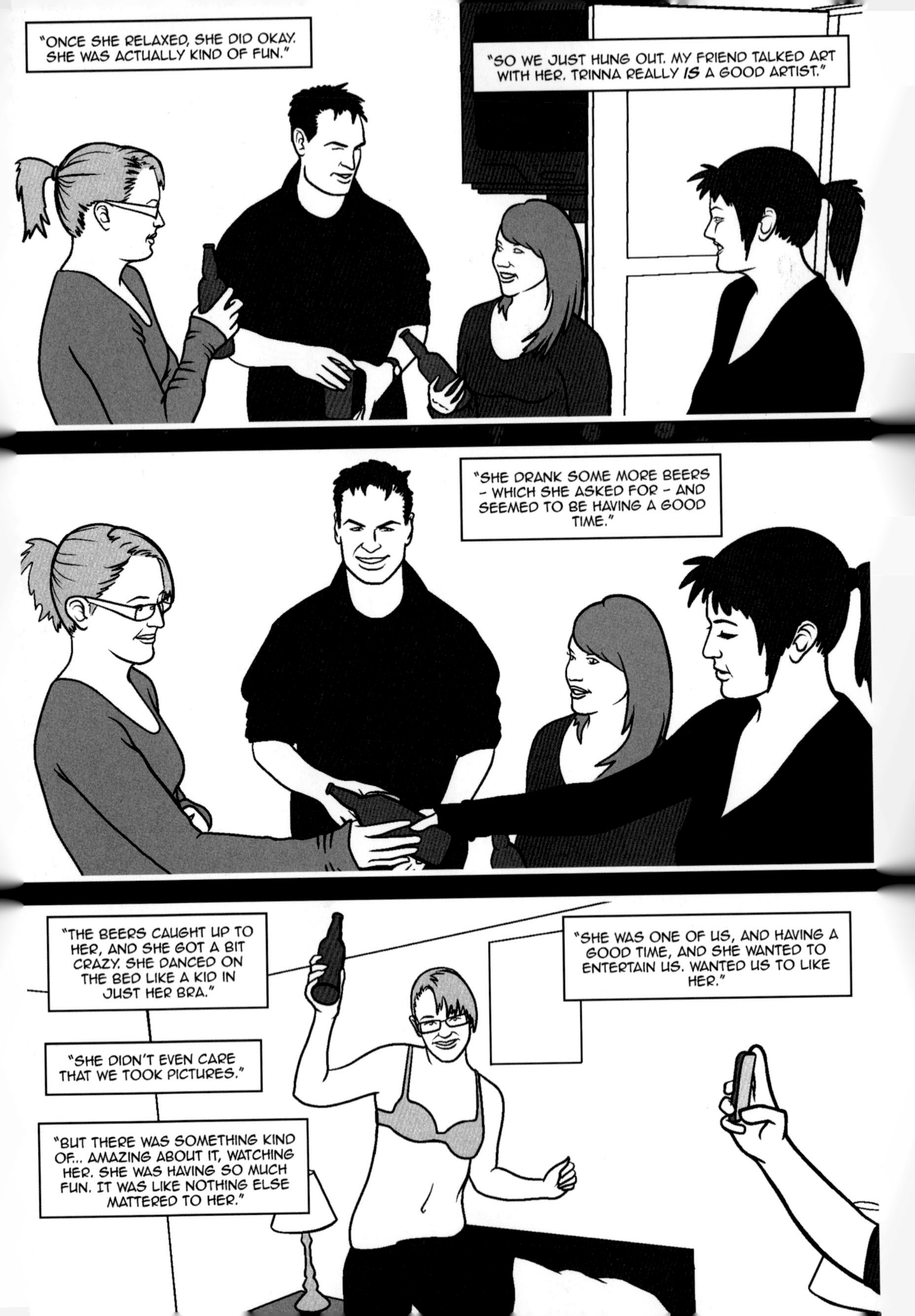
"ONCE SHE RELAXED, SHE DID OKAY. SHE WAS ACTUALLY KIND OF FUN."
"SO WE JUST HUNG OUT. MY FRIEND TALKED ART WITH HER. TRINNA REALLY *IS* A GOOD ARTIST."
"SHE DRANK SOME MORE BEERS - WHICH SHE ASKED FOR - AND SEEMED TO BE HAVING A GOOD TIME."
"THE BEERS CAUGHT UP TO HER, AND SHE GOT A BIT CRAZY. SHE DANCED ON THE BED LIKE A KID IN JUST HER BRA."
"SHE WAS ONE OF US, AND HAVING A GOOD TIME, AND SHE WANTED TO ENTERTAIN US. WANTED US TO LIKE HER."
"SHE DIDN'T EVEN CARE THAT WE TOOK PICTURES."
"BUT THERE WAS SOMETHING KIND OF... AMAZING ABOUT IT, WATCHING HER. SHE WAS HAVING SO MUCH FUN. IT WAS LIKE NOTHING ELSE MATTERED TO HER."

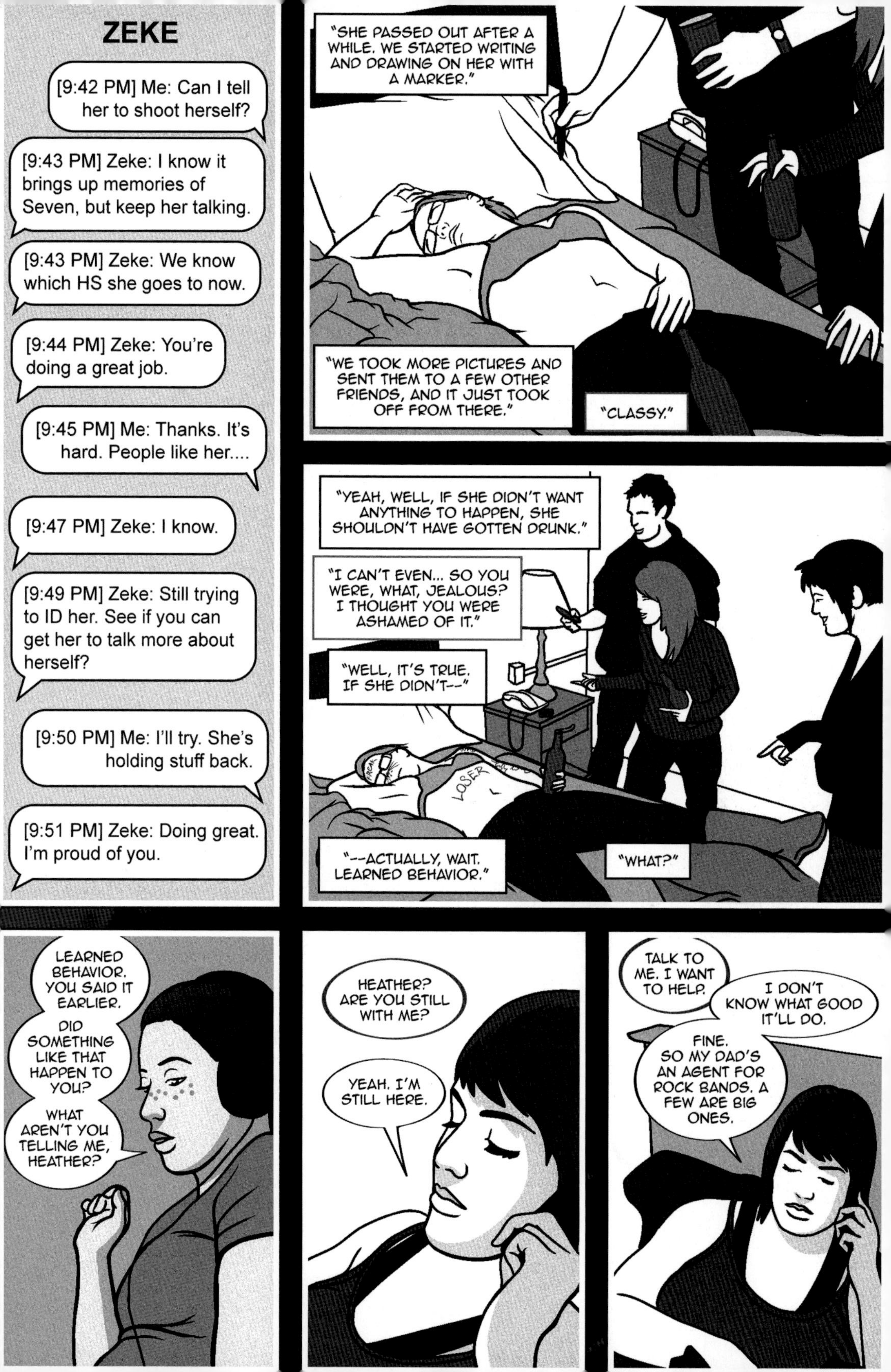
ZEKE
[9:42 PM] Me: Can I tell her to shoot herself?
[9:43 PM] Zeke: I know it brings up memories of Seven, but keep her talking.
[9:43 PM] Zeke: We know which HS she goes to now.
[9:44 PM] Zeke: You're doing a great job.
[9:45 PM] Me: Thanks. It's hard. People like her....
[9:47 PM] Zeke: I know.
[9:49 PM] Zeke: Still trying to ID her. See if you can get her to talk more about herself?
[9:50 PM] Me: I'll try. She's holding stuff back.
[9:51 PM] Zeke: Doing great. I'm proud of you.
"SHE PASSED OUT AFTER A WHILE. WE STARTED WRITING AND DRAWING ON HER WITH A MARKER."
"WE TOOK MORE PICTURES AND SENT THEM TO A FEW OTHER FRIENDS, AND IT JUST TOOK OFF FROM THERE."
"CLASSY."
"YEAH, WELL, IF SHE DIDN'T WANT ANYTHING TO HAPPEN, SHE SHOULDN'T HAVE GOTTEN DRUNK."
"I CAN'T EVEN... SO YOU WERE, WHAT, JEALOUS? I THOUGHT YOU WERE ASHAMED OF IT."
"WELL, IT'S TRUE. IF SHE DIDN'T--"
LOSER
"--ACTUALLY, WAIT. LEARNED BEHAVIOR."
"WHAT?"
LEARNED BEHAVIOR. YOU SAID IT EARLIER.
DID SOMETHING LIKE THAT HAPPEN TO YOU?
WHAT AREN'T YOU TELLING ME, HEATHER?
HEATHER? ARE YOU STILL WITH ME?
YEAH. I'M STILL HERE.
TALK TO ME. I WANT TO HELP.
I DON'T KNOW WHAT GOOD IT'LL DO.
FINE. SO MY DAD'S AN AGENT FOR ROCK BANDS. A FEW ARE BIG ONES.

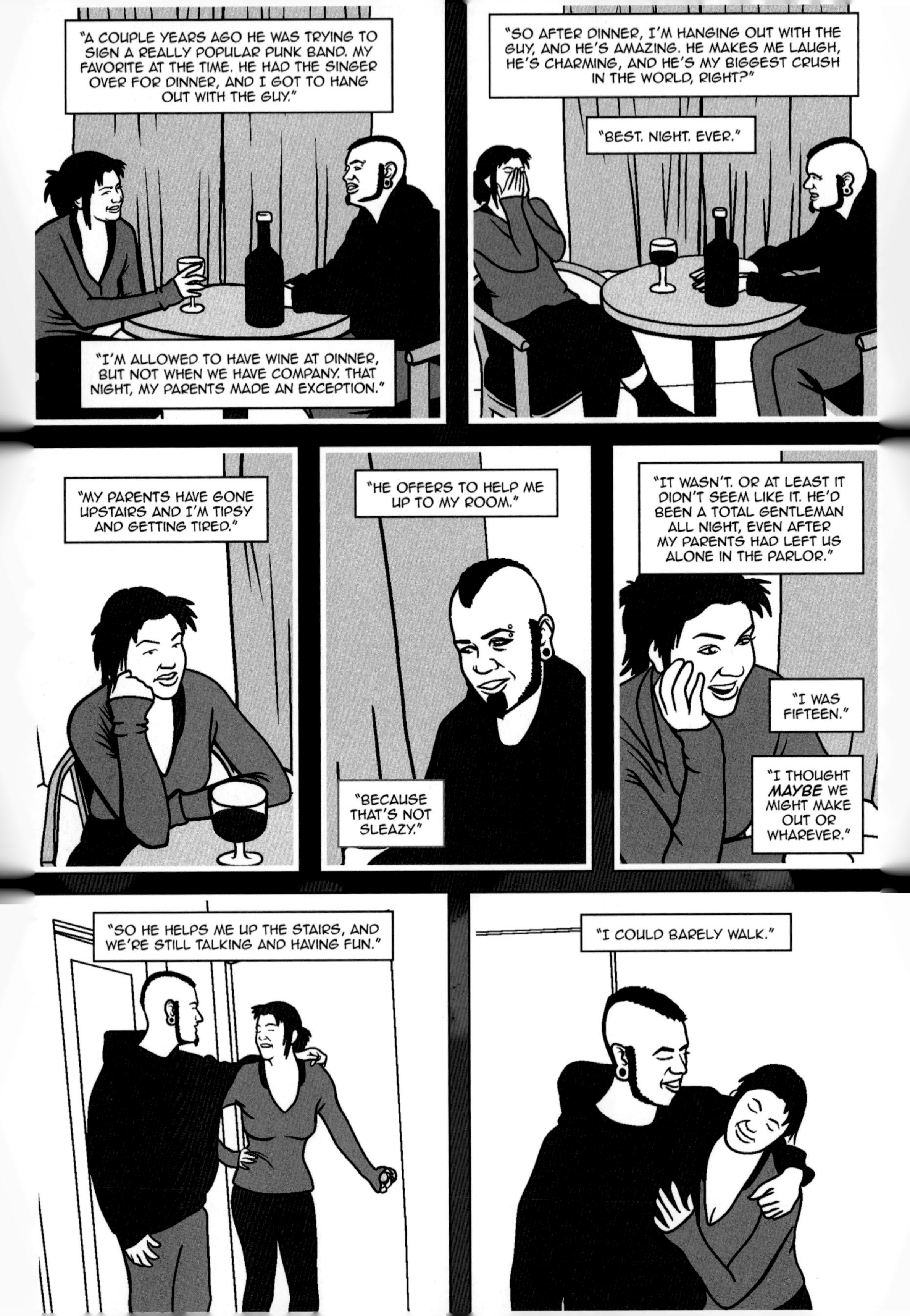
"A COUPLE YEARS AGO HE WAS TRYING TO SIGN A REALLY POPULAR PUNK BAND. MY FAVORITE AT THE TIME. HE HAD THE SINGER OVER FOR DINNER, AND I GOT TO HANG OUT WITH THE GUY."
"I'M ALLOWED TO HAVE WINE AT DINNER, BUT NOT WHEN WE HAVE COMPANY. THAT NIGHT, MY PARENTS MADE AN EXCEPTION."
"SO AFTER DINNER, I'M HANGING OUT WITH THE GUY, AND HE'S AMAZING. HE MAKES ME LAUGH, HE'S CHARMING, AND HE'S MY BIGGEST CRUSH IN THE WORLD, RIGHT?"
"BEST. NIGHT. EVER."
"MY PARENTS HAVE GONE UPSTAIRS AND I'M TIPSY AND GETTING TIRED."
"HE OFFERS TO HELP ME UP TO MY ROOM."
"BECAUSE THAT'S NOT SLEAZY."
"IT WASN'T. OR AT LEAST IT DIDN'T SEEM LIKE IT. HE'D BEEN A TOTAL GENTLEMAN ALL NIGHT, EVEN AFTER MY PARENTS HAD LEFT US ALONE IN THE PARLOR."
"I WAS FIFTEEN."
"I THOUGHT *MAYBE* WE MIGHT MAKE OUT OR WHAREVER."
"SO HE HELPS ME UP THE STAIRS, AND WE'RE STILL TALKING AND HAVING FUN."
"I COULD BARELY WALK."

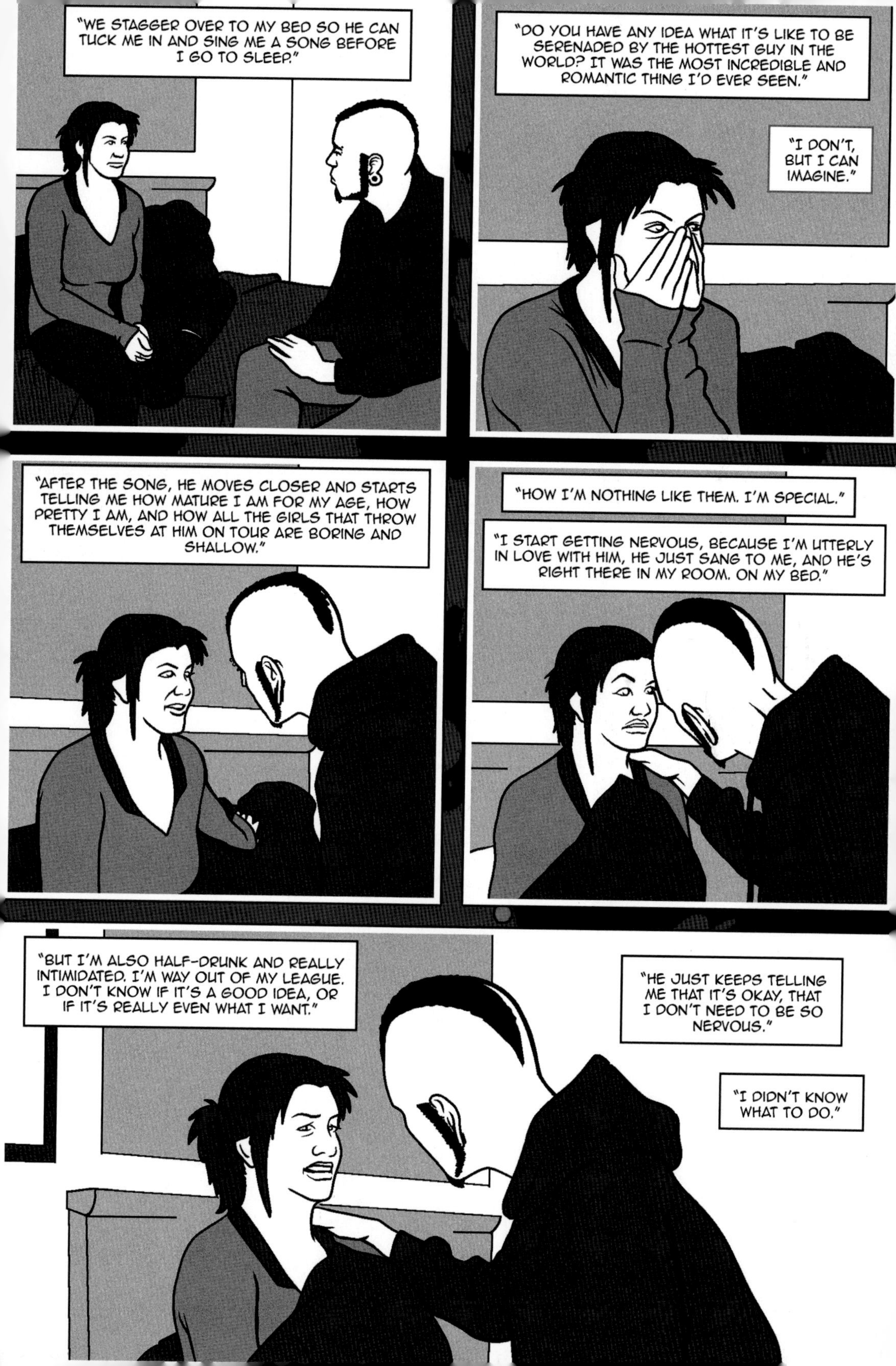
"WE STAGGER OVER TO MY BED SO HE CAN TUCK ME IN AND SING ME A SONG BEFORE I GO TO SLEEP."
"DO YOU HAVE ANY IDEA WHAT IT'S LIKE TO BE SERENADED BY THE HOTTEST GUY IN THE WORLD? IT WAS THE MOST INCREDIBLE AND ROMANTIC THING I'D EVER SEEN."
"I DON'T, BUT I CAN IMAGINE."
"AFTER THE SONG, HE MOVES CLOSER AND STARTS TELLING ME HOW MATURE I AM FOR MY AGE, HOW PRETTY I AM, AND HOW ALL THE GIRLS THAT THROW THEMSELVES AT HIM ON TOUR ARE BORING AND SHALLOW."
"HOW I'M NOTHING LIKE THEM. I'M SPECIAL."
"I START GETTING NERVOUS, BECAUSE I'M UTTERLY IN LOVE WITH HIM, HE JUST SANG TO ME, AND HE'S RIGHT THERE IN MY ROOM. ON MY BED."
"BUT I'M ALSO HALF-DRUNK AND REALLY INTIMIDATED. I'M WAY OUT OF MY LEAGUE. I DON'T KNOW IF IT'S A GOOD IDEA, OR IF IT'S REALLY EVEN WHAT I WANT."
"HE JUST KEEPS TELLING ME THAT IT'S OKAY, THAT I DON'T NEED TO BE SO NERVOUS."
"I DIDN'T KNOW WHAT TO DO."

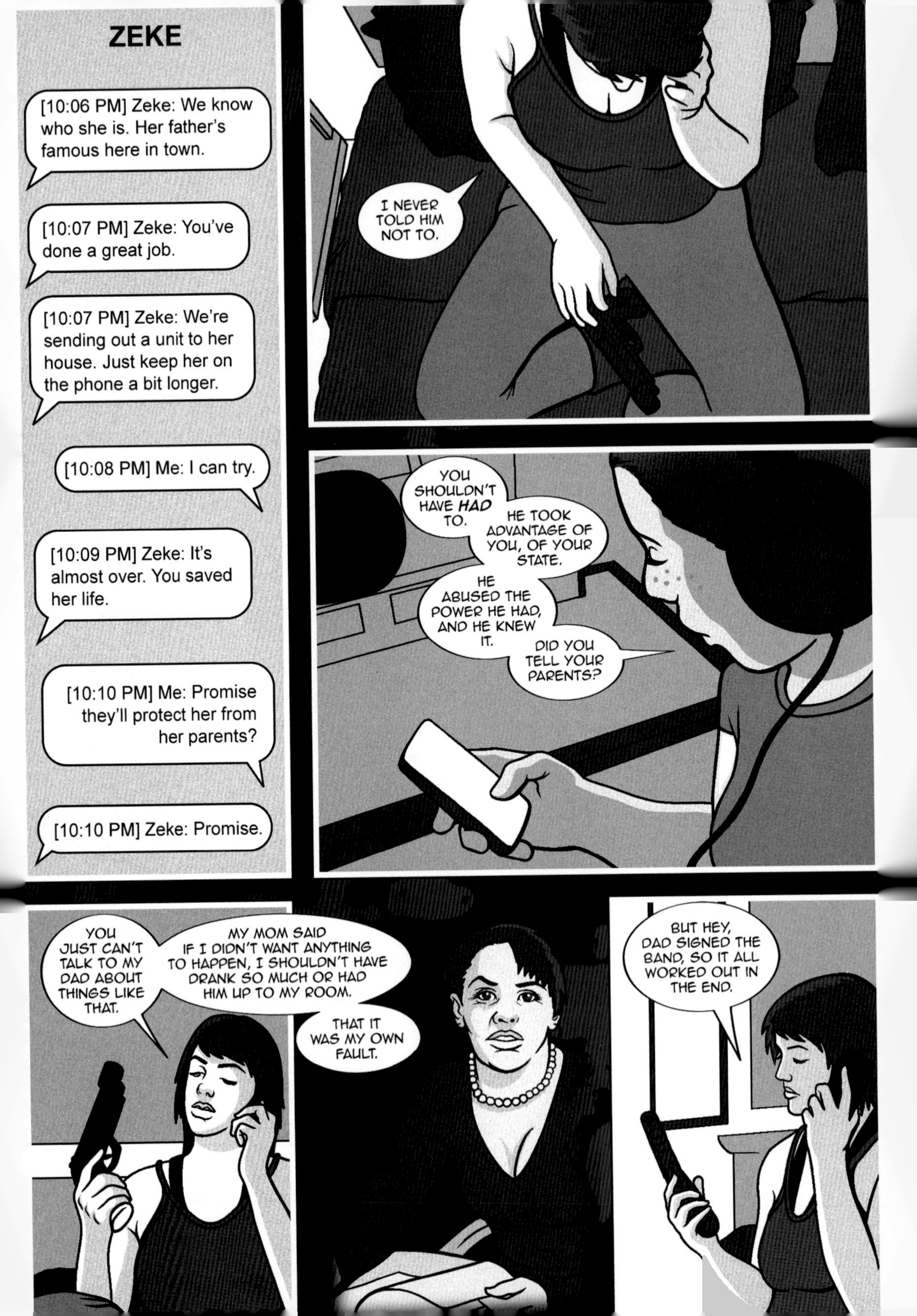
ZEKE
[10:06 PM] Zeke: We know who she is. Her father's famous here in town.
[10:07 PM] Zeke: You've done a great job.
[10:07 PM] Zeke: We're sending out a unit to her house. Just keep her on the phone a bit longer.
[10:08 PM] Me: I can try.
[10:09 PM] Zeke: It's almost over. You saved her life.
[10:10 PM] Me: Promise they'll protect her from her parents?
[10:10 PM] Zeke: Promise.
I NEVER TOLD HIM NOT TO.
YOU SHOULDN'T HAVE ***HAD*** TO.
HE TOOK ADVANTAGE OF YOU, OF YOUR STATE.
HE ABUSED THE POWER HE HAD, AND HE KNEW IT.
DID YOU TELL YOUR PARENTS?
YOU JUST CAN'T TALK TO MY DAD ABOUT THINGS LIKE THAT.
MY MOM SAID IF I DIDN'T WANT ANYTHING TO HAPPEN, I SHOULDN'T HAVE DRANK SO MUCH OR HAD HIM UP TO MY ROOM.
THAT IT WAS MY OWN FAULT.
BUT HEY, DAD SIGNED THE BAND, SO IT ALL WORKED OUT IN THE END.

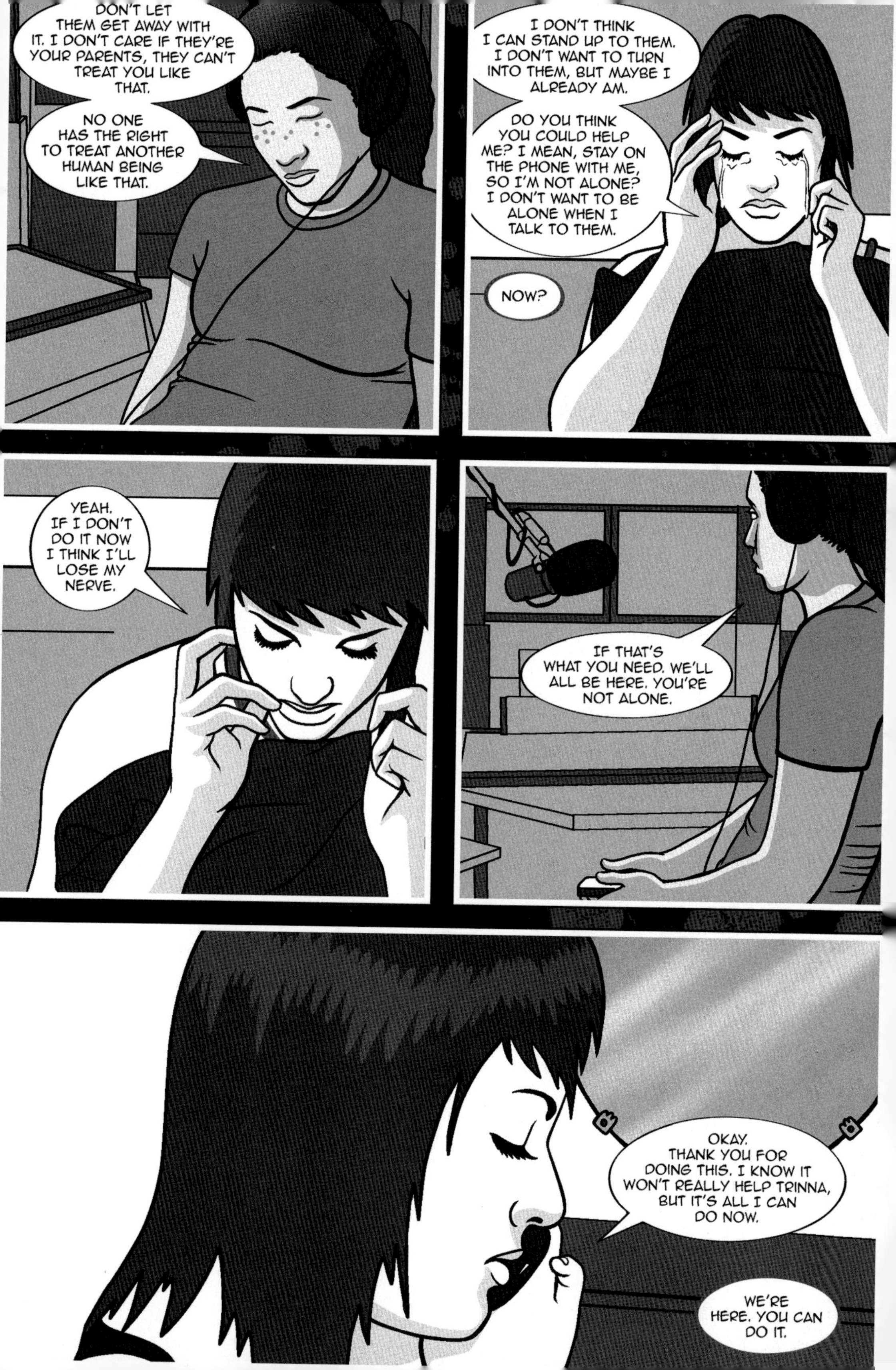
DON'T LET THEM GET AWAY WITH IT. I DON'T CARE IF THEY'RE YOUR PARENTS, THEY CAN'T TREAT YOU LIKE THAT.
NO ONE HAS THE RIGHT TO TREAT ANOTHER HUMAN BEING LIKE THAT.
I DON'T THINK I CAN STAND UP TO THEM. I DON'T WANT TO TURN INTO THEM, BUT MAYBE I ALREADY AM.
DO YOU THINK YOU COULD HELP ME? I MEAN, STAY ON THE PHONE WITH ME, SO I'M NOT ALONE? I DON'T WANT TO BE ALONE WHEN I TALK TO THEM.
NOW?
YEAH. IF I DON'T DO IT NOW I THINK I'LL LOSE MY NERVE.
IF THAT'S WHAT YOU NEED. WE'LL ALL BE HERE. YOU'RE NOT ALONE.
OKAY. THANK YOU FOR DOING THIS. I KNOW IT WON'T REALLY HELP TRINNA, BUT IT'S ALL I CAN DO NOW.
WE'RE HERE. YOU CAN DO IT.

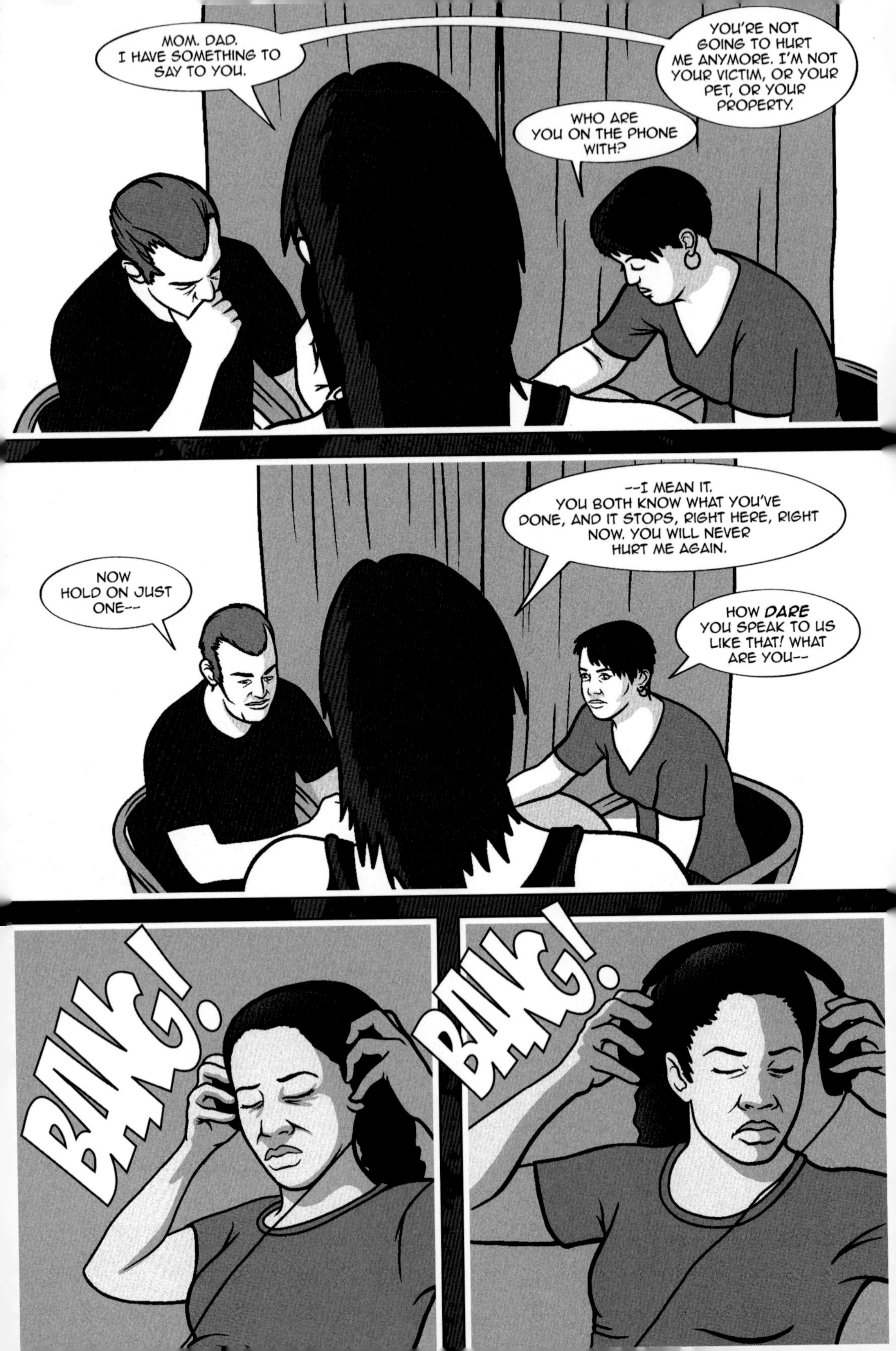
MOM. DAD. I HAVE SOMETHING TO SAY TO YOU.
YOU'RE NOT GOING TO HURT ME ANYMORE. I'M NOT YOUR VICTIM, OR YOUR PET, OR YOUR PROPERTY.
WHO ARE YOU ON THE PHONE WITH?
--I MEAN IT. YOU BOTH KNOW WHAT YOU'VE DONE, AND IT STOPS, RIGHT HERE, RIGHT NOW. YOU WILL NEVER HURT ME AGAIN.
NOW HOLD ON JUST ONE--
HOW *DARE* YOU SPEAK TO US LIKE THAT! WHAT ARE YOU--
BANG!
BANG!

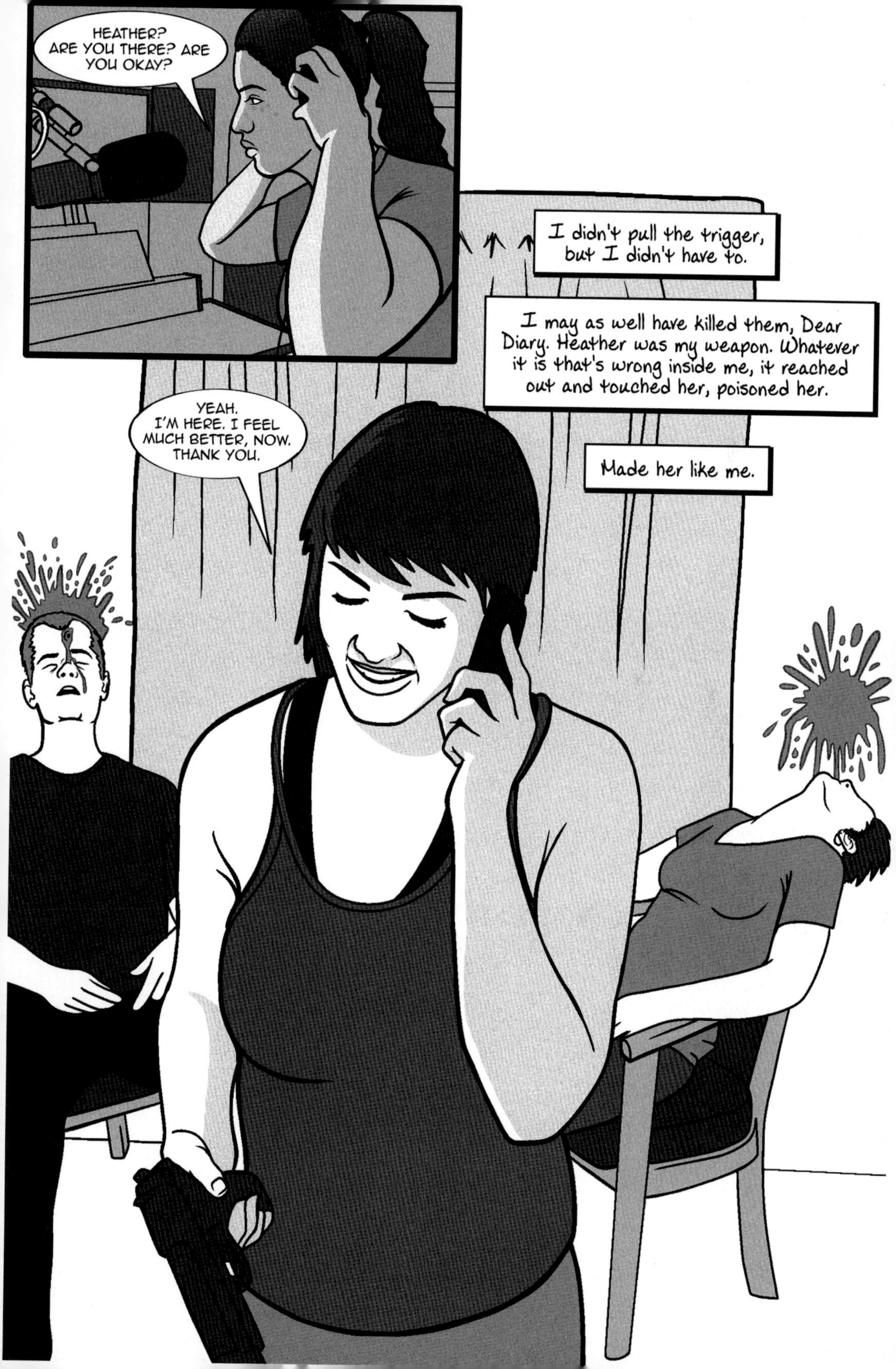
HEATHER? ARE YOU THERE? ARE YOU OKAY?
I didn't pull the trigger, but I didn't have to.
I may as well have killed them, Dear Diary. Heather was my weapon. Whatever it is that's wrong inside me, it reached out and touched her, poisoned her.
Made her like me.
YEAH. I'M HERE. I FEEL MUCH BETTER, NOW. THANK YOU.

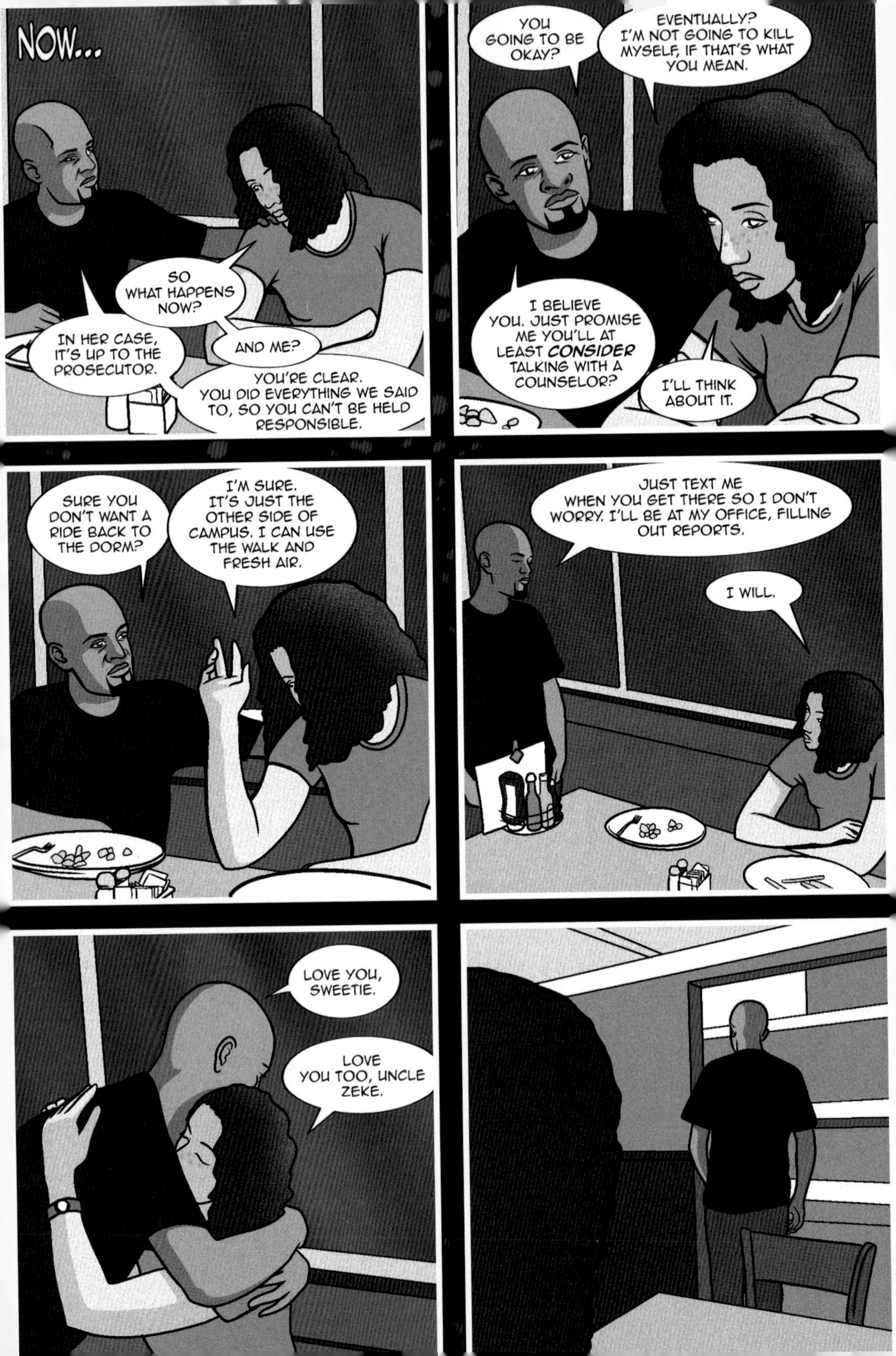
NOW...
SO WHAT HAPPENS NOW?
IN HER CASE, IT'S UP TO THE PROSECUTOR.
AND ME?
YOU'RE CLEAR. YOU DID EVERYTHING WE SAID TO, SO YOU CAN'T BE HELD RESPONSIBLE.
YOU GOING TO BE OKAY?
EVENTUALLY? I'M NOT GOING TO KILL MYSELF, IF THAT'S WHAT YOU MEAN.
I BELIEVE YOU. JUST PROMISE ME YOU'LL AT LEAST CONSIDER TALKING WITH A COUNSELOR?
I'LL THINK ABOUT IT.
SURE YOU DON'T WANT A RIDE BACK TO THE DORM?
I'M SURE. IT'S JUST THE OTHER SIDE OF CAMPUS. I CAN USE THE WALK AND FRESH AIR.
JUST TEXT ME WHEN YOU GET THERE SO I DON'T WORRY. I'LL BE AT MY OFFICE, FILLING OUT REPORTS.
I WILL.
LOVE YOU, SWEETIE.
LOVE YOU TOO, UNCLE ZEKE.

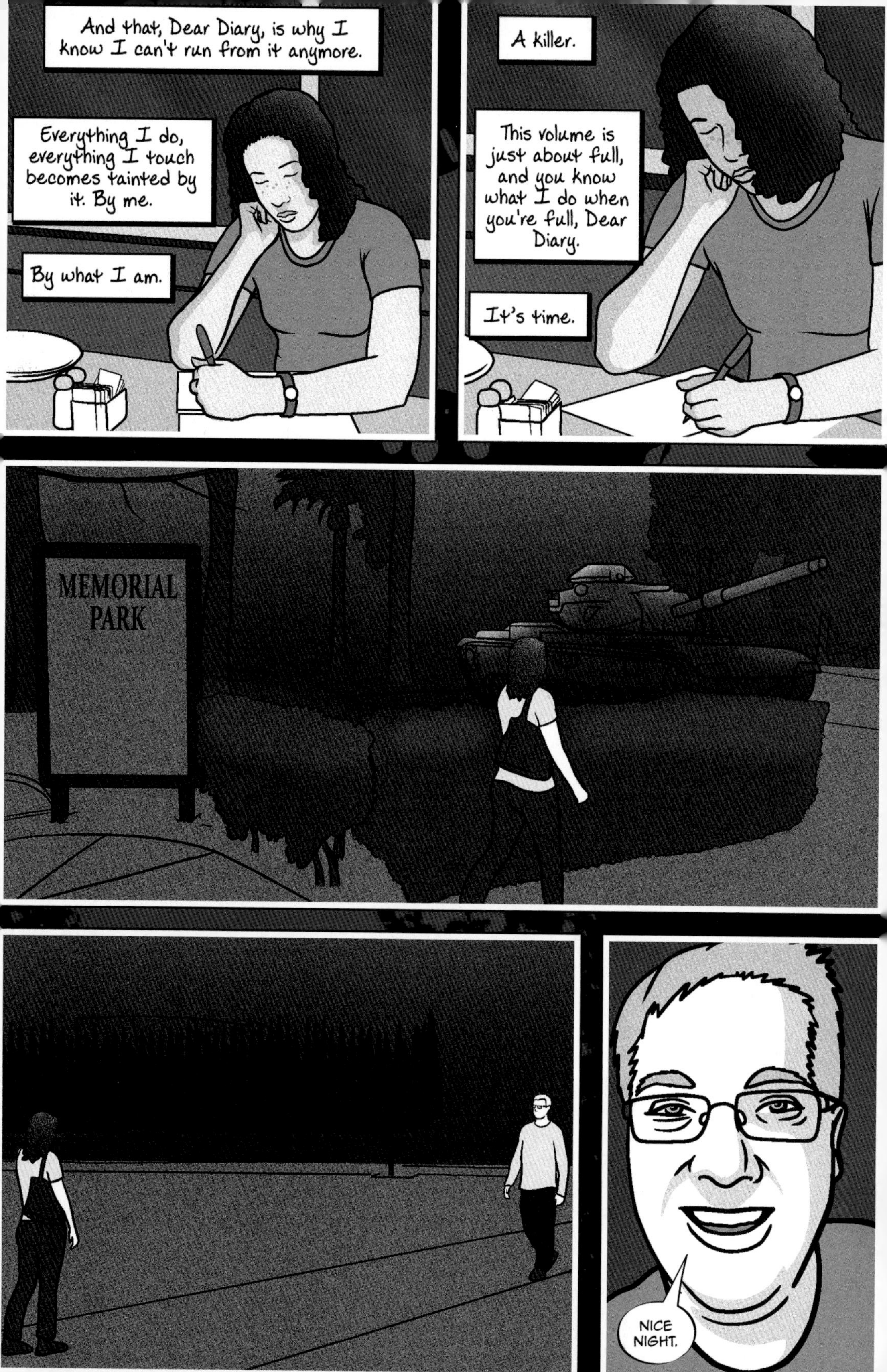
And that, Dear Diary, is why I know I can't run from it anymore.
Everything I do, everything I touch becomes tainted by it. By me.
By what I am.
A killer.
This volume is just about full, and you know what I do when you're full, Dear Diary.
It's time.
MEMORIAL PARK
NICE NIGHT.

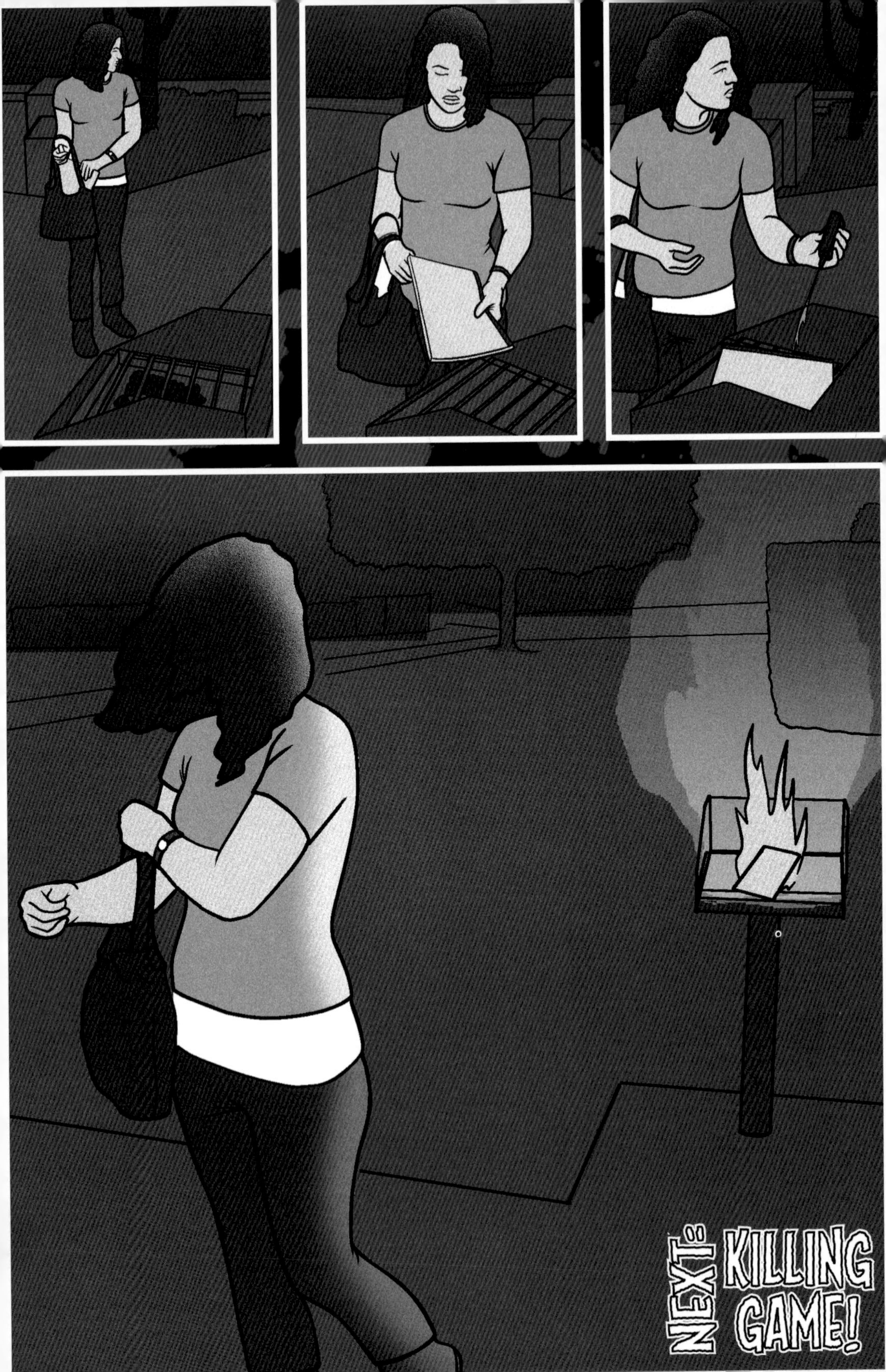
NEXT: KILLING GAME!

Blair Student Found Dead

Staff Writer | August 28, 2013 | <u>0 comments</u>

CUTTER'S CIRCLE - A Blair student was found dead in the early morning hours on Monday, August 26th, off a jogging trail near the Southern shore of Cutter's Lake.

Katelyn Miller, 19, of Mobile, Alabama, was discovered by a jogger who immediately called 911. She was declared dead by EMS on arrival.

Pictured above: Katelyn Miller

A sophomore at Blair University, Miller was a communications major, a member of the cheer squad, and an aspiring model. A spokesperson for the university described her as an exemplary student who was well liked by her fellow students and teachers alike. Members of the cheer squad are holding a memorial on Wednesday at 7pm at the Rue Marjory Gymnasium.

Detective Sergeant Ezekiel Aarons of the Cutter's Circle Police Department indicated that Miller's death is being ruled a homicide, and that the case is currently under investigation.

"We have ample reason to believe that Ms. Miller was the victim of homicide," Aarons said. "At this time, we are unable to disclose any details of the crime. We'll let you all know what we can, when we can."

The identity of the jogger who found Miller's body is currently being withheld.

Lakeside High Student Remains In Coma After Suicide Attempt

Staff Writer | August 28, 2013 | <u>11 comments</u>

CUTTER'S CIRCLE - 17-year-old Trinna Goff remains in a coma at Desert Regional Medical Center after attempting suicide on Sunday. Doctors say that she is in critical but stable condition in the ICU.

The circumstances surrounding Goff's suicide attempt are unknown, though school officials have suggested that she may have been the recipient of bullying. Friends of the family have said that Goff has been bullied since grade school.

Police are asking that anyone with information contact THE CCPD tip line at 555-8344.

a VOICE in the DARK

"KILLING GAME, PT. 1"

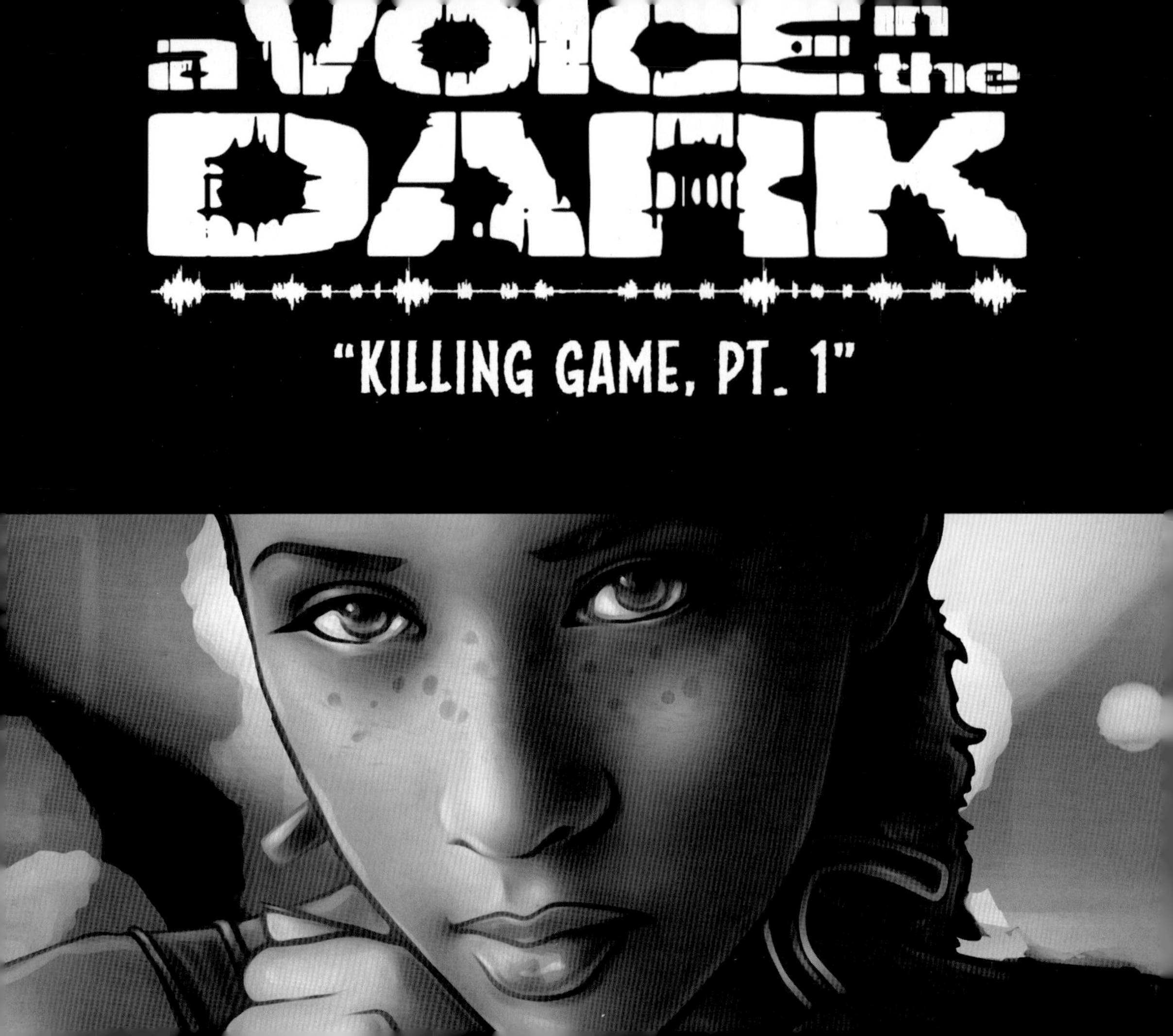

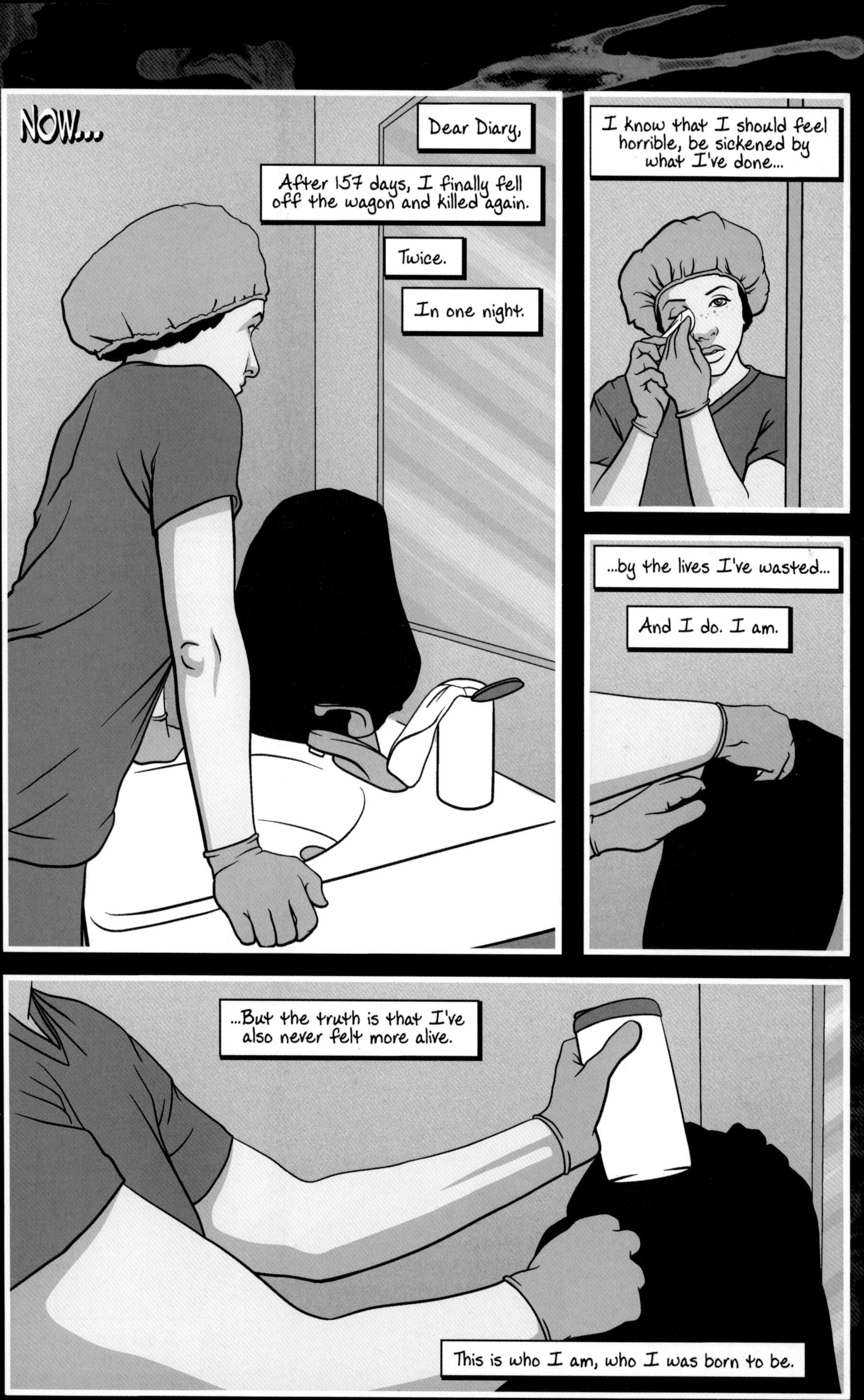
NOW...
Dear Diary,
After 157 days, I finally fell off the wagon and killed again.
Twice.
In one night.
I know that I should feel horrible, be sickened by what I've done...
...by the lives I've wasted...
And I do. I am.
...But the truth is that I've also never felt more alive.
This is who I am, who I was born to be.

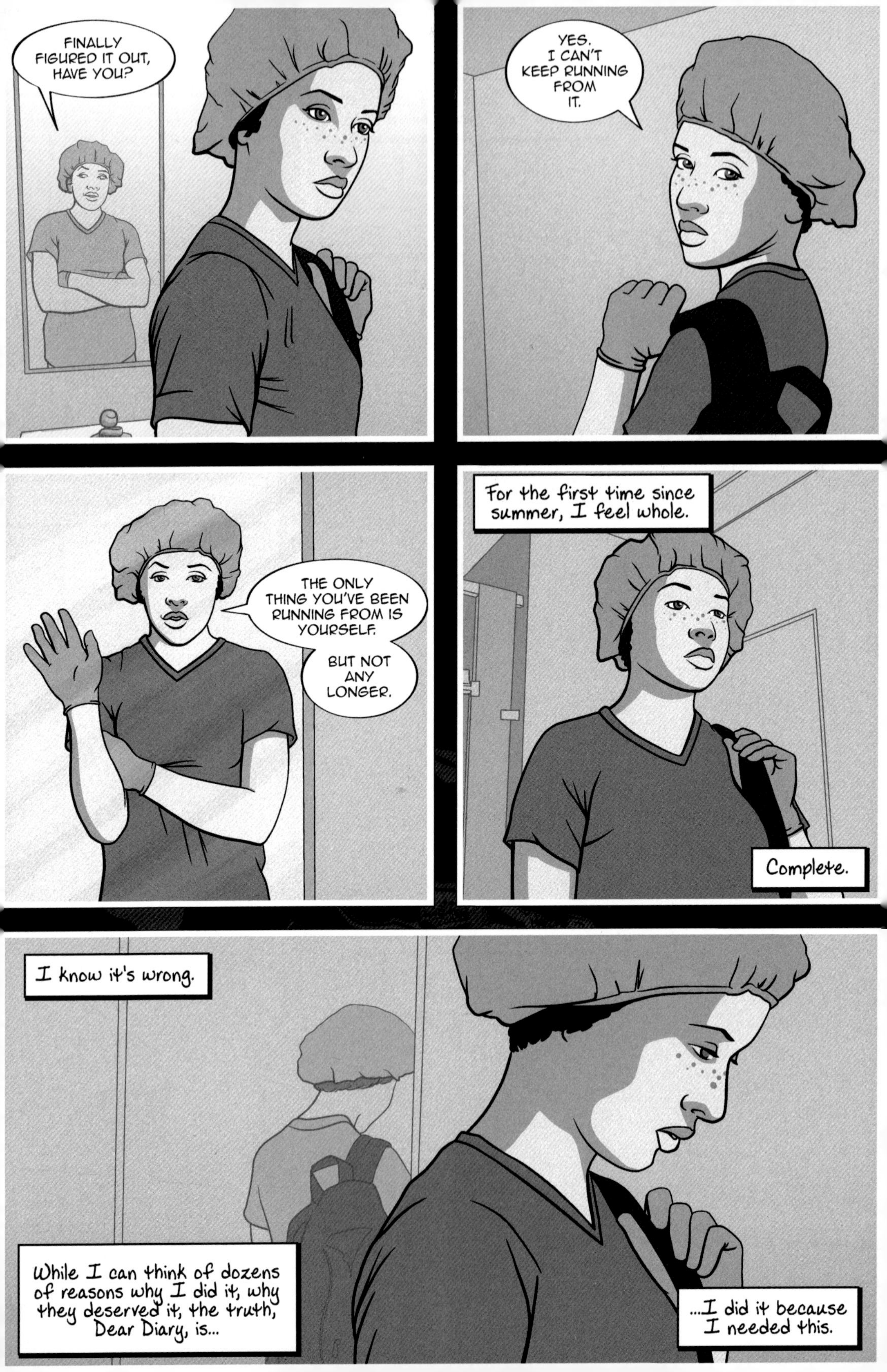

FINALLY FIGURED IT OUT, HAVE YOU?
YES. I CAN'T KEEP RUNNING FROM IT.
THE ONLY THING YOU'VE BEEN RUNNING FROM IS YOURSELF.
BUT NOT ANY LONGER.
For the first time since summer, I feel whole.
Complete.
I know it's wrong.
While I can think of dozens of reasons why I did it, why they deserved it, the truth, Dear Diary, is...
...I did it because I needed this.

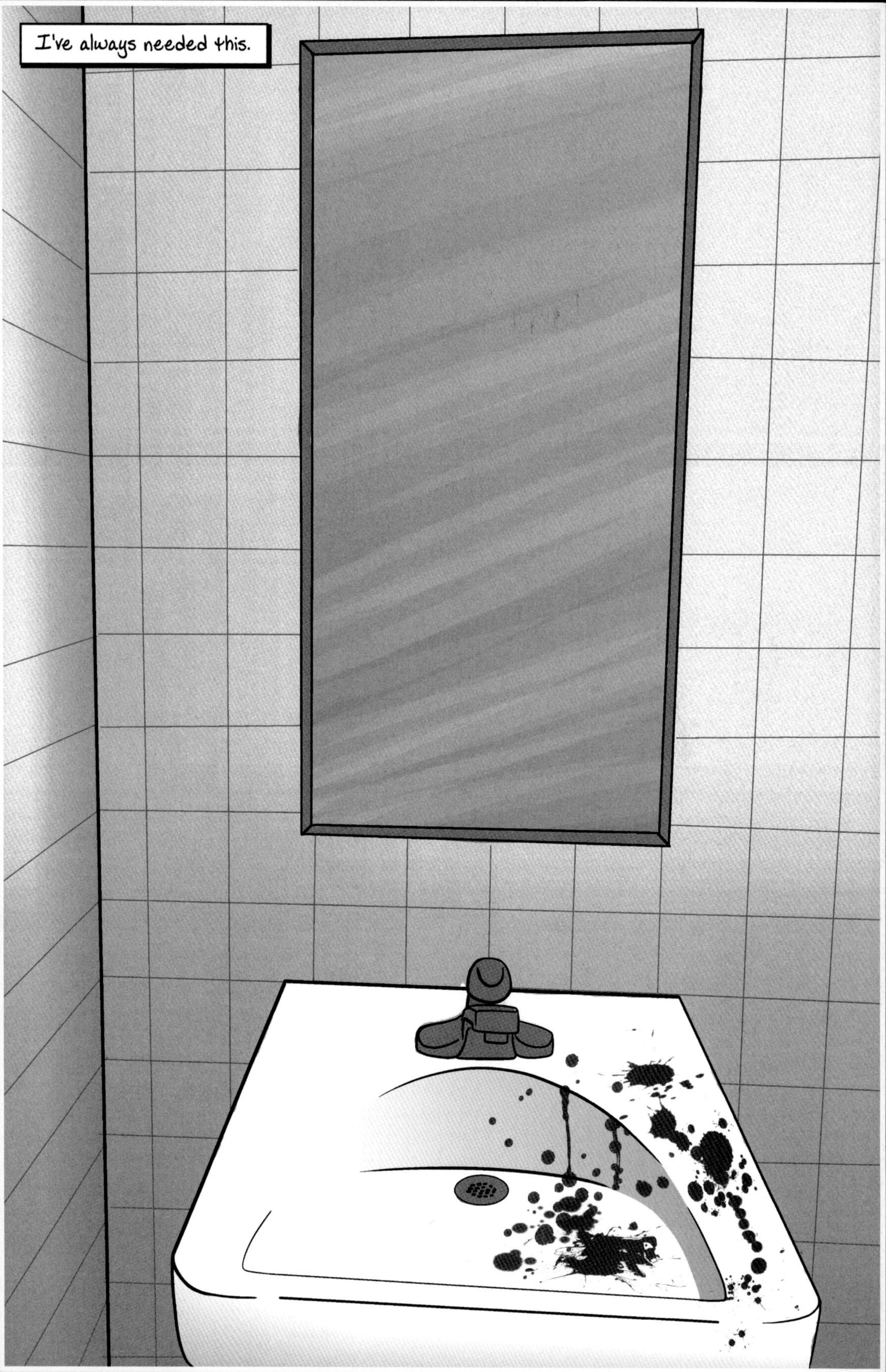
I've always needed this.

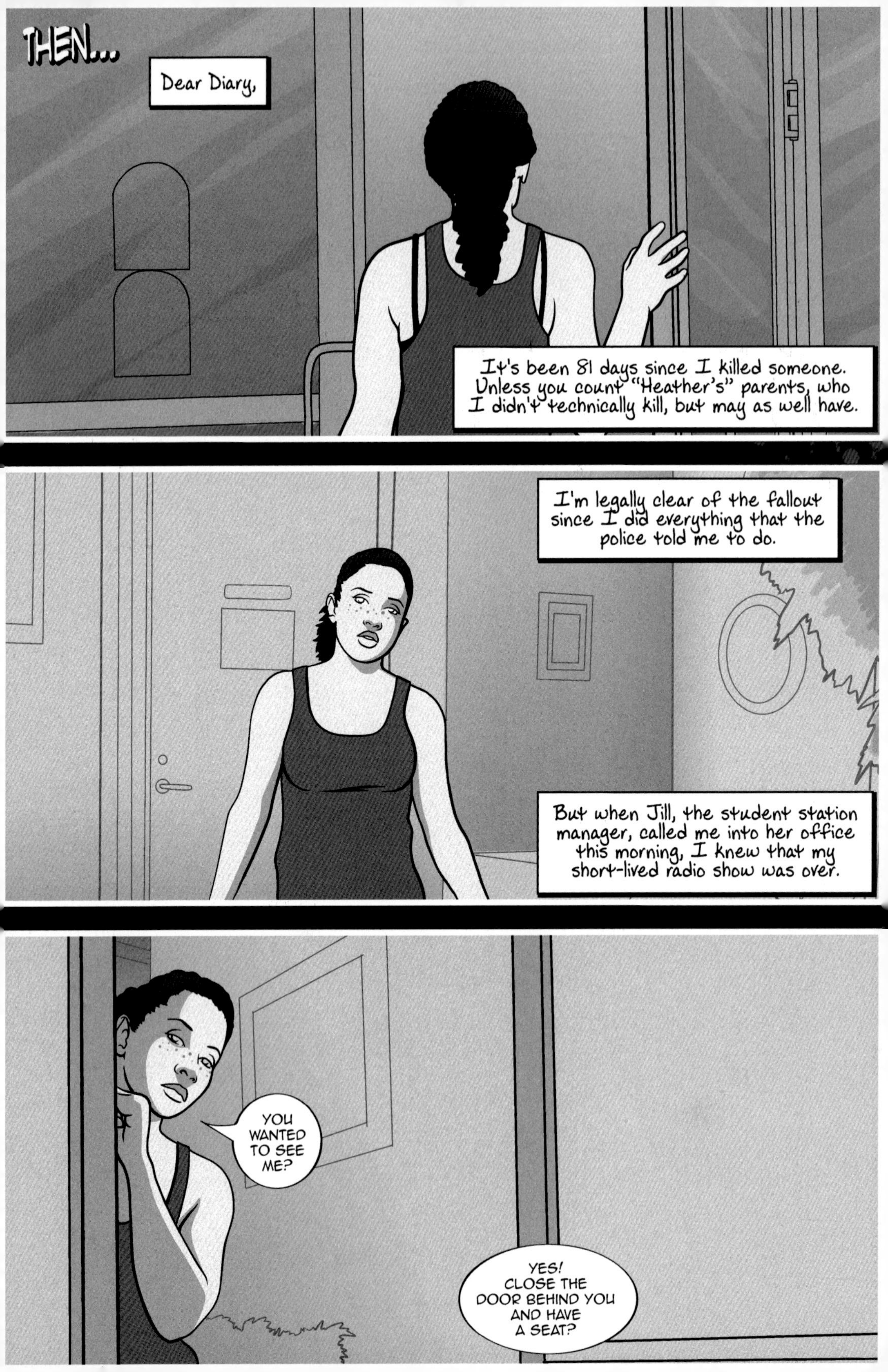
THEN...
Dear Diary,
It's been 81 days since I killed someone. Unless you count "Heather's" parents, who I didn't technically kill, but may as well have.
I'm legally clear of the fallout since I did everything that the police told me to do.
But when Jill, the student station manager, called me into her office this morning, I knew that my short-lived radio show was over.
YOU WANTED TO SEE ME?
YES! CLOSE THE DOOR BEHIND YOU AND HAVE A SEAT?

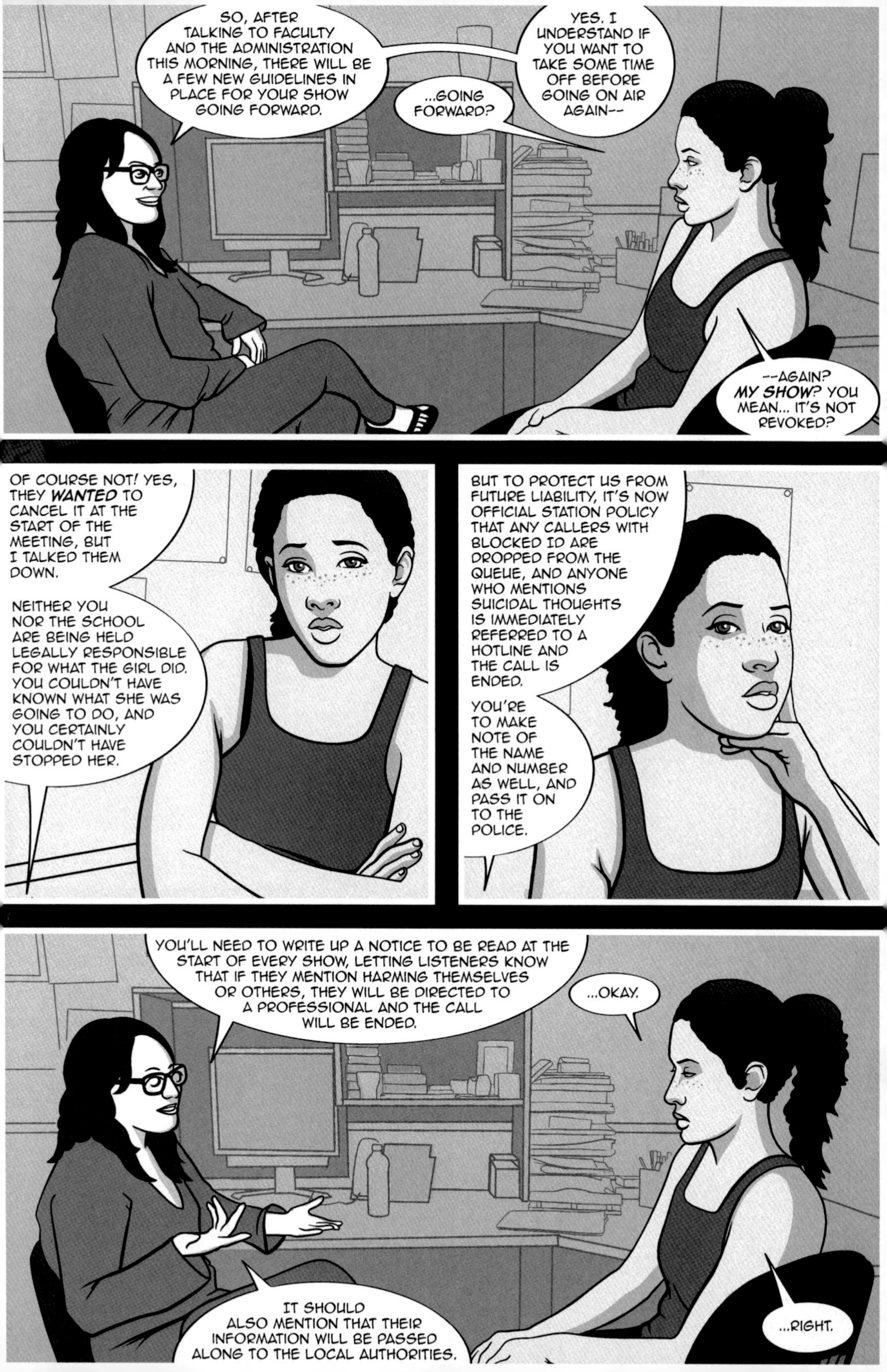
SO, AFTER TALKING TO FACULTY AND THE ADMINISTRATION THIS MORNING, THERE WILL BE A FEW NEW GUIDELINES IN PLACE FOR YOUR SHOW GOING FORWARD.
...GOING FORWARD?
YES. I UNDERSTAND IF YOU WANT TO TAKE SOME TIME OFF BEFORE GOING ON AIR AGAIN--
--AGAIN? ***MY SHOW***? YOU MEAN... IT'S NOT REVOKED?
OF COURSE NOT! YES, THEY ***WANTED*** TO CANCEL IT AT THE START OF THE MEETING, BUT I TALKED THEM DOWN.
NEITHER YOU NOR THE SCHOOL ARE BEING HELD LEGALLY RESPONSIBLE FOR WHAT THE GIRL DID. YOU COULDN'T HAVE KNOWN WHAT SHE WAS GOING TO DO, AND YOU CERTAINLY COULDN'T HAVE STOPPED HER.
BUT TO PROTECT US FROM FUTURE LIABILITY, IT'S NOW OFFICIAL STATION POLICY THAT ANY CALLERS WITH BLOCKED ID ARE DROPPED FROM THE QUEUE, AND ANYONE WHO MENTIONS SUICIDAL THOUGHTS IS IMMEDIATELY REFERRED TO A HOTLINE AND THE CALL IS ENDED.
YOU'RE TO MAKE NOTE OF THE NAME AND NUMBER AS WELL, AND PASS IT ON TO THE POLICE.
YOU'LL NEED TO WRITE UP A NOTICE TO BE READ AT THE START OF EVERY SHOW, LETTING LISTENERS KNOW THAT IF THEY MENTION HARMING THEMSELVES OR OTHERS, THEY WILL BE DIRECTED TO A PROFESSIONAL AND THE CALL WILL BE ENDED.
...OKAY.
IT SHOULD ALSO MENTION THAT THEIR INFORMATION WILL BE PASSED ALONG TO THE LOCAL AUTHORITIES.
...RIGHT.

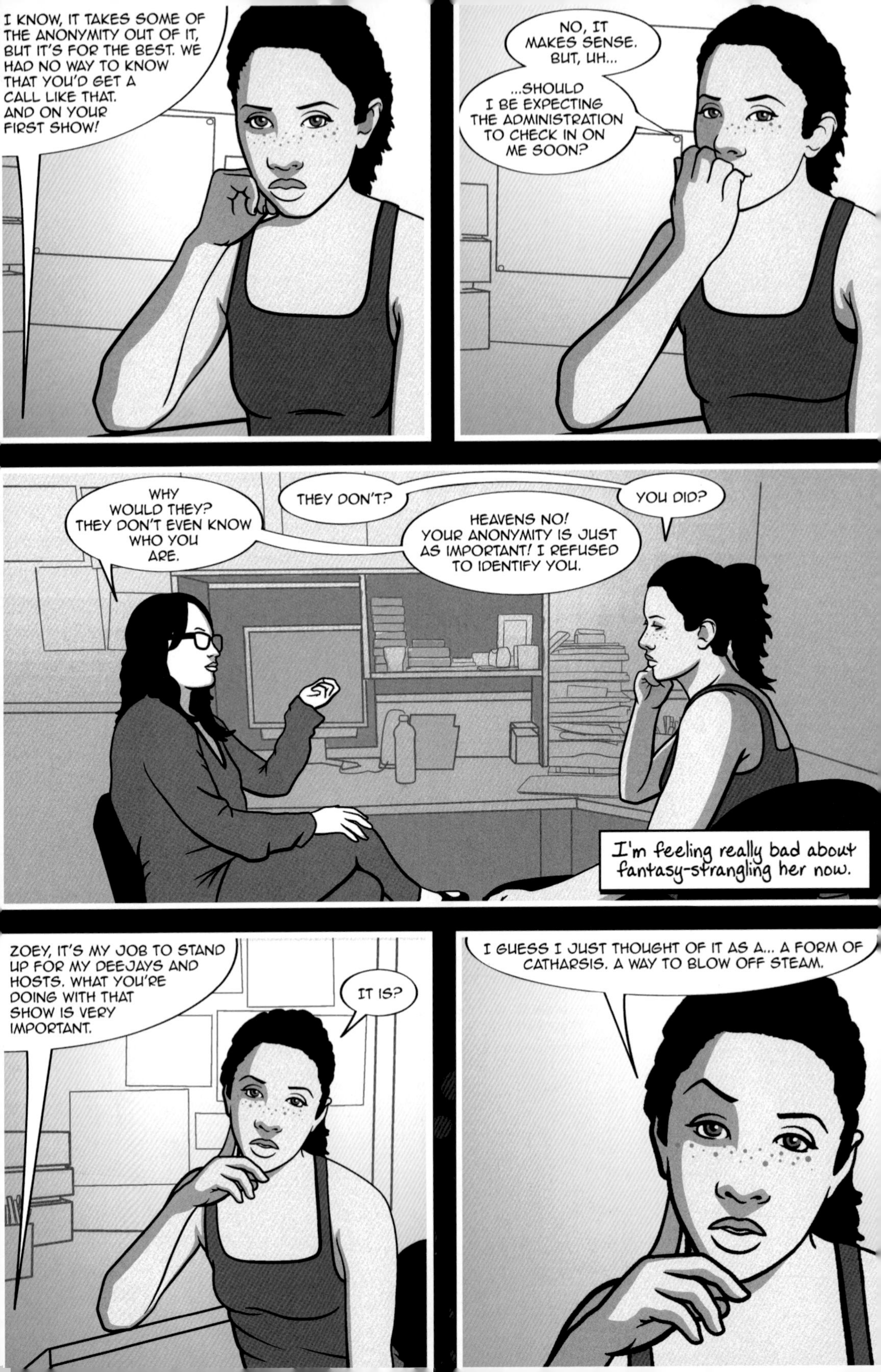
I KNOW, IT TAKES SOME OF THE ANONYMITY OUT OF IT, BUT IT'S FOR THE BEST. WE HAD NO WAY TO KNOW THAT YOU'D GET A CALL LIKE THAT. AND ON YOUR FIRST SHOW!
NO, IT MAKES SENSE. BUT, UH...
...SHOULD I BE EXPECTING THE ADMINISTRATION TO CHECK IN ON ME SOON?
WHY WOULD THEY? THEY DON'T EVEN KNOW WHO YOU ARE.
THEY DON'T?
HEAVENS NO! YOUR ANONYMITY IS JUST AS IMPORTANT! I REFUSED TO IDENTIFY YOU.
YOU DID?
I'm feeling really bad about fantasy-strangling her now.
ZOEY, IT'S MY JOB TO STAND UP FOR MY DEEJAYS AND HOSTS. WHAT YOU'RE DOING WITH THAT SHOW IS VERY IMPORTANT.
IT IS?
I GUESS I JUST THOUGHT OF IT AS A... A FORM OF CATHARSIS. A WAY TO BLOW OFF STEAM.

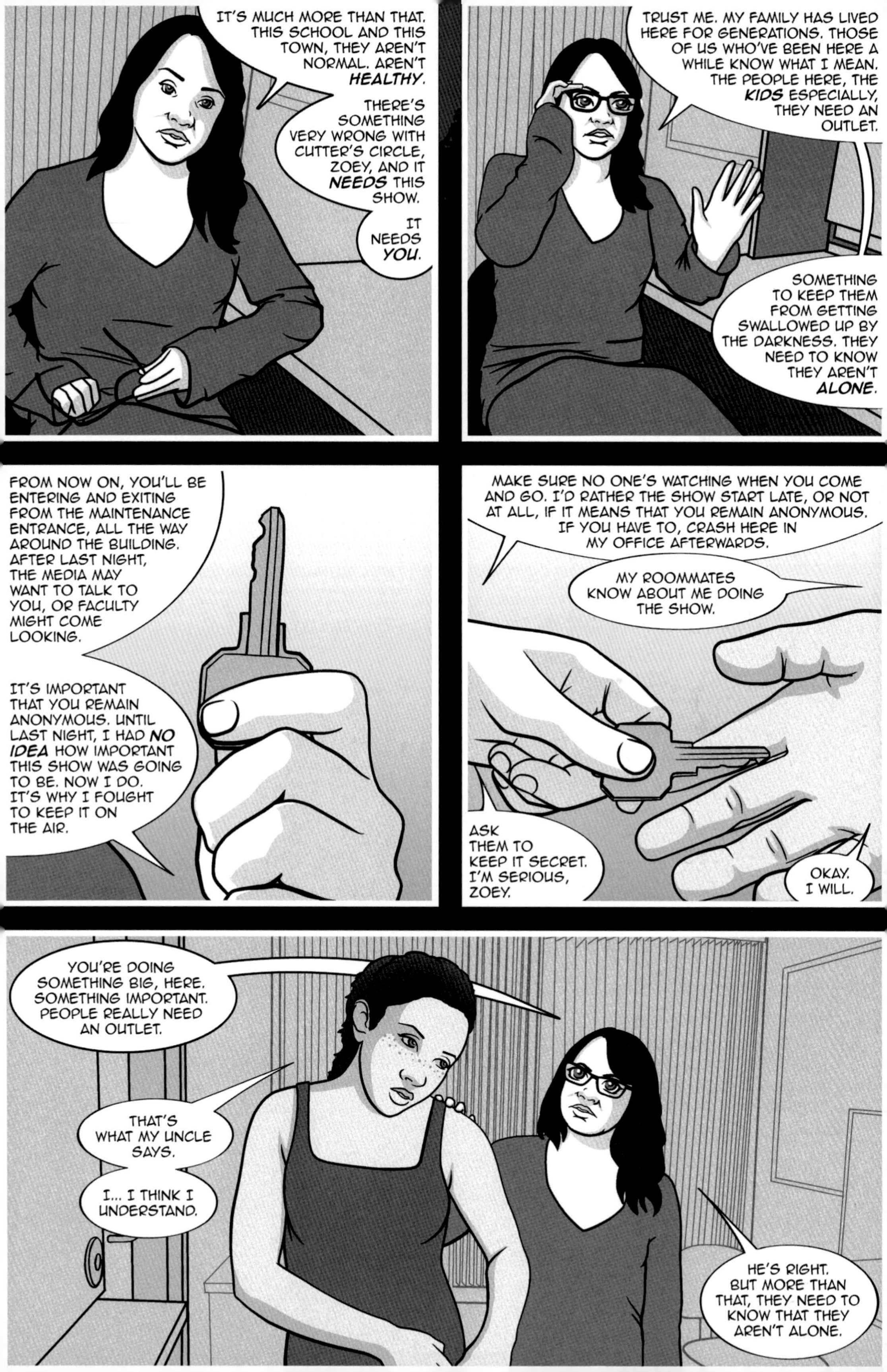
IT'S MUCH MORE THAN THAT. THIS SCHOOL AND THIS TOWN, THEY AREN'T NORMAL. AREN'T **HEALTHY**.
THERE'S SOMETHING VERY WRONG WITH CUTTER'S CIRCLE, ZOEY, AND IT **NEEDS** THIS SHOW.
IT NEEDS **YOU**.
TRUST ME. MY FAMILY HAS LIVED HERE FOR GENERATIONS. THOSE OF US WHO'VE BEEN HERE A WHILE KNOW WHAT I MEAN. THE PEOPLE HERE, THE **KIDS** ESPECIALLY, THEY NEED AN OUTLET.
SOMETHING TO KEEP THEM FROM GETTING SWALLOWED UP BY THE DARKNESS. THEY NEED TO KNOW THEY AREN'T **ALONE**.
FROM NOW ON, YOU'LL BE ENTERING AND EXITING FROM THE MAINTENANCE ENTRANCE, ALL THE WAY AROUND THE BUILDING. AFTER LAST NIGHT, THE MEDIA MAY WANT TO TALK TO YOU, OR FACULTY MIGHT COME LOOKING.
IT'S IMPORTANT THAT YOU REMAIN ANONYMOUS. UNTIL LAST NIGHT, I HAD **NO IDEA** HOW IMPORTANT THIS SHOW WAS GOING TO BE. NOW I DO. IT'S WHY I FOUGHT TO KEEP IT ON THE AIR.
MAKE SURE NO ONE'S WATCHING WHEN YOU COME AND GO. I'D RATHER THE SHOW START LATE, OR NOT AT ALL, IF IT MEANS THAT YOU REMAIN ANONYMOUS. IF YOU HAVE TO, CRASH HERE IN MY OFFICE AFTERWARDS.
MY ROOMMATES KNOW ABOUT ME DOING THE SHOW.
ASK THEM TO KEEP IT SECRET. I'M SERIOUS, ZOEY.
OKAY. I WILL.
YOU'RE DOING SOMETHING BIG, HERE. SOMETHING IMPORTANT. PEOPLE REALLY NEED AN OUTLET.
THAT'S WHAT MY UNCLE SAYS.
I... I THINK I UNDERSTAND.
HE'S RIGHT. BUT MORE THAN THAT, THEY NEED TO KNOW THAT THEY AREN'T ALONE.

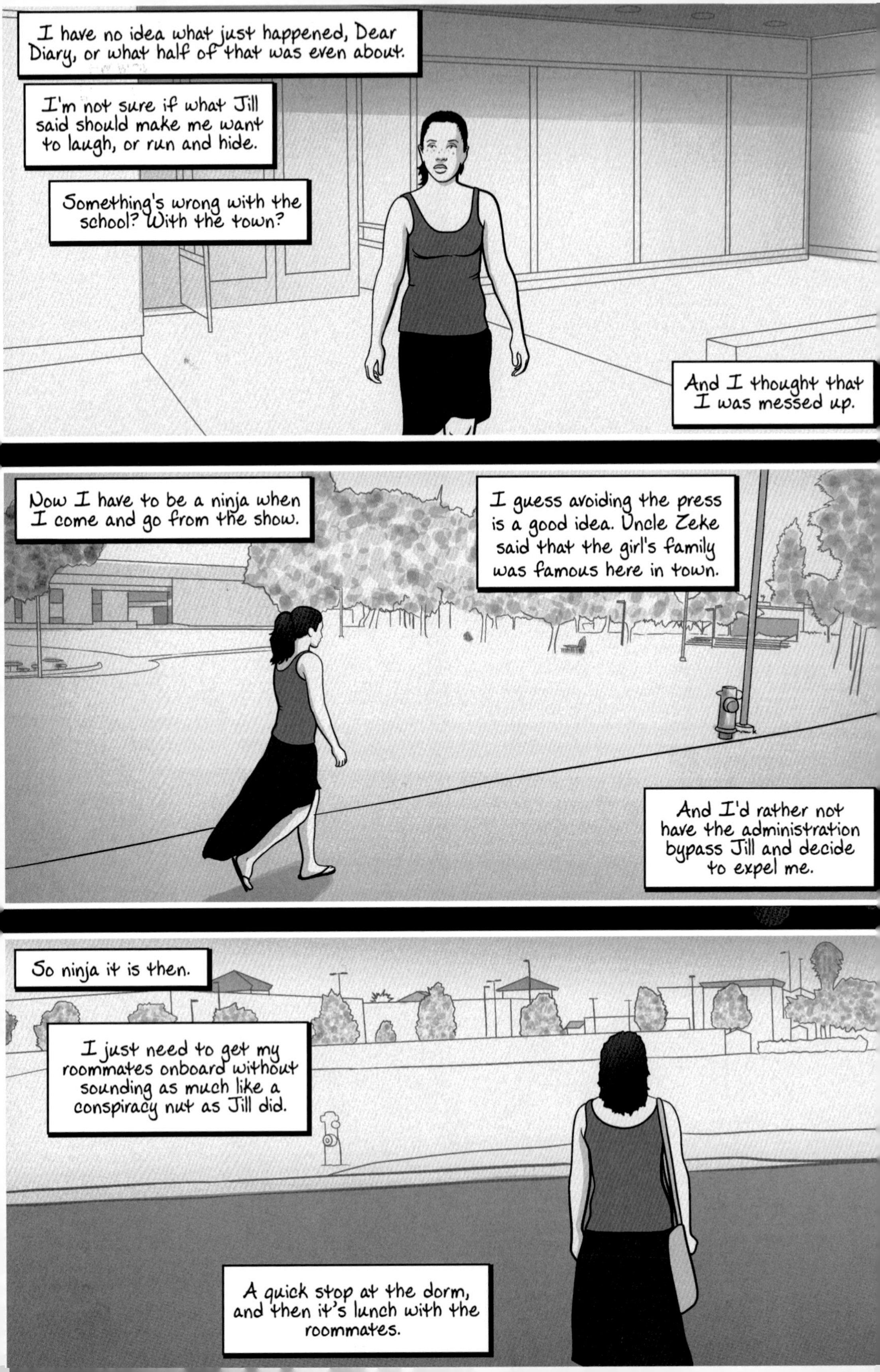
I have no idea what just happened, Dear Diary, or what half of that was even about.
I'm not sure if what Jill said should make me want to laugh, or run and hide.
Something's wrong with the school? With the town?
And I thought that I was messed up.
Now I have to be a ninja when I come and go from the show.
I guess avoiding the press is a good idea. Uncle Zeke said that the girl's family was famous here in town.
And I'd rather not have the administration bypass Jill and decide to expel me.
So ninja it is then.
I just need to get my roommates onboard without sounding as much like a conspiracy nut as Jill did.
A quick stop at the dorm, and then it's lunch with the roommates.

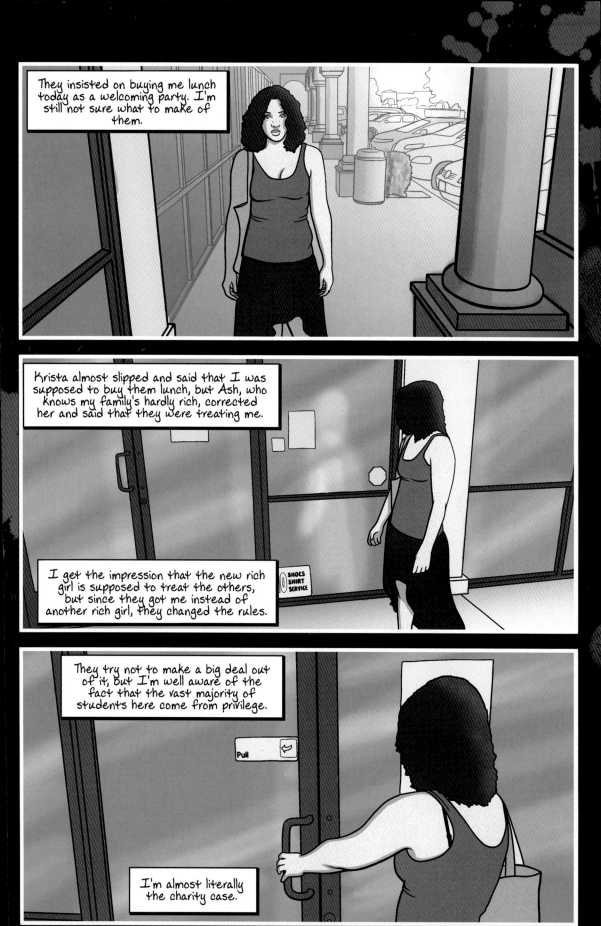

They insisted on buying me lunch today as a welcoming party. I'm still not sure what to make of them.

Krista almost slipped and said that I was supposed to buy them lunch, but Ash, who knows my family's hardly rich, corrected her and said that they were treating me.

I get the impression that the new rich girl is supposed to treat the others, but since they got me instead of another rich girl, they changed the rules.

SHOES
SHIRT
SERVICE

They try not to make a big deal out of it, but I'm well aware of the fact that the vast majority of students here come from privilege.

Pull ⬅

I'm almost literally the charity case.

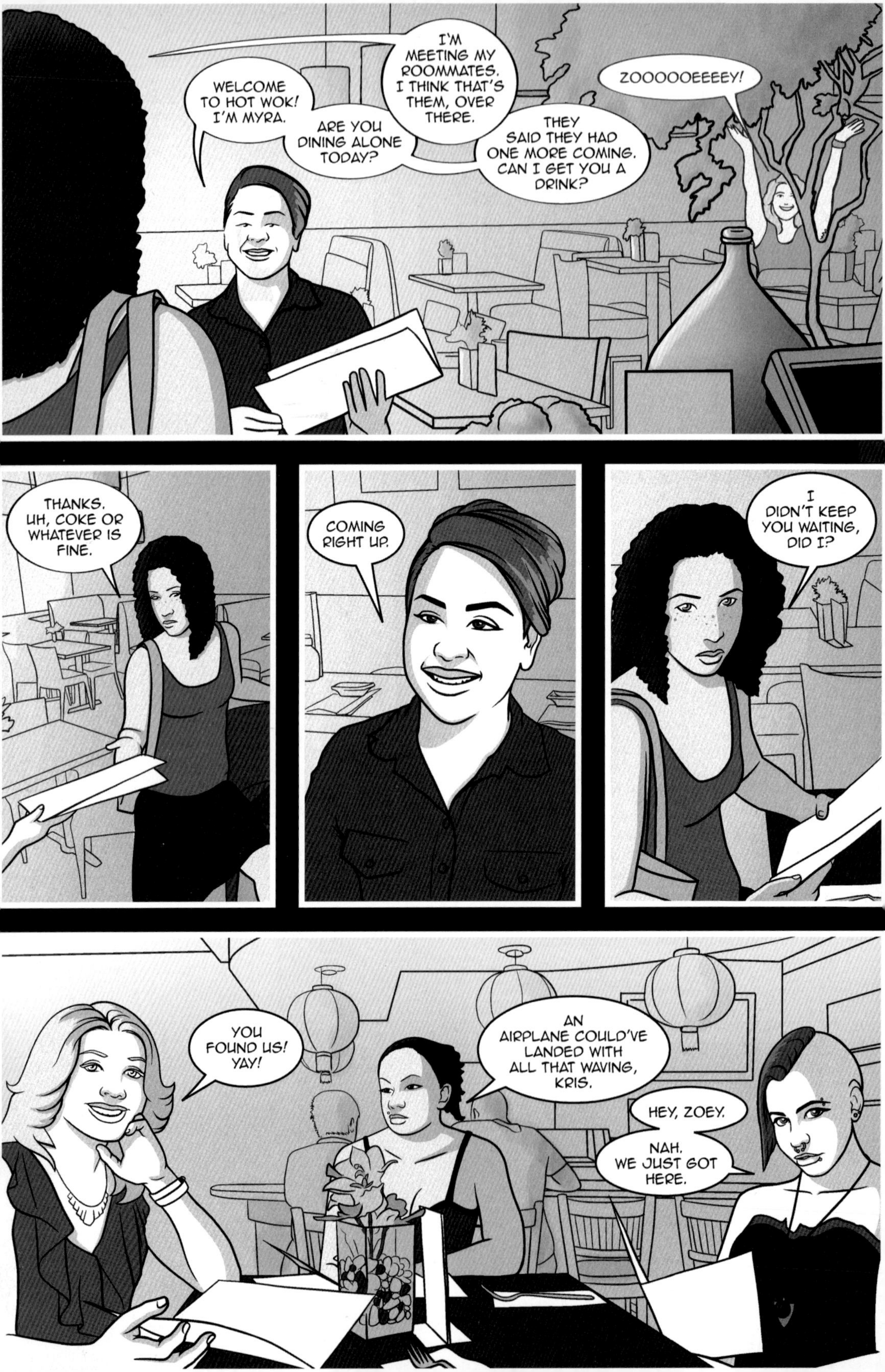
WELCOME TO HOT WOK! I'M MYRA.
ARE YOU DINING ALONE TODAY?
I'M MEETING MY ROOMMATES. I THINK THAT'S THEM, OVER THERE.
THEY SAID THEY HAD ONE MORE COMING. CAN I GET YOU A DRINK?
ZOOOOOEEEEY!
THANKS. UH, COKE OR WHATEVER IS FINE.
COMING RIGHT UP.
I DIDN'T KEEP YOU WAITING, DID I?
YOU FOUND US! YAY!
AN AIRPLANE COULD'VE LANDED WITH ALL THAT WAVING, KRIS.
HEY, ZOEY.
NAH. WE JUST GOT HERE.

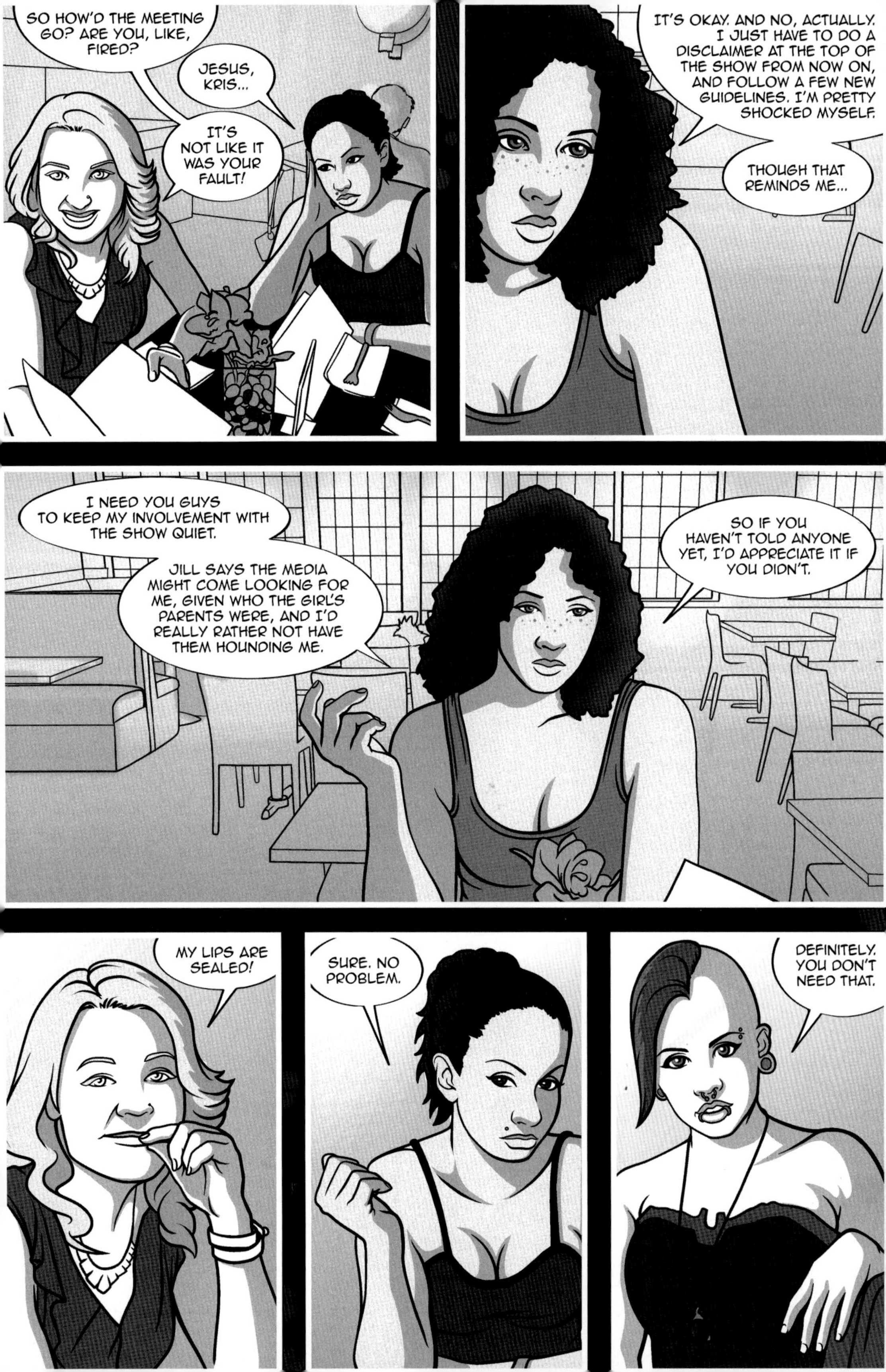
SO HOW'D THE MEETING GO? ARE YOU, LIKE, FIRED?
JESUS, KRIS...
IT'S NOT LIKE IT WAS YOUR FAULT!
IT'S OKAY. AND NO, ACTUALLY. I JUST HAVE TO DO A DISCLAIMER AT THE TOP OF THE SHOW FROM NOW ON, AND FOLLOW A FEW NEW GUIDELINES. I'M PRETTY SHOCKED MYSELF.
THOUGH THAT REMINDS ME...
I NEED YOU GUYS TO KEEP MY INVOLVEMENT WITH THE SHOW QUIET.
JILL SAYS THE MEDIA MIGHT COME LOOKING FOR ME, GIVEN WHO THE GIRL'S PARENTS WERE, AND I'D REALLY RATHER NOT HAVE THEM HOUNDING ME.
SO IF YOU HAVEN'T TOLD ANYONE YET, I'D APPRECIATE IT IF YOU DIDN'T.
MY LIPS ARE SEALED!
SURE. NO PROBLEM.
DEFINITELY. YOU DON'T NEED THAT.

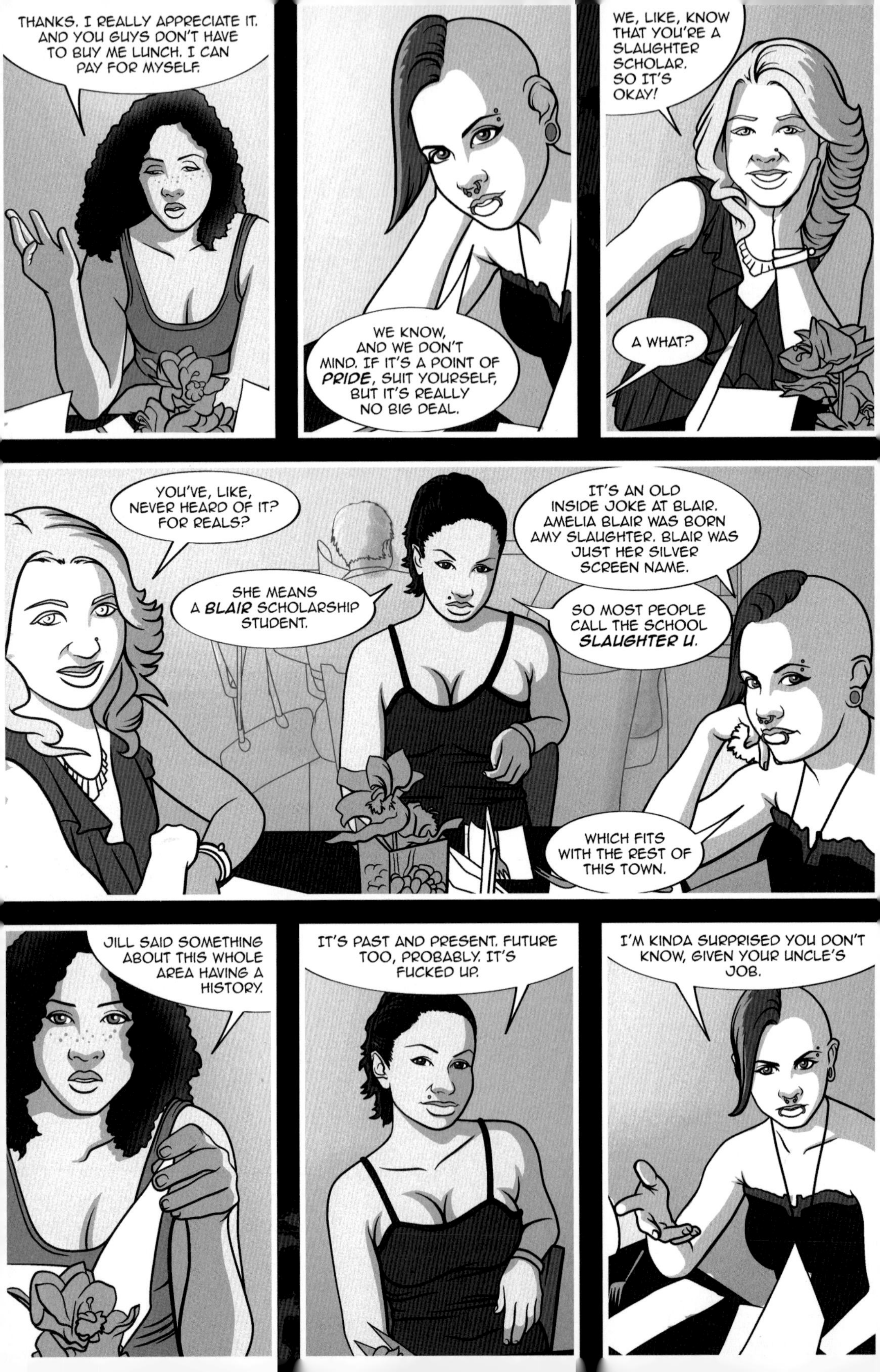
THANKS. I REALLY APPRECIATE IT. AND YOU GUYS DON'T HAVE TO BUY ME LUNCH. I CAN PAY FOR MYSELF.
WE KNOW, AND WE DON'T MIND. IF IT'S A POINT OF *PRIDE*, SUIT YOURSELF, BUT IT'S REALLY NO BIG DEAL.
WE, LIKE, KNOW THAT YOU'RE A SLAUGHTER SCHOLAR. SO IT'S OKAY!
A WHAT?
YOU'VE, LIKE, NEVER HEARD OF IT? FOR REALS?
SHE MEANS A **BLAIR** SCHOLARSHIP STUDENT.
IT'S AN OLD INSIDE JOKE AT BLAIR. AMELIA BLAIR WAS BORN AMY SLAUGHTER. BLAIR WAS JUST HER SILVER SCREEN NAME.
SO MOST PEOPLE CALL THE SCHOOL **SLAUGHTER U**.
WHICH FITS WITH THE REST OF THIS TOWN.
JILL SAID SOMETHING ABOUT THIS WHOLE AREA HAVING A HISTORY.
IT'S PAST AND PRESENT. FUTURE TOO, PROBABLY. IT'S FUCKED UP.
I'M KINDA SURPRISED YOU DON'T KNOW, GIVEN YOUR UNCLE'S JOB.

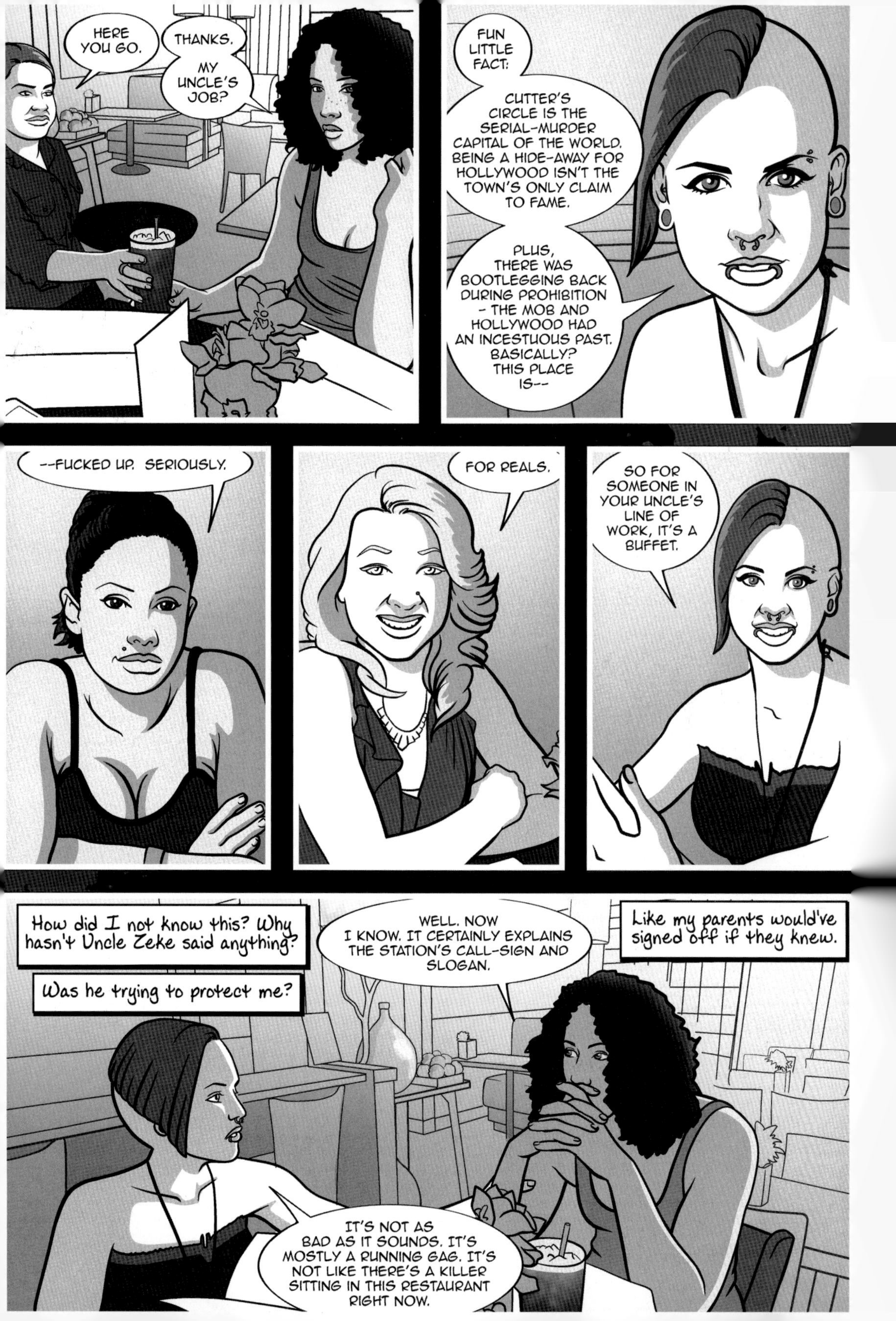
HERE YOU GO.
THANKS.
MY UNCLE'S JOB?
FUN LITTLE FACT:
CUTTER'S CIRCLE IS THE SERIAL-MURDER CAPITAL OF THE WORLD. BEING A HIDE-AWAY FOR HOLLYWOOD ISN'T THE TOWN'S ONLY CLAIM TO FAME.
PLUS, THERE WAS BOOTLEGGING BACK DURING PROHIBITION - THE MOB AND HOLLYWOOD HAD AN INCESTUOUS PAST. BASICALLY? THIS PLACE IS--
--FUCKED UP. SERIOUSLY.
FOR REALS.
SO FOR SOMEONE IN YOUR UNCLE'S LINE OF WORK, IT'S A BUFFET.
How did I not know this? Why hasn't Uncle Zeke said anything?
Was he trying to protect me?
WELL. NOW I KNOW. IT CERTAINLY EXPLAINS THE STATION'S CALL-SIGN AND SLOGAN.
Like my parents would've signed off if they knew.
IT'S NOT AS BAD AS IT SOUNDS. IT'S MOSTLY A RUNNING GAG. IT'S NOT LIKE THERE'S A KILLER SITTING IN THIS RESTAURANT RIGHT NOW.

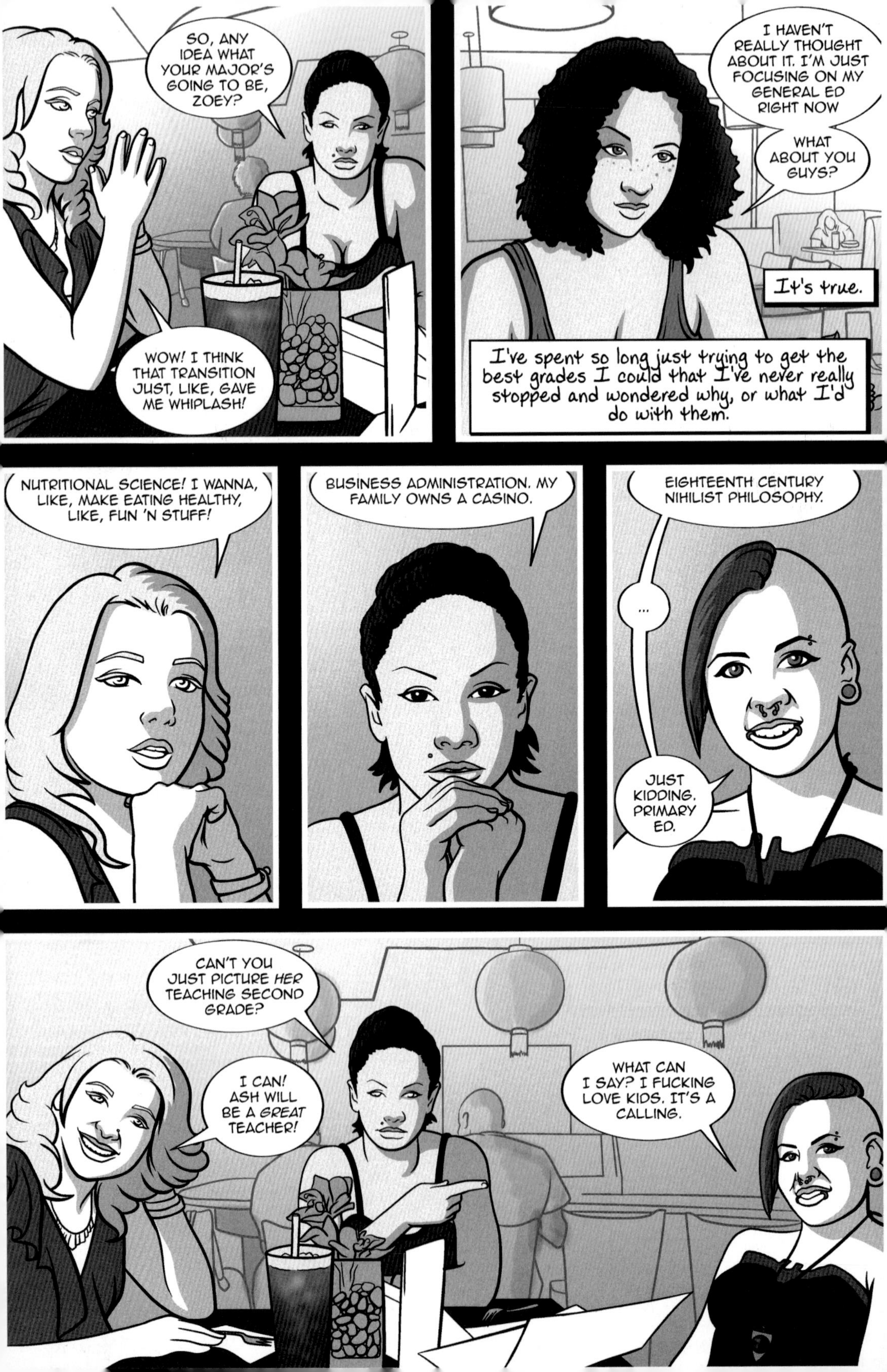
SO, ANY IDEA WHAT YOUR MAJOR'S GOING TO BE, ZOEY?
WOW! I THINK THAT TRANSITION JUST, LIKE, GAVE ME WHIPLASH!
I HAVEN'T REALLY THOUGHT ABOUT IT. I'M JUST FOCUSING ON MY GENERAL ED RIGHT NOW
WHAT ABOUT YOU GUYS?
It's true.
I've spent so long just trying to get the best grades I could that I've never really stopped and wondered why, or what I'd do with them.
NUTRITIONAL SCIENCE! I WANNA, LIKE, MAKE EATING HEALTHY, LIKE, FUN 'N STUFF!
BUSINESS ADMINISTRATION. MY FAMILY OWNS A CASINO.
EIGHTEENTH CENTURY NIHILIST PHILOSOPHY.
...
JUST KIDDING. PRIMARY ED.
CAN'T YOU JUST PICTURE *HER* TEACHING SECOND GRADE?
I CAN! ASH WILL BE A *GREAT* TEACHER!
WHAT CAN I SAY? I FUCKING LOVE KIDS. IT'S A CALLING.

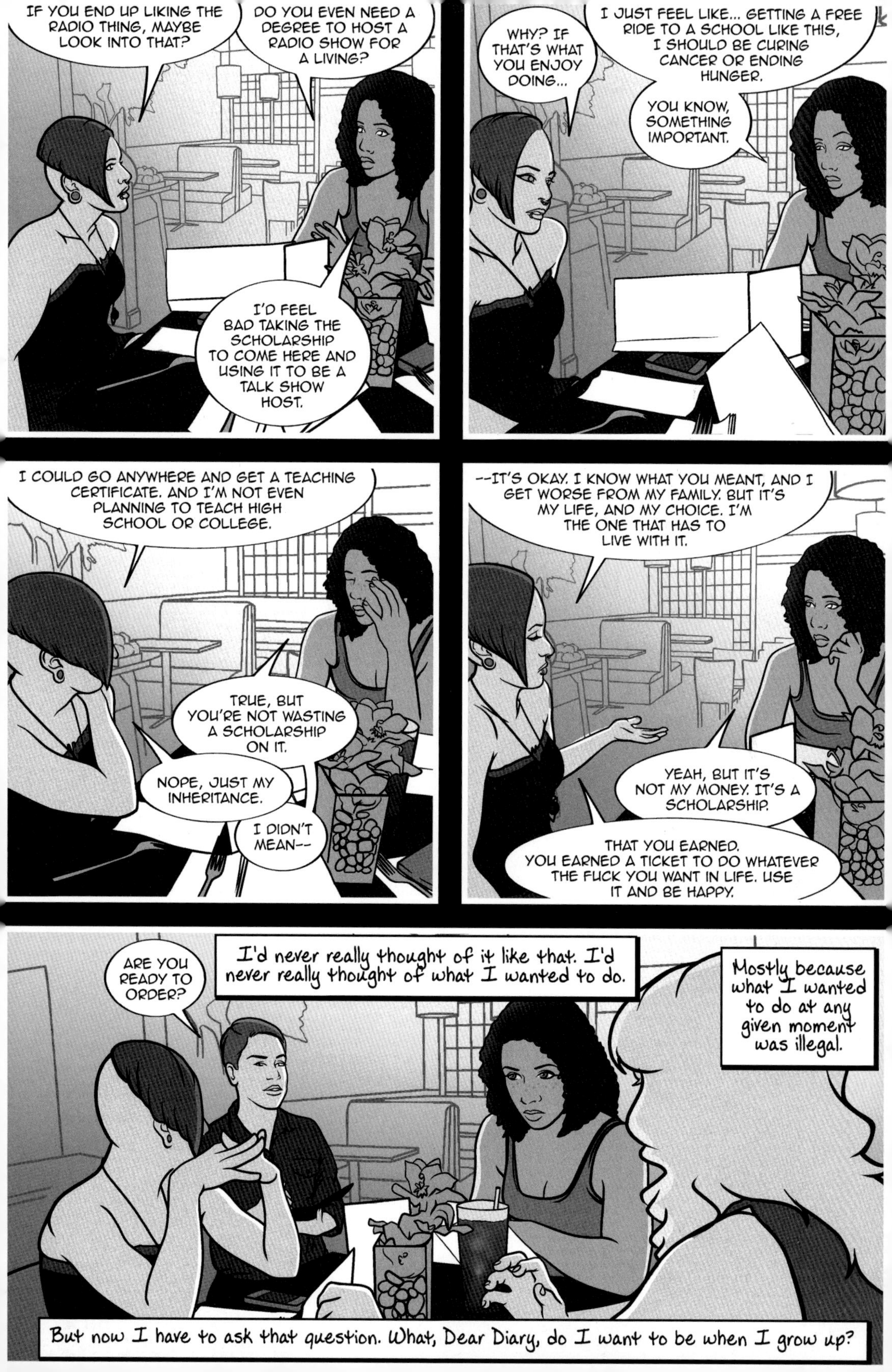
IF YOU END UP LIKING THE RADIO THING, MAYBE LOOK INTO THAT?
DO YOU EVEN NEED A DEGREE TO HOST A RADIO SHOW FOR A LIVING?
I'D FEEL BAD TAKING THE SCHOLARSHIP TO COME HERE AND USING IT TO BE A TALK SHOW HOST.
WHY? IF THAT'S WHAT YOU ENJOY DOING...
I JUST FEEL LIKE... GETTING A FREE RIDE TO A SCHOOL LIKE THIS, I SHOULD BE CURING CANCER OR ENDING HUNGER.
YOU KNOW, SOMETHING IMPORTANT.
I COULD GO ANYWHERE AND GET A TEACHING CERTIFICATE. AND I'M NOT EVEN PLANNING TO TEACH HIGH SCHOOL OR COLLEGE.
TRUE, BUT YOU'RE NOT WASTING A SCHOLARSHIP ON IT.
NOPE, JUST MY INHERITANCE.
I DIDN'T MEAN--
--IT'S OKAY. I KNOW WHAT YOU MEANT, AND I GET WORSE FROM MY FAMILY. BUT IT'S MY LIFE, AND MY CHOICE. I'M THE ONE THAT HAS TO LIVE WITH IT.
YEAH, BUT IT'S NOT MY MONEY. IT'S A SCHOLARSHIP.
THAT YOU EARNED. YOU EARNED A TICKET TO DO WHATEVER THE FUCK YOU WANT IN LIFE. USE IT AND BE HAPPY.
ARE YOU READY TO ORDER?
I'd never really thought of it like that. I'd never really thought of what I wanted to do.
Mostly because what I wanted to do at any given moment was illegal.
But now I have to ask that question. What, Dear Diary, do I want to be when I grow up?

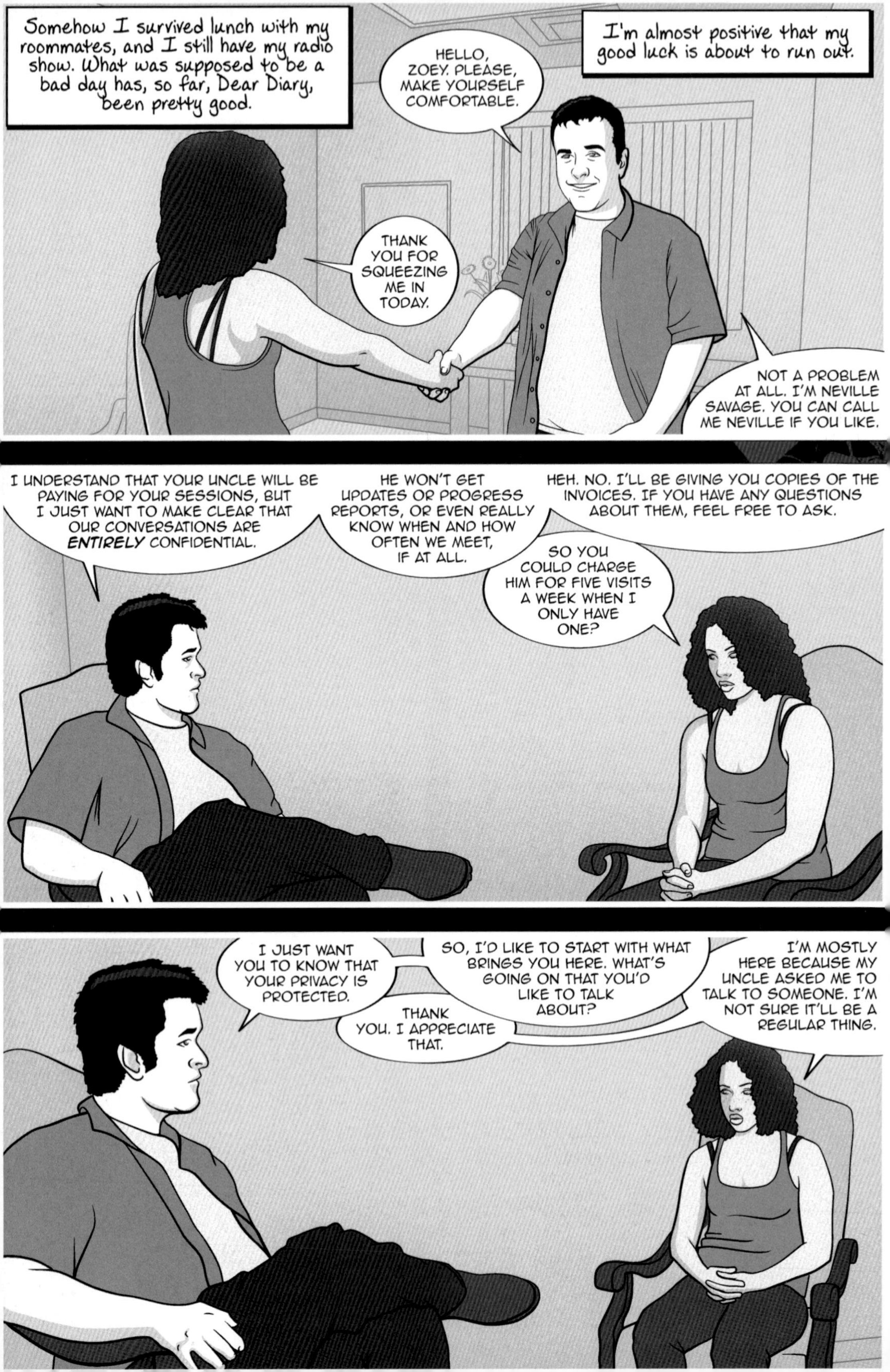
Somehow I survived lunch with my roommates, and I still have my radio show. What was supposed to be a bad day has, so far, Dear Diary, been pretty good.
HELLO, ZOEY. PLEASE, MAKE YOURSELF COMFORTABLE.
I'm almost positive that my good luck is about to run out.
THANK YOU FOR SQUEEZING ME IN TODAY.
NOT A PROBLEM AT ALL. I'M NEVILLE SAVAGE. YOU CAN CALL ME NEVILLE IF YOU LIKE.
I UNDERSTAND THAT YOUR UNCLE WILL BE PAYING FOR YOUR SESSIONS, BUT I JUST WANT TO MAKE CLEAR THAT OUR CONVERSATIONS ARE *ENTIRELY* CONFIDENTIAL.
HE WON'T GET UPDATES OR PROGRESS REPORTS, OR EVEN REALLY KNOW WHEN AND HOW OFTEN WE MEET, IF AT ALL.
SO YOU COULD CHARGE HIM FOR FIVE VISITS A WEEK WHEN I ONLY HAVE ONE?
HEH. NO. I'LL BE GIVING YOU COPIES OF THE INVOICES. IF YOU HAVE ANY QUESTIONS ABOUT THEM, FEEL FREE TO ASK.
I JUST WANT YOU TO KNOW THAT YOUR PRIVACY IS PROTECTED.
THANK YOU. I APPRECIATE THAT.
SO, I'D LIKE TO START WITH WHAT BRINGS YOU HERE. WHAT'S GOING ON THAT YOU'D LIKE TO TALK ABOUT?
I'M MOSTLY HERE BECAUSE MY UNCLE ASKED ME TO TALK TO SOMEONE. I'M NOT SURE IT'LL BE A REGULAR THING.

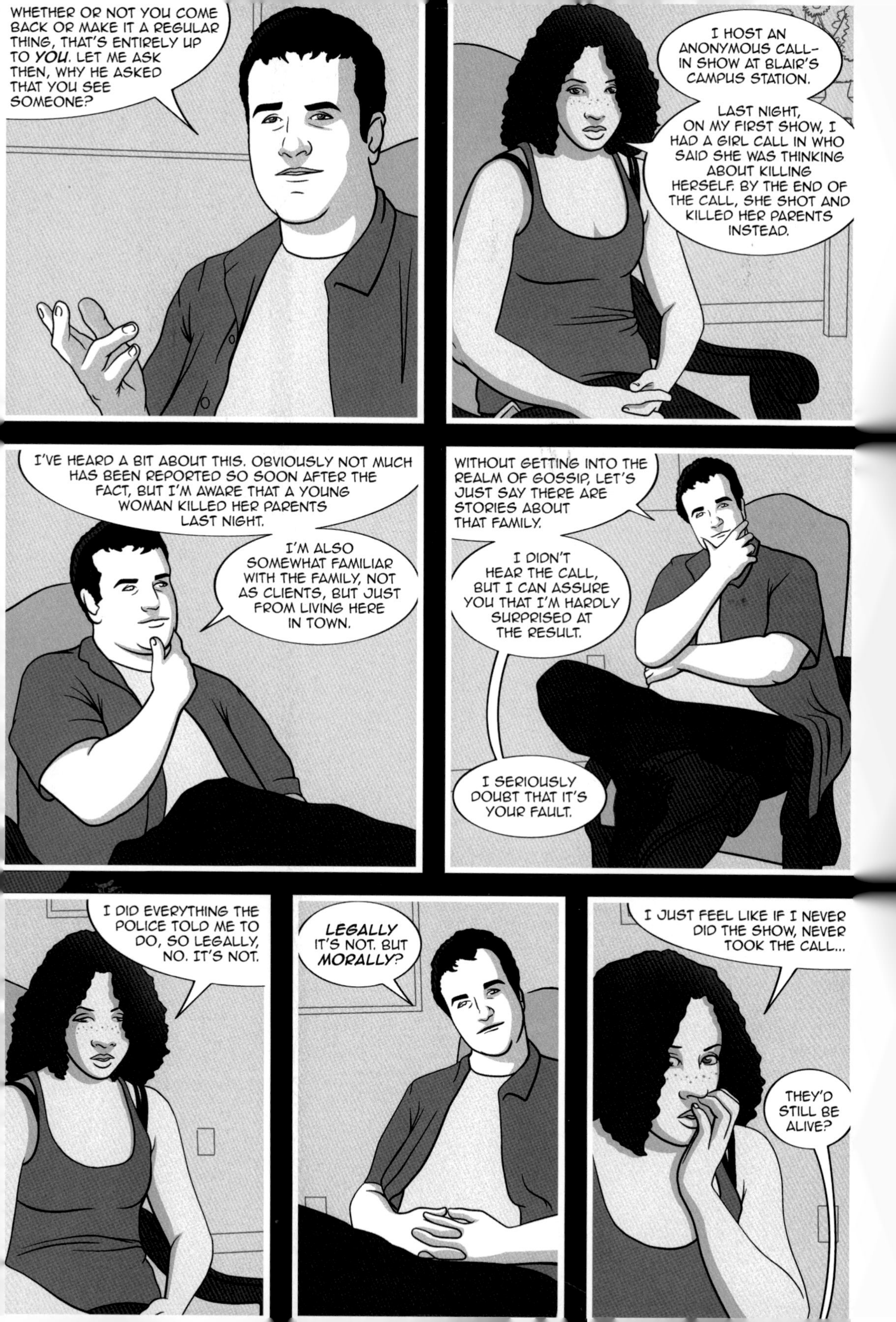
WHETHER OR NOT YOU COME BACK OR MAKE IT A REGULAR THING, THAT'S ENTIRELY UP TO *YOU*. LET ME ASK THEN, WHY HE ASKED THAT YOU SEE SOMEONE?
I HOST AN ANONYMOUS CALL-IN SHOW AT BLAIR'S CAMPUS STATION.
LAST NIGHT, ON MY FIRST SHOW, I HAD A GIRL CALL IN WHO SAID SHE WAS THINKING ABOUT KILLING HERSELF. BY THE END OF THE CALL, SHE SHOT AND KILLED HER PARENTS INSTEAD.
I'VE HEARD A BIT ABOUT THIS. OBVIOUSLY NOT MUCH HAS BEEN REPORTED SO SOON AFTER THE FACT, BUT I'M AWARE THAT A YOUNG WOMAN KILLED HER PARENTS LAST NIGHT.
I'M ALSO SOMEWHAT FAMILIAR WITH THE FAMILY, NOT AS CLIENTS, BUT JUST FROM LIVING HERE IN TOWN.
WITHOUT GETTING INTO THE REALM OF GOSSIP, LET'S JUST SAY THERE ARE STORIES ABOUT THAT FAMILY.
I DIDN'T HEAR THE CALL, BUT I CAN ASSURE YOU THAT I'M HARDLY SURPRISED AT THE RESULT.
I SERIOUSLY DOUBT THAT IT'S YOUR FAULT.
I DID EVERYTHING THE POLICE TOLD ME TO DO, SO LEGALLY, NO. IT'S NOT.
LEGALLY IT'S NOT. BUT *MORALLY*?
I JUST FEEL LIKE IF I NEVER DID THE SHOW, NEVER TOOK THE CALL...
THEY'D STILL BE ALIVE?

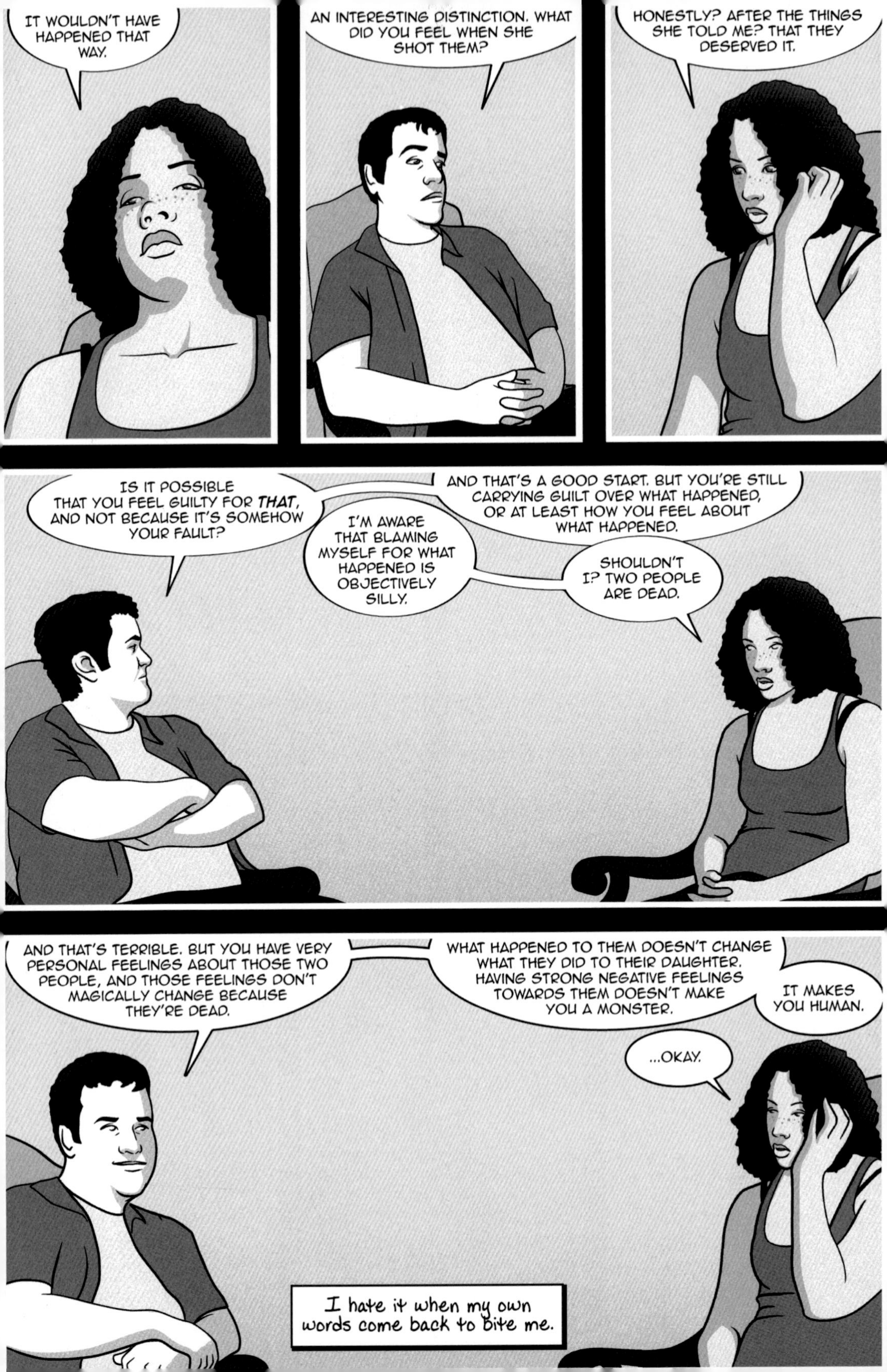
IT WOULDN'T HAVE HAPPENED THAT WAY.
AN INTERESTING DISTINCTION. WHAT DID YOU FEEL WHEN SHE SHOT THEM?
HONESTLY? AFTER THE THINGS SHE TOLD ME? THAT THEY DESERVED IT.
IS IT POSSIBLE THAT YOU FEEL GUILTY FOR THAT, AND NOT BECAUSE IT'S SOMEHOW YOUR FAULT?
I'M AWARE THAT BLAMING MYSELF FOR WHAT HAPPENED IS OBJECTIVELY SILLY.
AND THAT'S A GOOD START. BUT YOU'RE STILL CARRYING GUILT OVER WHAT HAPPENED, OR AT LEAST HOW YOU FEEL ABOUT WHAT HAPPENED.
SHOULDN'T I? TWO PEOPLE ARE DEAD.
AND THAT'S TERRIBLE. BUT YOU HAVE VERY PERSONAL FEELINGS ABOUT THOSE TWO PEOPLE, AND THOSE FEELINGS DON'T MAGICALLY CHANGE BECAUSE THEY'RE DEAD.
WHAT HAPPENED TO THEM DOESN'T CHANGE WHAT THEY DID TO THEIR DAUGHTER. HAVING STRONG NEGATIVE FEELINGS TOWARDS THEM DOESN'T MAKE YOU A MONSTER.
IT MAKES YOU HUMAN.
...OKAY.
I hate it when my own words come back to bite me.

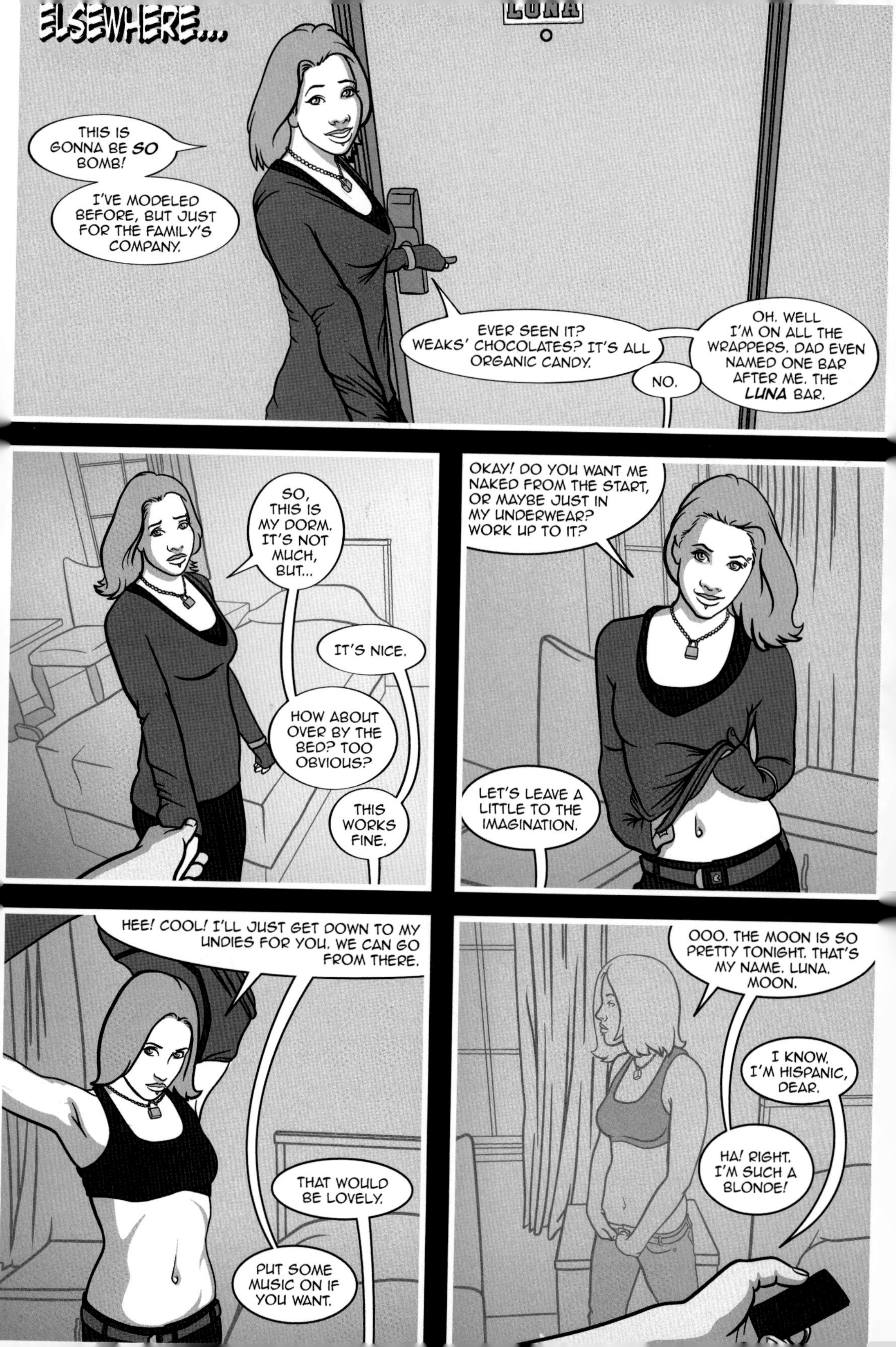
ELSEWHERE...
LUNA
THIS IS GONNA BE SO BOMB!
I'VE MODELED BEFORE, BUT JUST FOR THE FAMILY'S COMPANY.
EVER SEEN IT? WEAKS' CHOCOLATES? IT'S ALL ORGANIC CANDY.
NO.
OH. WELL I'M ON ALL THE WRAPPERS. DAD EVEN NAMED ONE BAR AFTER ME. THE LUNA BAR.
SO, THIS IS MY DORM. IT'S NOT MUCH, BUT...
IT'S NICE.
HOW ABOUT OVER BY THE BED? TOO OBVIOUS?
THIS WORKS FINE.
OKAY! DO YOU WANT ME NAKED FROM THE START, OR MAYBE JUST IN MY UNDERWEAR? WORK UP TO IT?
LET'S LEAVE A LITTLE TO THE IMAGINATION.
HEE! COOL! I'LL JUST GET DOWN TO MY UNDIES FOR YOU. WE CAN GO FROM THERE.
THAT WOULD BE LOVELY.
PUT SOME MUSIC ON IF YOU WANT.
OOO. THE MOON IS SO PRETTY TONIGHT. THAT'S MY NAME. LUNA. MOON.
I KNOW. I'M HISPANIC, DEAR.
HA! RIGHT. I'M SUCH A BLONDE!

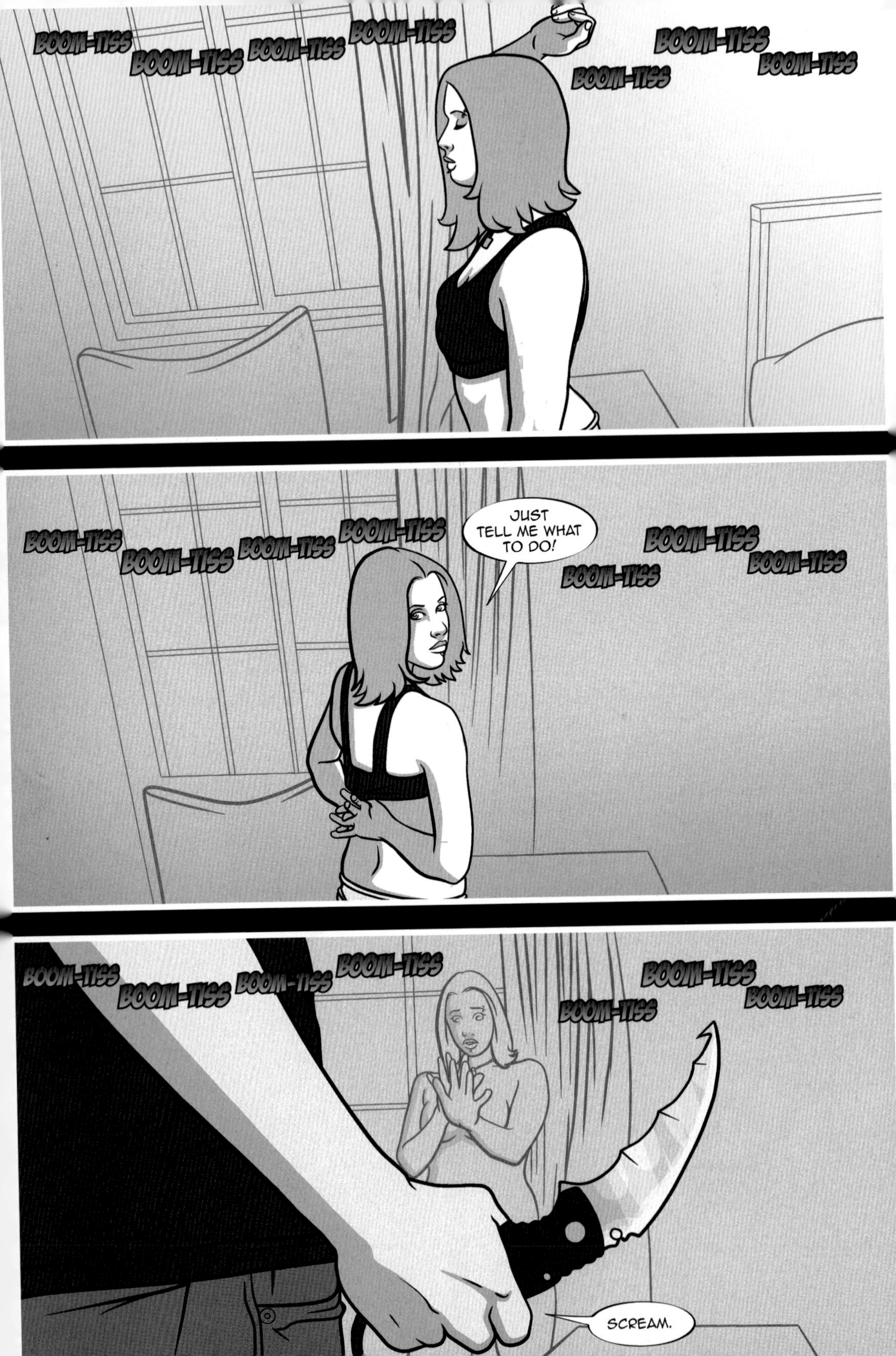
BOOM-TISS
BOOM-TISS
BOOM-TISS
BOOM-TISS
BOOM-TISS
BOOM-TISS
BOOM-TISS
BOOM-TISS
BOOM-TISS
BOOM-TISS
BOOM-TISS
JUST TELL ME WHAT TO DO!
BOOM-TISS
BOOM-TISS
BOOM-TISS
BOOM-TISS
BOOM-TISS
BOOM-TISS
BOOM-TISS
BOOM-TISS
BOOM-TISS
BOOM-TISS
SCREAM.

a VOICE in the DARK

"KILLING GAME, PT. 2"

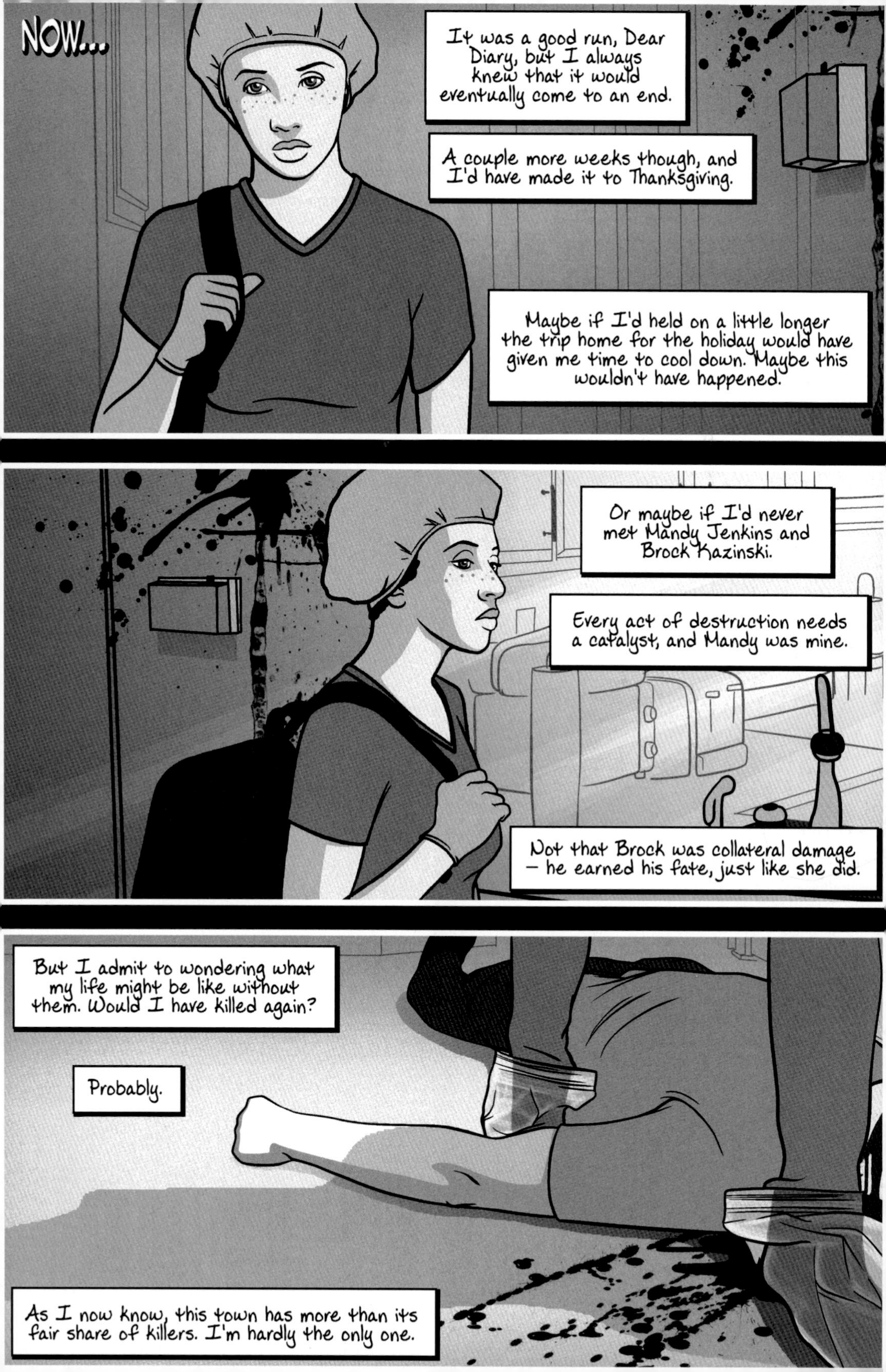
NOW...
It was a good run, Dear Diary, but I always knew that it would eventually come to an end.
A couple more weeks though, and I'd have made it to Thanksgiving.
Maybe if I'd held on a little longer the trip home for the holiday would have given me time to cool down. Maybe this wouldn't have happened.
Or maybe if I'd never met Mandy Jenkins and Brock Kazinski.
Every act of destruction needs a catalyst, and Mandy was mine.
Not that Brock was collateral damage – he earned his fate, just like she did.
But I admit to wondering what my life might be like without them. Would I have killed again?
Probably.
As I now know, this town has more than its fair share of killers. I'm hardly the only one.

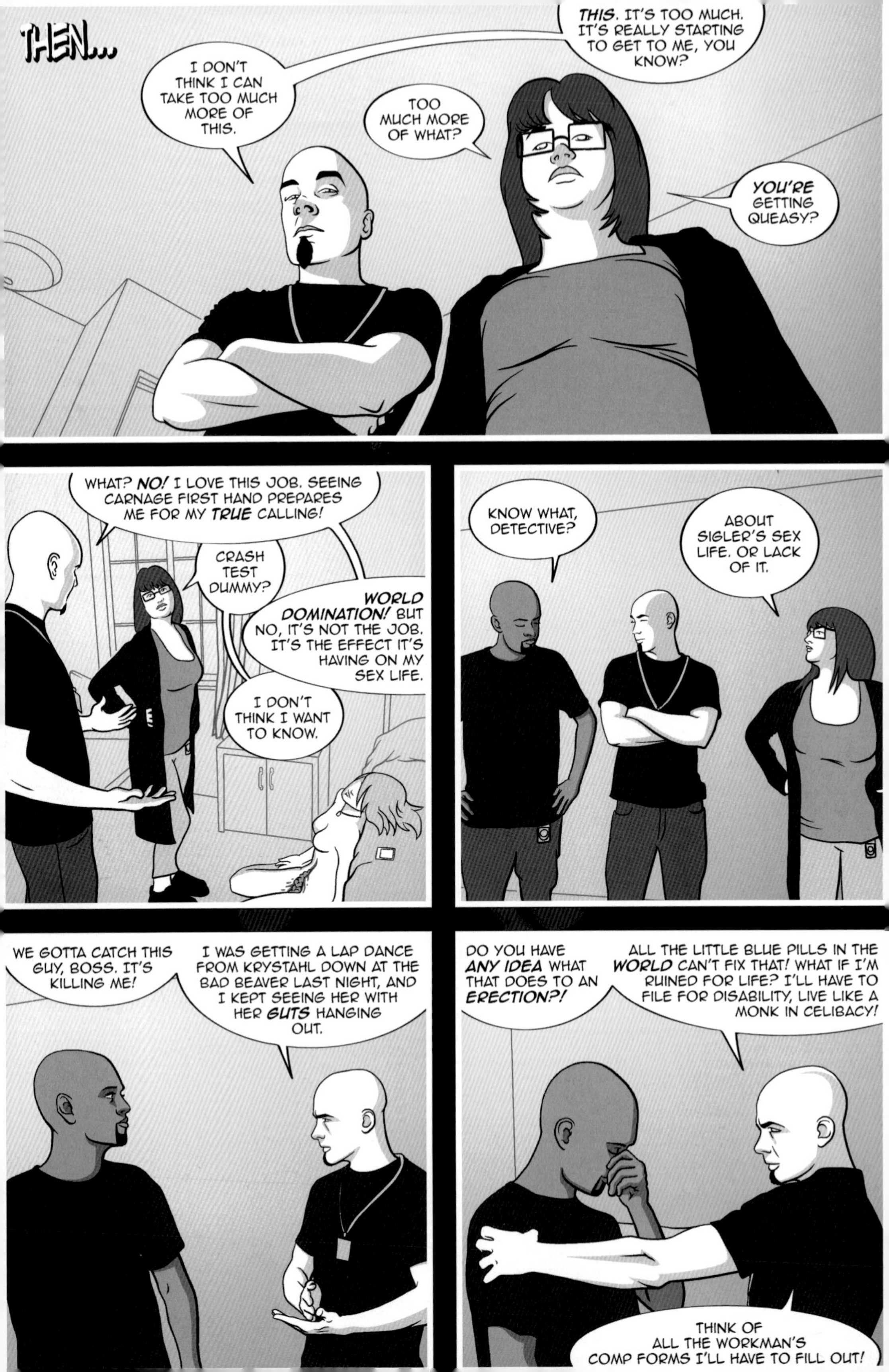
THEN...
I DON'T THINK I CAN TAKE TOO MUCH MORE OF THIS.
TOO MUCH MORE OF WHAT?
THIS. IT'S TOO MUCH. IT'S REALLY STARTING TO GET TO ME, YOU KNOW?
YOU'RE GETTING QUEASY?
WHAT? NO! I LOVE THIS JOB. SEEING CARNAGE FIRST HAND PREPARES ME FOR MY TRUE CALLING!
CRASH TEST DUMMY?
WORLD DOMINATION! BUT NO, IT'S NOT THE JOB. IT'S THE EFFECT IT'S HAVING ON MY SEX LIFE.
I DON'T THINK I WANT TO KNOW.
KNOW WHAT, DETECTIVE?
ABOUT SIGLER'S SEX LIFE. OR LACK OF IT.
WE GOTTA CATCH THIS GUY, BOSS. IT'S KILLING ME!
I WAS GETTING A LAP DANCE FROM KRYSTAHL DOWN AT THE BAD BEAVER LAST NIGHT, AND I KEPT SEEING HER WITH HER GUTS HANGING OUT.
DO YOU HAVE ANY IDEA WHAT THAT DOES TO AN ERECTION?!
ALL THE LITTLE BLUE PILLS IN THE WORLD CAN'T FIX THAT! WHAT IF I'M RUINED FOR LIFE? I'LL HAVE TO FILE FOR DISABILITY, LIVE LIKE A MONK IN CELIBACY!
THINK OF ALL THE WORKMAN'S COMP FORMS I'LL HAVE TO FILL OUT!

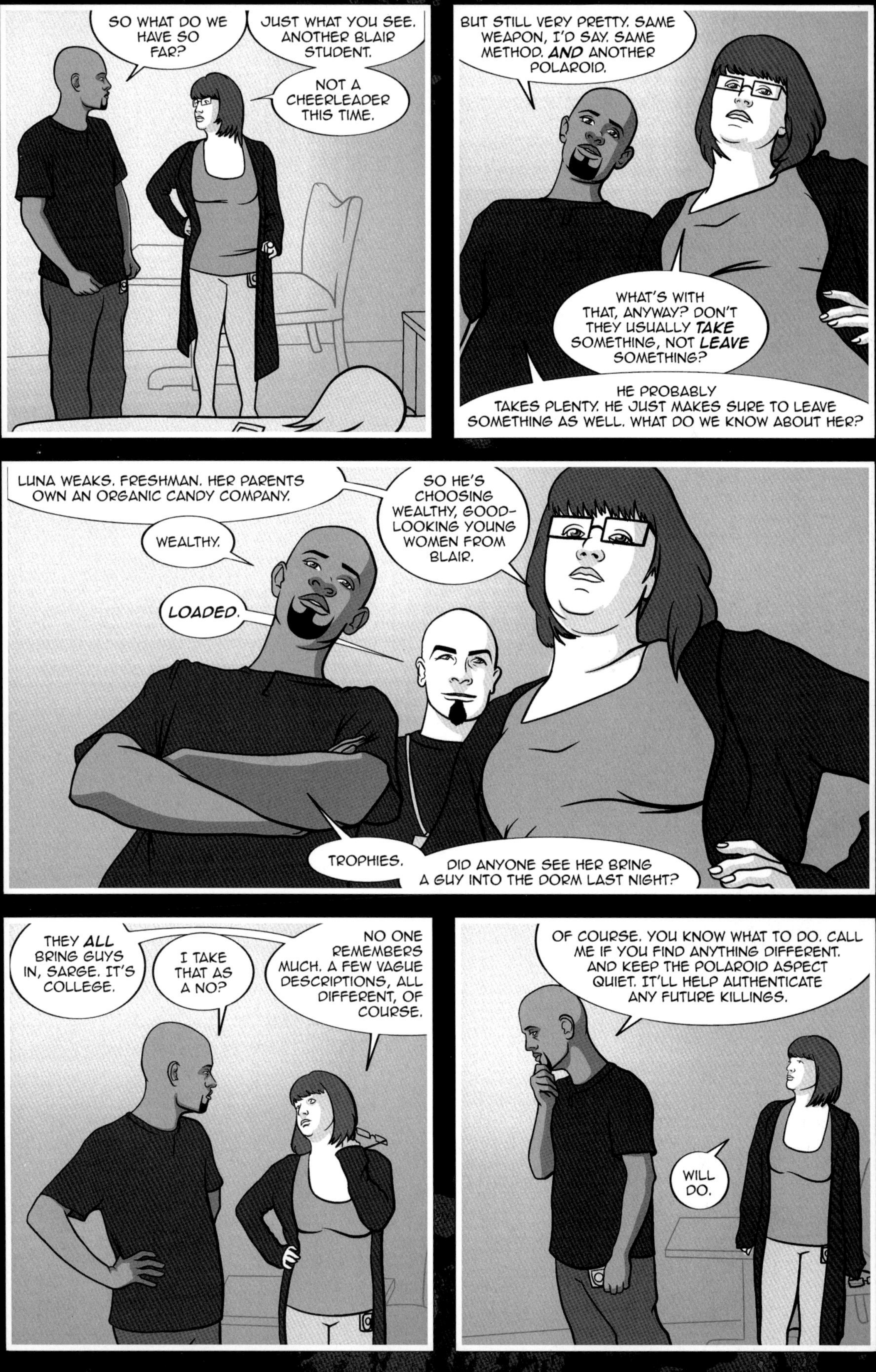
SO WHAT DO WE HAVE SO FAR?
JUST WHAT YOU SEE. ANOTHER BLAIR STUDENT.
NOT A CHEERLEADER THIS TIME.
BUT STILL VERY PRETTY. SAME WEAPON, I'D SAY. SAME METHOD. AND ANOTHER POLAROID.
WHAT'S WITH THAT, ANYWAY? DON'T THEY USUALLY TAKE SOMETHING, NOT LEAVE SOMETHING?
HE PROBABLY TAKES PLENTY. HE JUST MAKES SURE TO LEAVE SOMETHING AS WELL. WHAT DO WE KNOW ABOUT HER?
LUNA WEAKS. FRESHMAN. HER PARENTS OWN AN ORGANIC CANDY COMPANY.
WEALTHY.
LOADED.
SO HE'S CHOOSING WEALTHY, GOOD-LOOKING YOUNG WOMEN FROM BLAIR.
TROPHIES.
DID ANYONE SEE HER BRING A GUY INTO THE DORM LAST NIGHT?
THEY ALL BRING GUYS IN, SARGE. IT'S COLLEGE.
I TAKE THAT AS A NO?
NO ONE REMEMBERS MUCH. A FEW VAGUE DESCRIPTIONS, ALL DIFFERENT, OF COURSE.
OF COURSE. YOU KNOW WHAT TO DO. CALL ME IF YOU FIND ANYTHING DIFFERENT. AND KEEP THE POLAROID ASPECT QUIET. IT'LL HELP AUTHENTICATE ANY FUTURE KILLINGS.
WILL DO.

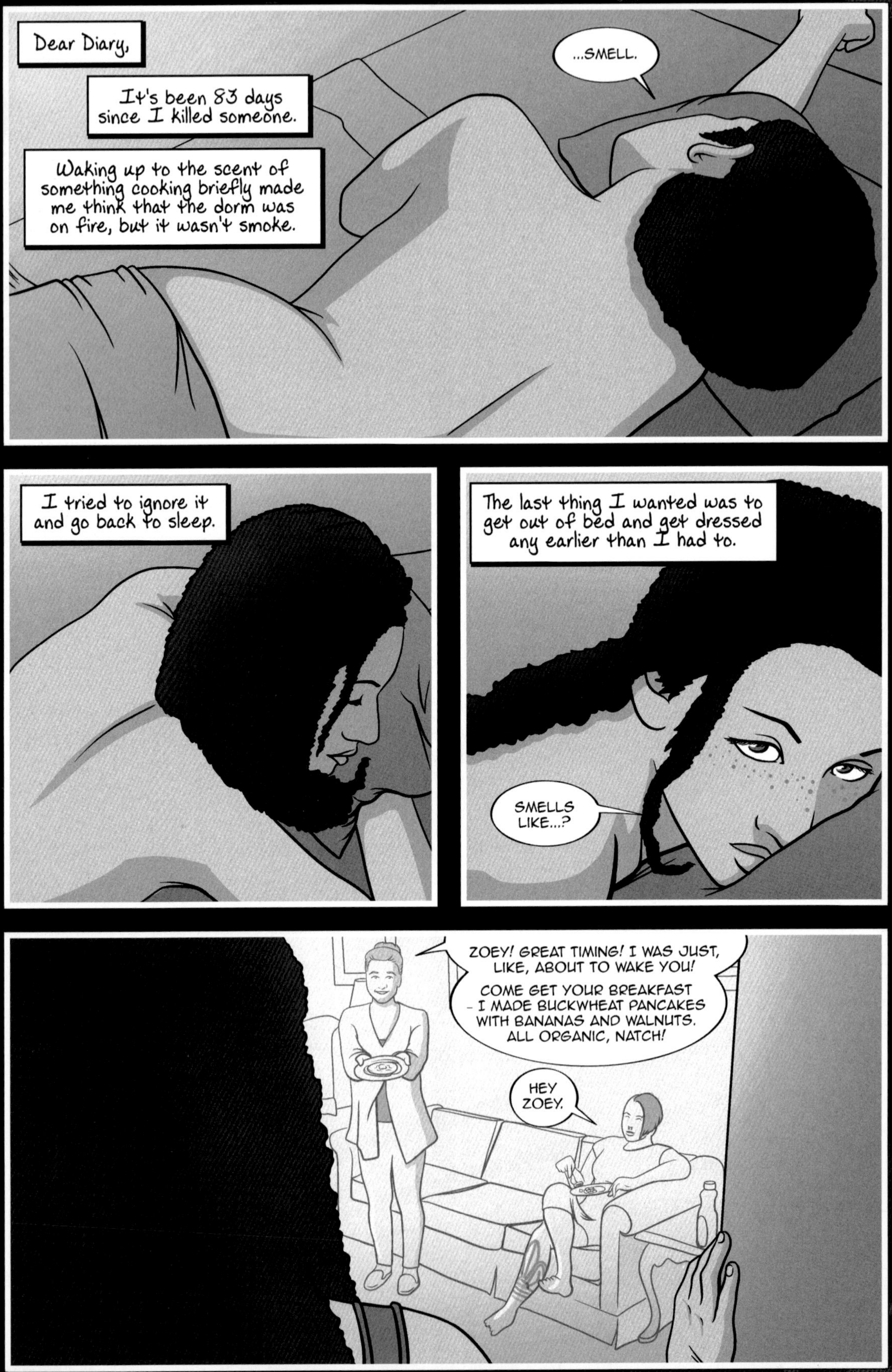
Dear Diary,
It's been 83 days since I killed someone.
Waking up to the scent of something cooking briefly made me think that the dorm was on fire, but it wasn't smoke.
...SMELL.
I tried to ignore it and go back to sleep.
The last thing I wanted was to get out of bed and get dressed any earlier than I had to.
SMELLS LIKE...?
ZOEY! GREAT TIMING! I WAS JUST, LIKE, ABOUT TO WAKE YOU!
COME GET YOUR BREAKFAST - I MADE BUCKWHEAT PANCAKES WITH BANANAS AND WALNUTS. ALL ORGANIC, NATCH!
HEY ZOEY.

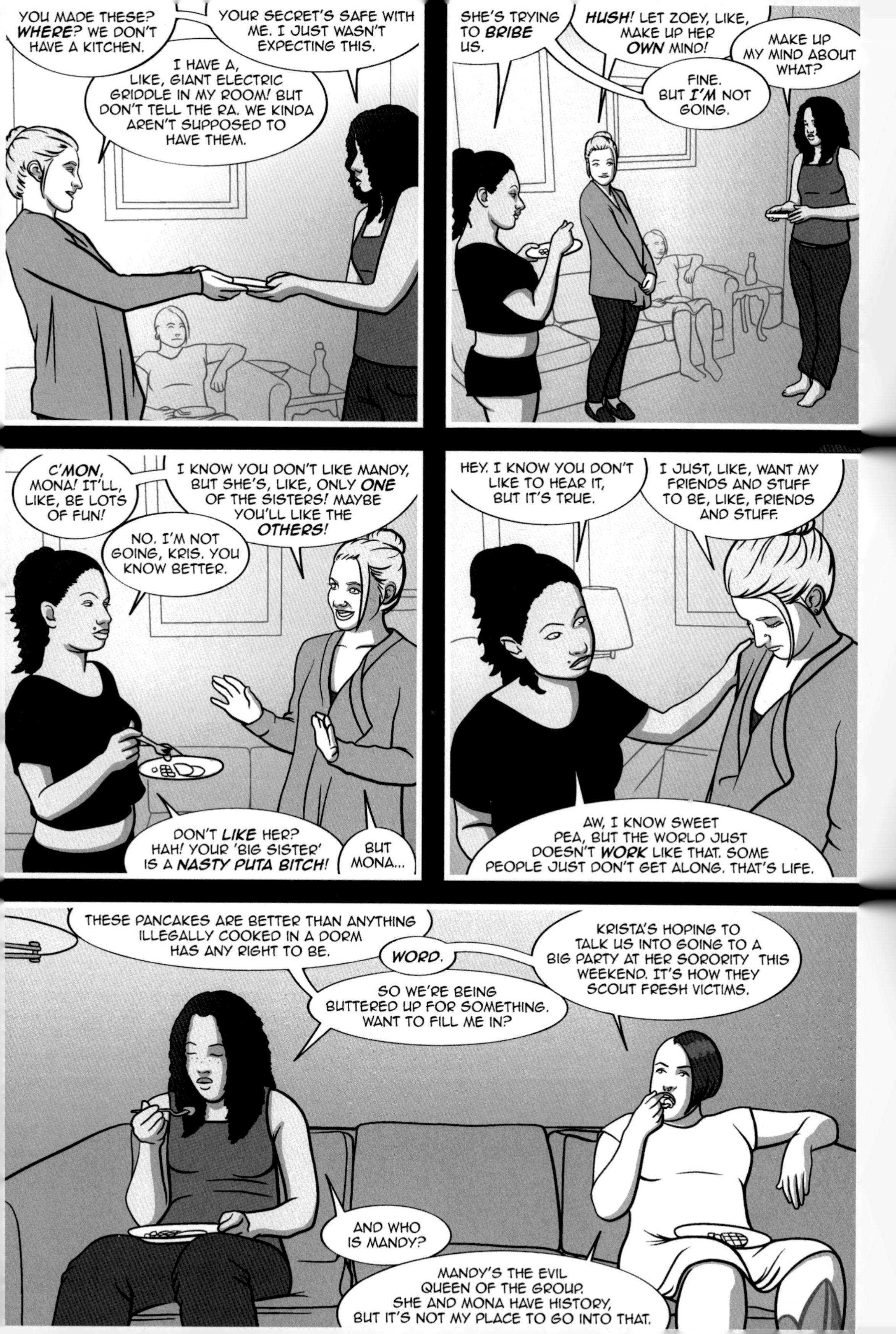
YOU MADE THESE? WHERE? WE DON'T HAVE A KITCHEN.
YOUR SECRET'S SAFE WITH ME. I JUST WASN'T EXPECTING THIS.
I HAVE A, LIKE, GIANT ELECTRIC GRIDDLE IN MY ROOM! BUT DON'T TELL THE RA. WE KINDA AREN'T SUPPOSED TO HAVE THEM.
SHE'S TRYING TO BRIBE US.
HUSH! LET ZOEY, LIKE, MAKE UP HER OWN MIND!
FINE. BUT I'M NOT GOING.
MAKE UP MY MIND ABOUT WHAT?
C'MON, MONA! IT'LL, LIKE, BE LOTS OF FUN!
I KNOW YOU DON'T LIKE MANDY, BUT SHE'S, LIKE, ONLY ONE OF THE SISTERS! MAYBE YOU'LL LIKE THE OTHERS!
NO. I'M NOT GOING, KRIS. YOU KNOW BETTER.
DON'T LIKE HER? HAH! YOUR 'BIG SISTER' IS A NASTY PUTA BITCH!
BUT MONA...
HEY. I KNOW YOU DON'T LIKE TO HEAR IT, BUT IT'S TRUE.
I JUST, LIKE, WANT MY FRIENDS AND STUFF TO BE, LIKE, FRIENDS AND STUFF.
AW, I KNOW SWEET PEA, BUT THE WORLD JUST DOESN'T WORK LIKE THAT. SOME PEOPLE JUST DON'T GET ALONG. THAT'S LIFE.
THESE PANCAKES ARE BETTER THAN ANYTHING ILLEGALLY COOKED IN A DORM HAS ANY RIGHT TO BE.
WORD.
SO WE'RE BEING BUTTERED UP FOR SOMETHING. WANT TO FILL ME IN?
KRISTA'S HOPING TO TALK US INTO GOING TO A BIG PARTY AT HER SORORITY THIS WEEKEND. IT'S HOW THEY SCOUT FRESH VICTIMS.
AND WHO IS MANDY?
MANDY'S THE EVIL QUEEN OF THE GROUP. SHE AND MONA HAVE HISTORY, BUT IT'S NOT MY PLACE TO GO INTO THAT.

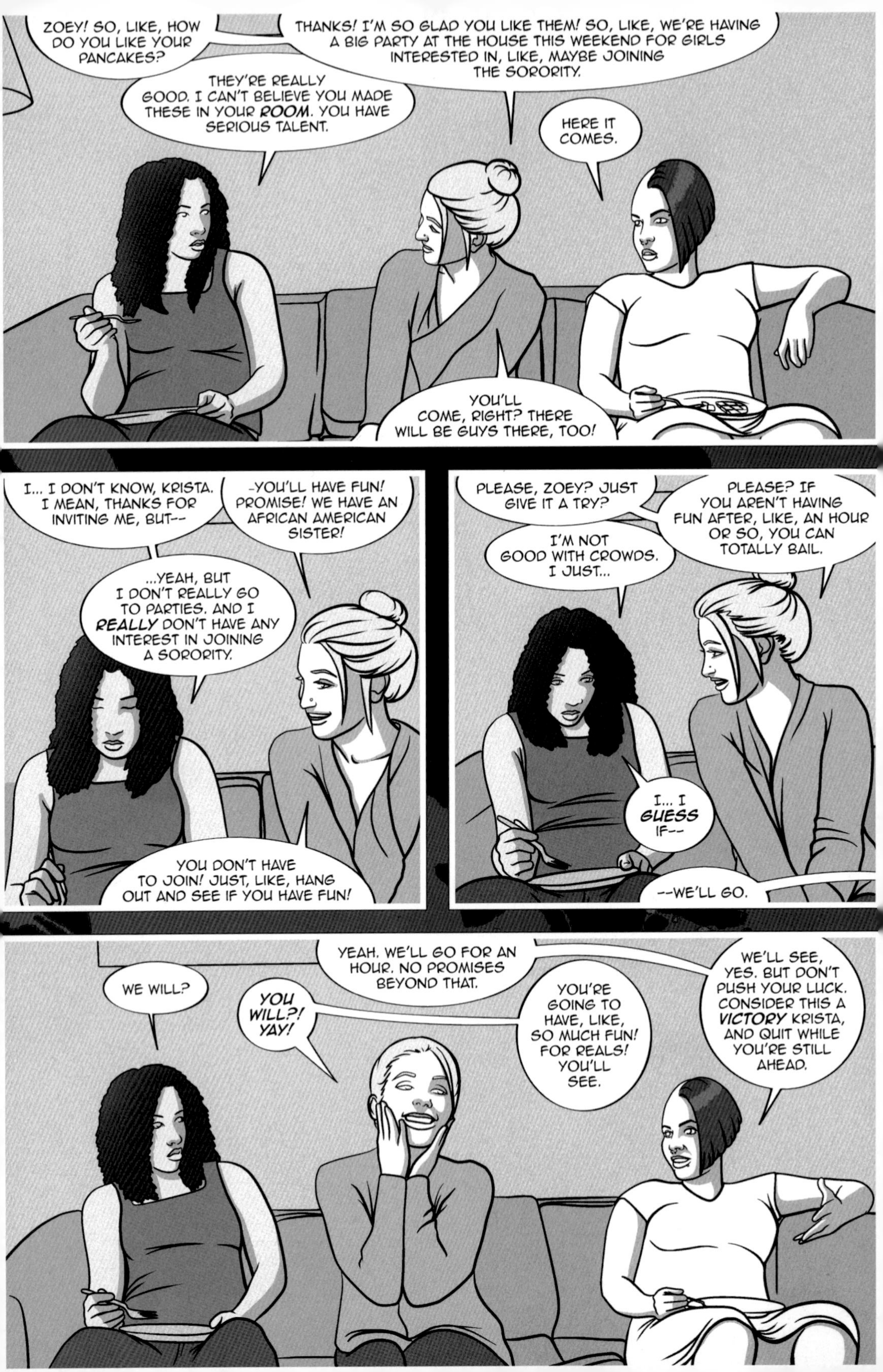
ZOEY! SO, LIKE, HOW DO YOU LIKE YOUR PANCAKES?
THEY'RE REALLY GOOD. I CAN'T BELIEVE YOU MADE THESE IN YOUR ROOM. YOU HAVE SERIOUS TALENT.
THANKS! I'M SO GLAD YOU LIKE THEM! SO, LIKE, WE'RE HAVING A BIG PARTY AT THE HOUSE THIS WEEKEND FOR GIRLS INTERESTED IN, LIKE, MAYBE JOINING THE SORORITY.
HERE IT COMES.
YOU'LL COME, RIGHT? THERE WILL BE GUYS THERE, TOO!
I... I DON'T KNOW, KRISTA. I MEAN, THANKS FOR INVITING ME, BUT--
-YOU'LL HAVE FUN! PROMISE! WE HAVE AN AFRICAN AMERICAN SISTER!
...YEAH, BUT I DON'T REALLY GO TO PARTIES. AND I REALLY DON'T HAVE ANY INTEREST IN JOINING A SORORITY.
YOU DON'T HAVE TO JOIN! JUST, LIKE, HANG OUT AND SEE IF YOU HAVE FUN!
PLEASE, ZOEY? JUST GIVE IT A TRY?
I'M NOT GOOD WITH CROWDS. I JUST...
PLEASE? IF YOU AREN'T HAVING FUN AFTER, LIKE, AN HOUR OR SO, YOU CAN TOTALLY BAIL.
I... I GUESS IF--
--WE'LL GO.
WE WILL?
YEAH. WE'LL GO FOR AN HOUR. NO PROMISES BEYOND THAT.
YOU WILL?! YAY!
YOU'RE GOING TO HAVE, LIKE, SO MUCH FUN! FOR REALS! YOU'LL SEE.
WE'LL SEE, YES. BUT DON'T PUSH YOUR LUCK. CONSIDER THIS A VICTORY KRISTA, AND QUIT WHILE YOU'RE STILL AHEAD.

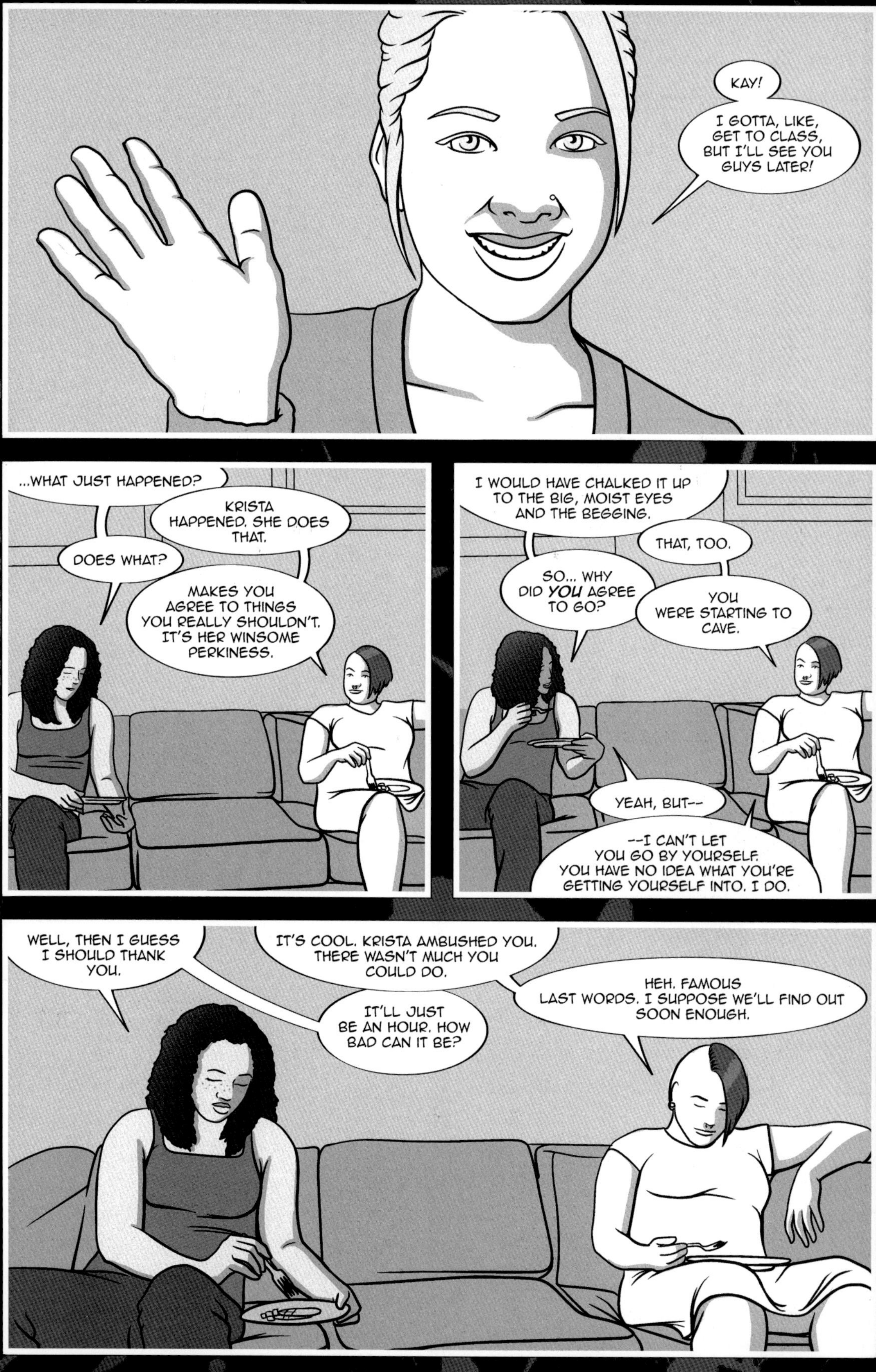
KAY!
I GOTTA, LIKE, GET TO CLASS, BUT I'LL SEE YOU GUYS LATER!
...WHAT JUST HAPPENED?
KRISTA HAPPENED. SHE DOES THAT.
DOES WHAT?
MAKES YOU AGREE TO THINGS YOU REALLY SHOULDN'T. IT'S HER WINSOME PERKINESS.
I WOULD HAVE CHALKED IT UP TO THE BIG, MOIST EYES AND THE BEGGING.
THAT, TOO.
SO... WHY DID *YOU* AGREE TO GO?
YOU WERE STARTING TO CAVE.
YEAH, BUT--
--I CAN'T LET YOU GO BY YOURSELF. YOU HAVE NO IDEA WHAT YOU'RE GETTING YOURSELF INTO. I DO.
WELL, THEN I GUESS I SHOULD THANK YOU.
IT'S COOL. KRISTA AMBUSHED YOU. THERE WASN'T MUCH YOU COULD DO.
IT'LL JUST BE AN HOUR. HOW BAD CAN IT BE?
HEH. FAMOUS LAST WORDS. I SUPPOSE WE'LL FIND OUT SOON ENOUGH.

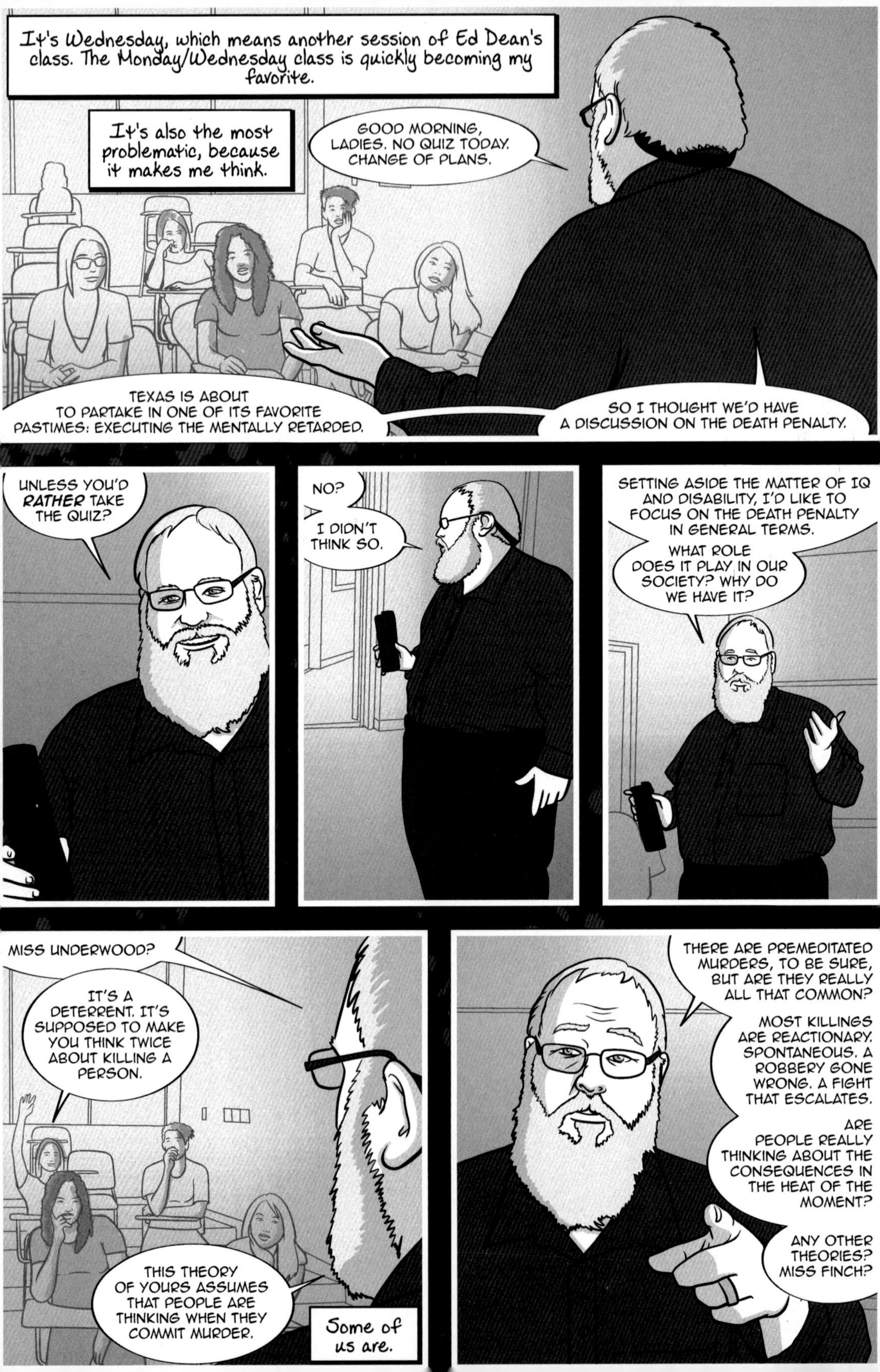
It's Wednesday, which means another session of Ed Dean's class. The Monday/Wednesday class is quickly becoming my favorite.
It's also the most problematic, because it makes me think.
GOOD MORNING, LADIES. NO QUIZ TODAY. CHANGE OF PLANS.
TEXAS IS ABOUT TO PARTAKE IN ONE OF ITS FAVORITE PASTIMES: EXECUTING THE MENTALLY RETARDED.
SO I THOUGHT WE'D HAVE A DISCUSSION ON THE DEATH PENALTY.
UNLESS YOU'D RATHER TAKE THE QUIZ?
NO?
I DIDN'T THINK SO.
SETTING ASIDE THE MATTER OF IQ AND DISABILITY, I'D LIKE TO FOCUS ON THE DEATH PENALTY IN GENERAL TERMS.
WHAT ROLE DOES IT PLAY IN OUR SOCIETY? WHY DO WE HAVE IT?
MISS UNDERWOOD?
IT'S A DETERRENT. IT'S SUPPOSED TO MAKE YOU THINK TWICE ABOUT KILLING A PERSON.
THIS THEORY OF YOURS ASSUMES THAT PEOPLE ARE THINKING WHEN THEY COMMIT MURDER.
Some of us are.
THERE ARE PREMEDITATED MURDERS, TO BE SURE, BUT ARE THEY REALLY ALL THAT COMMON?
MOST KILLINGS ARE REACTIONARY. SPONTANEOUS. A ROBBERY GONE WRONG. A FIGHT THAT ESCALATES.
ARE PEOPLE REALLY THINKING ABOUT THE CONSEQUENCES IN THE HEAT OF THE MOMENT?
ANY OTHER THEORIES? MISS FINCH?

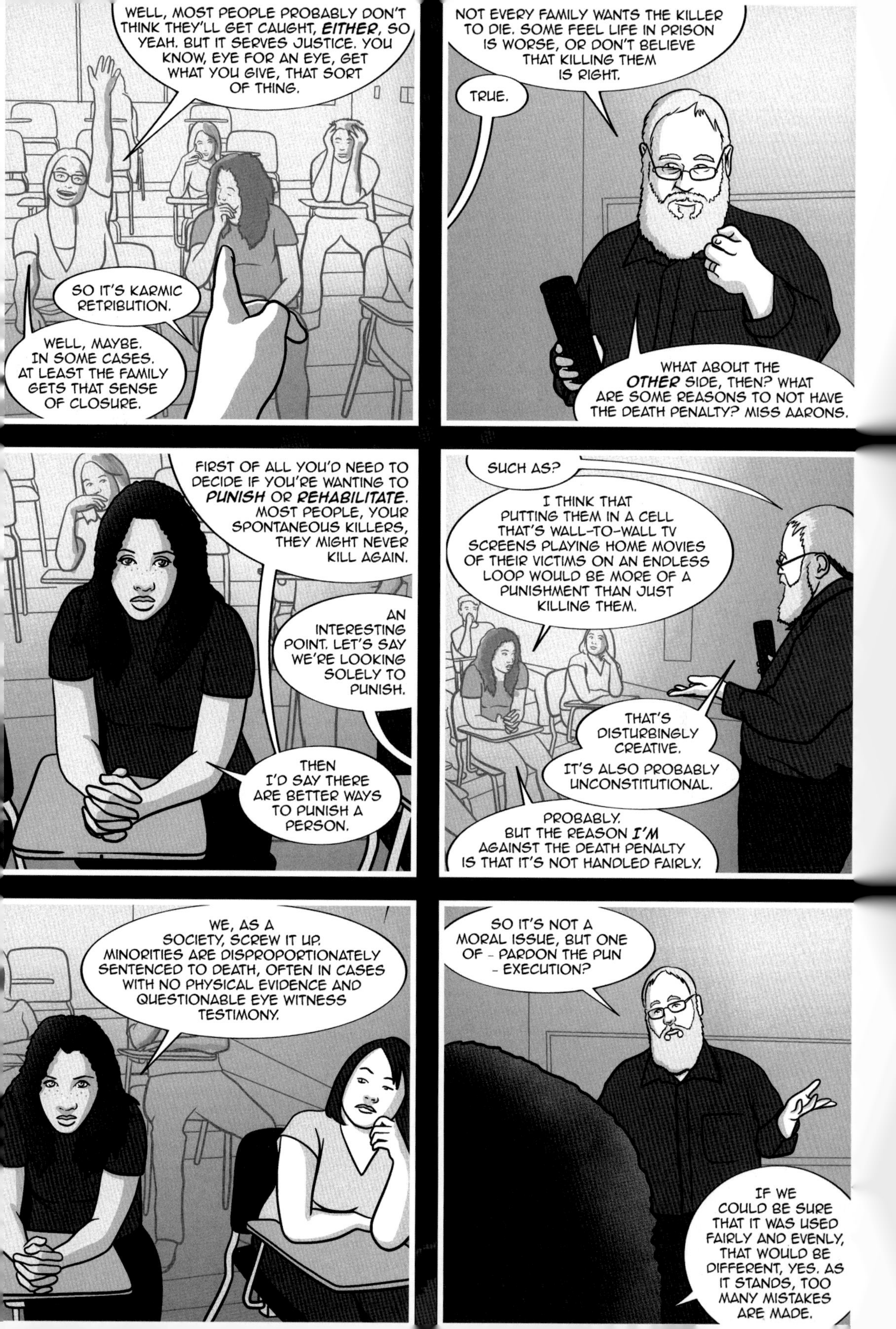
WELL, MOST PEOPLE PROBABLY DON'T THINK THEY'LL GET CAUGHT, *EITHER*, SO YEAH. BUT IT SERVES JUSTICE. YOU KNOW, EYE FOR AN EYE, GET WHAT YOU GIVE, THAT SORT OF THING.
SO IT'S KARMIC RETRIBUTION.
WELL, MAYBE. IN SOME CASES. AT LEAST THE FAMILY GETS THAT SENSE OF CLOSURE.
NOT EVERY FAMILY WANTS THE KILLER TO DIE. SOME FEEL LIFE IN PRISON IS WORSE, OR DON'T BELIEVE THAT KILLING THEM IS RIGHT.
TRUE.
WHAT ABOUT THE *OTHER* SIDE, THEN? WHAT ARE SOME REASONS TO NOT HAVE THE DEATH PENALTY? MISS AARONS.
FIRST OF ALL YOU'D NEED TO DECIDE IF YOU'RE WANTING TO *PUNISH* OR *REHABILITATE*. MOST PEOPLE, YOUR SPONTANEOUS KILLERS, THEY MIGHT NEVER KILL AGAIN.
AN INTERESTING POINT. LET'S SAY WE'RE LOOKING SOLELY TO PUNISH.
THEN I'D SAY THERE ARE BETTER WAYS TO PUNISH A PERSON.
SUCH AS?
I THINK THAT PUTTING THEM IN A CELL THAT'S WALL-TO-WALL TV SCREENS PLAYING HOME MOVIES OF THEIR VICTIMS ON AN ENDLESS LOOP WOULD BE MORE OF A PUNISHMENT THAN JUST KILLING THEM.
THAT'S DISTURBINGLY CREATIVE.
IT'S ALSO PROBABLY UNCONSTITUTIONAL.
PROBABLY. BUT THE REASON *I'M* AGAINST THE DEATH PENALTY IS THAT IT'S NOT HANDLED FAIRLY.
WE, AS A SOCIETY, SCREW IT UP. MINORITIES ARE DISPROPORTIONATELY SENTENCED TO DEATH, OFTEN IN CASES WITH NO PHYSICAL EVIDENCE AND QUESTIONABLE EYE WITNESS TESTIMONY.
SO IT'S NOT A MORAL ISSUE, BUT ONE OF - PARDON THE PUN - EXECUTION?
IF WE COULD BE SURE THAT IT WAS USED FAIRLY AND EVENLY, THAT WOULD BE DIFFERENT, YES. AS IT STANDS, TOO MANY MISTAKES ARE MADE.

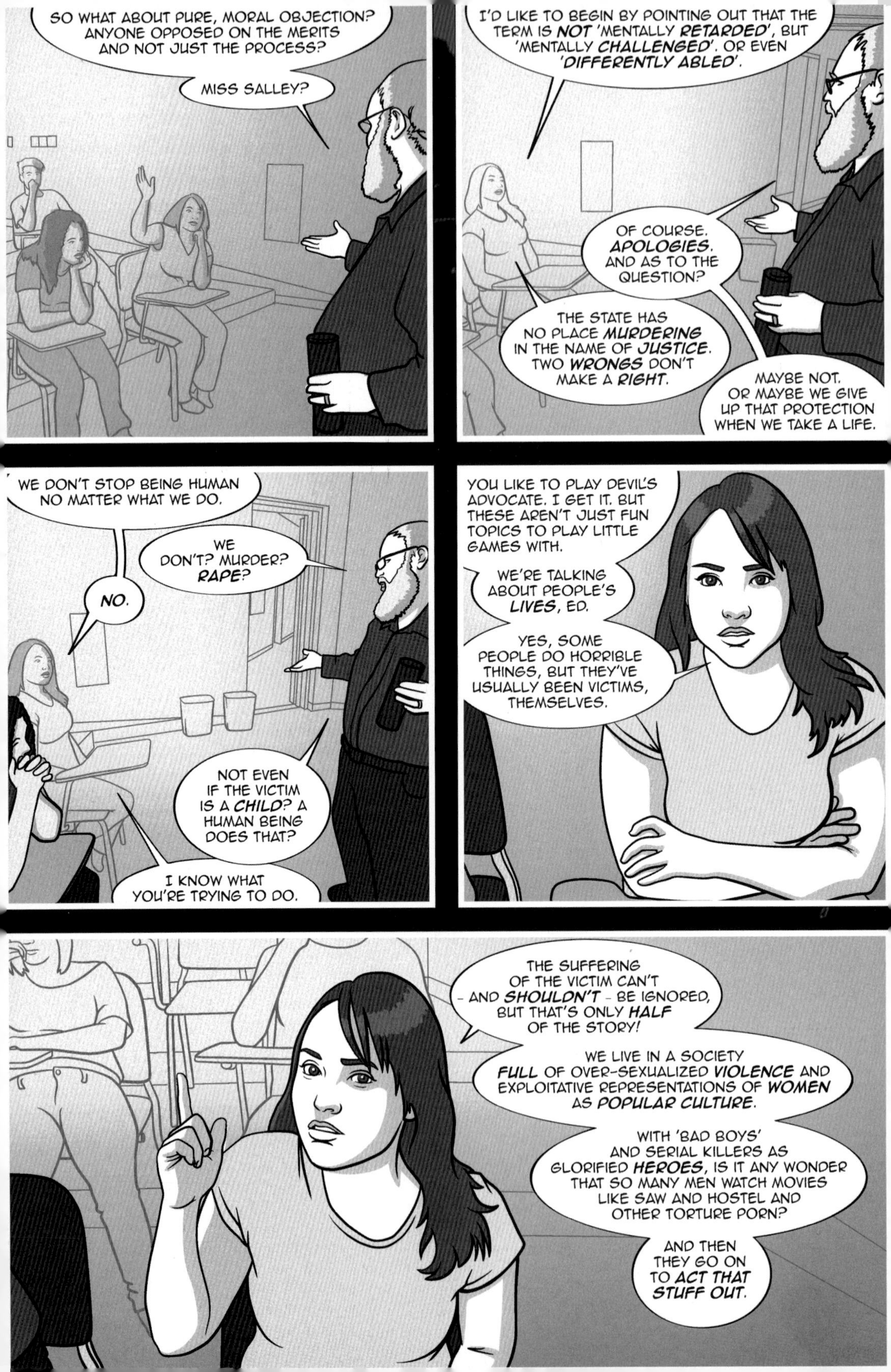
SO WHAT ABOUT PURE, MORAL OBJECTION? ANYONE OPPOSED ON THE MERITS AND NOT JUST THE PROCESS?
MISS SALLEY?
I'D LIKE TO BEGIN BY POINTING OUT THAT THE TERM IS NOT 'MENTALLY RETARDED', BUT 'MENTALLY CHALLENGED'. OR EVEN 'DIFFERENTLY ABLED'.
OF COURSE. APOLOGIES. AND AS TO THE QUESTION?
THE STATE HAS NO PLACE MURDERING IN THE NAME OF JUSTICE. TWO WRONGS DON'T MAKE A RIGHT.
MAYBE NOT. OR MAYBE WE GIVE UP THAT PROTECTION WHEN WE TAKE A LIFE.
WE DON'T STOP BEING HUMAN NO MATTER WHAT WE DO.
WE DON'T? MURDER? RAPE?
NO.
NOT EVEN IF THE VICTIM IS A CHILD? A HUMAN BEING DOES THAT?
I KNOW WHAT YOU'RE TRYING TO DO.
YOU LIKE TO PLAY DEVIL'S ADVOCATE. I GET IT. BUT THESE AREN'T JUST FUN TOPICS TO PLAY LITTLE GAMES WITH.
WE'RE TALKING ABOUT PEOPLE'S LIVES, ED.
YES, SOME PEOPLE DO HORRIBLE THINGS, BUT THEY'VE USUALLY BEEN VICTIMS, THEMSELVES.
THE SUFFERING OF THE VICTIM CAN'T - AND SHOULDN'T - BE IGNORED, BUT THAT'S ONLY HALF OF THE STORY!
WE LIVE IN A SOCIETY FULL OF OVER-SEXUALIZED VIOLENCE AND EXPLOITATIVE REPRESENTATIONS OF WOMEN AS POPULAR CULTURE.
WITH 'BAD BOYS' AND SERIAL KILLERS AS GLORIFIED HEROES, IS IT ANY WONDER THAT SO MANY MEN WATCH MOVIES LIKE SAW AND HOSTEL AND OTHER TORTURE PORN?
AND THEN THEY GO ON TO ACT THAT STUFF OUT.

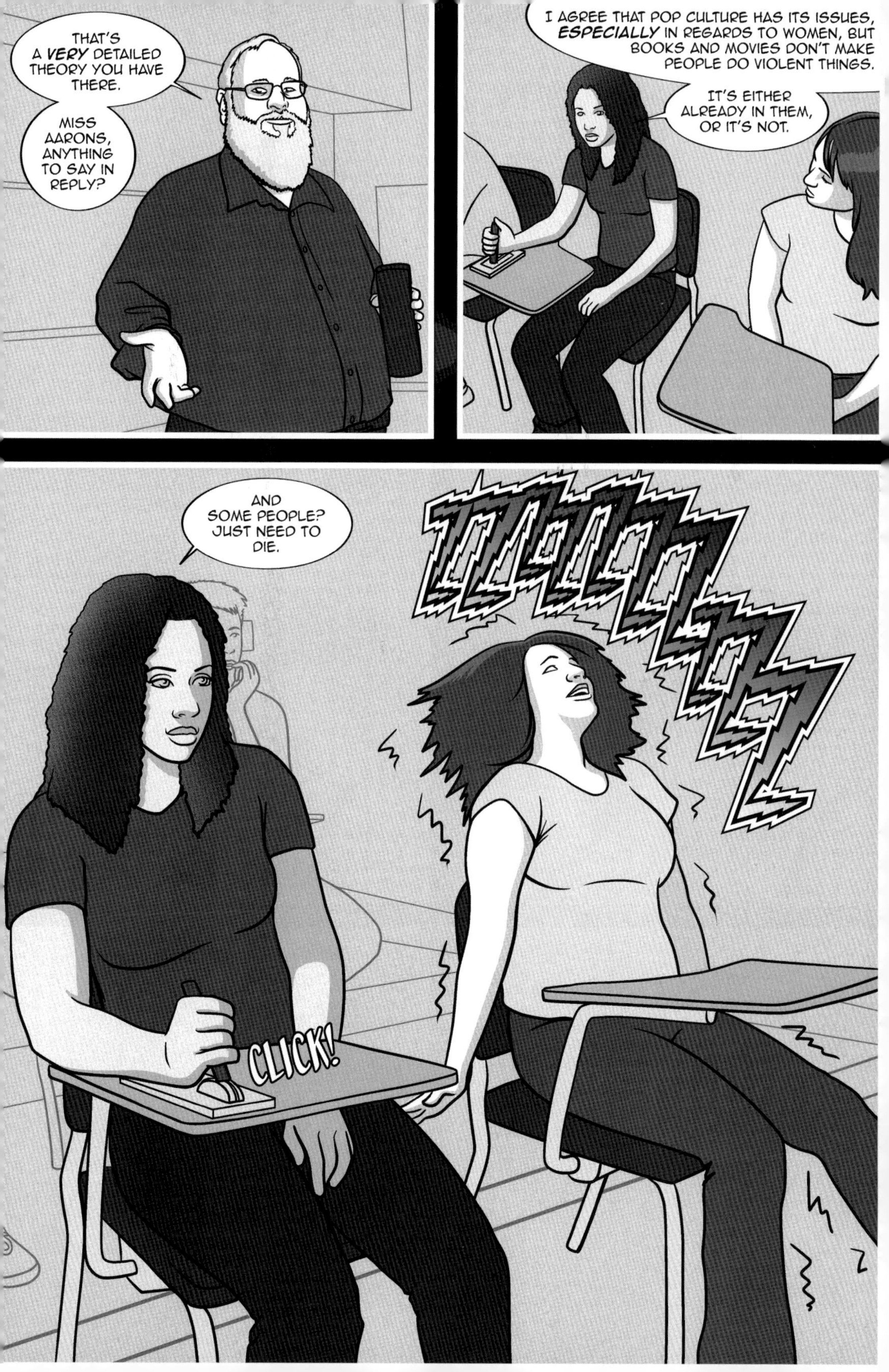
THAT'S A *VERY* DETAILED THEORY YOU HAVE THERE.
MISS AARONS, ANYTHING TO SAY IN REPLY?
I AGREE THAT POP CULTURE HAS ITS ISSUES, *ESPECIALLY* IN REGARDS TO WOMEN, BUT BOOKS AND MOVIES DON'T MAKE PEOPLE DO VIOLENT THINGS.
IT'S EITHER ALREADY IN THEM, OR IT'S NOT.
AND SOME PEOPLE? JUST NEED TO DIE.
CLICK!

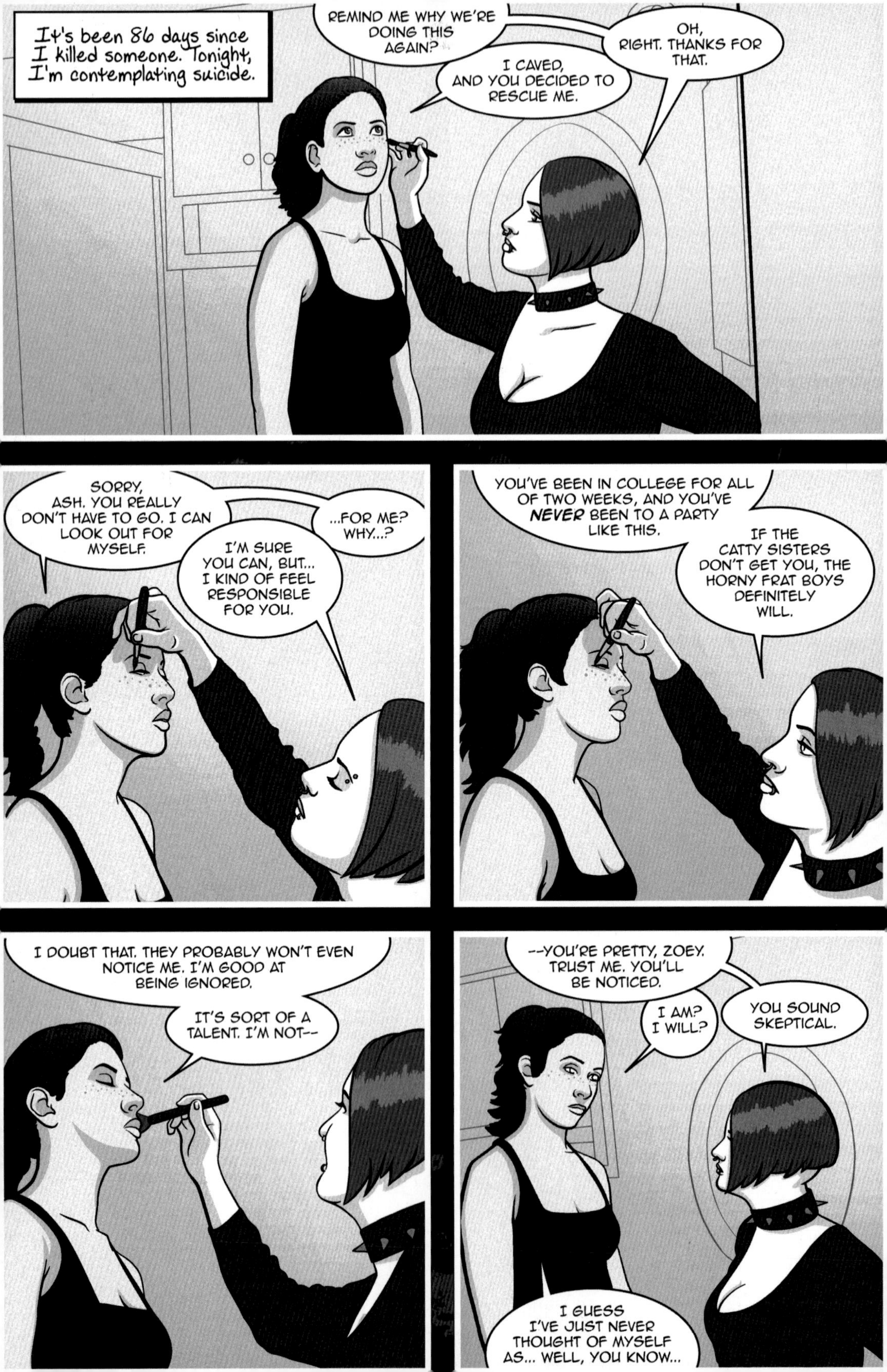
It's been 86 days since I killed someone. Tonight, I'm contemplating suicide.
REMIND ME WHY WE'RE DOING THIS AGAIN?
I CAVED, AND YOU DECIDED TO RESCUE ME.
OH, RIGHT. THANKS FOR THAT.
SORRY, ASH. YOU REALLY DON'T HAVE TO GO. I CAN LOOK OUT FOR MYSELF.
I'M SURE YOU CAN, BUT... I KIND OF FEEL RESPONSIBLE FOR YOU.
...FOR ME? WHY...?
YOU'VE BEEN IN COLLEGE FOR ALL OF TWO WEEKS, AND YOU'VE NEVER BEEN TO A PARTY LIKE THIS.
IF THE CATTY SISTERS DON'T GET YOU, THE HORNY FRAT BOYS DEFINITELY WILL.
I DOUBT THAT. THEY PROBABLY WON'T EVEN NOTICE ME. I'M GOOD AT BEING IGNORED.
IT'S SORT OF A TALENT. I'M NOT--
--YOU'RE PRETTY, ZOEY. TRUST ME. YOU'LL BE NOTICED.
I AM? I WILL?
YOU SOUND SKEPTICAL.
I GUESS I'VE JUST NEVER THOUGHT OF MYSELF AS... WELL, YOU KNOW...

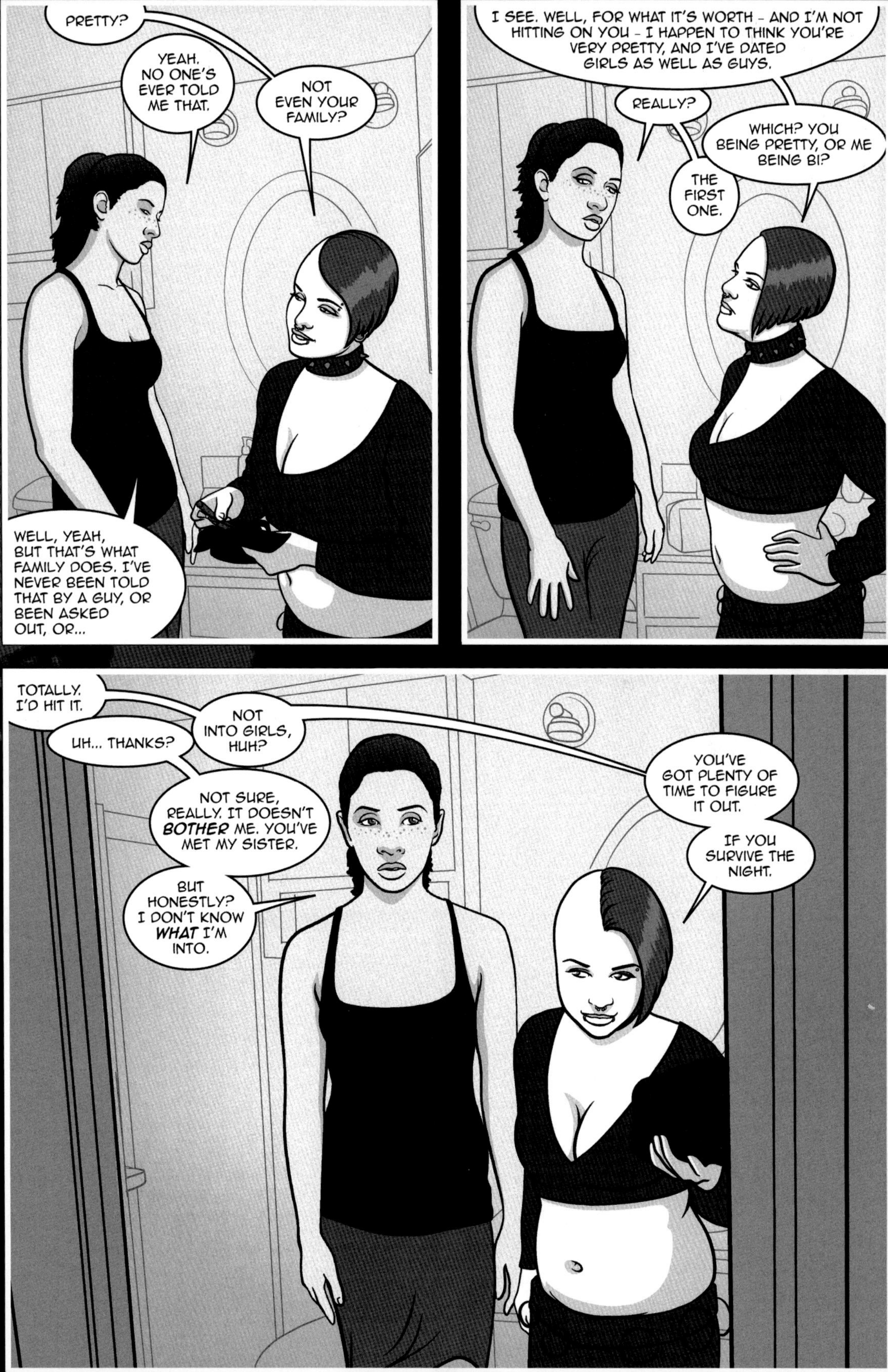
PRETTY?
YEAH. NO ONE'S EVER TOLD ME THAT.
NOT EVEN YOUR FAMILY?
WELL, YEAH, BUT THAT'S WHAT FAMILY DOES. I'VE NEVER BEEN TOLD THAT BY A GUY, OR BEEN ASKED OUT, OR...
I SEE. WELL, FOR WHAT IT'S WORTH - AND I'M NOT HITTING ON YOU - I HAPPEN TO THINK YOU'RE VERY PRETTY, AND I'VE DATED GIRLS AS WELL AS GUYS.
REALLY?
WHICH? YOU BEING PRETTY, OR ME BEING BI?
THE FIRST ONE.
TOTALLY. I'D HIT IT.
UH... THANKS?
NOT INTO GIRLS, HUH?
NOT SURE, REALLY. IT DOESN'T BOTHER ME. YOU'VE MET MY SISTER.
BUT HONESTLY? I DON'T KNOW WHAT I'M INTO.
YOU'VE GOT PLENTY OF TIME TO FIGURE IT OUT.
IF YOU SURVIVE THE NIGHT.

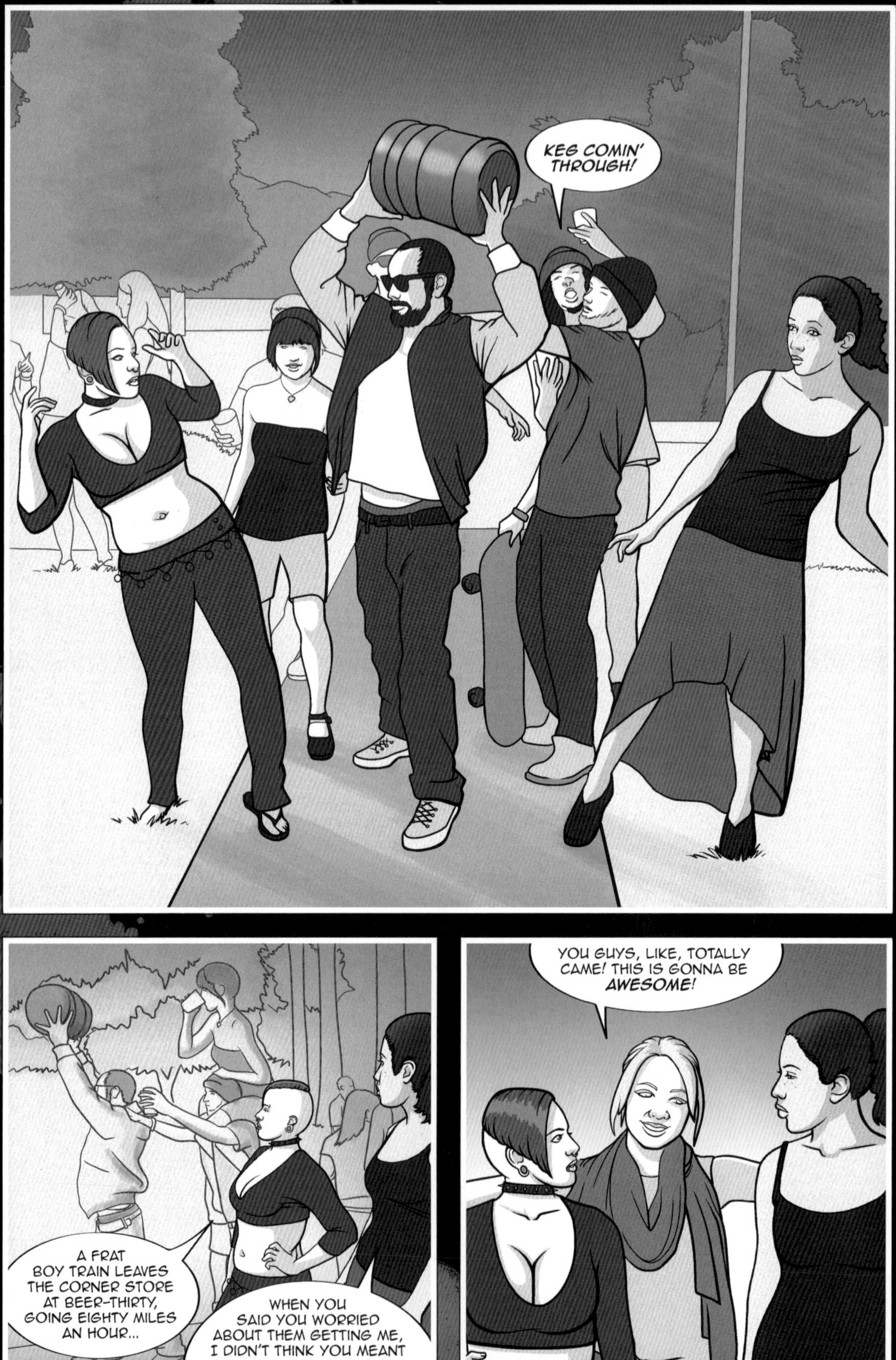
KEG COMIN' THROUGH!
A FRAT BOY TRAIN LEAVES THE CORNER STORE AT BEER-THIRTY, GOING EIGHTY MILES AN HOUR...
WHEN YOU SAID YOU WORRIED ABOUT THEM GETTING ME, I DIDN'T THINK YOU MEANT THEY MIGHT RUN ME OVER.
YOU GUYS, LIKE, TOTALLY CAME! THIS IS GONNA BE *AWESOME!*

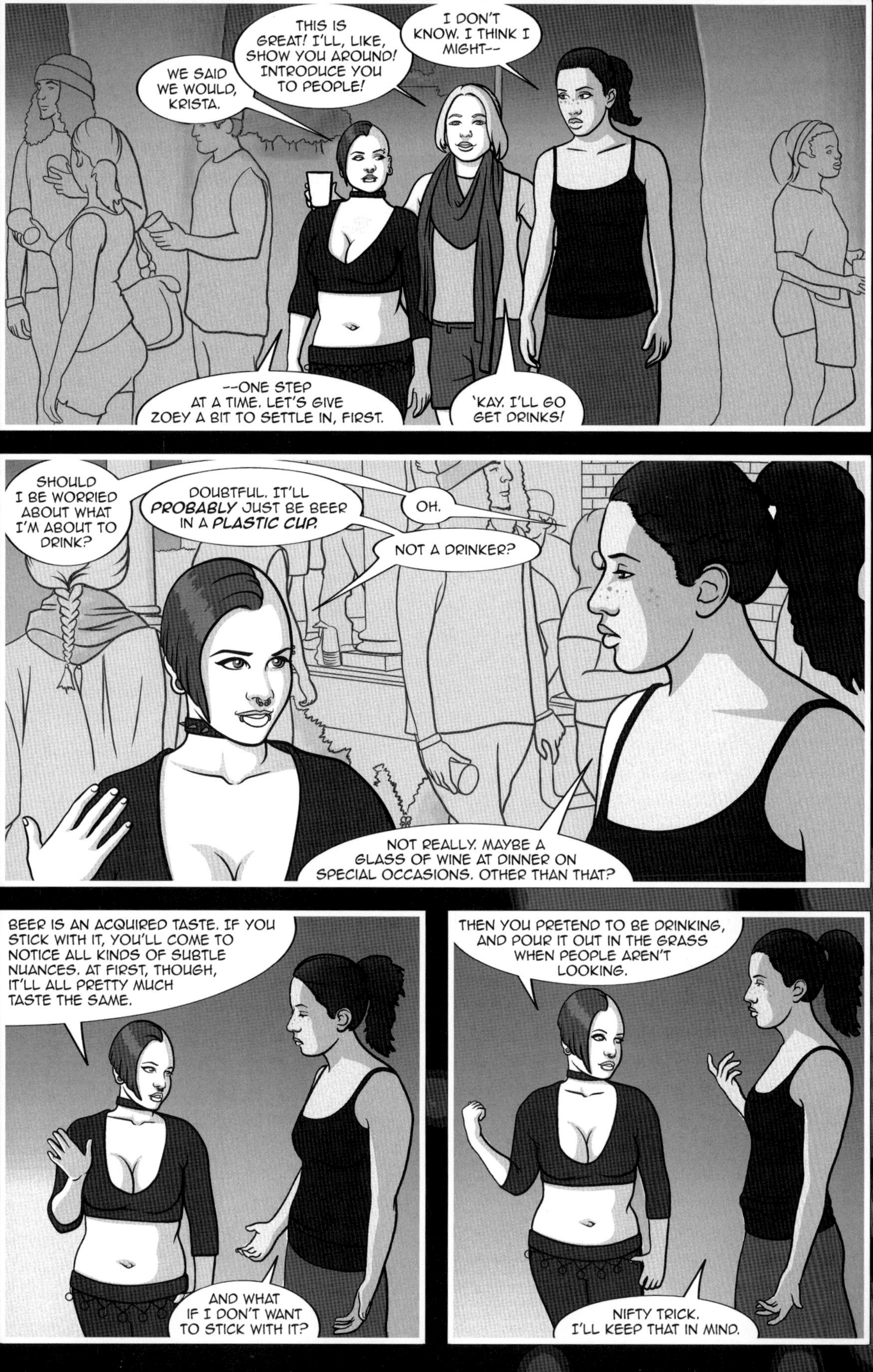
WE SAID WE WOULD, KRISTA.
THIS IS GREAT! I'LL, LIKE, SHOW YOU AROUND! INTRODUCE YOU TO PEOPLE!
I DON'T KNOW. I THINK I MIGHT--
--ONE STEP AT A TIME. LET'S GIVE ZOEY A BIT TO SETTLE IN, FIRST.
'KAY. I'LL GO GET DRINKS!
SHOULD I BE WORRIED ABOUT WHAT I'M ABOUT TO DRINK?
DOUBTFUL. IT'LL *PROBABLY* JUST BE BEER IN A *PLASTIC CUP.*
OH.
NOT A DRINKER?
NOT REALLY. MAYBE A GLASS OF WINE AT DINNER ON SPECIAL OCCASIONS. OTHER THAN THAT?
BEER IS AN ACQUIRED TASTE. IF YOU STICK WITH IT, YOU'LL COME TO NOTICE ALL KINDS OF SUBTLE NUANCES. AT FIRST, THOUGH, IT'LL ALL PRETTY MUCH TASTE THE SAME.
AND WHAT IF I DON'T WANT TO STICK WITH IT?
THEN YOU PRETEND TO BE DRINKING, AND POUR IT OUT IN THE GRASS WHEN PEOPLE AREN'T LOOKING.
NIFTY TRICK. I'LL KEEP THAT IN MIND.

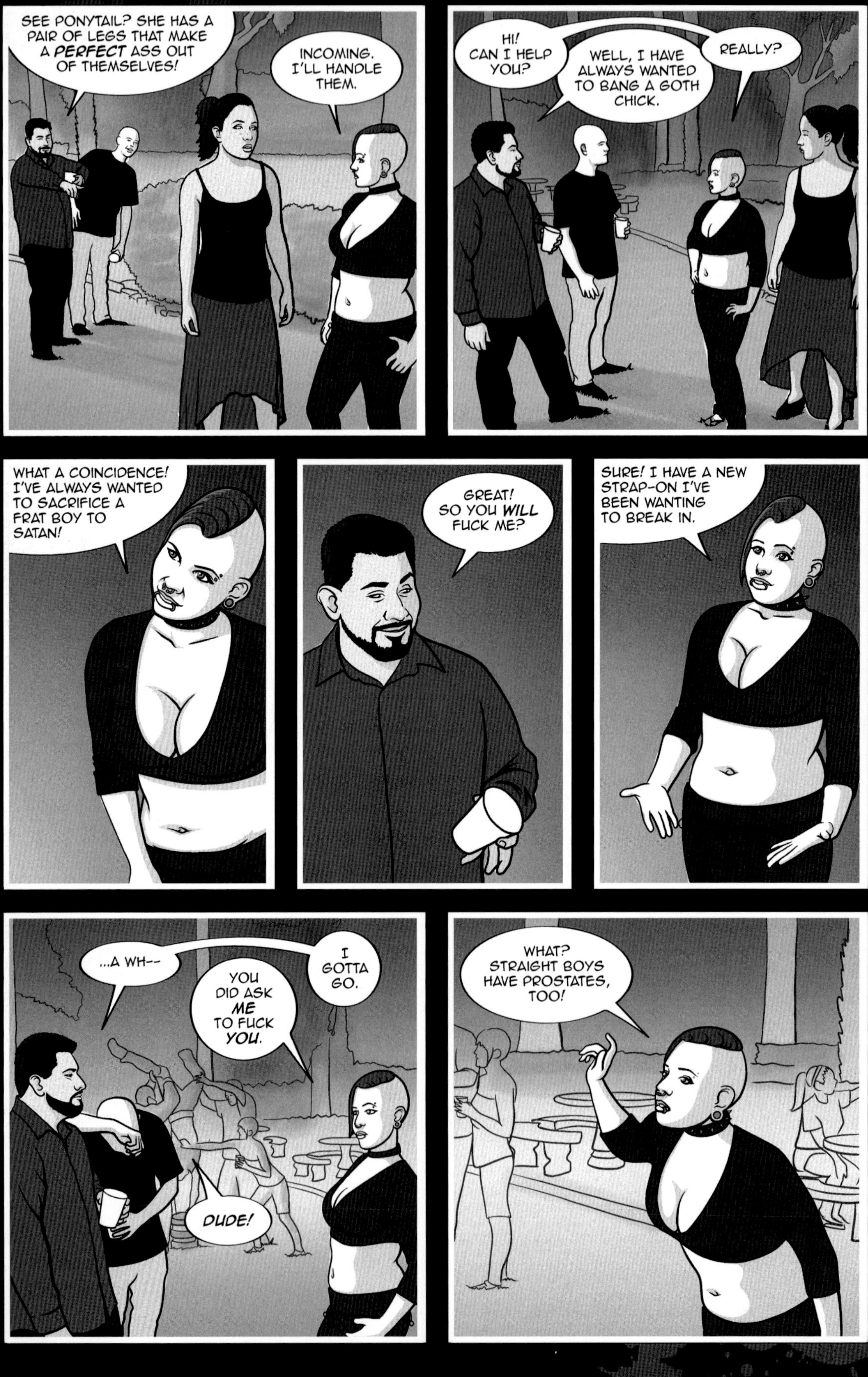

SEE PONYTAIL? SHE HAS A PAIR OF LEGS THAT MAKE A *PERFECT* ASS OUT OF THEMSELVES!
INCOMING. I'LL HANDLE THEM.
HI! CAN I HELP YOU?
WELL, I HAVE ALWAYS WANTED TO BANG A GOTH CHICK.
REALLY?
WHAT A COINCIDENCE! I'VE ALWAYS WANTED TO SACRIFICE A FRAT BOY TO SATAN!
GREAT! SO YOU *WILL* FUCK ME?
SURE! I HAVE A NEW STRAP-ON I'VE BEEN WANTING TO BREAK IN.
...A WH--
I GOTTA GO.
YOU DID ASK *ME* TO FUCK *YOU*.
DUDE!
WHAT? STRAIGHT BOYS HAVE PROSTATES, TOO!

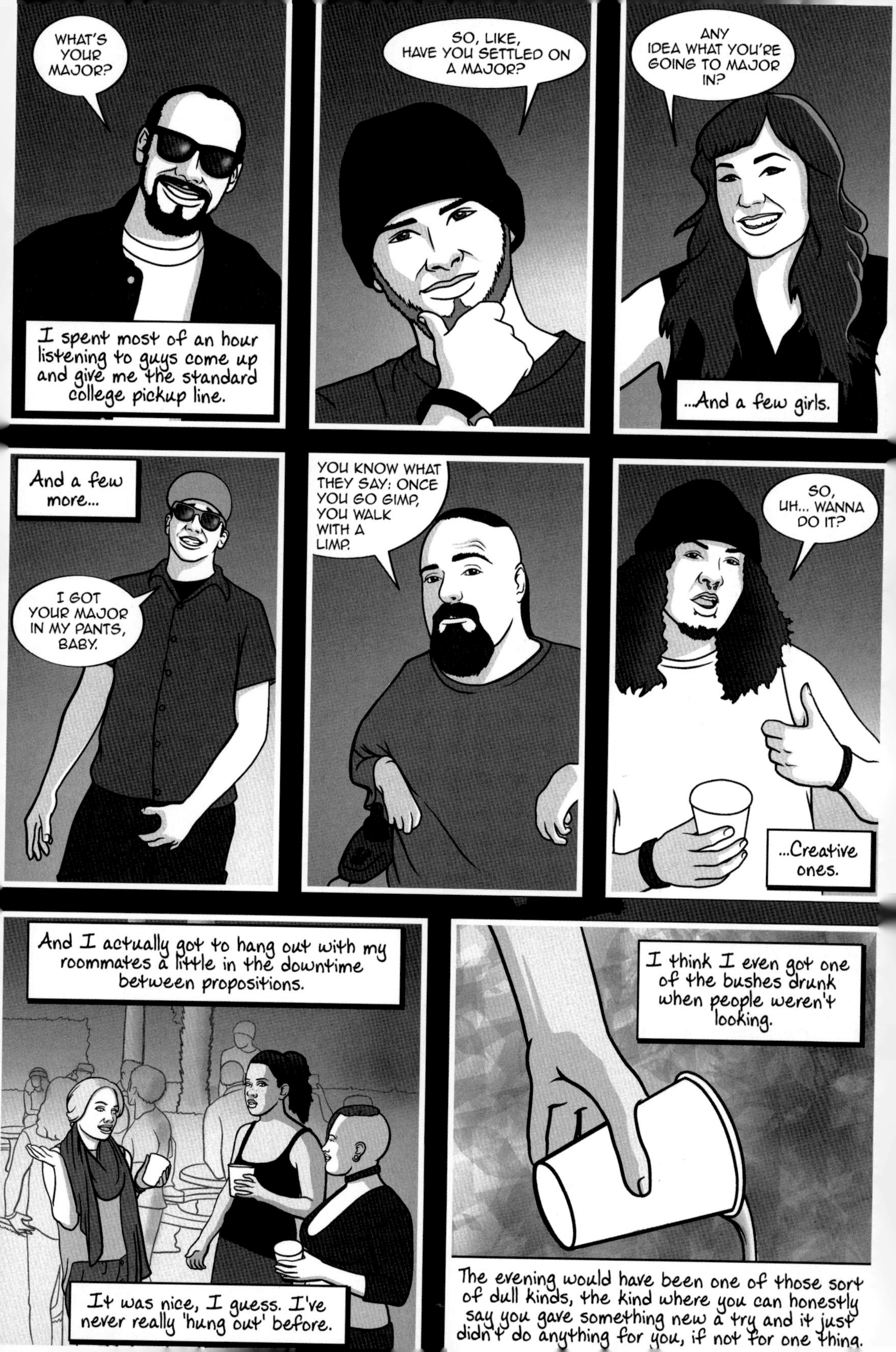
WHAT'S YOUR MAJOR?
I spent most of an hour listening to guys come up and give me the standard college pickup line.
SO, LIKE, HAVE YOU SETTLED ON A MAJOR?
ANY IDEA WHAT YOU'RE GOING TO MAJOR IN?
...And a few girls.
And a few more...
I GOT YOUR MAJOR IN MY PANTS, BABY.
YOU KNOW WHAT THEY SAY: ONCE YOU GO GIMP, YOU WALK WITH A LIMP.
SO, UH... WANNA DO IT?
...Creative ones.
And I actually got to hang out with my roommates a little in the downtime between propositions.
It was nice, I guess. I've never really 'hung out' before.
I think I even got one of the bushes drunk when people weren't looking.
The evening would have been one of those sort of dull kinds, the kind where you can honestly say you gave something new a try and it just didn't do anything for you, if not for one thing.

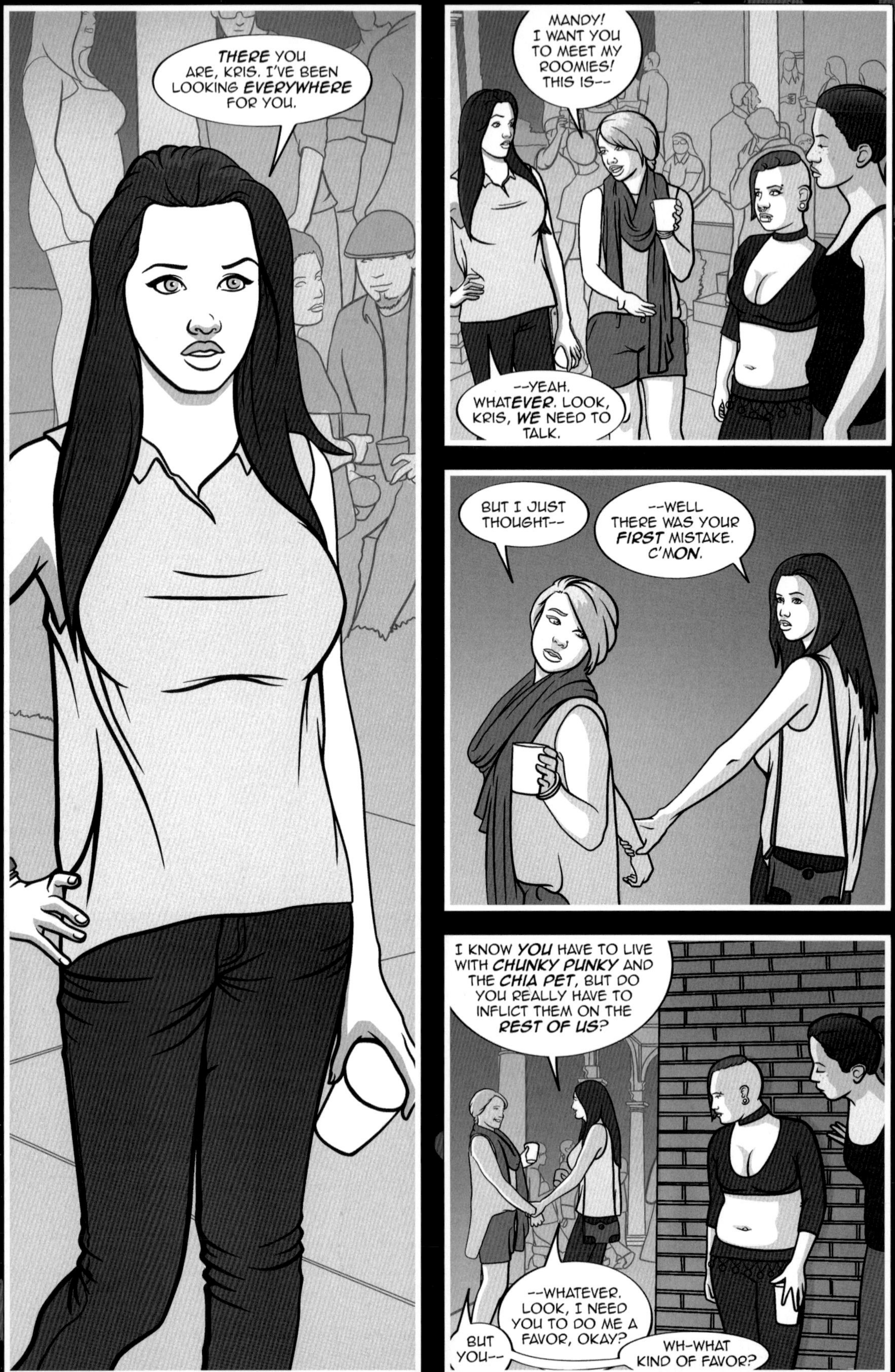
THERE YOU ARE, KRIS. I'VE BEEN LOOKING EVERYWHERE FOR YOU.
MANDY! I WANT YOU TO MEET MY ROOMIES! THIS IS--
--YEAH. WHATEVER. LOOK, KRIS, WE NEED TO TALK.
BUT I JUST THOUGHT--
--WELL THERE WAS YOUR FIRST MISTAKE. C'MON.
I KNOW YOU HAVE TO LIVE WITH CHUNKY PUNKY AND THE CHIA PET, BUT DO YOU REALLY HAVE TO INFLICT THEM ON THE REST OF US?
BUT YOU--
--WHATEVER. LOOK, I NEED YOU TO DO ME A FAVOR, OKAY?
WH-WHAT KIND OF FAVOR?

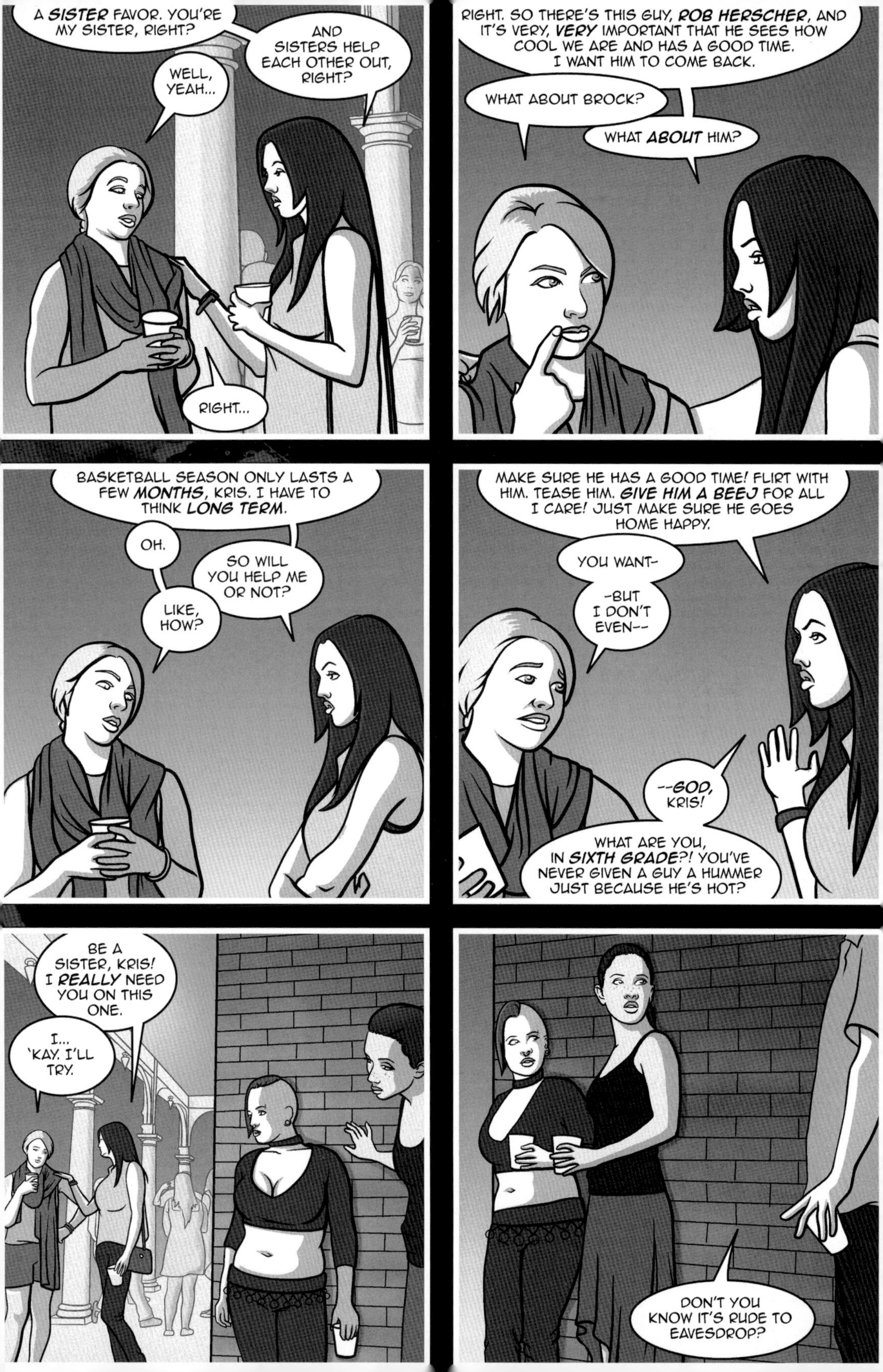
A SISTER FAVOR. YOU'RE MY SISTER, RIGHT?
WELL, YEAH...
AND SISTERS HELP EACH OTHER OUT, RIGHT?
RIGHT...
RIGHT. SO THERE'S THIS GUY, ROB HERSCHER, AND IT'S VERY, VERY IMPORTANT THAT HE SEES HOW COOL WE ARE AND HAS A GOOD TIME. I WANT HIM TO COME BACK.
WHAT ABOUT BROCK?
WHAT ABOUT HIM?
BASKETBALL SEASON ONLY LASTS A FEW MONTHS, KRIS. I HAVE TO THINK LONG TERM.
OH.
LIKE, HOW?
SO WILL YOU HELP ME OR NOT?
MAKE SURE HE HAS A GOOD TIME! FLIRT WITH HIM. TEASE HIM. GIVE HIM A BEEJ FOR ALL I CARE! JUST MAKE SURE HE GOES HOME HAPPY.
YOU WANT-
-BUT I DON'T EVEN--
--GOD, KRIS!
WHAT ARE YOU, IN SIXTH GRADE?! YOU'VE NEVER GIVEN A GUY A HUMMER JUST BECAUSE HE'S HOT?
BE A SISTER, KRIS! I REALLY NEED YOU ON THIS ONE.
I... 'KAY. I'LL TRY.
DON'T YOU KNOW IT'S RUDE TO EAVESDROP?

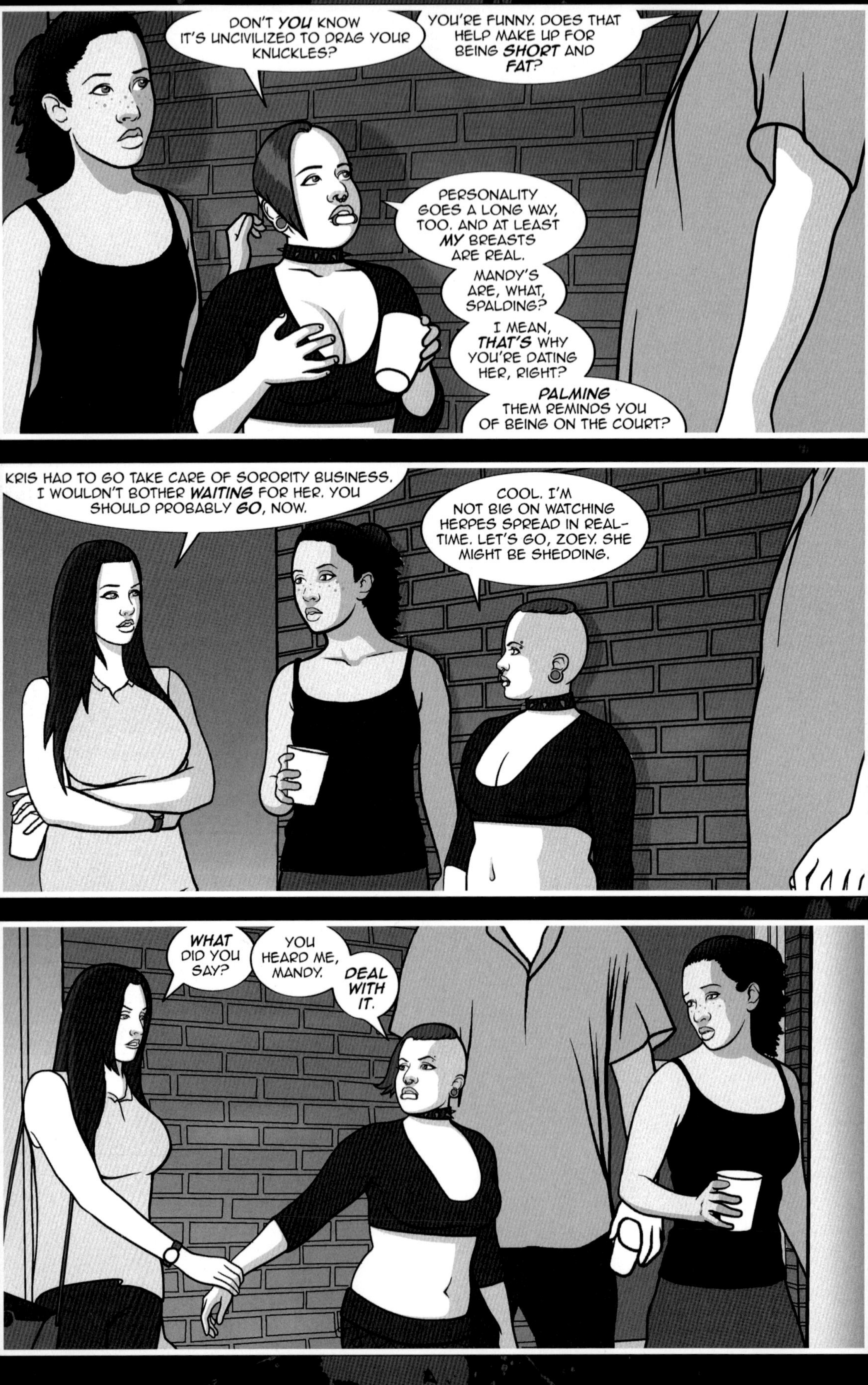
DON'T *YOU* KNOW IT'S UNCIVILIZED TO DRAG YOUR KNUCKLES?
YOU'RE FUNNY. DOES THAT HELP MAKE UP FOR BEING *SHORT* AND *FAT*?
PERSONALITY GOES A LONG WAY, TOO. AND AT LEAST *MY* BREASTS ARE REAL.
MANDY'S ARE, WHAT, SPALDING?
I MEAN, *THAT'S* WHY YOU'RE DATING HER, RIGHT?
PALMING THEM REMINDS YOU OF BEING ON THE COURT?
KRIS HAD TO GO TAKE CARE OF SORORITY BUSINESS. I WOULDN'T BOTHER *WAITING* FOR HER. YOU SHOULD PROBABLY *GO*, NOW.
COOL. I'M NOT BIG ON WATCHING HERPES SPREAD IN REAL-TIME. LET'S GO, ZOEY. SHE MIGHT BE SHEDDING.
WHAT DID YOU SAY?
YOU HEARD ME, MANDY.
DEAL WITH IT.

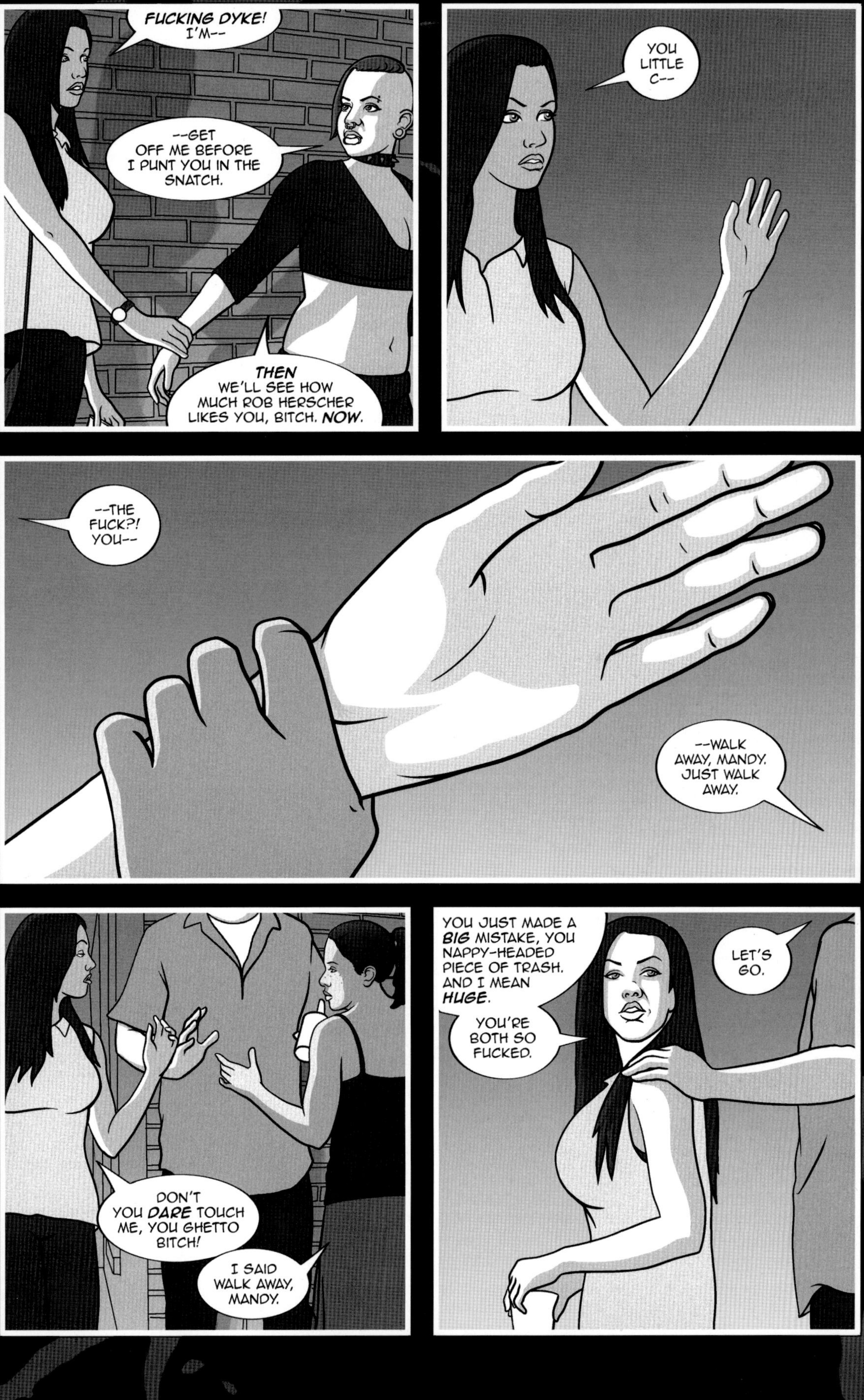
FUCKING DYKE! I'M--
--GET OFF ME BEFORE I PUNT YOU IN THE SNATCH.
THEN WE'LL SEE HOW MUCH ROB HERSCHER LIKES YOU, BITCH. NOW.
YOU LITTLE C--
--THE FUCK?! YOU--
--WALK AWAY, MANDY. JUST WALK AWAY.
DON'T YOU DARE TOUCH ME, YOU GHETTO BITCH!
I SAID WALK AWAY, MANDY.
YOU JUST MADE A BIG MISTAKE, YOU NAPPY-HEADED PIECE OF TRASH. AND I MEAN HUGE.
YOU'RE BOTH SO FUCKED.
LET'S GO.

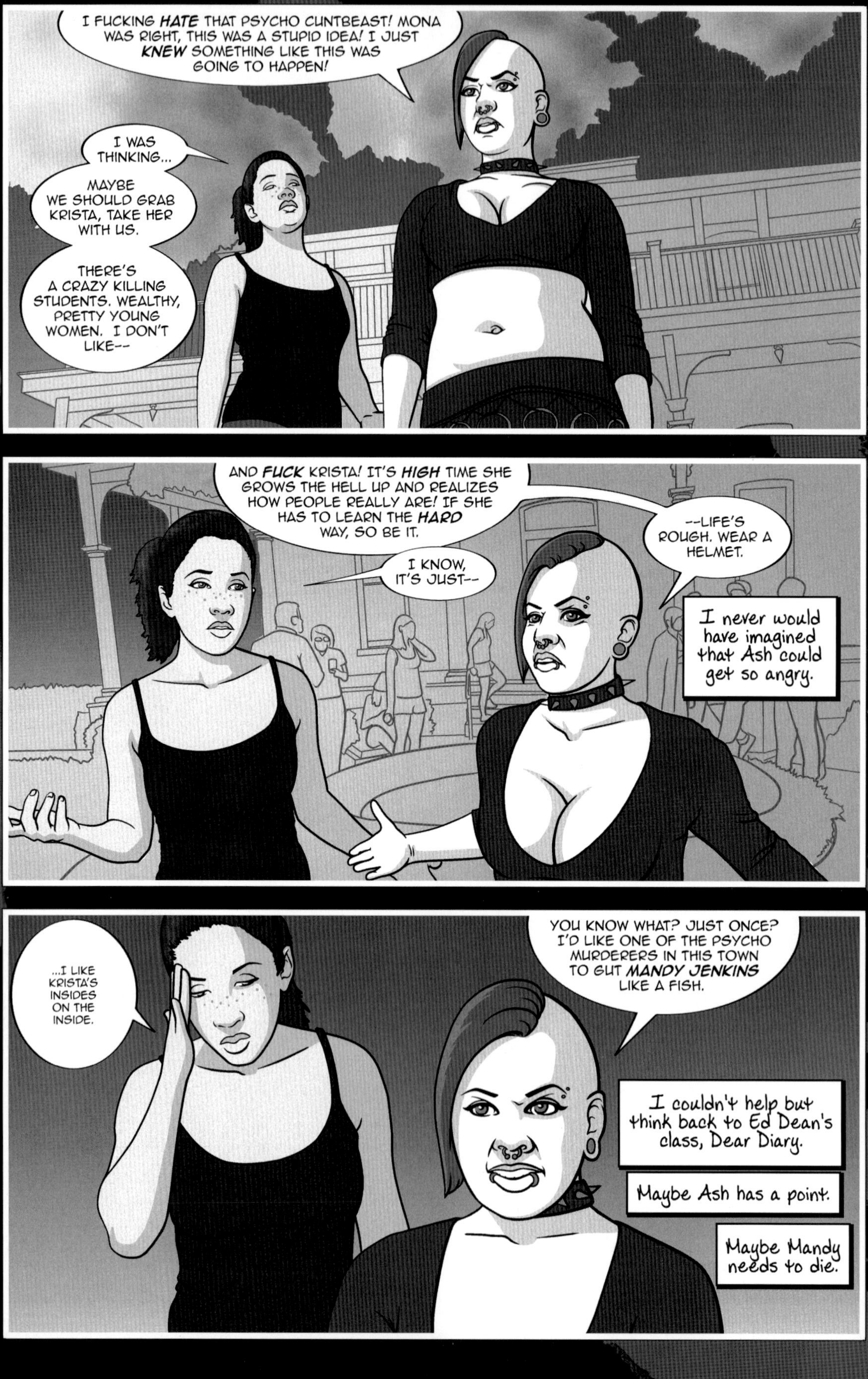
I FUCKING HATE THAT PSYCHO CUNTBEAST! MONA WAS RIGHT, THIS WAS A STUPID IDEA! I JUST KNEW SOMETHING LIKE THIS WAS GOING TO HAPPEN!
I WAS THINKING...
MAYBE WE SHOULD GRAB KRISTA, TAKE HER WITH US.
THERE'S A CRAZY KILLING STUDENTS. WEALTHY, PRETTY YOUNG WOMEN. I DON'T LIKE--
AND FUCK KRISTA! IT'S HIGH TIME SHE GROWS THE HELL UP AND REALIZES HOW PEOPLE REALLY ARE! IF SHE HAS TO LEARN THE HARD WAY, SO BE IT.
I KNOW, IT'S JUST--
--LIFE'S ROUGH. WEAR A HELMET.
I never would have imagined that Ash could get so angry.
...I LIKE KRISTA'S INSIDES ON THE INSIDE.
YOU KNOW WHAT? JUST ONCE? I'D LIKE ONE OF THE PSYCHO MURDERERS IN THIS TOWN TO GUT MANDY JENKINS LIKE A FISH.
I couldn't help but think back to Ed Dean's class, Dear Diary.
Maybe Ash has a point.
Maybe Mandy needs to die.

Dead Student Found In Dorm

Staff Writer | September 5, 2013 | 26 comments

CUTTER'S CIRCLE - A second Blair student was found dead late Tuesday night, in her dorm room, by a Resident Advisor following up on a noise complaint. The murder comes only one week after the murder of Katelyn Miller.

Luna Weaks, 18, of Portland, Oregon, was discovered by the RA after neighbors made complaints about a loud stereo. Knocks on the door went unanswered. Upon obtaining a key, the RA found Weaks' body.

Pictured above: Luna Weaks

Weaks, a freshman, was the daughter of organic candy magnate Rory Weaks.

"We have reason to believe that the same person or persons responsible for the death of Katelyn Miller also killed Ms. Weaks," said Detective Sergeant Ezekiel Aarons, lead homicide investigator for the Cutter's Circle Police Department. "Certain aspects of the crime scenes are similar. We believe we are dealing with a serial killer."

Aarons advised Blair students to take extra precautions. "It's too early to form a solid profile," said Aarons, "but what we do know is that the suspect is probably an artist of some sort, perhaps a photographer, and that the victims believed they were modeling. All young women in Cutter's Circle should be extra careful of where they go and with whom, but Blair students in particular need to be aware of the danger."

A vigil has been planned for both young women tomorrow night, September 6th, at 6pm at the Blair University mall lawn. Several women's groups working in the fields of domestic violence and self-defense will be on hand to offer their assistance to interested persons.

Anyone who may have seen either young woman the night before their deaths is encouraged to call the CCPD tip line at 555-8344.

Katelyn Miller was found last week by a jogger near the lake.

a VOICE in the DARK

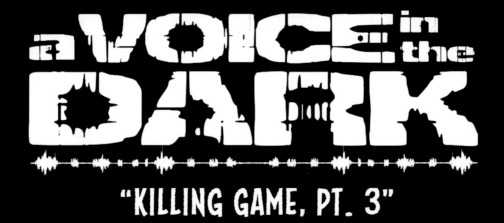

"KILLING GAME, PT. 3"

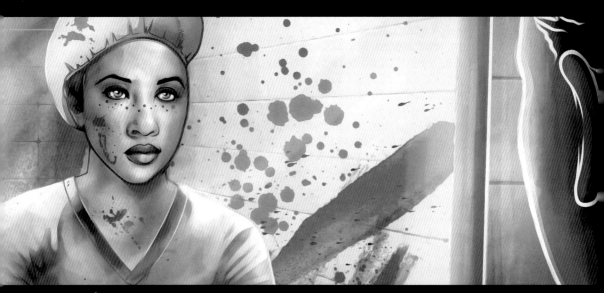

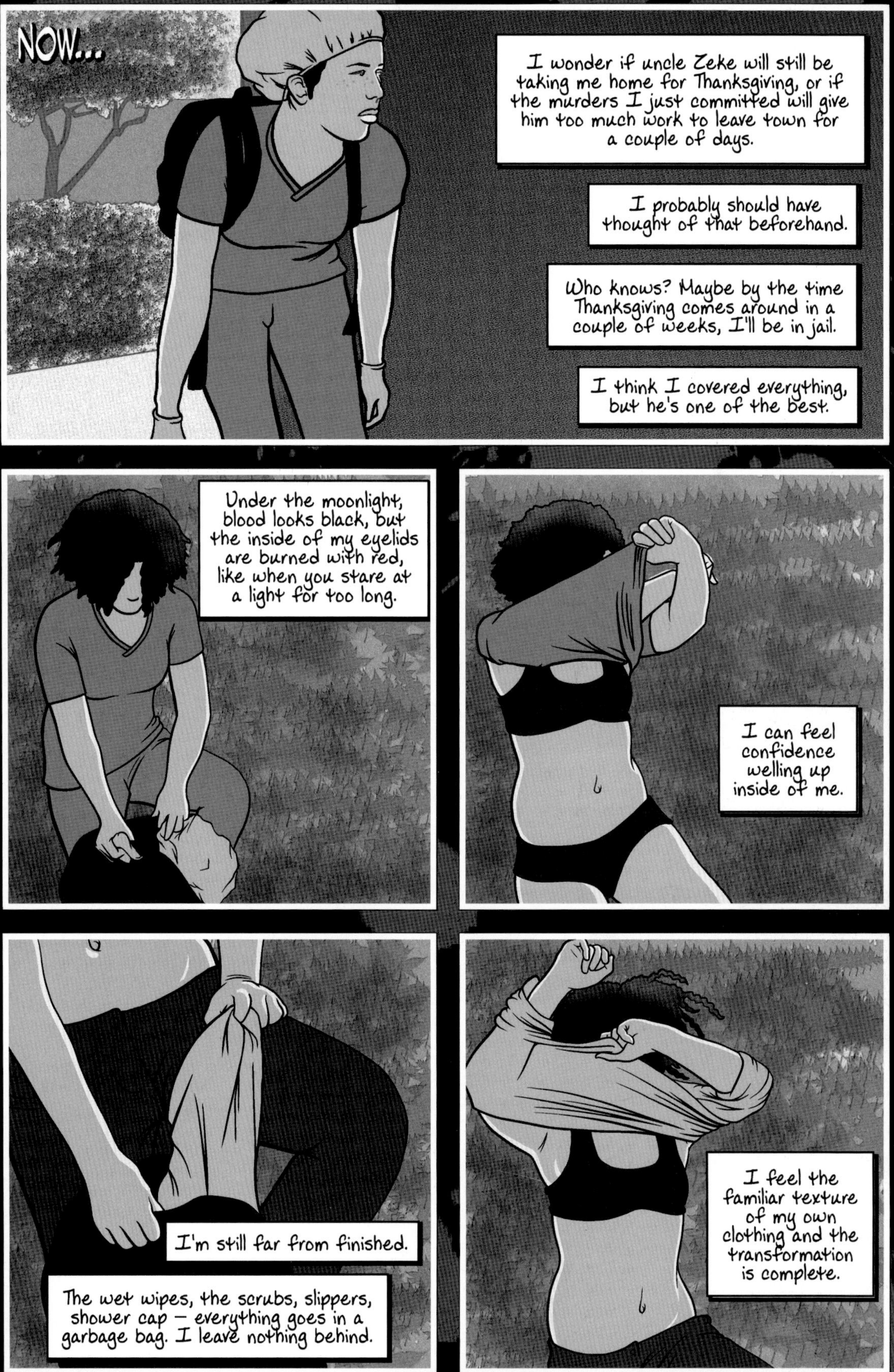
NOW...
I wonder if uncle Zeke will still be taking me home for Thanksgiving, or if the murders I just committed will give him too much work to leave town for a couple of days.
I probably should have thought of that beforehand.
Who knows? Maybe by the time Thanksgiving comes around in a couple of weeks, I'll be in jail.
I think I covered everything, but he's one of the best.
Under the moonlight, blood looks black, but the inside of my eyelids are burned with red, like when you stare at a light for too long.
I can feel confidence welling up inside of me.
I'm still far from finished.
The wet wipes, the scrubs, slippers, shower cap — everything goes in a garbage bag. I leave nothing behind.
I feel the familiar texture of my own clothing and the transformation is complete.

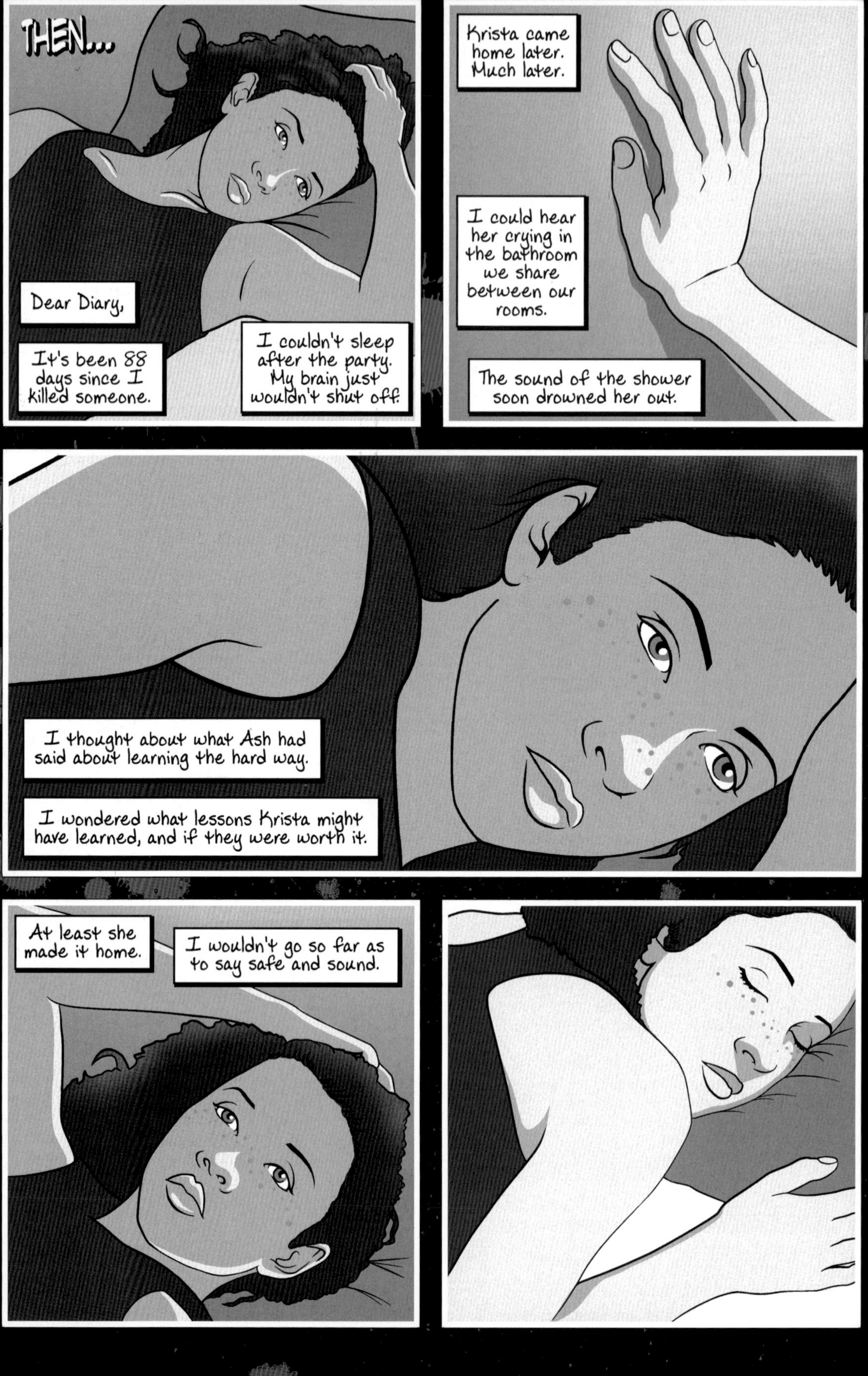
THEN...
Dear Diary,
It's been 88 days since I killed someone.
I couldn't sleep after the party. My brain just wouldn't shut off.
Krista came home later. Much later.
I could hear her crying in the bathroom we share between our rooms.
The sound of the shower soon drowned her out.
I thought about what Ash had said about learning the hard way.
I wondered what lessons Krista might have learned, and if they were worth it.
At least she made it home.
I wouldn't go so far as to say safe and sound.

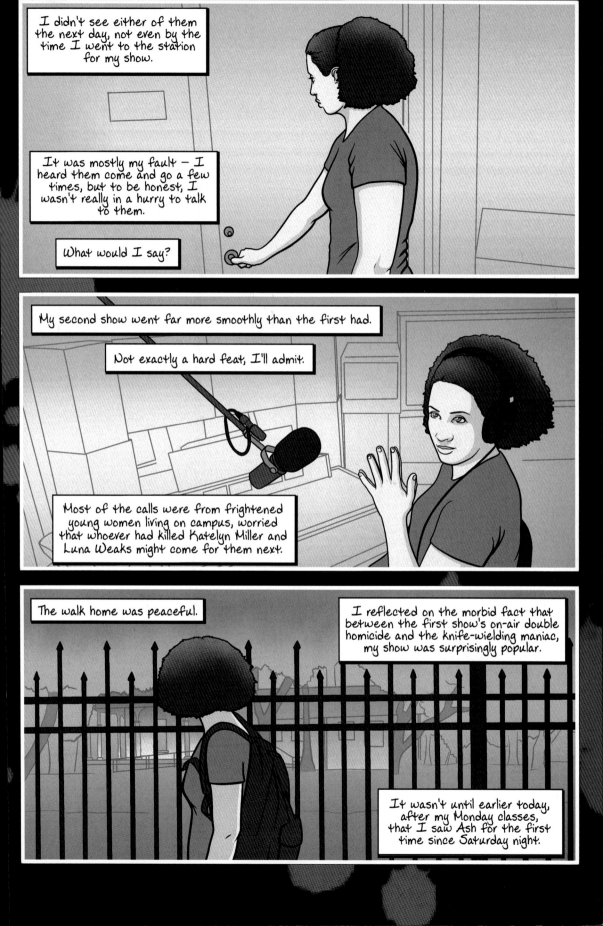

I didn't see either of them the next day, not even by the time I went to the station for my show.

It was mostly my fault — I heard them come and go a few times, but to be honest, I wasn't really in a hurry to talk to them.

What would I say?

My second show went far more smoothly than the first had.

Not exactly a hard feat, I'll admit.

Most of the calls were from frightened young women living on campus, worried that whoever had killed Katelyn Miller and Luna Weaks might come for them next.

The walk home was peaceful.

I reflected on the morbid fact that between the first show's on-air double homicide and the knife-wielding maniac, my show was surprisingly popular.

It wasn't until earlier today, after my Monday classes, that I saw Ash for the first time since Saturday night.

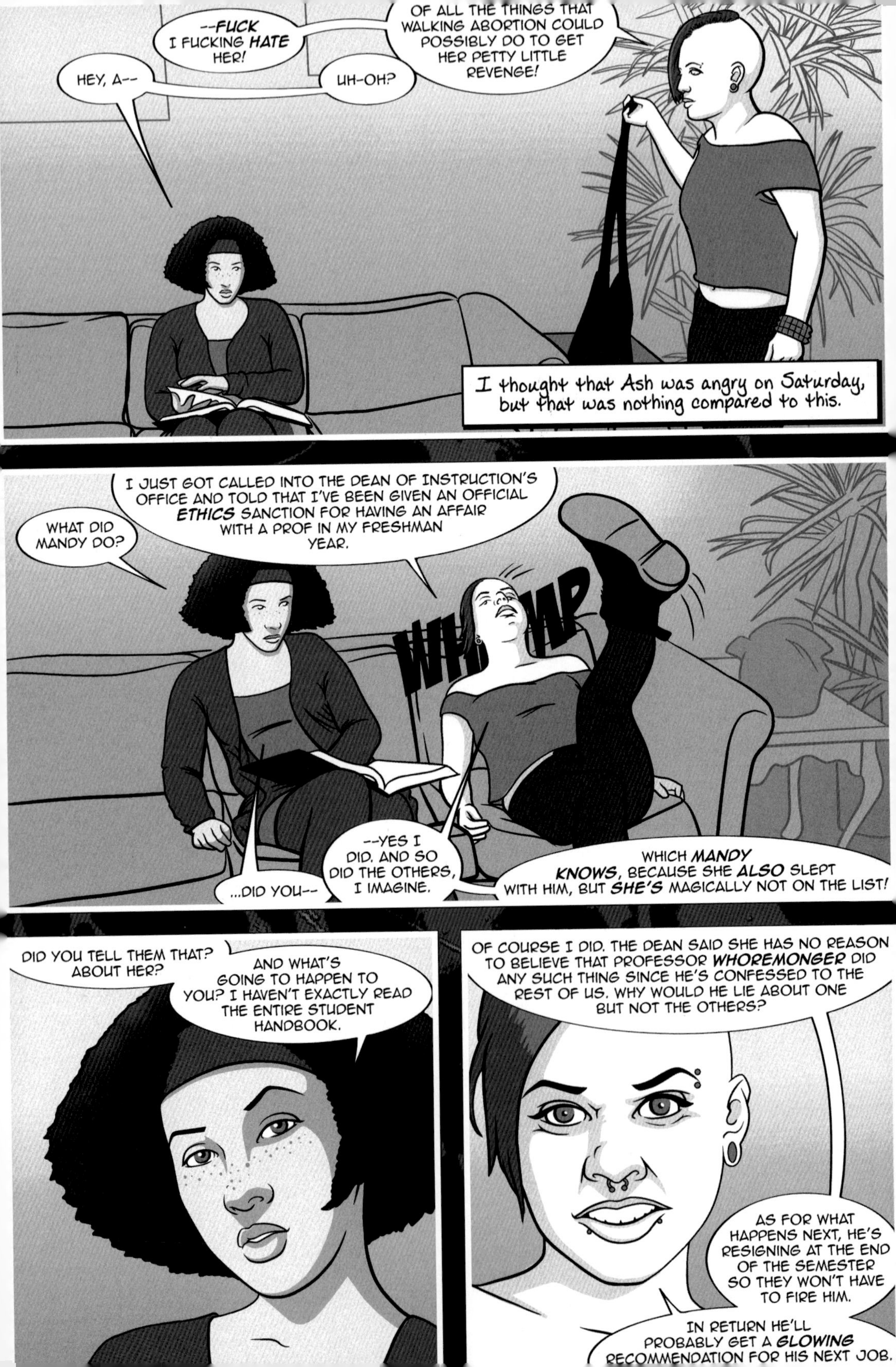
HEY, A--
--FUCK I FUCKING HATE HER!
UH-OH?
OF ALL THE THINGS THAT WALKING ABORTION COULD POSSIBLY DO TO GET HER PETTY LITTLE REVENGE!
I thought that Ash was angry on Saturday, but that was nothing compared to this.
WHAT DID MANDY DO?
I JUST GOT CALLED INTO THE DEAN OF INSTRUCTION'S OFFICE AND TOLD THAT I'VE BEEN GIVEN AN OFFICIAL ETHICS SANCTION FOR HAVING AN AFFAIR WITH A PROF IN MY FRESHMAN YEAR.
...DID YOU--
--YES I DID. AND SO DID THE OTHERS, I IMAGINE.
WHICH MANDY KNOWS, BECAUSE SHE ALSO SLEPT WITH HIM, BUT SHE'S MAGICALLY NOT ON THE LIST!
DID YOU TELL THEM THAT? ABOUT HER?
AND WHAT'S GOING TO HAPPEN TO YOU? I HAVEN'T EXACTLY READ THE ENTIRE STUDENT HANDBOOK.
OF COURSE I DID. THE DEAN SAID SHE HAS NO REASON TO BELIEVE THAT PROFESSOR WHOREMONGER DID ANY SUCH THING SINCE HE'S CONFESSED TO THE REST OF US. WHY WOULD HE LIE ABOUT ONE BUT NOT THE OTHERS?
AS FOR WHAT HAPPENS NEXT, HE'S RESIGNING AT THE END OF THE SEMESTER SO THEY WON'T HAVE TO FIRE HIM.
IN RETURN HE'LL PROBABLY GET A GLOWING RECOMMENDATION FOR HIS NEXT JOB.

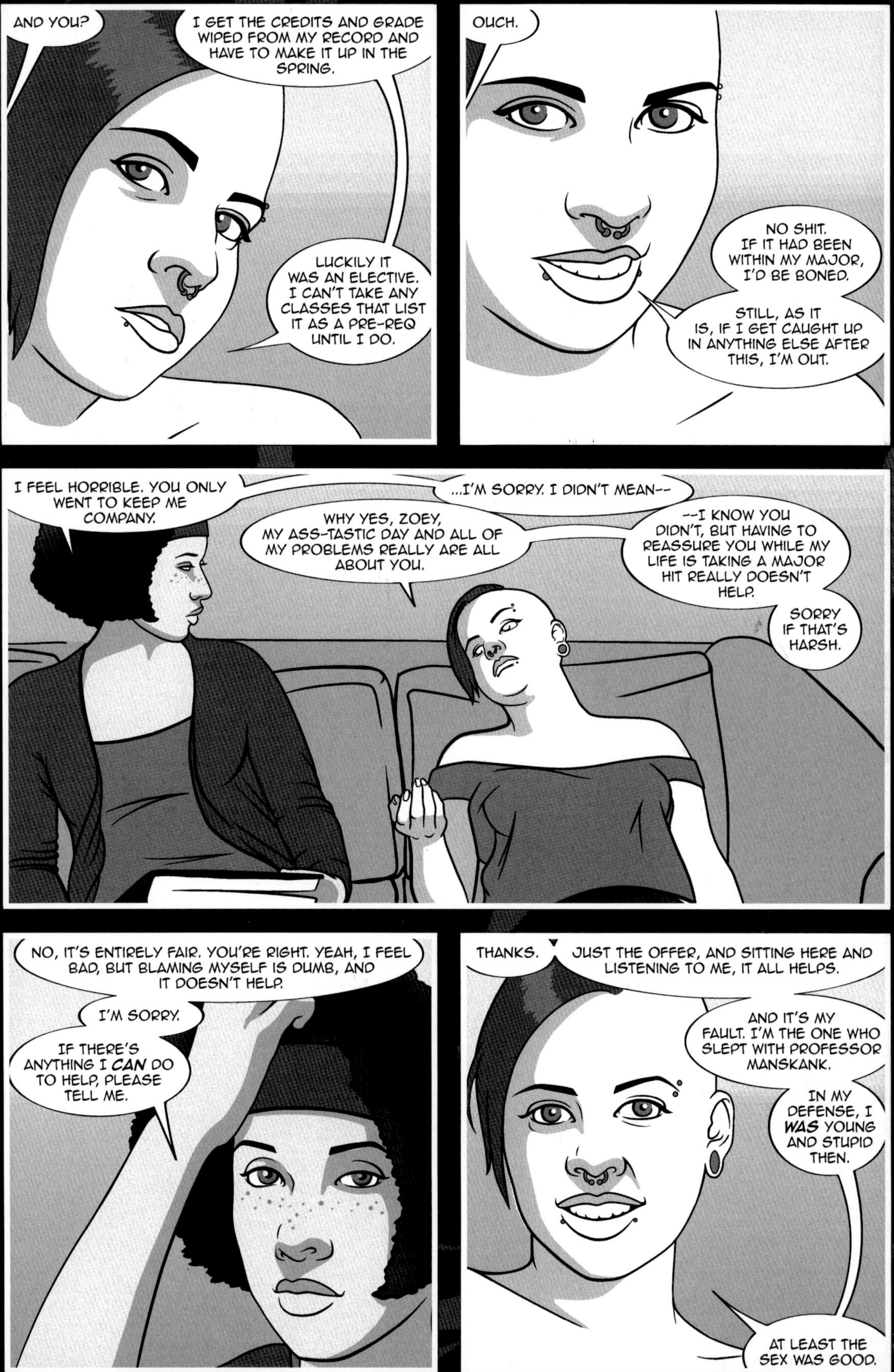
AND YOU?
I GET THE CREDITS AND GRADE WIPED FROM MY RECORD AND HAVE TO MAKE IT UP IN THE SPRING.
LUCKILY IT WAS AN ELECTIVE. I CAN'T TAKE ANY CLASSES THAT LIST IT AS A PRE-REQ UNTIL I DO.
OUCH.
NO SHIT. IF IT HAD BEEN WITHIN MY MAJOR, I'D BE BONED.
STILL, AS IT IS, IF I GET CAUGHT UP IN ANYTHING ELSE AFTER THIS, I'M OUT.
I FEEL HORRIBLE. YOU ONLY WENT TO KEEP ME COMPANY.
...I'M SORRY. I DIDN'T MEAN--
WHY YES, ZOEY, MY ASS-TASTIC DAY AND ALL OF MY PROBLEMS REALLY ARE ALL ABOUT YOU.
--I KNOW YOU DIDN'T, BUT HAVING TO REASSURE YOU WHILE MY LIFE IS TAKING A MAJOR HIT REALLY DOESN'T HELP.
SORRY IF THAT'S HARSH.
NO, IT'S ENTIRELY FAIR. YOU'RE RIGHT. YEAH, I FEEL BAD, BUT BLAMING MYSELF IS DUMB, AND IT DOESN'T HELP.
I'M SORRY.
IF THERE'S ANYTHING I *CAN* DO TO HELP, PLEASE TELL ME.
THANKS.
JUST THE OFFER, AND SITTING HERE AND LISTENING TO ME, IT ALL HELPS.
AND IT'S MY FAULT. I'M THE ONE WHO SLEPT WITH PROFESSOR MANSKANK.
IN MY DEFENSE, I *WAS* YOUNG AND STUPID THEN.
AT LEAST THE SEX WAS GOOD.

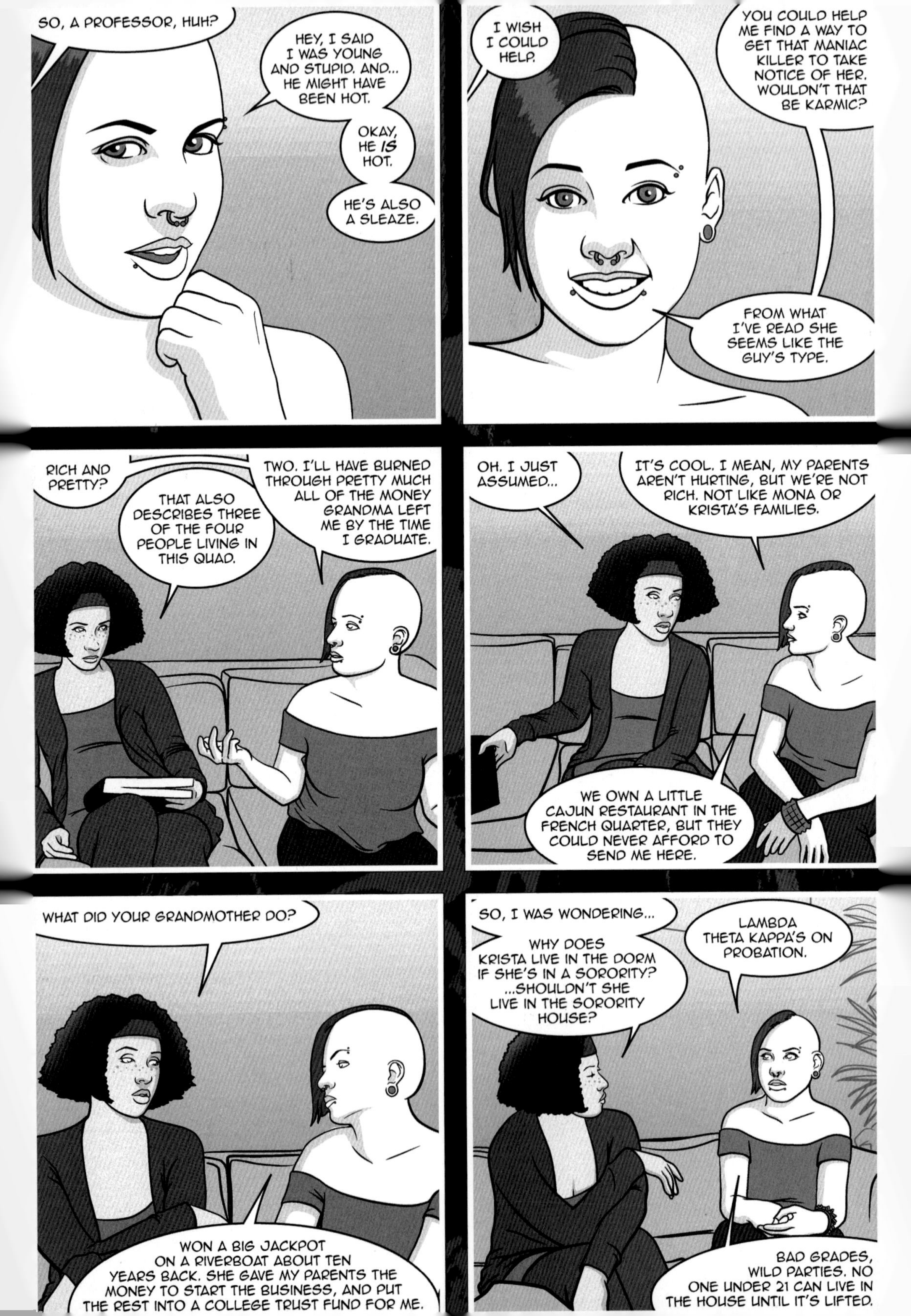
SO, A PROFESSOR, HUH?
HEY, I SAID I WAS YOUNG AND STUPID. AND... HE MIGHT HAVE BEEN HOT.
OKAY, HE *IS* HOT.
HE'S ALSO A SLEAZE.
I WISH I COULD HELP.
YOU COULD HELP ME FIND A WAY TO GET THAT MANIAC KILLER TO TAKE NOTICE OF HER. WOULDN'T THAT BE KARMIC?
FROM WHAT I'VE READ SHE SEEMS LIKE THE GUY'S TYPE.
RICH AND PRETTY?
THAT ALSO DESCRIBES THREE OF THE FOUR PEOPLE LIVING IN THIS QUAD.
TWO. I'LL HAVE BURNED THROUGH PRETTY MUCH ALL OF THE MONEY GRANDMA LEFT ME BY THE TIME I GRADUATE.
OH. I JUST ASSUMED...
IT'S COOL. I MEAN, MY PARENTS AREN'T HURTING, BUT WE'RE NOT RICH. NOT LIKE MONA OR KRISTA'S FAMILIES.
WE OWN A LITTLE CAJUN RESTAURANT IN THE FRENCH QUARTER, BUT THEY COULD NEVER AFFORD TO SEND ME HERE.
WHAT DID YOUR GRANDMOTHER DO?
WON A BIG JACKPOT ON A RIVERBOAT ABOUT TEN YEARS BACK. SHE GAVE MY PARENTS THE MONEY TO START THE BUSINESS, AND PUT THE REST INTO A COLLEGE TRUST FUND FOR ME.
SO, I WAS WONDERING...
WHY DOES KRISTA LIVE IN THE DORM IF SHE'S IN A SORORITY? ...SHOULDN'T SHE LIVE IN THE SORORITY HOUSE?
LAMBDA THETA KAPPA'S ON PROBATION.
BAD GRADES, WILD PARTIES. NO ONE UNDER 21 CAN LIVE IN THE HOUSE UNTIL IT'S LIFTED.

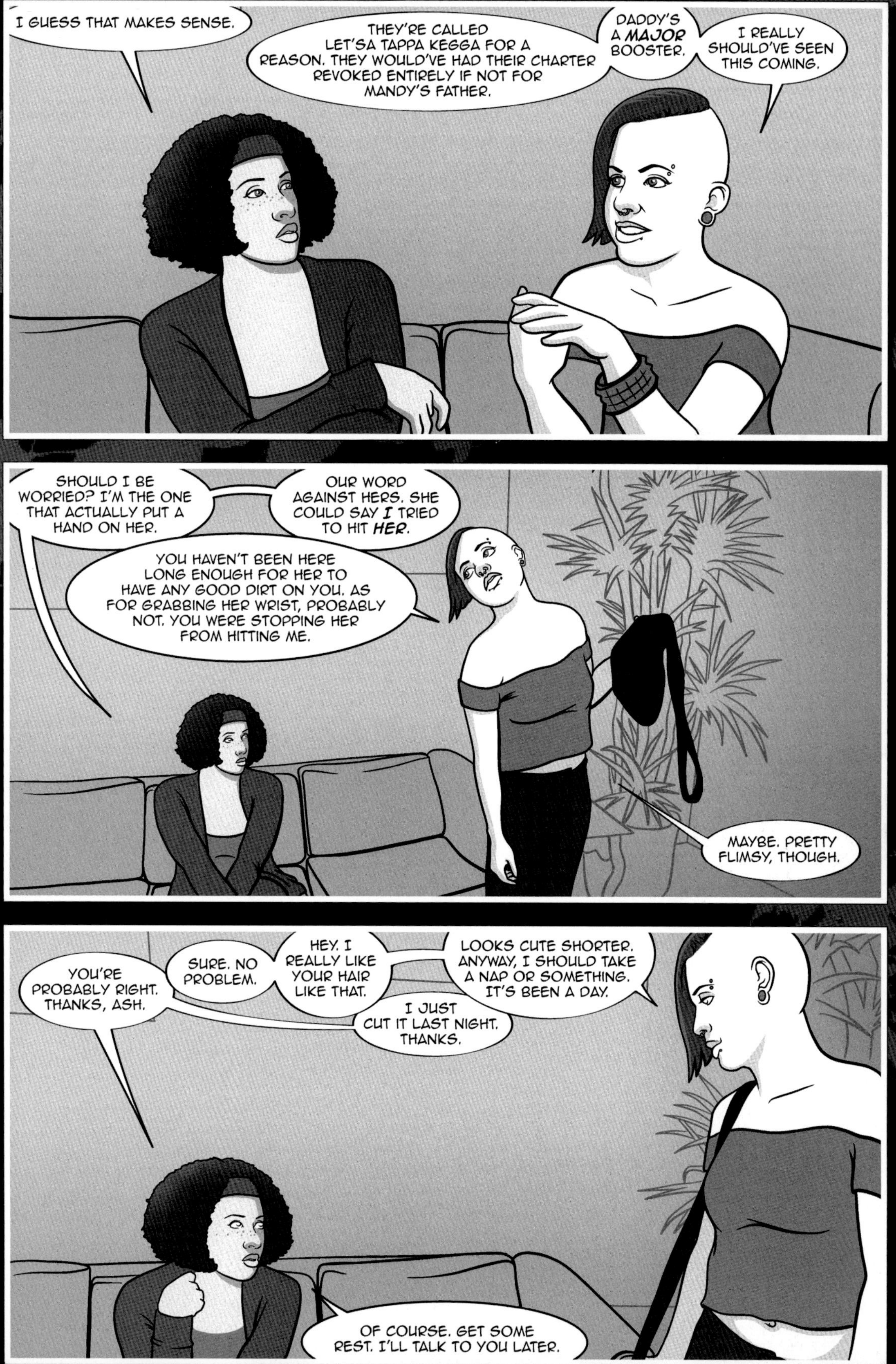

I GUESS THAT MAKES SENSE.
THEY'RE CALLED LET'SA TAPPA KEGGA FOR A REASON. THEY WOULD'VE HAD THEIR CHARTER REVOKED ENTIRELY IF NOT FOR MANDY'S FATHER.
DADDY'S A *MAJOR* BOOSTER.
I REALLY SHOULD'VE SEEN THIS COMING.
SHOULD I BE WORRIED? I'M THE ONE THAT ACTUALLY PUT A HAND ON HER.
OUR WORD AGAINST HERS. SHE COULD SAY *I* TRIED TO HIT *HER*.
YOU HAVEN'T BEEN HERE LONG ENOUGH FOR HER TO HAVE ANY GOOD DIRT ON YOU. AS FOR GRABBING HER WRIST, PROBABLY NOT. YOU WERE STOPPING HER FROM HITTING ME.
MAYBE. PRETTY FLIMSY, THOUGH.
YOU'RE PROBABLY RIGHT. THANKS, ASH.
SURE. NO PROBLEM.
HEY. I REALLY LIKE YOUR HAIR LIKE THAT.
I JUST CUT IT LAST NIGHT. THANKS.
LOOKS CUTE SHORTER. ANYWAY, I SHOULD TAKE A NAP OR SOMETHING. IT'S BEEN A DAY.
OF COURSE. GET SOME REST. I'LL TALK TO YOU LATER.

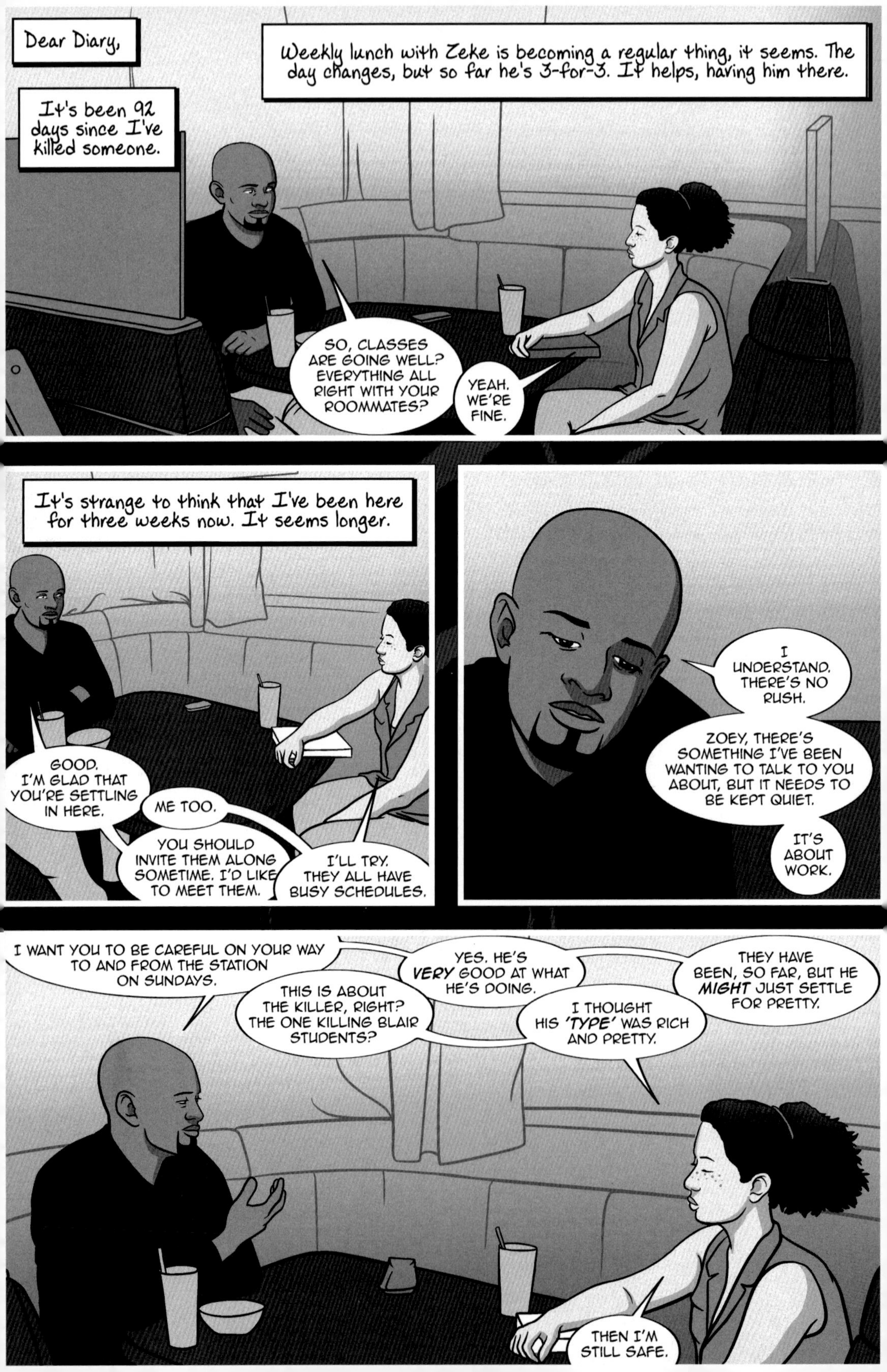

Dear Diary,
Weekly lunch with Zeke is becoming a regular thing, it seems. The day changes, but so far he's 3-for-3. It helps, having him there.
It's been 92 days since I've killed someone.
SO, CLASSES ARE GOING WELL? EVERYTHING ALL RIGHT WITH YOUR ROOMMATES?
YEAH. WE'RE FINE.
It's strange to think that I've been here for three weeks now. It seems longer.
GOOD. I'M GLAD THAT YOU'RE SETTLING IN HERE.
ME TOO.
YOU SHOULD INVITE THEM ALONG SOMETIME. I'D LIKE TO MEET THEM.
I'LL TRY. THEY ALL HAVE BUSY SCHEDULES.
I UNDERSTAND. THERE'S NO RUSH.
ZOEY, THERE'S SOMETHING I'VE BEEN WANTING TO TALK TO YOU ABOUT, BUT IT NEEDS TO BE KEPT QUIET.
IT'S ABOUT WORK.
I WANT YOU TO BE CAREFUL ON YOUR WAY TO AND FROM THE STATION ON SUNDAYS.
THIS IS ABOUT THE KILLER, RIGHT? THE ONE KILLING BLAIR STUDENTS?
YES. HE'S *VERY* GOOD AT WHAT HE'S DOING.
I THOUGHT HIS *'TYPE'* WAS RICH AND PRETTY.
THEY HAVE BEEN, SO FAR, BUT HE *MIGHT* JUST SETTLE FOR PRETTY.
THEN I'M STILL SAFE.

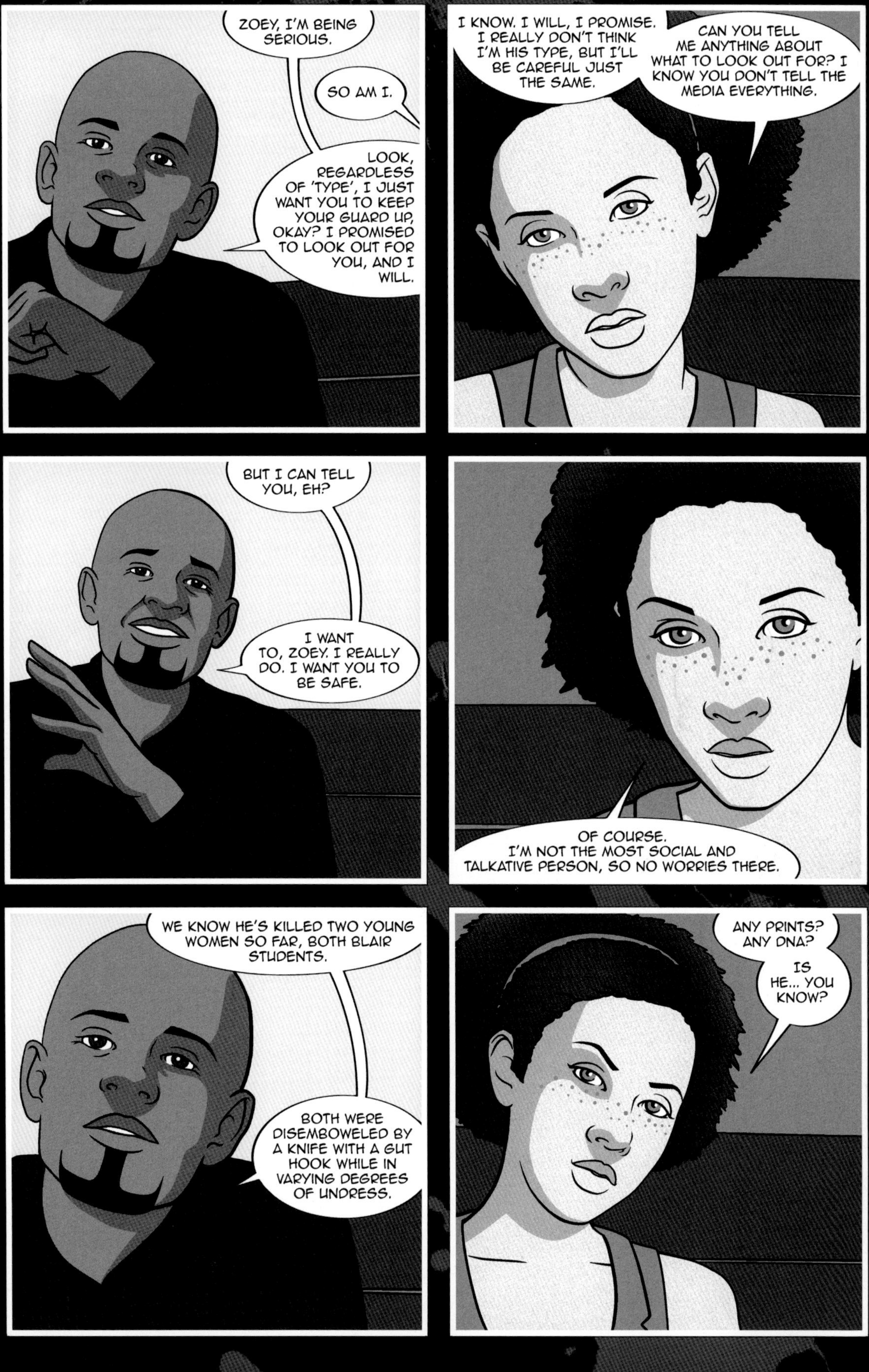
ZOEY, I'M BEING SERIOUS.
SO AM I.
LOOK, REGARDLESS OF 'TYPE', I JUST WANT YOU TO KEEP YOUR GUARD UP, OKAY? I PROMISED TO LOOK OUT FOR YOU, AND I WILL.
I KNOW. I WILL, I PROMISE. I REALLY DON'T THINK I'M HIS TYPE, BUT I'LL BE CAREFUL JUST THE SAME.
CAN YOU TELL ME ANYTHING ABOUT WHAT TO LOOK OUT FOR? I KNOW YOU DON'T TELL THE MEDIA EVERYTHING.
BUT I CAN TELL YOU, EH?
I WANT TO, ZOEY. I REALLY DO. I WANT YOU TO BE SAFE.
OF COURSE. I'M NOT THE MOST SOCIAL AND TALKATIVE PERSON, SO NO WORRIES THERE.
WE KNOW HE'S KILLED TWO YOUNG WOMEN SO FAR, BOTH BLAIR STUDENTS.
BOTH WERE DISEMBOWELED BY A KNIFE WITH A GUT HOOK WHILE IN VARYING DEGREES OF UNDRESS.
ANY PRINTS? ANY DNA?
IS HE... YOU KNOW?

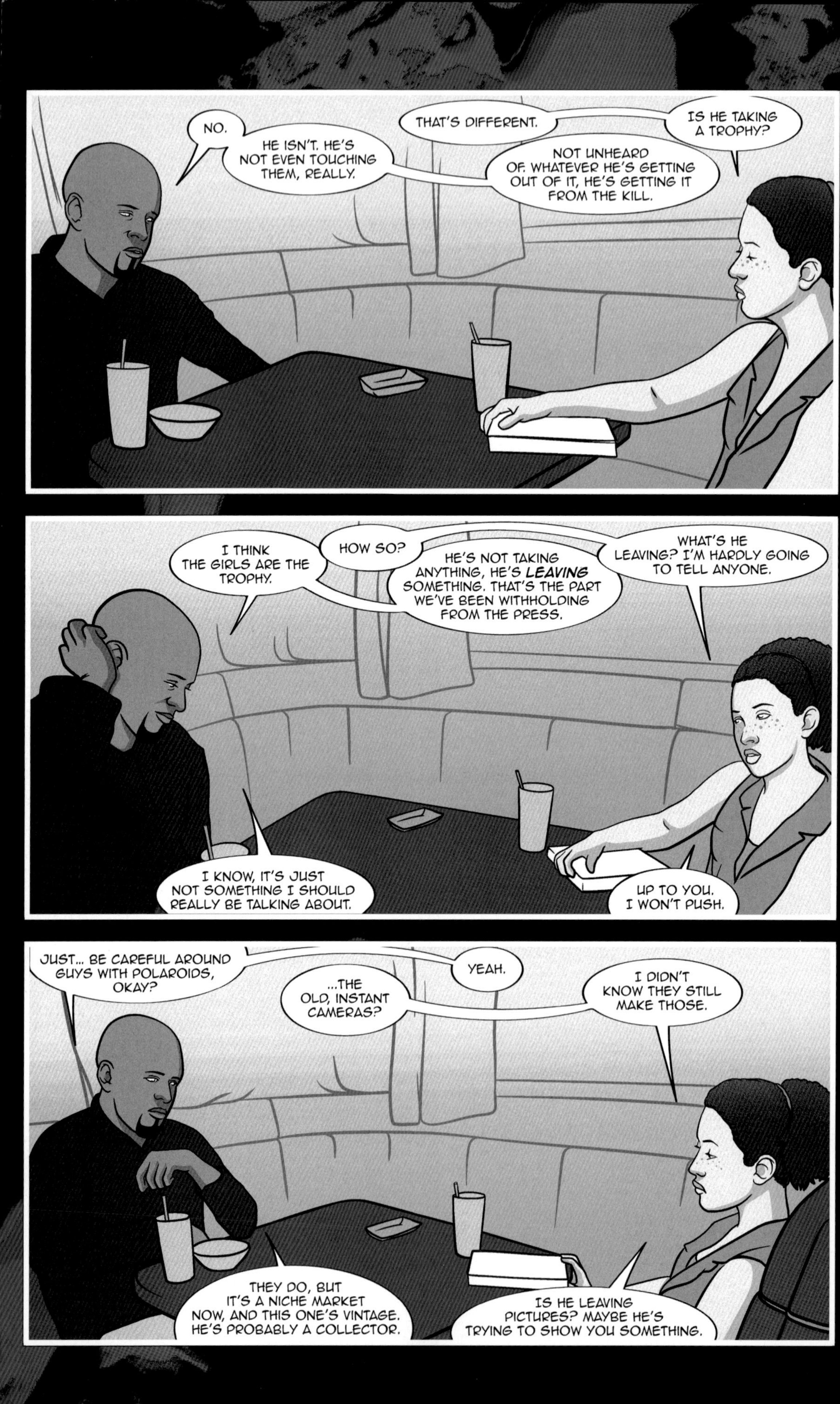
NO.
HE ISN'T. HE'S NOT EVEN TOUCHING THEM, REALLY.
THAT'S DIFFERENT.
IS HE TAKING A TROPHY?
NOT UNHEARD OF. WHATEVER HE'S GETTING OUT OF IT, HE'S GETTING IT FROM THE KILL.
I THINK THE GIRLS ARE THE TROPHY.
HOW SO?
HE'S NOT TAKING ANYTHING, HE'S *LEAVING* SOMETHING. THAT'S THE PART WE'VE BEEN WITHHOLDING FROM THE PRESS.
WHAT'S HE LEAVING? I'M HARDLY GOING TO TELL ANYONE.
I KNOW, IT'S JUST NOT SOMETHING I SHOULD REALLY BE TALKING ABOUT.
UP TO YOU. I WON'T PUSH.
JUST... BE CAREFUL AROUND GUYS WITH POLAROIDS, OKAY?
YEAH.
...THE OLD, INSTANT CAMERAS?
I DIDN'T KNOW THEY STILL MAKE THOSE.
THEY DO, BUT IT'S A NICHE MARKET NOW, AND THIS ONE'S VINTAGE. HE'S PROBABLY A COLLECTOR.
IS HE LEAVING PICTURES? MAYBE HE'S TRYING TO SHOW YOU SOMETHING.

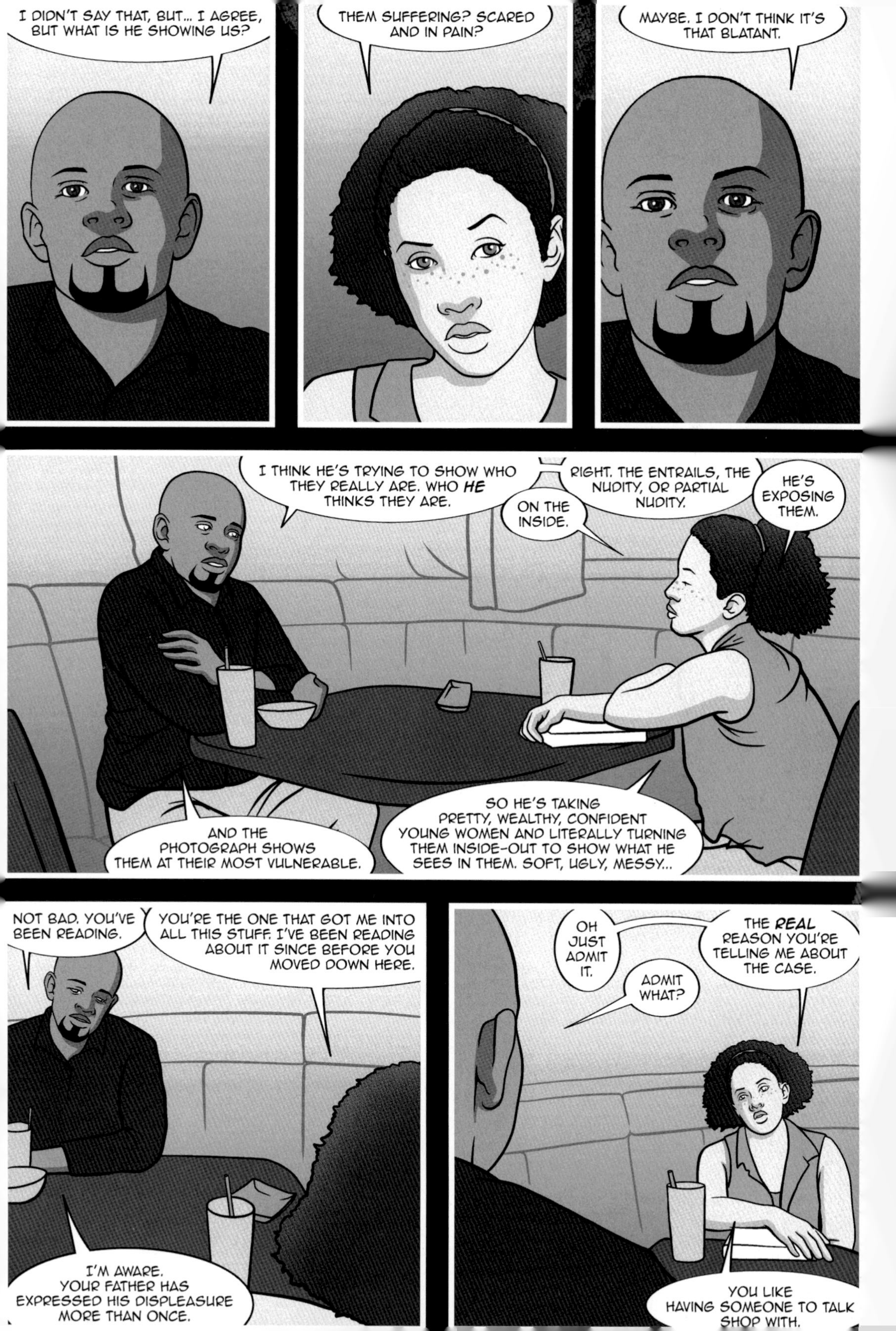
I DIDN'T SAY THAT, BUT... I AGREE, BUT WHAT IS HE SHOWING US?
THEM SUFFERING? SCARED AND IN PAIN?
MAYBE. I DON'T THINK IT'S THAT BLATANT.
I THINK HE'S TRYING TO SHOW WHO THEY REALLY ARE. WHO *HE* THINKS THEY ARE.
ON THE INSIDE.
RIGHT. THE ENTRAILS, THE NUDITY, OR PARTIAL NUDITY.
HE'S EXPOSING THEM.
AND THE PHOTOGRAPH SHOWS THEM AT THEIR MOST VULNERABLE.
SO HE'S TAKING PRETTY, WEALTHY, CONFIDENT YOUNG WOMEN AND LITERALLY TURNING THEM INSIDE-OUT TO SHOW WHAT HE SEES IN THEM. SOFT, UGLY, MESSY...
NOT BAD. YOU'VE BEEN READING.
YOU'RE THE ONE THAT GOT ME INTO ALL THIS STUFF. I'VE BEEN READING ABOUT IT SINCE BEFORE YOU MOVED DOWN HERE.
I'M AWARE. YOUR FATHER HAS EXPRESSED HIS DISPLEASURE MORE THAN ONCE.
OH JUST ADMIT IT.
ADMIT WHAT?
THE *REAL* REASON YOU'RE TELLING ME ABOUT THE CASE.
YOU LIKE HAVING SOMEONE TO TALK SHOP WITH.

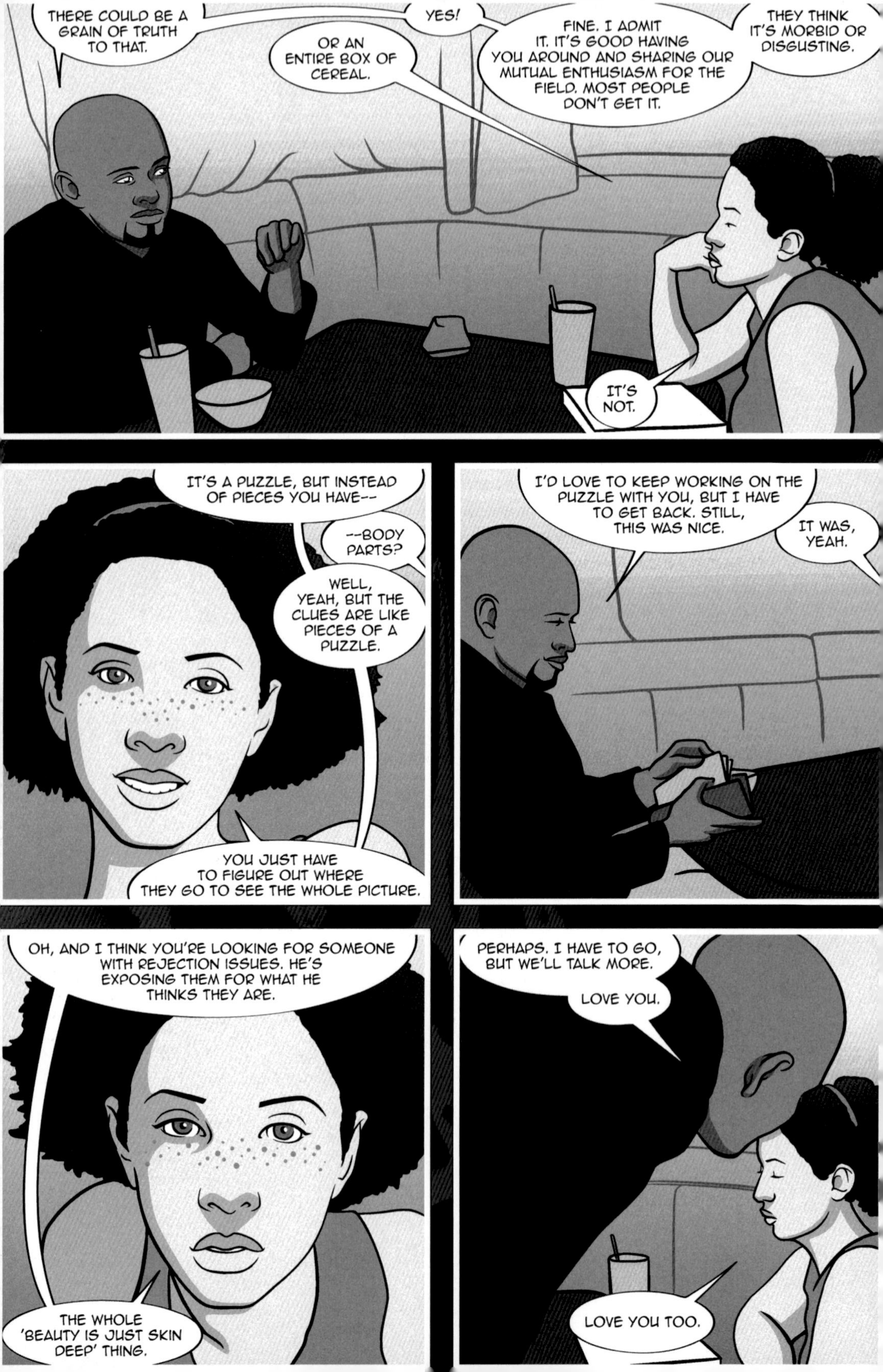
THERE COULD BE A GRAIN OF TRUTH TO THAT.
YES!
OR AN ENTIRE BOX OF CEREAL.
FINE. I ADMIT IT. IT'S GOOD HAVING YOU AROUND AND SHARING OUR MUTUAL ENTHUSIASM FOR THE FIELD. MOST PEOPLE DON'T GET IT.
THEY THINK IT'S MORBID OR DISGUSTING.
IT'S NOT.
IT'S A PUZZLE, BUT INSTEAD OF PIECES YOU HAVE--
--BODY PARTS?
WELL, YEAH, BUT THE CLUES ARE LIKE PIECES OF A PUZZLE.
YOU JUST HAVE TO FIGURE OUT WHERE THEY GO TO SEE THE WHOLE PICTURE.
I'D LOVE TO KEEP WORKING ON THE PUZZLE WITH YOU, BUT I HAVE TO GET BACK. STILL, THIS WAS NICE.
IT WAS, YEAH.
OH, AND I THINK YOU'RE LOOKING FOR SOMEONE WITH REJECTION ISSUES. HE'S EXPOSING THEM FOR WHAT HE THINKS THEY ARE.
THE WHOLE 'BEAUTY IS JUST SKIN DEEP' THING.
PERHAPS. I HAVE TO GO, BUT WE'LL TALK MORE.
LOVE YOU.
LOVE YOU TOO.

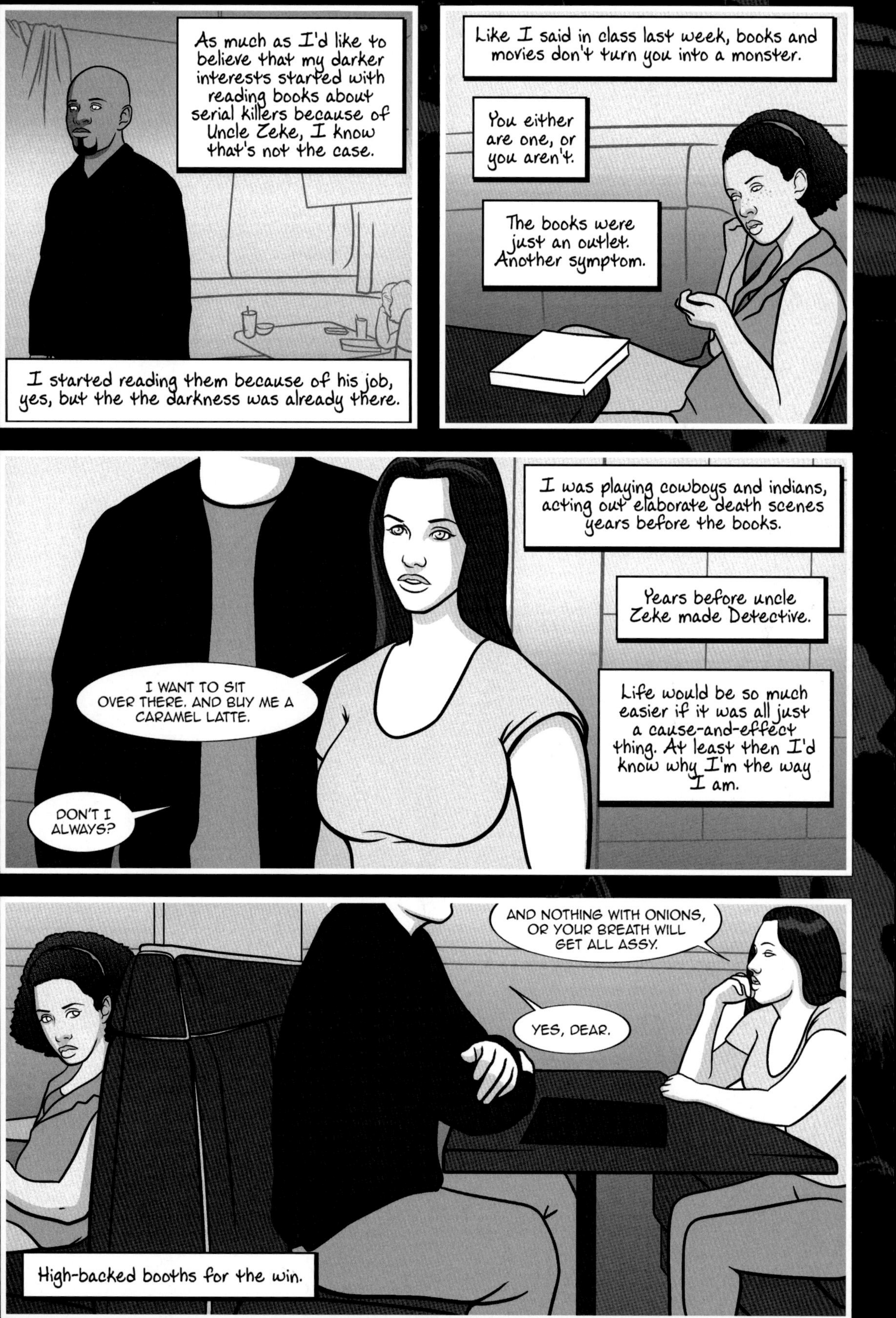
As much as I'd like to believe that my darker interests started with reading books about serial killers because of Uncle Zeke, I know that's not the case.
I started reading them because of his job, yes, but the the darkness was already there.
Like I said in class last week, books and movies don't turn you into a monster.
You either are one, or you aren't.
The books were just an outlet. Another symptom.
I was playing cowboys and indians, acting out elaborate death scenes years before the books.
Years before uncle Zeke made Detective.
Life would be so much easier if it was all just a cause-and-effect thing. At least then I'd know why I'm the way I am.
I WANT TO SIT OVER THERE. AND BUY ME A CARAMEL LATTE.
DON'T I ALWAYS?
AND NOTHING WITH ONIONS, OR YOUR BREATH WILL GET ALL ASSY.
YES, DEAR.
High-backed booths for the win.

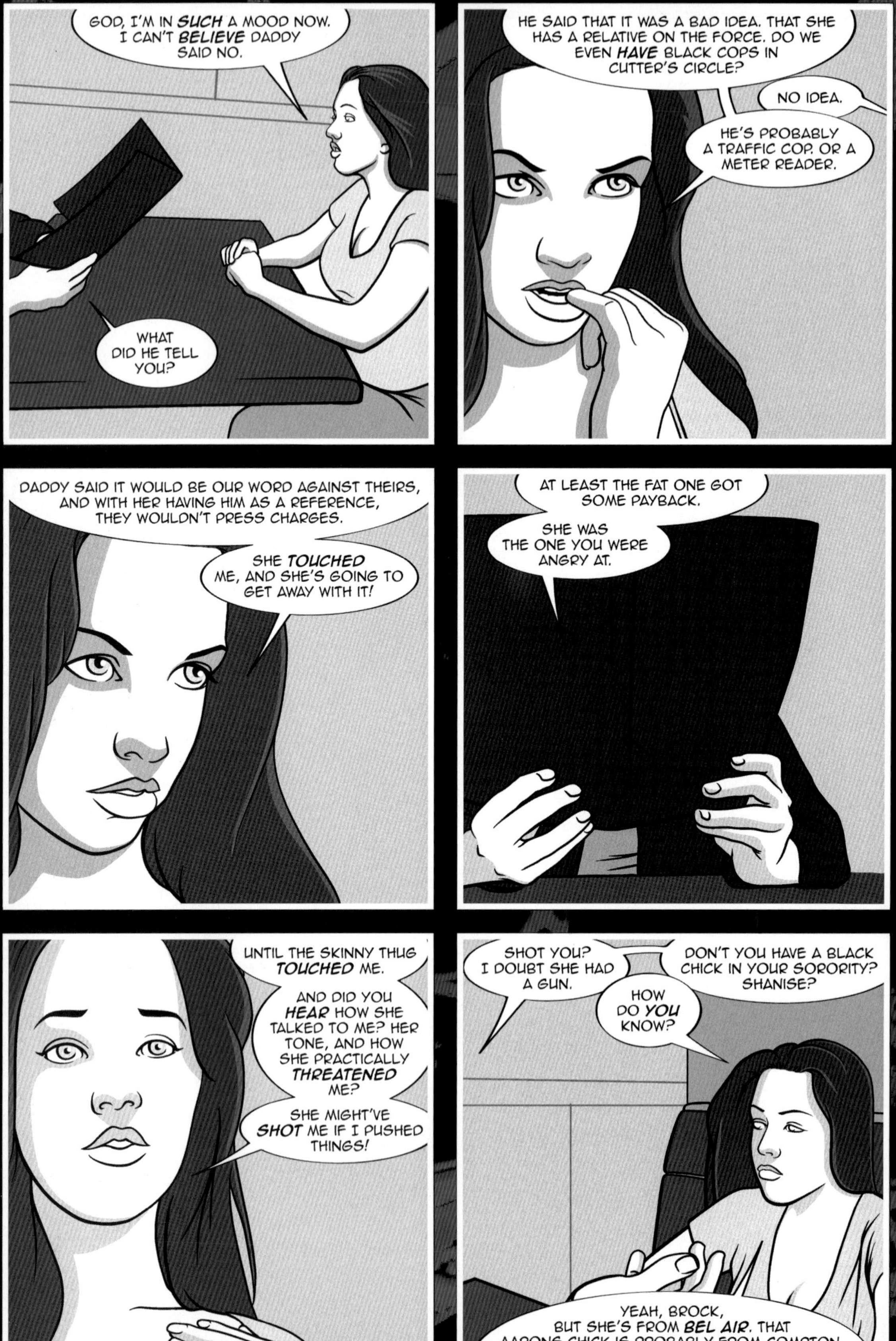
GOD, I'M IN SUCH A MOOD NOW. I CAN'T BELIEVE DADDY SAID NO.
WHAT DID HE TELL YOU?
HE SAID THAT IT WAS A BAD IDEA. THAT SHE HAS A RELATIVE ON THE FORCE. DO WE EVEN HAVE BLACK COPS IN CUTTER'S CIRCLE?
NO IDEA.
HE'S PROBABLY A TRAFFIC COP. OR A METER READER.
DADDY SAID IT WOULD BE OUR WORD AGAINST THEIRS, AND WITH HER HAVING HIM AS A REFERENCE, THEY WOULDN'T PRESS CHARGES.
SHE TOUCHED ME, AND SHE'S GOING TO GET AWAY WITH IT!
AT LEAST THE FAT ONE GOT SOME PAYBACK.
SHE WAS THE ONE YOU WERE ANGRY AT.
UNTIL THE SKINNY THUG TOUCHED ME.
AND DID YOU HEAR HOW SHE TALKED TO ME? HER TONE, AND HOW SHE PRACTICALLY THREATENED ME?
SHE MIGHT'VE SHOT ME IF I PUSHED THINGS!
SHOT YOU? I DOUBT SHE HAD A GUN.
DON'T YOU HAVE A BLACK CHICK IN YOUR SORORITY? SHANISE?
HOW DO YOU KNOW?
YEAH, BROCK, BUT SHE'S FROM BEL AIR. THAT AARONS CHICK IS PROBABLY FROM COMPTON, OR OAKLAND. OR VENICE! SOMEWHERE GHETTO.

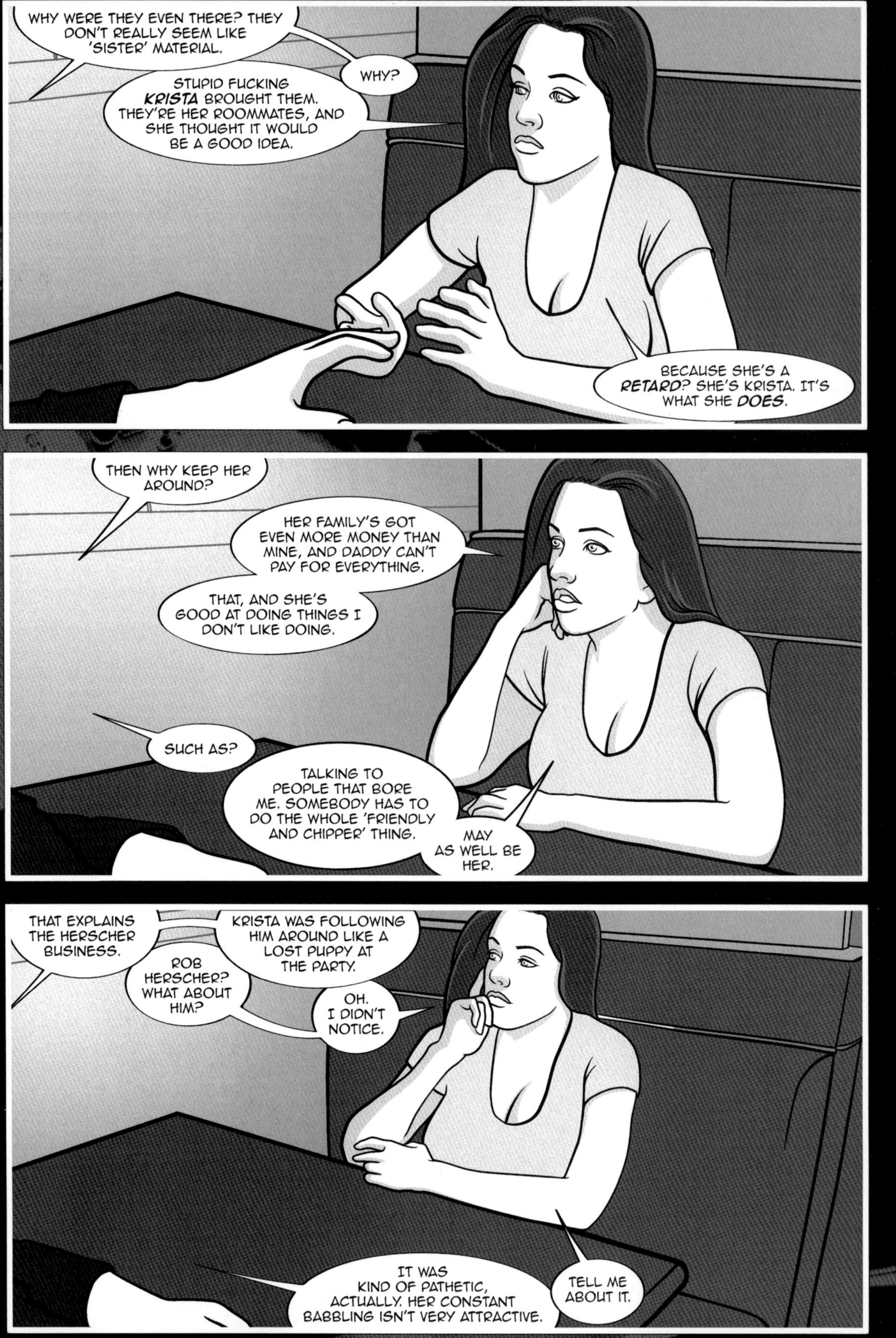

WHY WERE THEY EVEN THERE? THEY DON'T REALLY SEEM LIKE 'SISTER' MATERIAL.
WHY?
STUPID FUCKING KRISTA BROUGHT THEM. THEY'RE HER ROOMMATES, AND SHE THOUGHT IT WOULD BE A GOOD IDEA.
BECAUSE SHE'S A RETARD? SHE'S KRISTA. IT'S WHAT SHE DOES.
THEN WHY KEEP HER AROUND?
HER FAMILY'S GOT EVEN MORE MONEY THAN MINE, AND DADDY CAN'T PAY FOR EVERYTHING.
THAT, AND SHE'S GOOD AT DOING THINGS I DON'T LIKE DOING.
SUCH AS?
TALKING TO PEOPLE THAT BORE ME. SOMEBODY HAS TO DO THE WHOLE 'FRIENDLY AND CHIPPER' THING.
MAY AS WELL BE HER.
THAT EXPLAINS THE HERSCHER BUSINESS.
ROB HERSCHER? WHAT ABOUT HIM?
KRISTA WAS FOLLOWING HIM AROUND LIKE A LOST PUPPY AT THE PARTY.
OH. I DIDN'T NOTICE.
IT WAS KIND OF PATHETIC, ACTUALLY. HER CONSTANT BABBLING ISN'T VERY ATTRACTIVE.
TELL ME ABOUT IT.

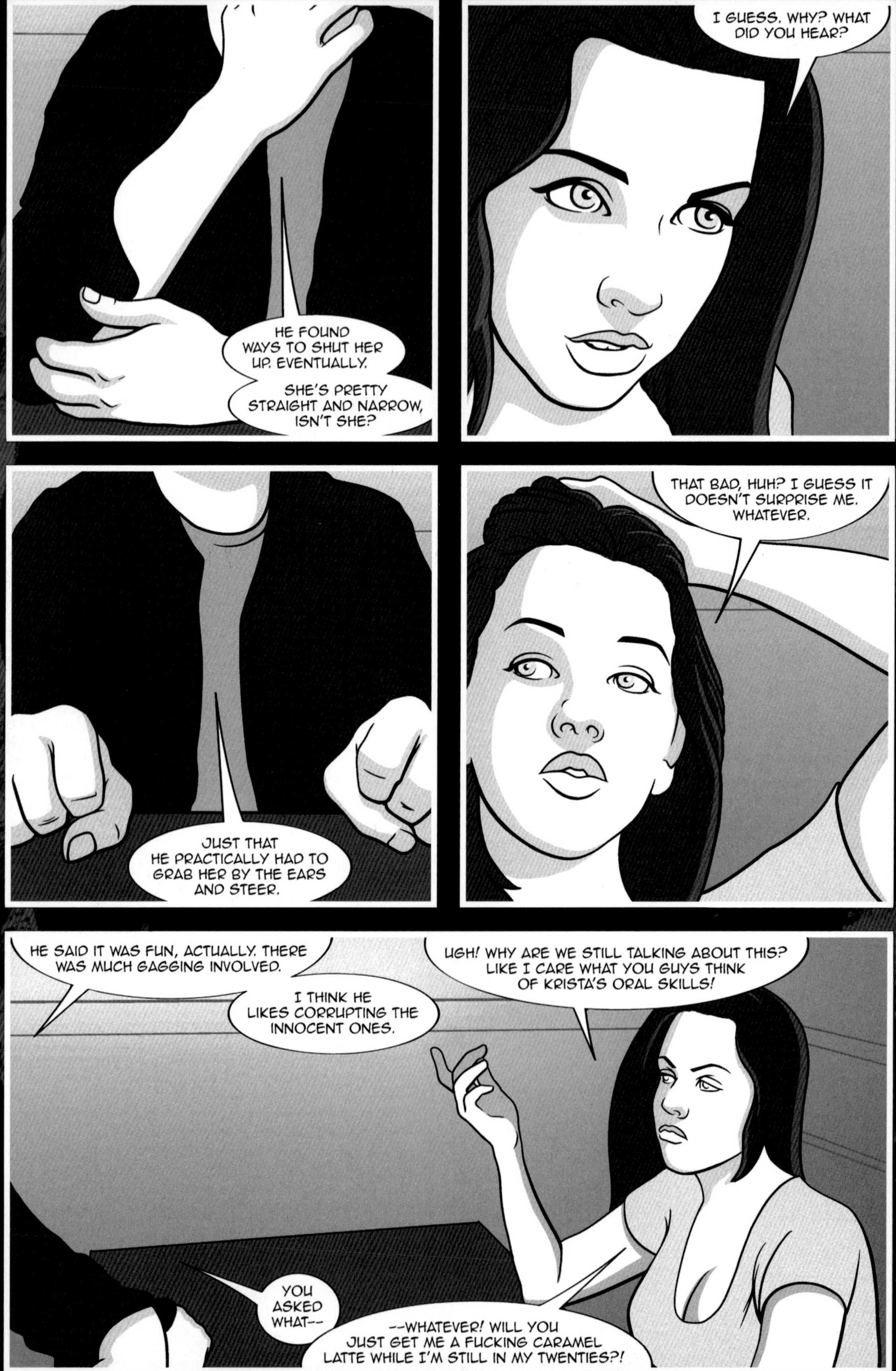
HE FOUND WAYS TO SHUT HER UP. EVENTUALLY.
SHE'S PRETTY STRAIGHT AND NARROW, ISN'T SHE?
I GUESS. WHY? WHAT DID YOU HEAR?
JUST THAT HE PRACTICALLY HAD TO GRAB HER BY THE EARS AND STEER.
THAT BAD, HUH? I GUESS IT DOESN'T SURPRISE ME. WHATEVER.
HE SAID IT WAS FUN, ACTUALLY. THERE WAS MUCH GAGGING INVOLVED.
I THINK HE LIKES CORRUPTING THE INNOCENT ONES.
UGH! WHY ARE WE STILL TALKING ABOUT THIS? LIKE I CARE WHAT YOU GUYS THINK OF KRISTA'S ORAL SKILLS!
YOU ASKED WHAT--
--WHATEVER! WILL YOU JUST GET ME A FUCKING CARAMEL LATTE WHILE I'M STILL IN MY TWENTIES?!

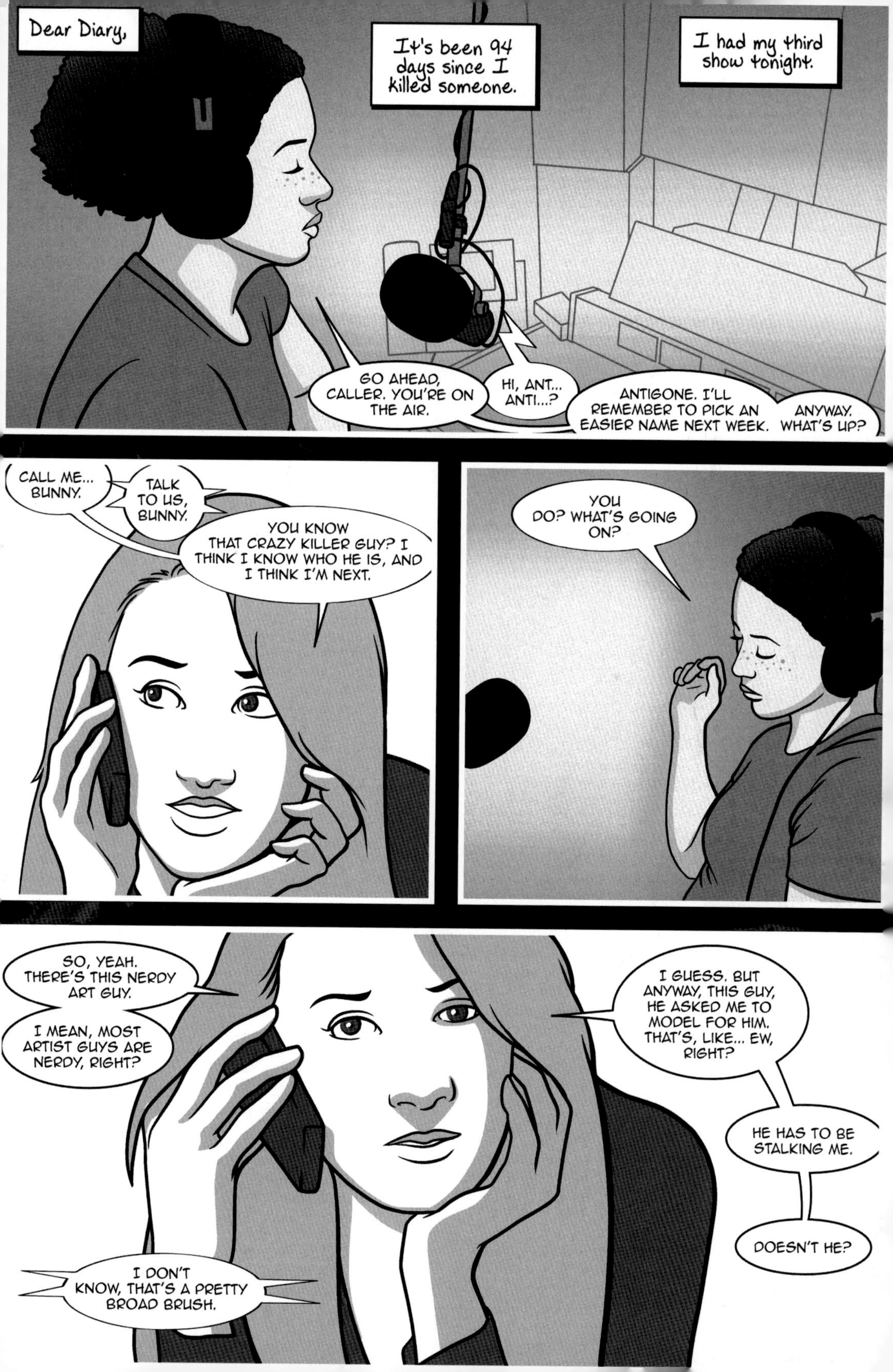
Dear Diary,
It's been 94 days since I killed someone.
I had my third show tonight.
GO AHEAD, CALLER. YOU'RE ON THE AIR.
HI, ANT... ANTI...?
ANTIGONE. I'LL REMEMBER TO PICK AN EASIER NAME NEXT WEEK.
ANYWAY. WHAT'S UP?
CALL ME... BUNNY.
TALK TO US, BUNNY.
YOU KNOW THAT CRAZY KILLER GUY? I THINK I KNOW WHO HE IS, AND I THINK I'M NEXT.
YOU DO? WHAT'S GOING ON?
SO, YEAH. THERE'S THIS NERDY ART GUY.
I MEAN, MOST ARTIST GUYS ARE NERDY, RIGHT?
I DON'T KNOW, THAT'S A PRETTY BROAD BRUSH.
I GUESS. BUT ANYWAY, THIS GUY, HE ASKED ME TO MODEL FOR HIM. THAT'S, LIKE... EW, RIGHT?
HE HAS TO BE STALKING ME.
DOESN'T HE?

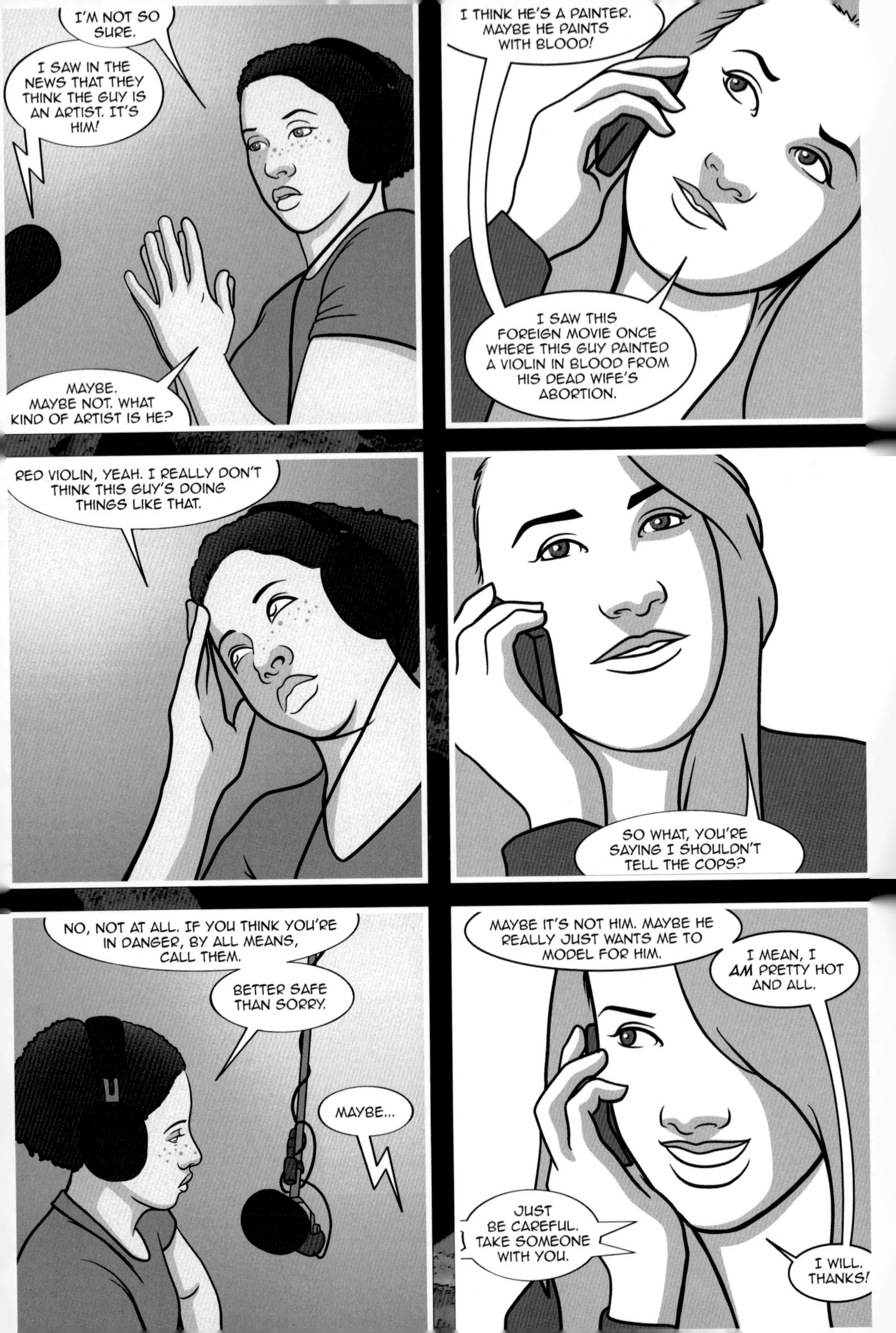
I'M NOT SO SURE.
I SAW IN THE NEWS THAT THEY THINK THE GUY IS AN ARTIST. IT'S HIM!
MAYBE. MAYBE NOT. WHAT KIND OF ARTIST IS HE?
I THINK HE'S A PAINTER. MAYBE HE PAINTS WITH BLOOD!
I SAW THIS FOREIGN MOVIE ONCE WHERE THIS GUY PAINTED A VIOLIN IN BLOOD FROM HIS DEAD WIFE'S ABORTION.
RED VIOLIN, YEAH. I REALLY DON'T THINK THIS GUY'S DOING THINGS LIKE THAT.
SO WHAT, YOU'RE SAYING I SHOULDN'T TELL THE COPS?
NO, NOT AT ALL. IF YOU THINK YOU'RE IN DANGER, BY ALL MEANS, CALL THEM.
BETTER SAFE THAN SORRY.
MAYBE...
MAYBE IT'S NOT HIM. MAYBE HE REALLY JUST WANTS ME TO MODEL FOR HIM.
I MEAN, I *AM* PRETTY HOT AND ALL.
JUST BE CAREFUL. TAKE SOMEONE WITH YOU.
I WILL. THANKS!

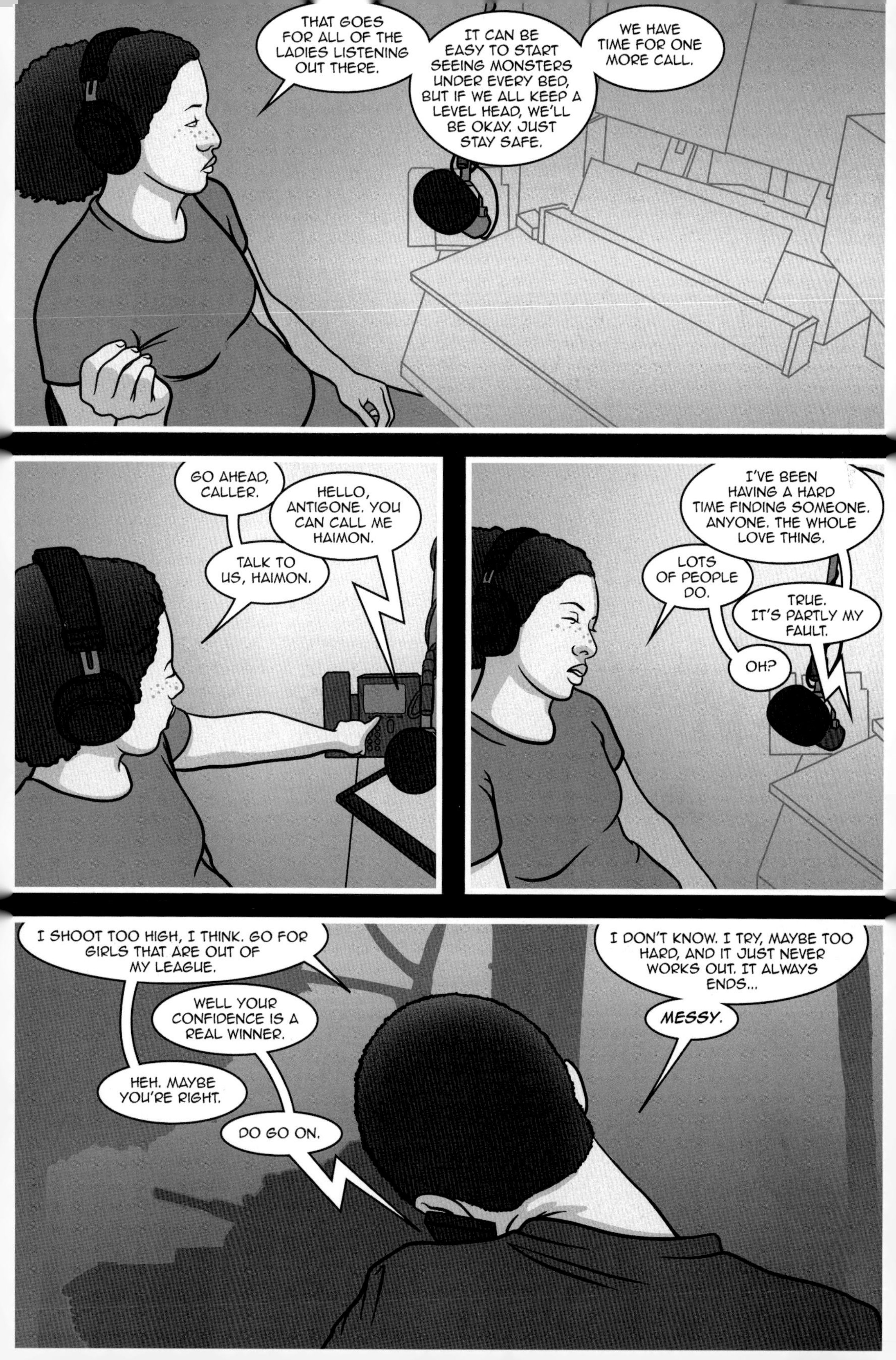
THAT GOES FOR ALL OF THE LADIES LISTENING OUT THERE.
IT CAN BE EASY TO START SEEING MONSTERS UNDER EVERY BED, BUT IF WE ALL KEEP A LEVEL HEAD, WE'LL BE OKAY. JUST STAY SAFE.
WE HAVE TIME FOR ONE MORE CALL.
GO AHEAD, CALLER.
HELLO, ANTIGONE. YOU CAN CALL ME HAIMON.
TALK TO US, HAIMON.
I'VE BEEN HAVING A HARD TIME FINDING SOMEONE. ANYONE. THE WHOLE LOVE THING.
LOTS OF PEOPLE DO.
TRUE. IT'S PARTLY MY FAULT.
OH?
I SHOOT TOO HIGH, I THINK. GO FOR GIRLS THAT ARE OUT OF MY LEAGUE.
WELL YOUR CONFIDENCE IS A REAL WINNER.
HEH. MAYBE YOU'RE RIGHT.
DO GO ON.
I DON'T KNOW. I TRY, MAYBE TOO HARD, AND IT JUST NEVER WORKS OUT. IT ALWAYS ENDS...
MESSY.

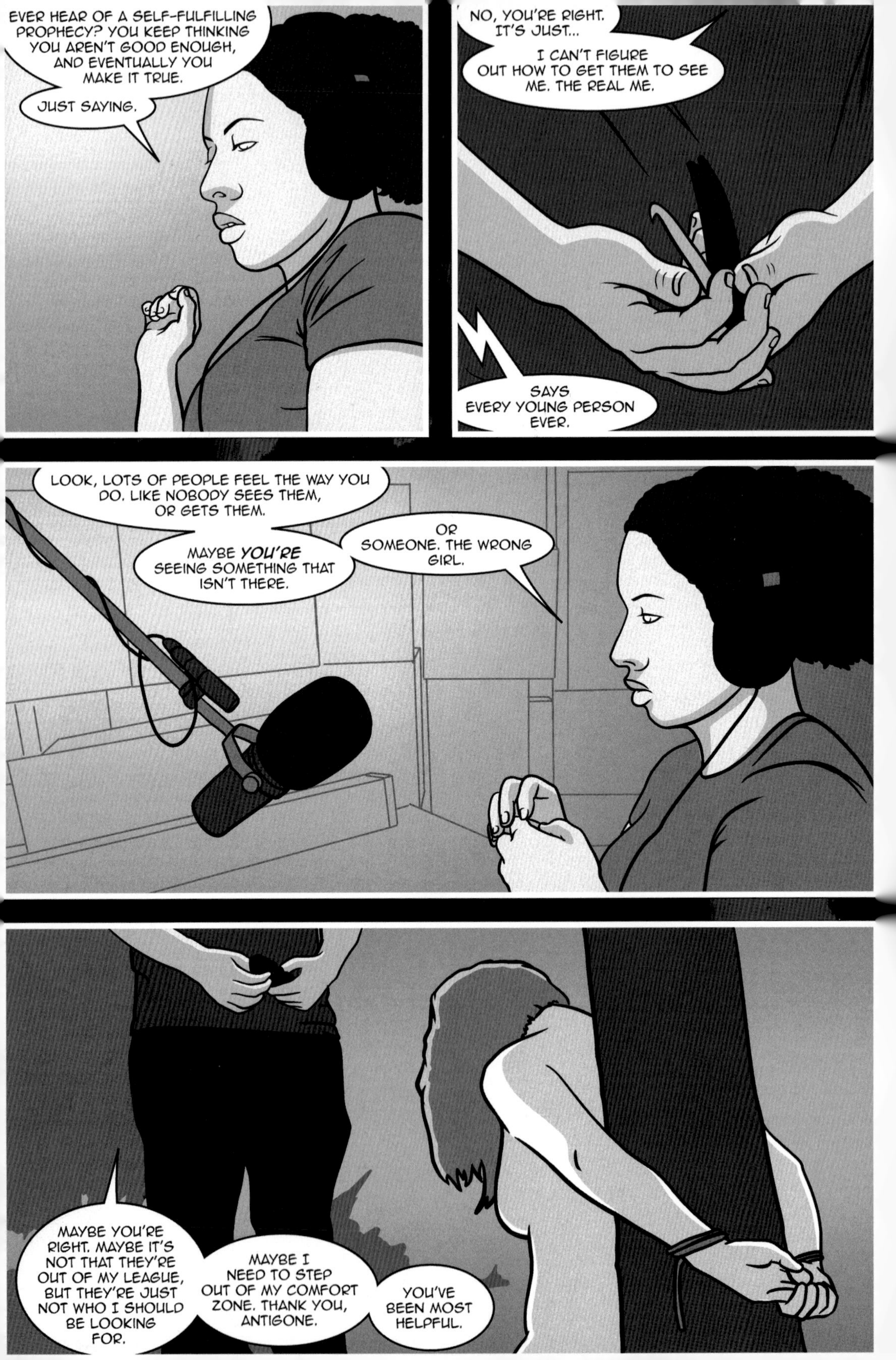
EVER HEAR OF A SELF-FULFILLING PROPHECY? YOU KEEP THINKING YOU AREN'T GOOD ENOUGH, AND EVENTUALLY YOU MAKE IT TRUE.
JUST SAYING.
NO, YOU'RE RIGHT. IT'S JUST...
I CAN'T FIGURE OUT HOW TO GET THEM TO SEE ME. THE REAL ME.
SAYS EVERY YOUNG PERSON EVER.
LOOK, LOTS OF PEOPLE FEEL THE WAY YOU DO. LIKE NOBODY SEES THEM, OR GETS THEM.
MAYBE *YOU'RE* SEEING SOMETHING THAT ISN'T THERE.
OR SOMEONE. THE WRONG GIRL.
MAYBE YOU'RE RIGHT. MAYBE IT'S NOT THAT THEY'RE OUT OF MY LEAGUE, BUT THEY'RE JUST NOT WHO I SHOULD BE LOOKING FOR.
MAYBE I NEED TO STEP OUT OF MY COMFORT ZONE. THANK YOU, ANTIGONE.
YOU'VE BEEN MOST HELPFUL.

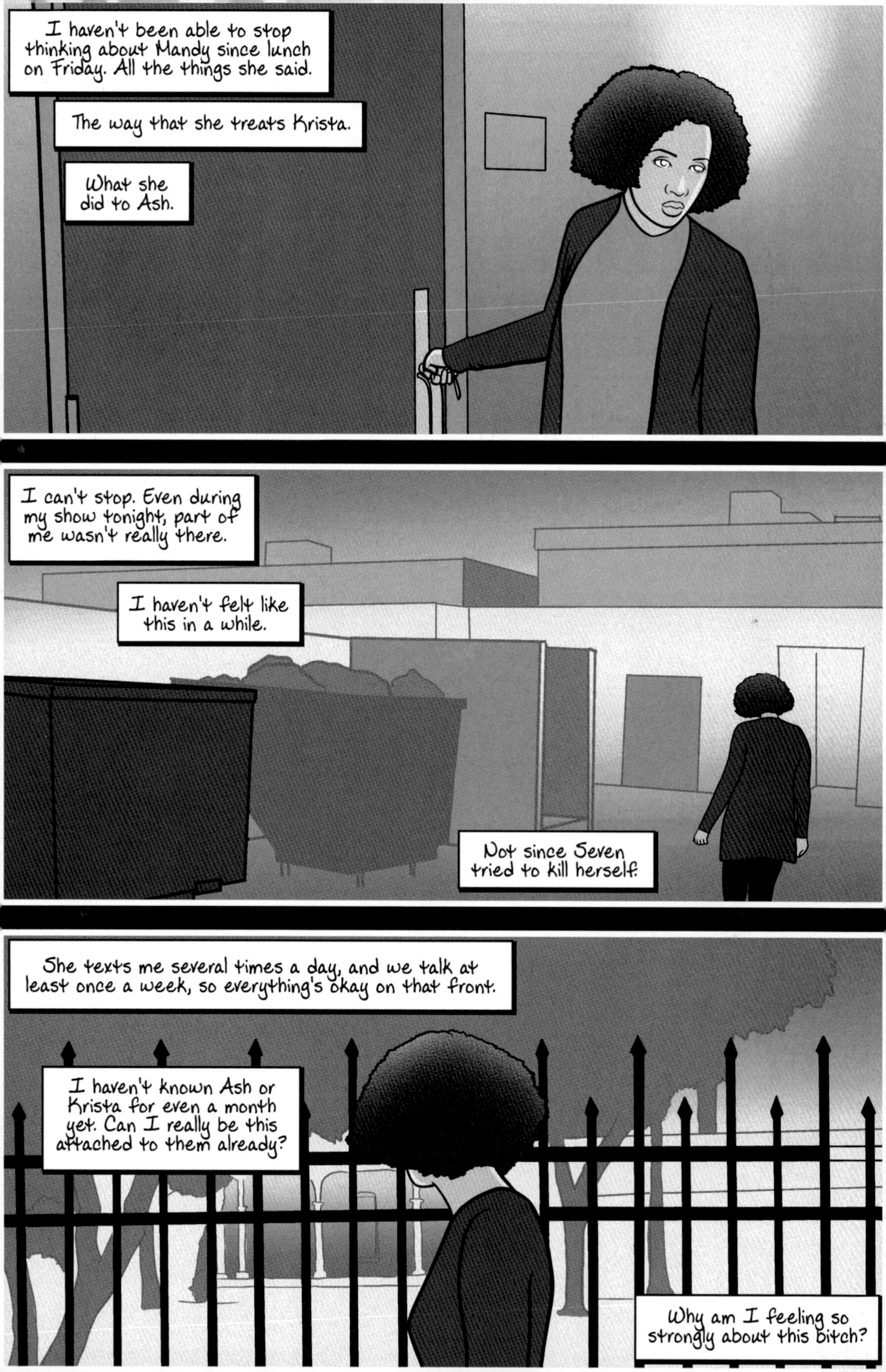
I haven't been able to stop thinking about Mandy since lunch on Friday. All the things she said.
The way that she treats Krista.
What she did to Ash.
I can't stop. Even during my show tonight, part of me wasn't really there.
I haven't felt like this in a while.
Not since Seven tried to kill herself.
She texts me several times a day, and we talk at least once a week, so everything's okay on that front.
I haven't known Ash or Krista for even a month yet. Can I really be this attached to them already?
Why am I feeling so strongly about this bitch?

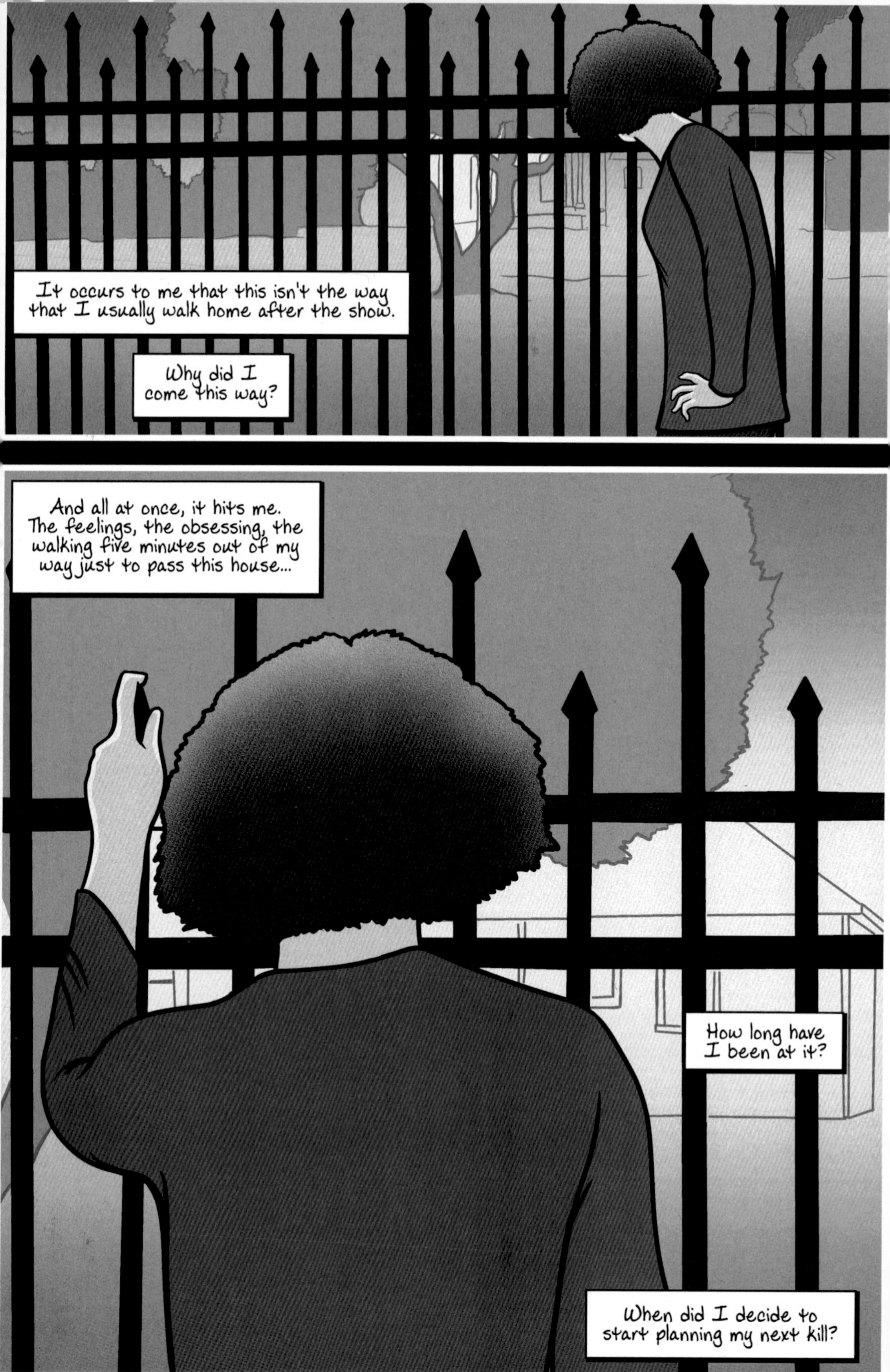
It occurs to me that this isn't the way that I usually walk home after the show.
Why did I come this way?
And all at once, it hits me. The feelings, the obsessing, the walking five minutes out of my way just to pass this house...
How long have I been at it?
When did I decide to start planning my next kill?

a VOICE in the DARK

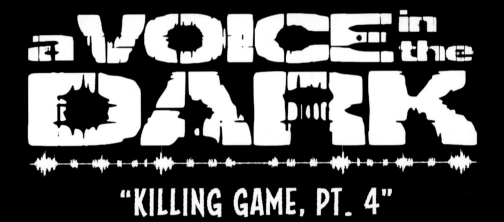

"KILLING GAME, PT. 4"

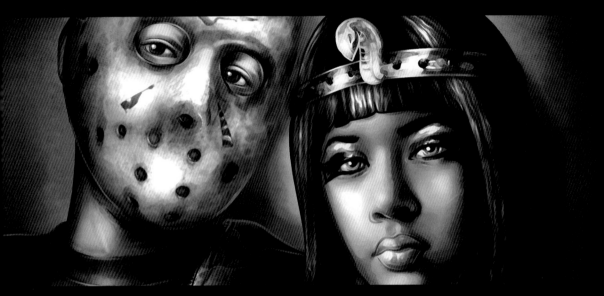

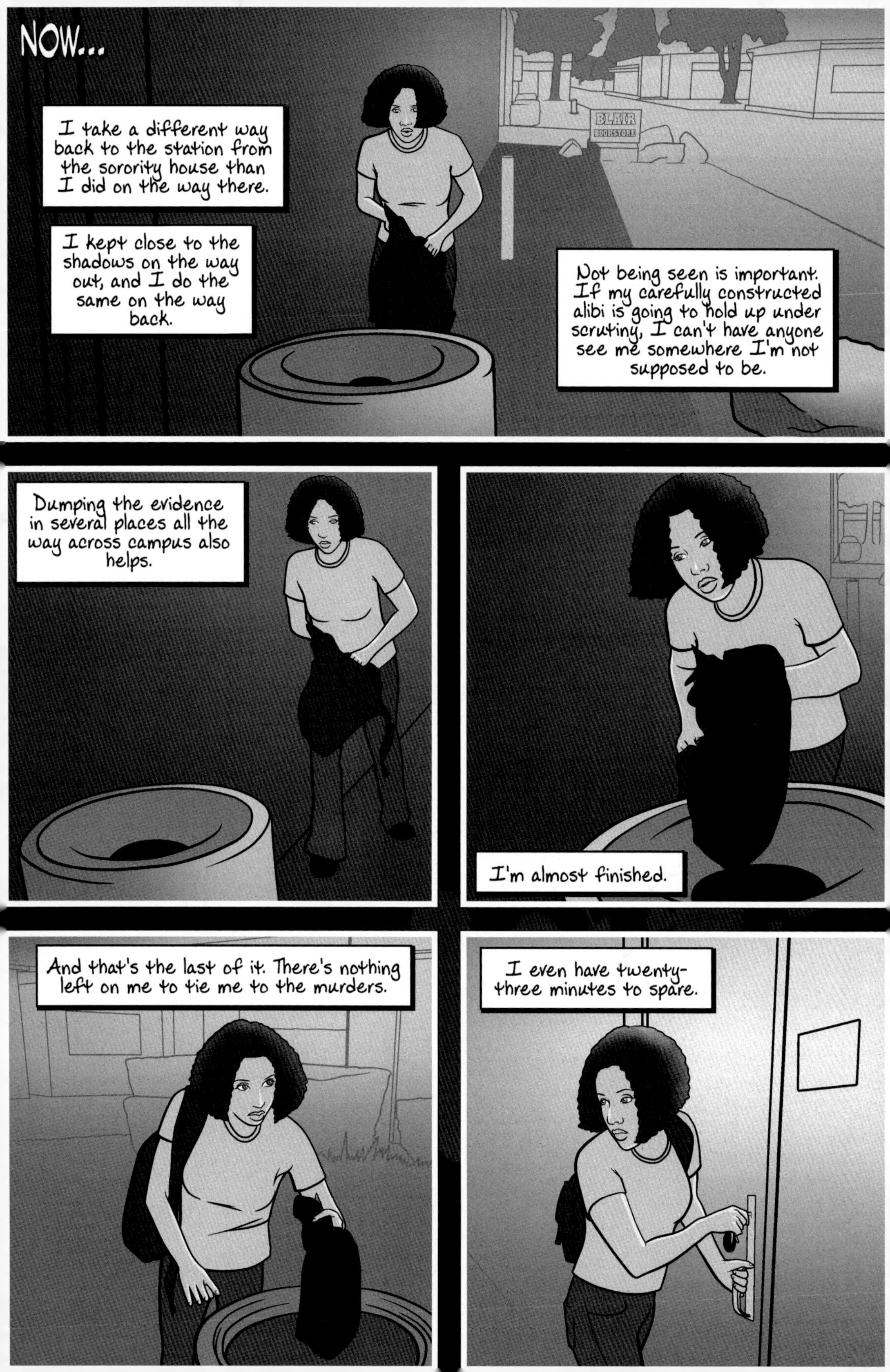
NOW...
I take a different way back to the station from the sorority house than I did on the way there.
I kept close to the shadows on the way out, and I do the same on the way back.
BLAIR BOOKSTORE
Not being seen is important. If my carefully constructed alibi is going to hold up under scrutiny, I can't have anyone see me somewhere I'm not supposed to be.
Dumping the evidence in several places all the way across campus also helps.
I'm almost finished.
And that's the last of it. There's nothing left on me to tie me to the murders.
I even have twenty-three minutes to spare.

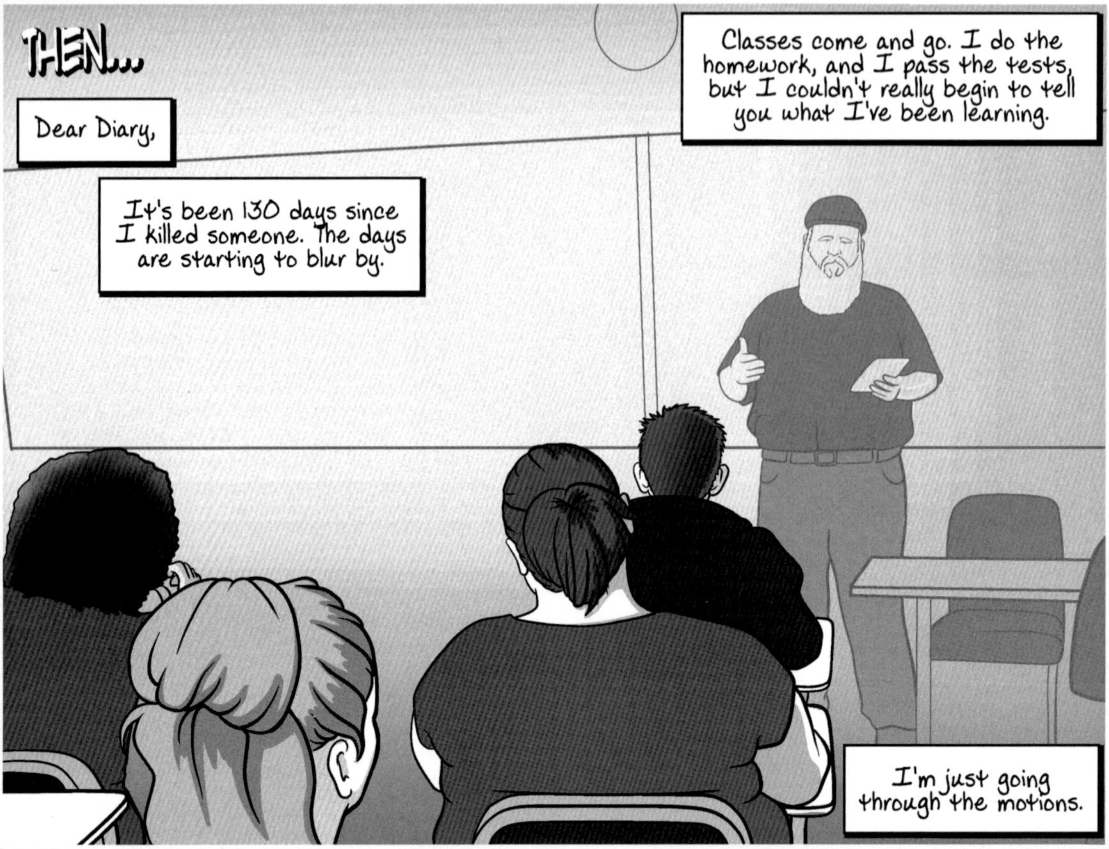
THEN...
Dear Diary,
It's been 130 days since I killed someone. The days are starting to blur by.
Classes come and go. I do the homework, and I pass the tests, but I couldn't really begin to tell you what I've been learning.
I'm just going through the motions.

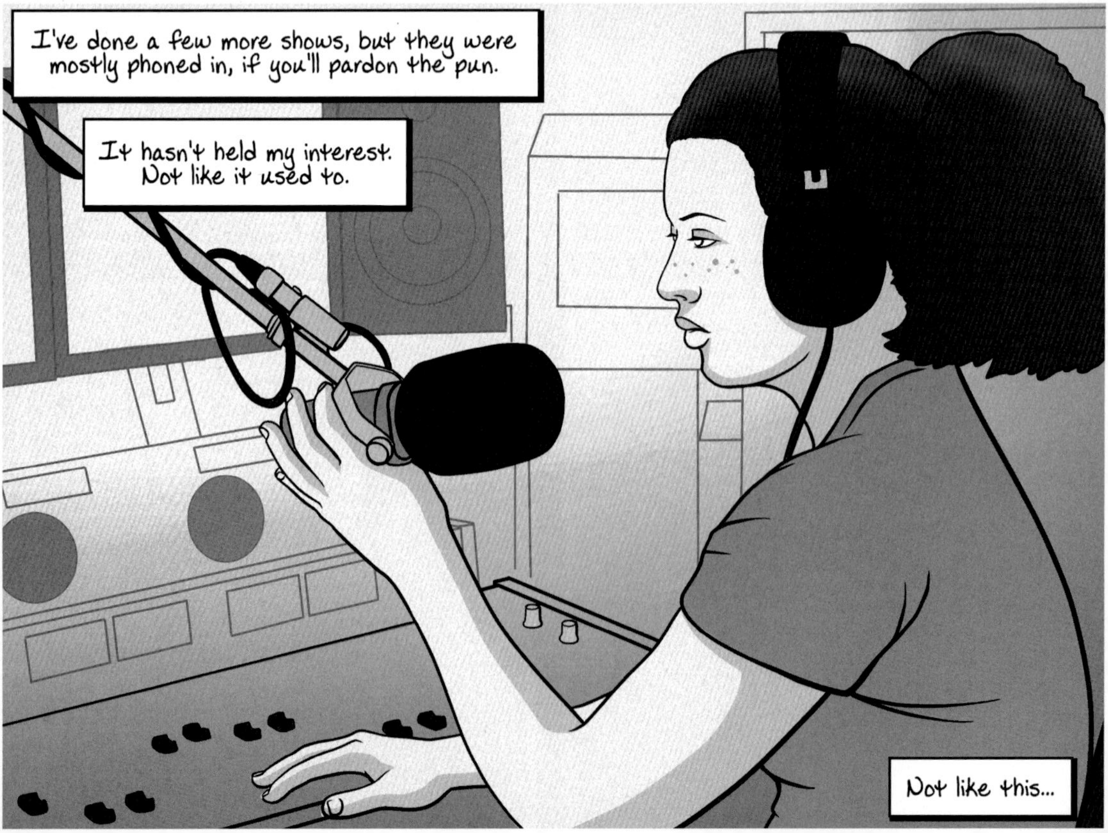
I've done a few more shows, but they were mostly phoned in, if you'll pardon the pun.
It hasn't held my interest. Not like it used to.
Not like this...

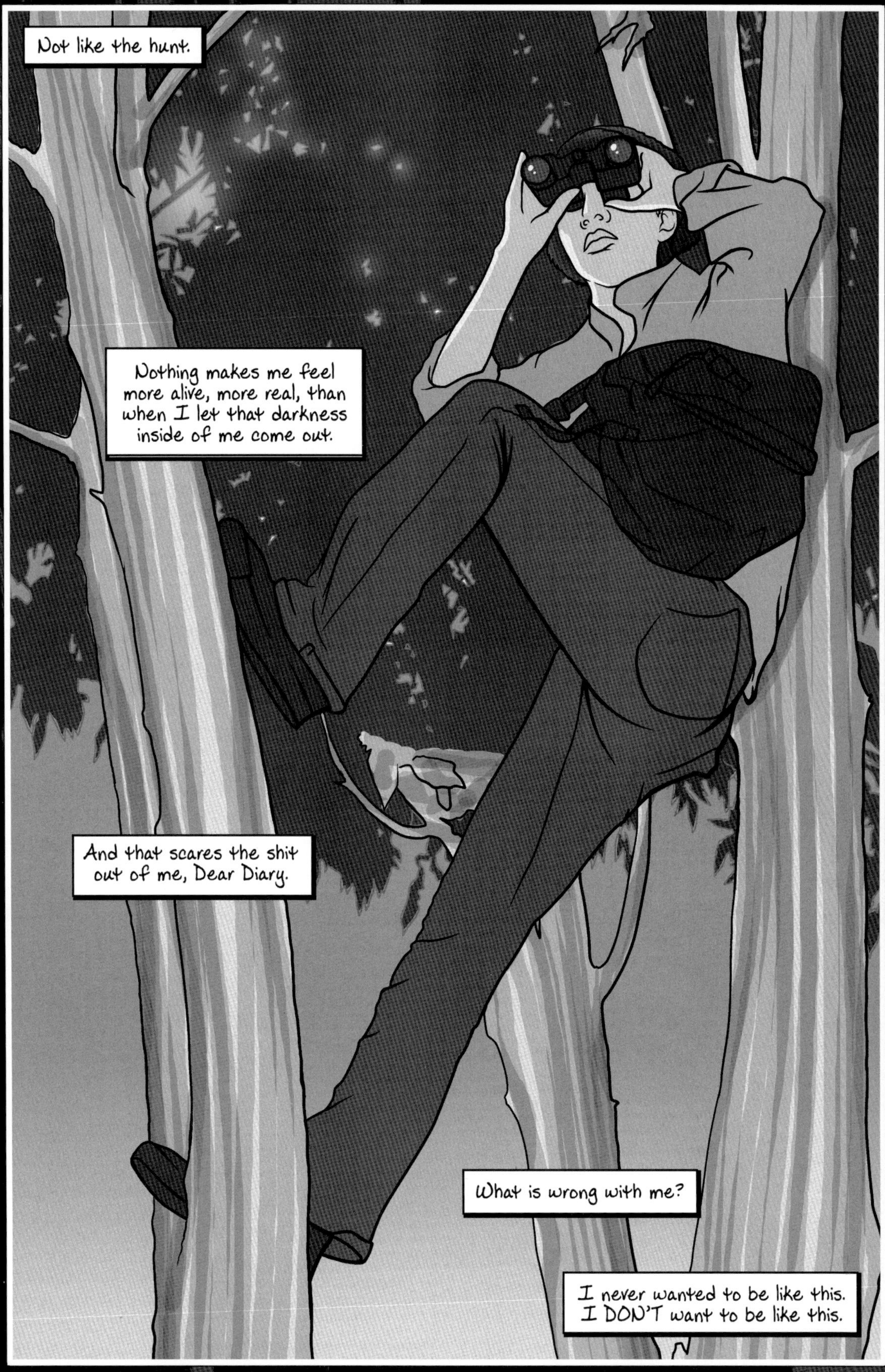
Not like the hunt.
Nothing makes me feel more alive, more real, than when I let that darkness inside of me come out.
And that scares the shit out of me, Dear Diary.
What is wrong with me?
I never wanted to be like this. I DON'T want to be like this.

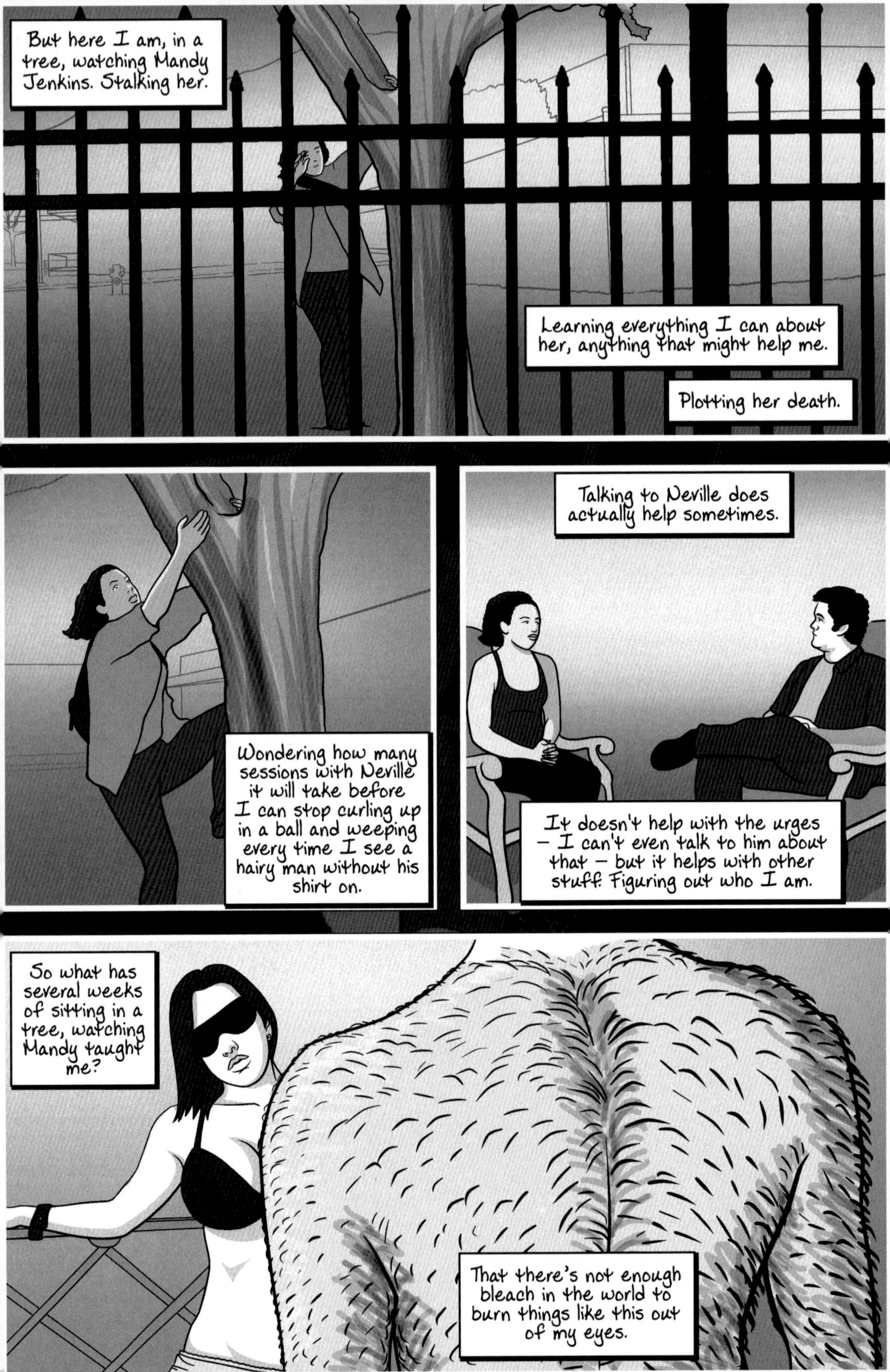
But here I am, in a tree, watching Mandy Jenkins. Stalking her.
Learning everything I can about her, anything that might help me.
Plotting her death.
Wondering how many sessions with Neville it will take before I can stop curling up in a ball and weeping every time I see a hairy man without his shirt on.
Talking to Neville does actually help sometimes.
It doesn't help with the urges – I can't even talk to him about that – but it helps with other stuff. Figuring out who I am.
So what has several weeks of sitting in a tree, watching Mandy taught me?
That there's not enough bleach in the world to burn things like this out of my eyes.

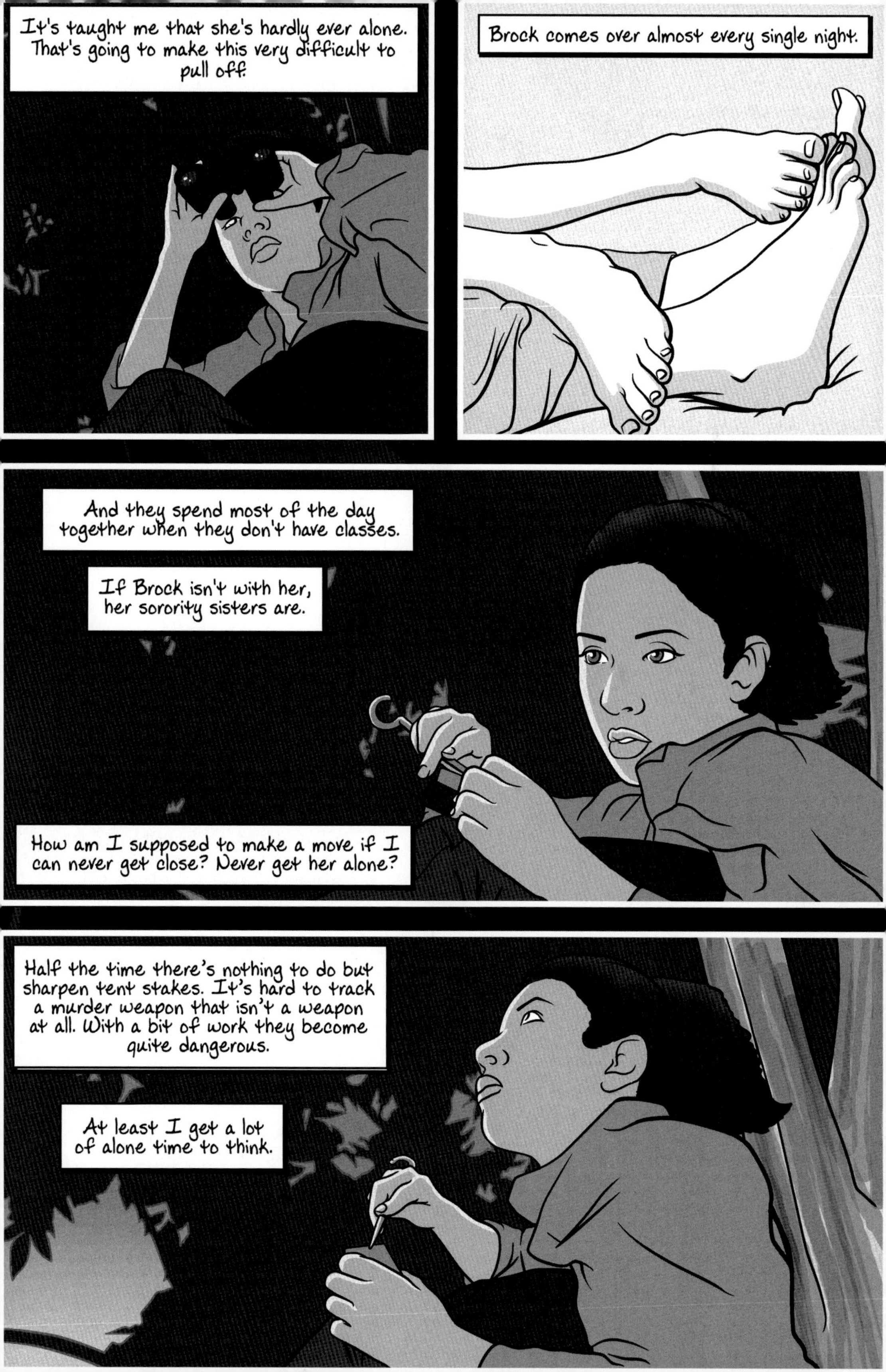
It's taught me that she's hardly ever alone. That's going to make this very difficult to pull off.
Brock comes over almost every single night.
And they spend most of the day together when they don't have classes.
If Brock isn't with her, her sorority sisters are.
How am I supposed to make a move if I can never get close? Never get her alone?
Half the time there's nothing to do but sharpen tent stakes. It's hard to track a murder weapon that isn't a weapon at all. With a bit of work they become quite dangerous.
At least I get a lot of alone time to think.

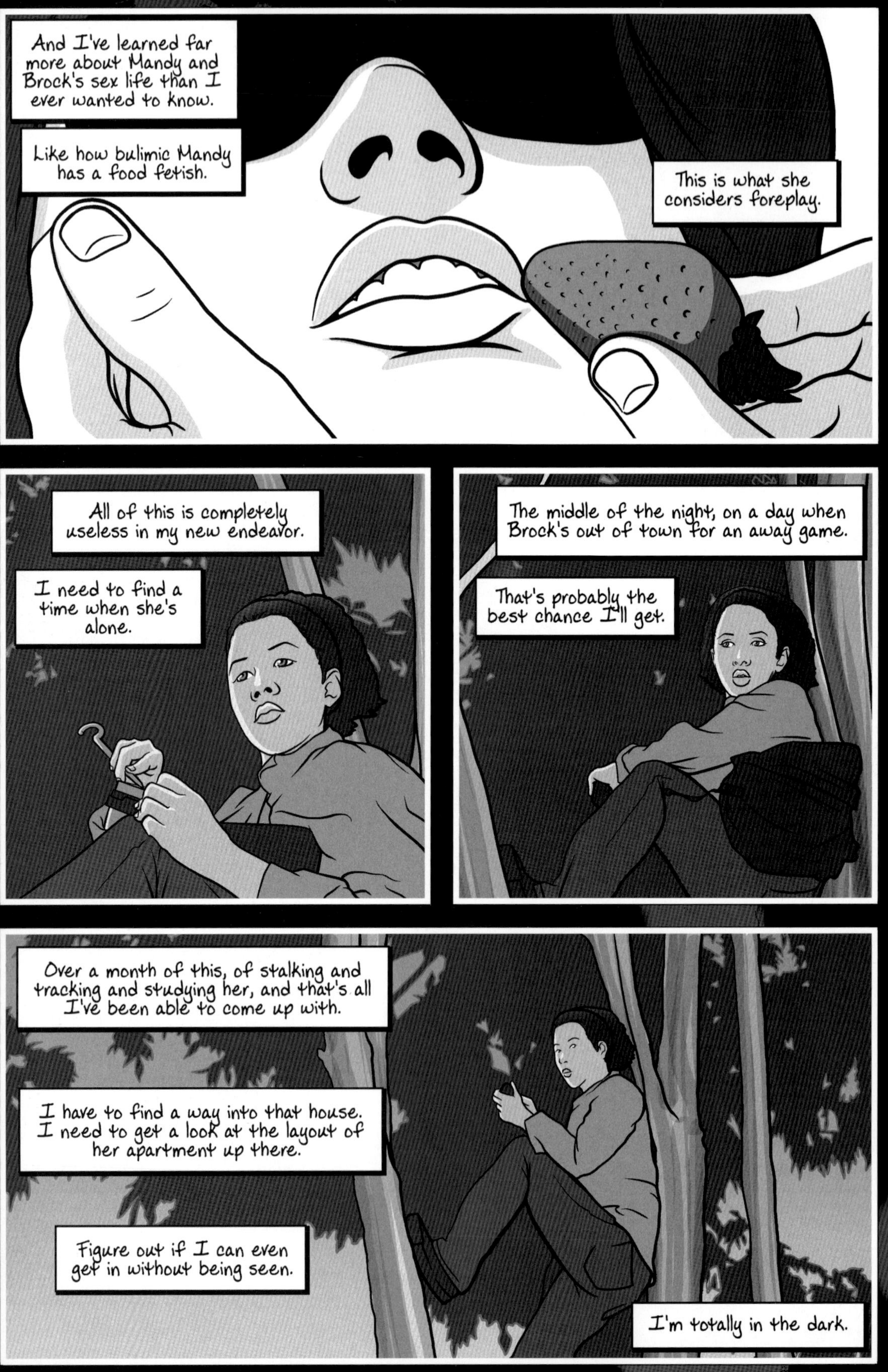
And I've learned far more about Mandy and Brock's sex life than I ever wanted to know.
Like how bulimic Mandy has a food fetish.
This is what she considers foreplay.
All of this is completely useless in my new endeavor.
I need to find a time when she's alone.
The middle of the night, on a day when Brock's out of town for an away game.
That's probably the best chance I'll get.
Over a month of this, of stalking and tracking and studying her, and that's all I've been able to come up with.
I have to find a way into that house. I need to get a look at the layout of her apartment up there.
Figure out if I can even get in without being seen.
I'm totally in the dark.

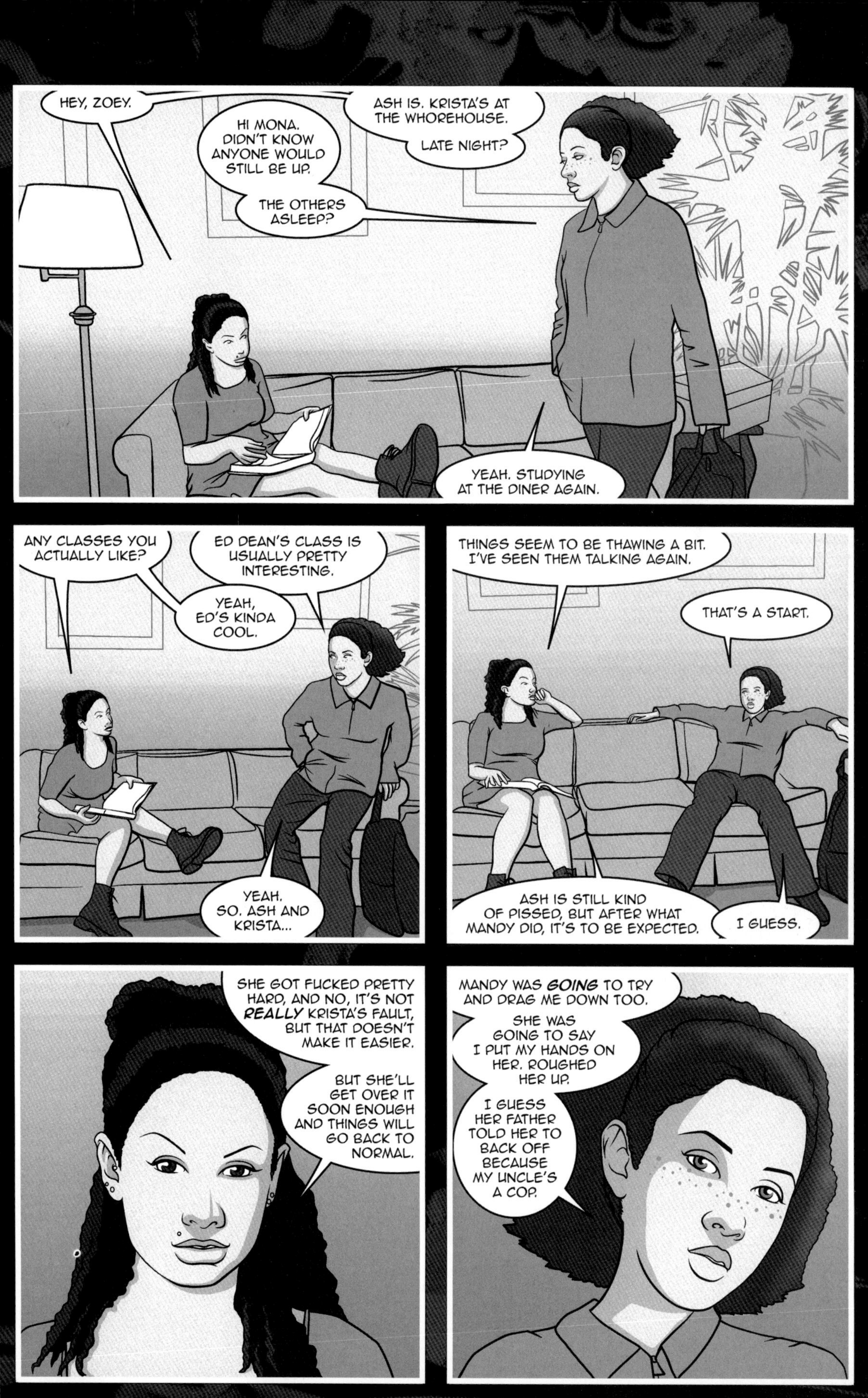
HEY, ZOEY.
HI MONA. DIDN'T KNOW ANYONE WOULD STILL BE UP.
THE OTHERS ASLEEP?
ASH IS. KRISTA'S AT THE WHOREHOUSE.
LATE NIGHT?
YEAH. STUDYING AT THE DINER AGAIN.
ANY CLASSES YOU ACTUALLY LIKE?
ED DEAN'S CLASS IS USUALLY PRETTY INTERESTING.
YEAH, ED'S KINDA COOL.
YEAH. SO. ASH AND KRISTA...
THINGS SEEM TO BE THAWING A BIT. I'VE SEEN THEM TALKING AGAIN.
THAT'S A START.
ASH IS STILL KIND OF PISSED, BUT AFTER WHAT MANDY DID, IT'S TO BE EXPECTED.
I GUESS.
SHE GOT FUCKED PRETTY HARD, AND NO, IT'S NOT REALLY KRISTA'S FAULT, BUT THAT DOESN'T MAKE IT EASIER.
BUT SHE'LL GET OVER IT SOON ENOUGH AND THINGS WILL GO BACK TO NORMAL.
MANDY WAS GOING TO TRY AND DRAG ME DOWN TOO.
SHE WAS GOING TO SAY I PUT MY HANDS ON HER. ROUGHED HER UP.
I GUESS HER FATHER TOLD HER TO BACK OFF BECAUSE MY UNCLE'S A COP.

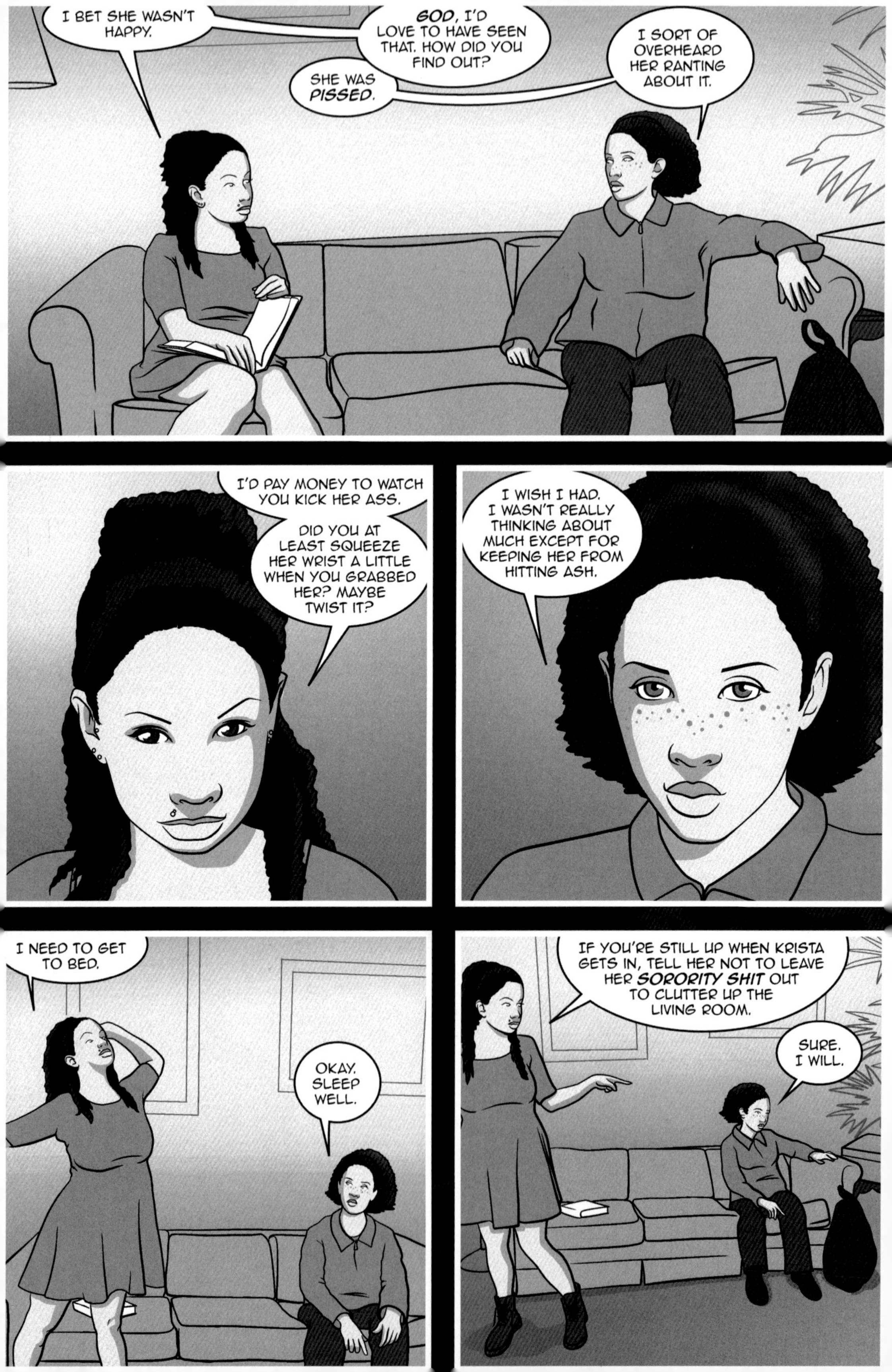
I BET SHE WASN'T HAPPY.
SHE WAS PISSED.
GOD, I'D LOVE TO HAVE SEEN THAT. HOW DID YOU FIND OUT?
I SORT OF OVERHEARD HER RANTING ABOUT IT.
I'D PAY MONEY TO WATCH YOU KICK HER ASS.
DID YOU AT LEAST SQUEEZE HER WRIST A LITTLE WHEN YOU GRABBED HER? MAYBE TWIST IT?
I WISH I HAD. I WASN'T REALLY THINKING ABOUT MUCH EXCEPT FOR KEEPING HER FROM HITTING ASH.
I NEED TO GET TO BED.
OKAY. SLEEP WELL.
IF YOU'RE STILL UP WHEN KRISTA GETS IN, TELL HER NOT TO LEAVE HER SORORITY SHIT OUT TO CLUTTER UP THE LIVING ROOM.
SURE. I WILL.

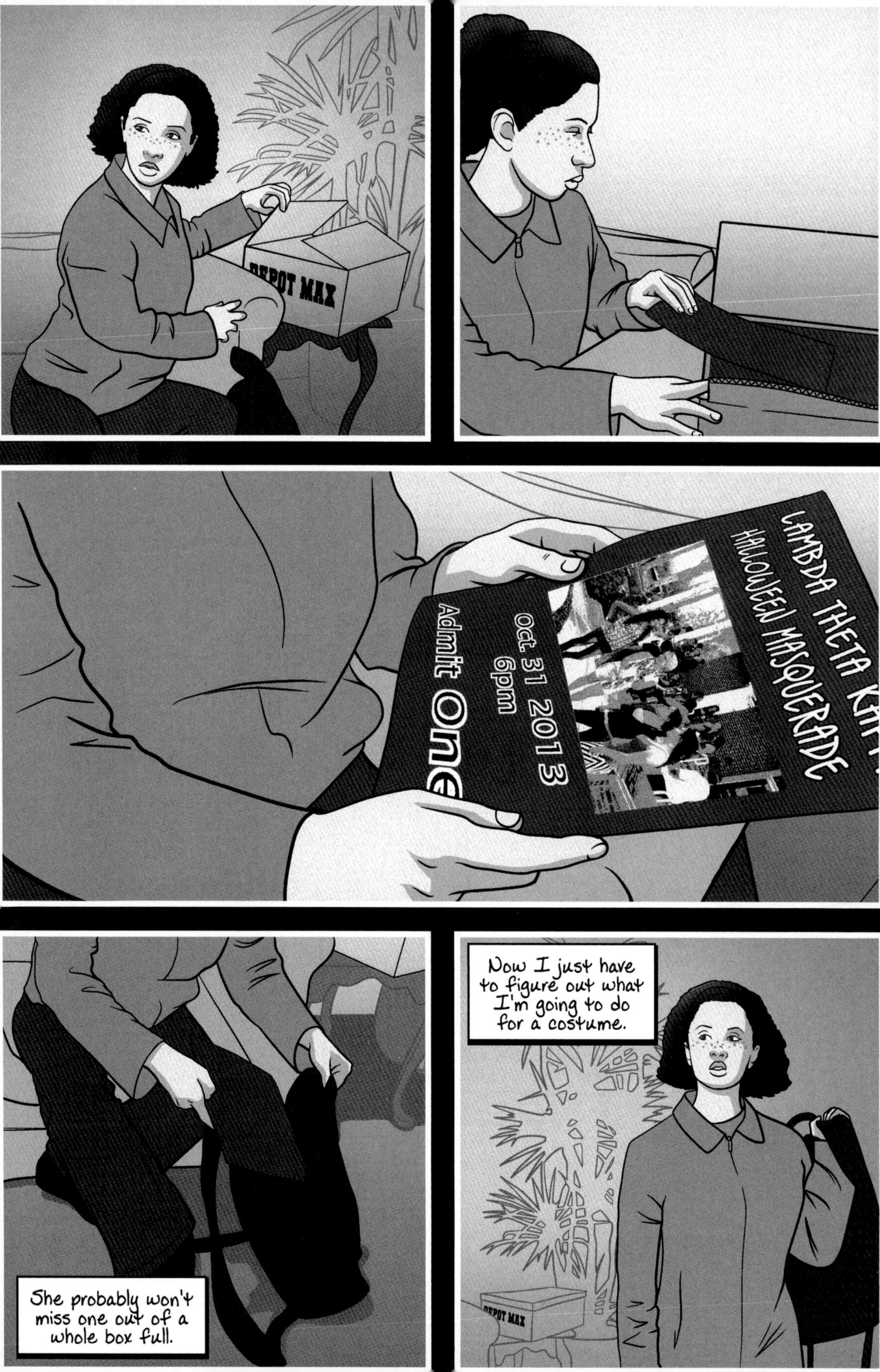
DEPOT MAX
LAMBDA THETA
HALLOWEEN MASQUERADE
Oct. 31 2013
6pm
Admit One
She probably won't miss one out of a whole box full.
Now I just have to figure out what I'm going to do for a costume.
DEPOT MAX

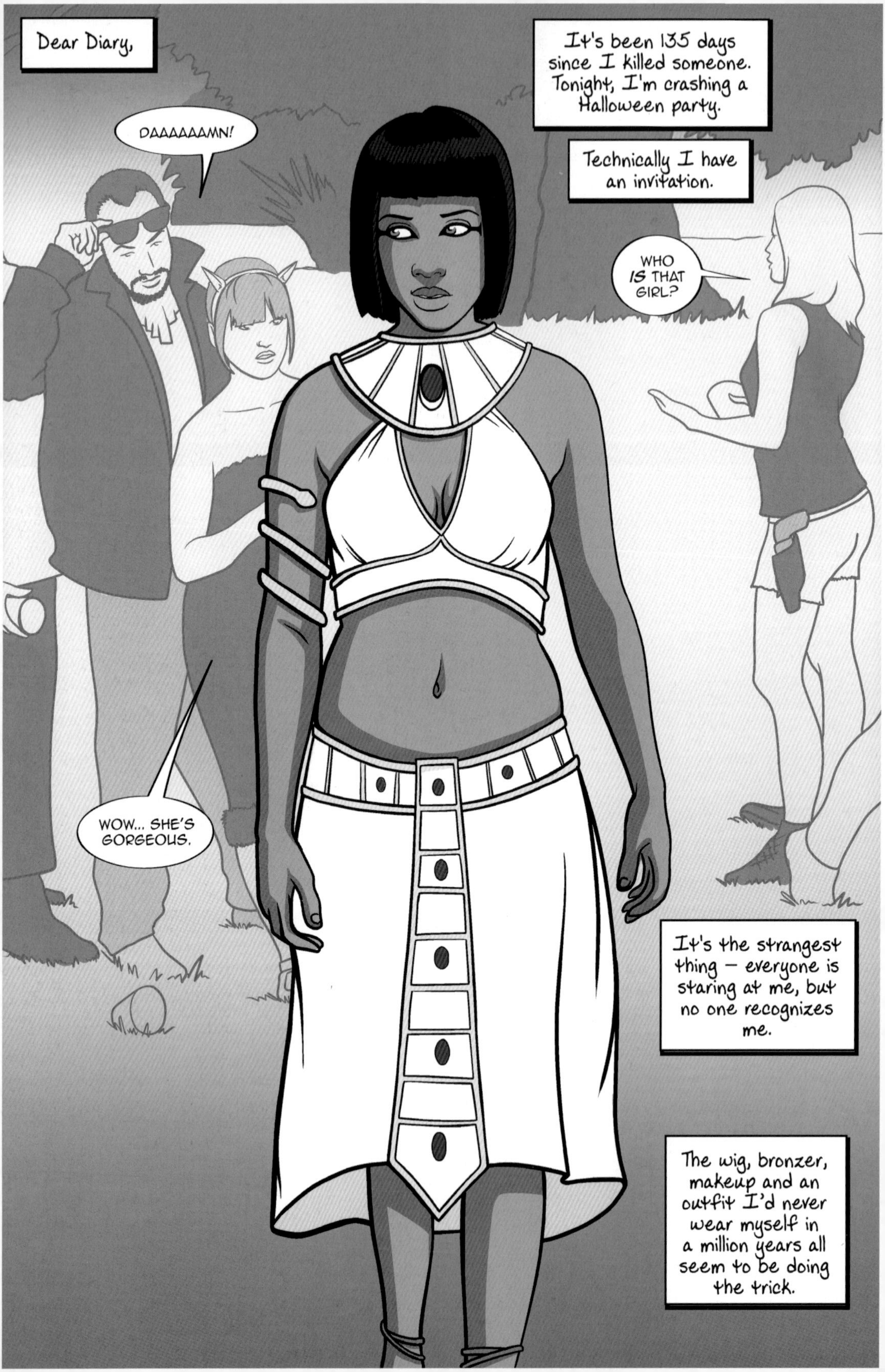
Dear Diary,
It's been 135 days since I killed someone. Tonight, I'm crashing a Halloween party.
DAAAAAAAMN!
Technically I have an invitation.
WHO IS THAT GIRL?
WOW... SHE'S GORGEOUS.
It's the strangest thing — everyone is staring at me, but no one recognizes me.
The wig, bronzer, makeup and an outfit I'd never wear myself in a million years all seem to be doing the trick.

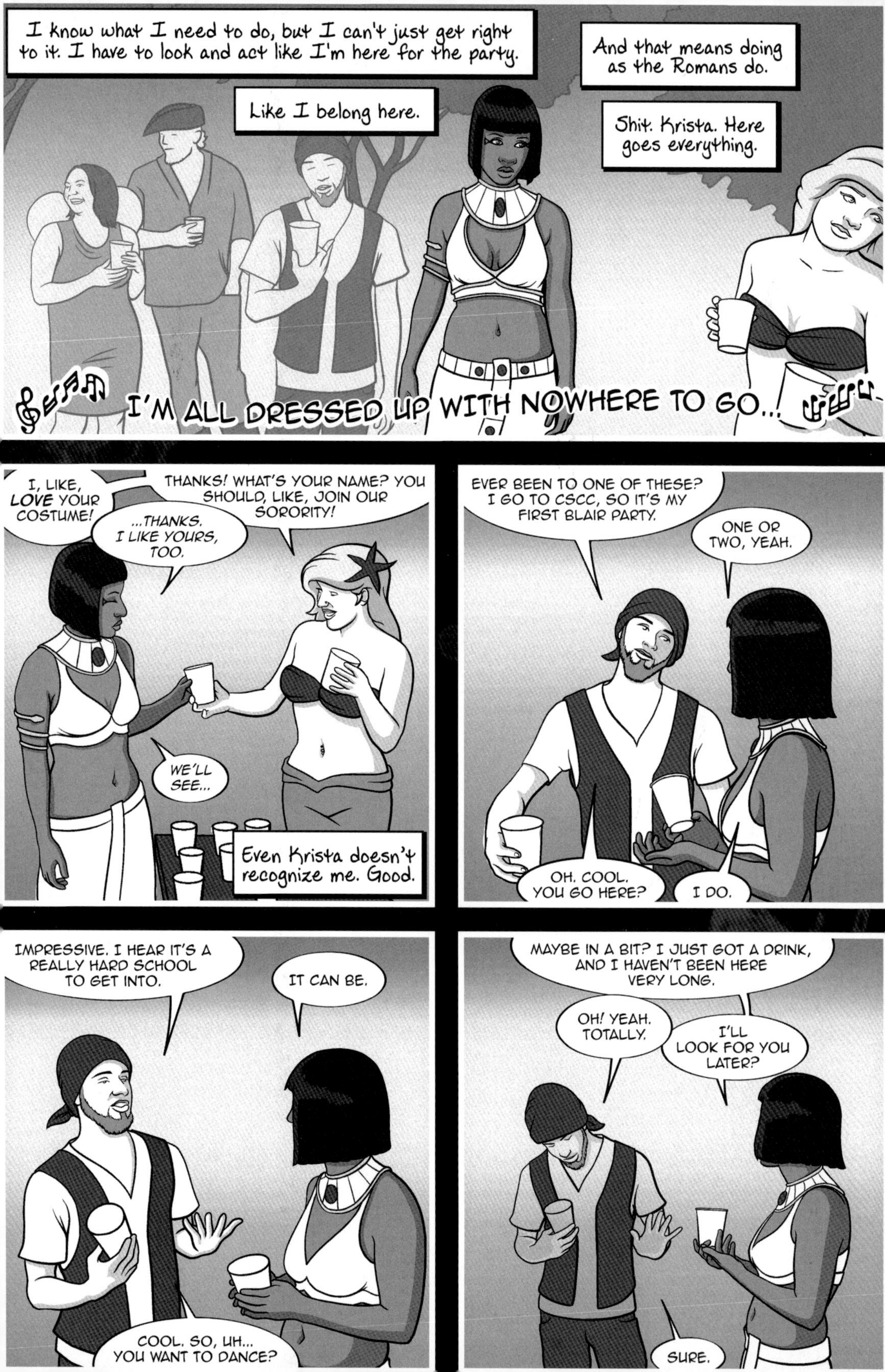
I know what I need to do, but I can't just get right to it. I have to look and act like I'm here for the party.
Like I belong here.
And that means doing as the Romans do.
Shit. Krista. Here goes everything.
I'M ALL DRESSED UP WITH NOWHERE TO GO...
I, LIKE, LOVE YOUR COSTUME!
...THANKS. I LIKE YOURS, TOO.
THANKS! WHAT'S YOUR NAME? YOU SHOULD, LIKE, JOIN OUR SORORITY!
WE'LL SEE...
Even Krista doesn't recognize me. Good.
EVER BEEN TO ONE OF THESE? I GO TO CSCC, SO IT'S MY FIRST BLAIR PARTY.
ONE OR TWO, YEAH.
OH. COOL. YOU GO HERE?
I DO.
IMPRESSIVE. I HEAR IT'S A REALLY HARD SCHOOL TO GET INTO.
IT CAN BE.
COOL. SO, UH... YOU WANT TO DANCE?
MAYBE IN A BIT? I JUST GOT A DRINK, AND I HAVEN'T BEEN HERE VERY LONG.
OH! YEAH. TOTALLY.
I'LL LOOK FOR YOU LATER?
SURE.

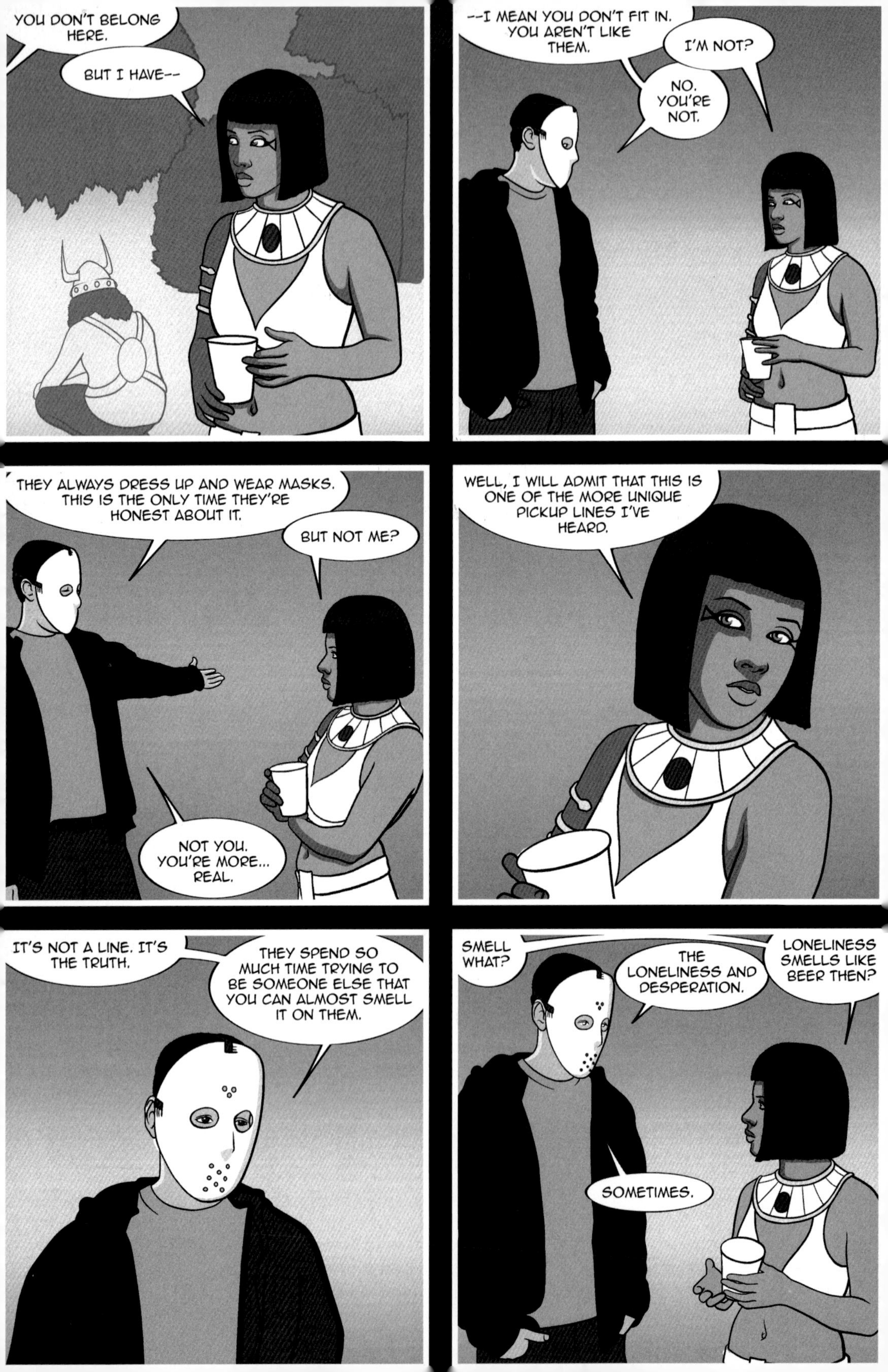

YOU DON'T BELONG HERE.
BUT I HAVE--
--I MEAN YOU DON'T FIT IN. YOU AREN'T LIKE THEM.
I'M NOT?
NO. YOU'RE NOT.
THEY ALWAYS DRESS UP AND WEAR MASKS. THIS IS THE ONLY TIME THEY'RE HONEST ABOUT IT.
BUT NOT ME?
NOT YOU. YOU'RE MORE... REAL.
WELL, I WILL ADMIT THAT THIS IS ONE OF THE MORE UNIQUE PICKUP LINES I'VE HEARD.
IT'S NOT A LINE. IT'S THE TRUTH.
THEY SPEND SO MUCH TIME TRYING TO BE SOMEONE ELSE THAT YOU CAN ALMOST SMELL IT ON THEM.
SMELL WHAT?
THE LONELINESS AND DESPERATION.
LONELINESS SMELLS LIKE BEER THEN?
SOMETIMES.

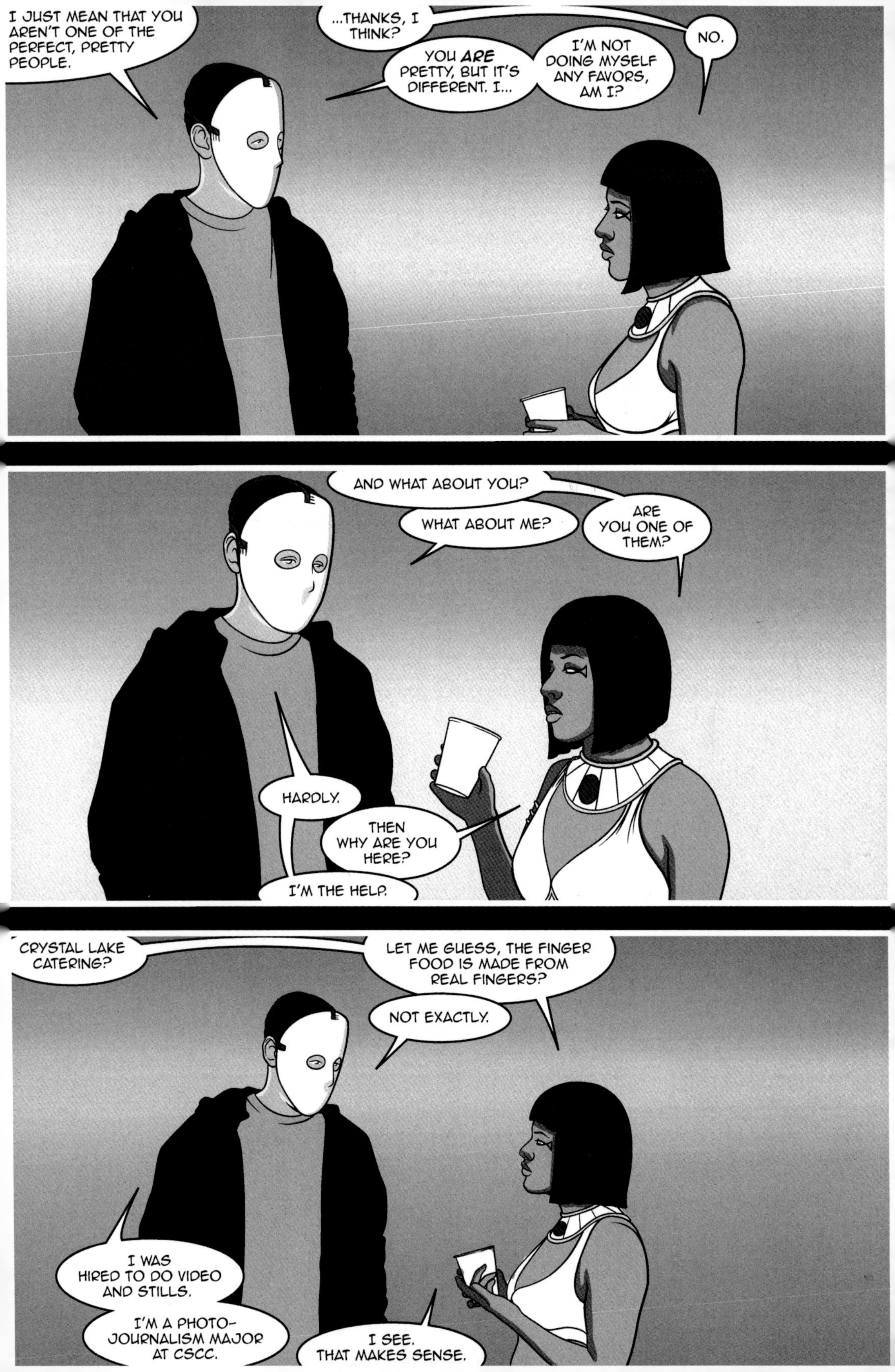
I JUST MEAN THAT YOU AREN'T ONE OF THE PERFECT, PRETTY PEOPLE.
...THANKS, I THINK?
YOU **ARE** PRETTY, BUT IT'S DIFFERENT. I...
I'M NOT DOING MYSELF ANY FAVORS, AM I?
NO.
AND WHAT ABOUT YOU?
WHAT ABOUT ME?
ARE YOU ONE OF THEM?
HARDLY.
THEN WHY ARE YOU HERE?
I'M THE HELP.
CRYSTAL LAKE CATERING?
LET ME GUESS, THE FINGER FOOD IS MADE FROM REAL FINGERS?
NOT EXACTLY.
I WAS HIRED TO DO VIDEO AND STILLS.
I'M A PHOTO-JOURNALISM MAJOR AT CSCC.
I SEE. THAT MAKES SENSE.

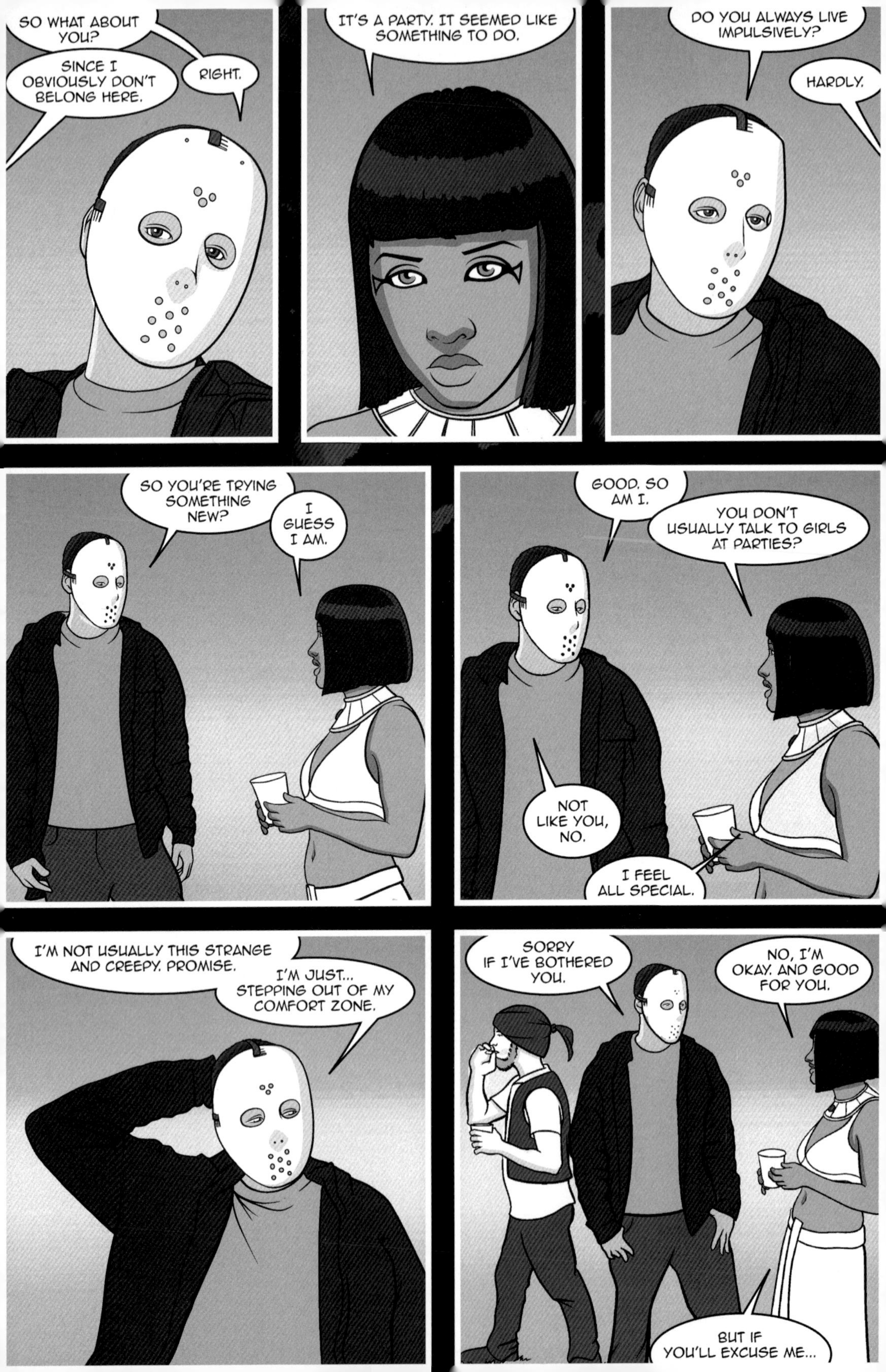
SO WHAT ABOUT YOU?
SINCE I OBVIOUSLY DON'T BELONG HERE.
RIGHT.
IT'S A PARTY. IT SEEMED LIKE SOMETHING TO DO.
DO YOU ALWAYS LIVE IMPULSIVELY?
HARDLY.
SO YOU'RE TRYING SOMETHING NEW?
I GUESS I AM.
GOOD. SO AM I.
YOU DON'T USUALLY TALK TO GIRLS AT PARTIES?
NOT LIKE YOU, NO.
I FEEL ALL SPECIAL.
I'M NOT USUALLY THIS STRANGE AND CREEPY. PROMISE.
I'M JUST... STEPPING OUT OF MY COMFORT ZONE.
SORRY IF I'VE BOTHERED YOU.
NO, I'M OKAY. AND GOOD FOR YOU.
BUT IF YOU'LL EXCUSE ME...

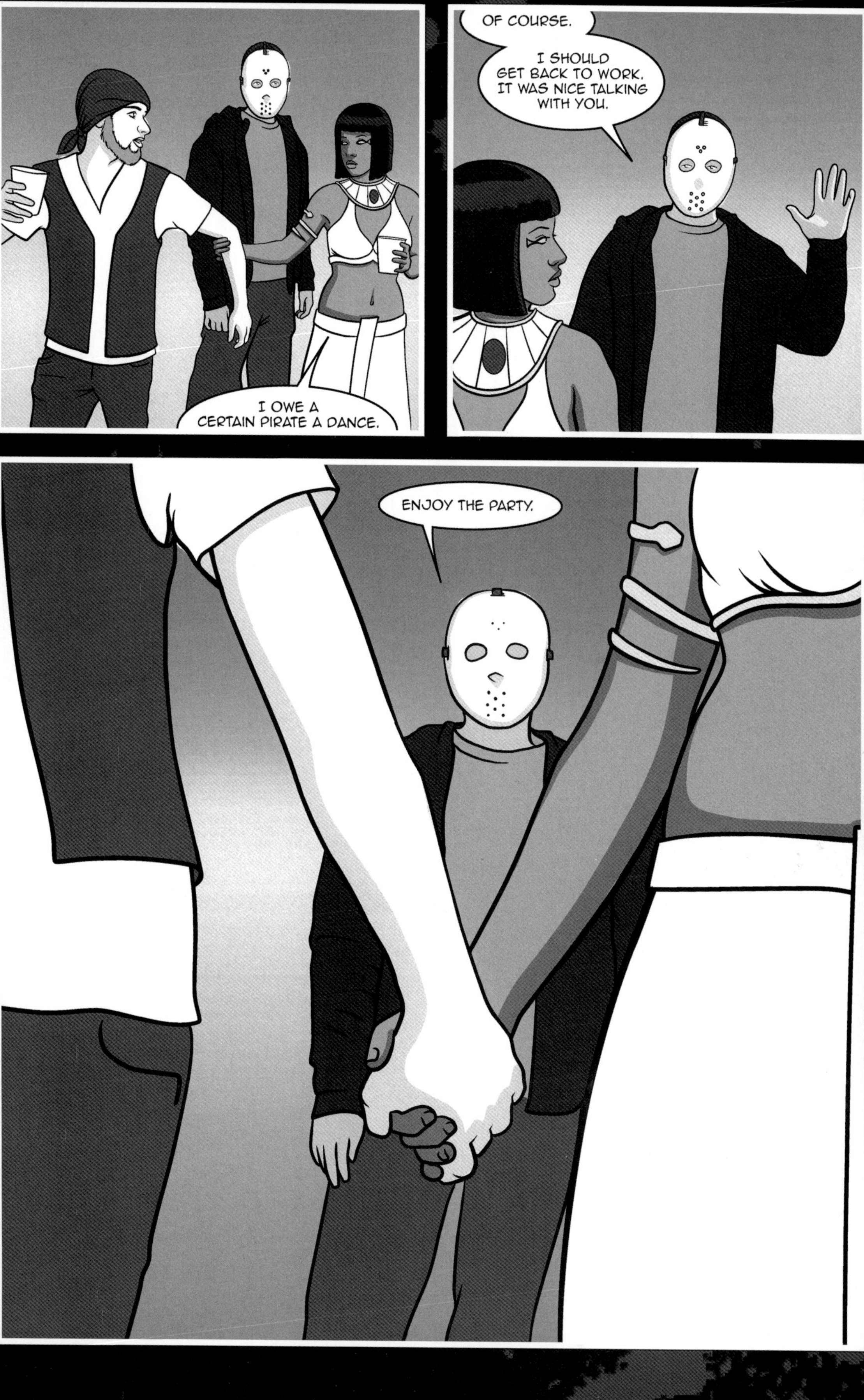
I OWE A CERTAIN PIRATE A DANCE.
OF COURSE.
I SHOULD GET BACK TO WORK. IT WAS NICE TALKING WITH YOU.
ENJOY THE PARTY.

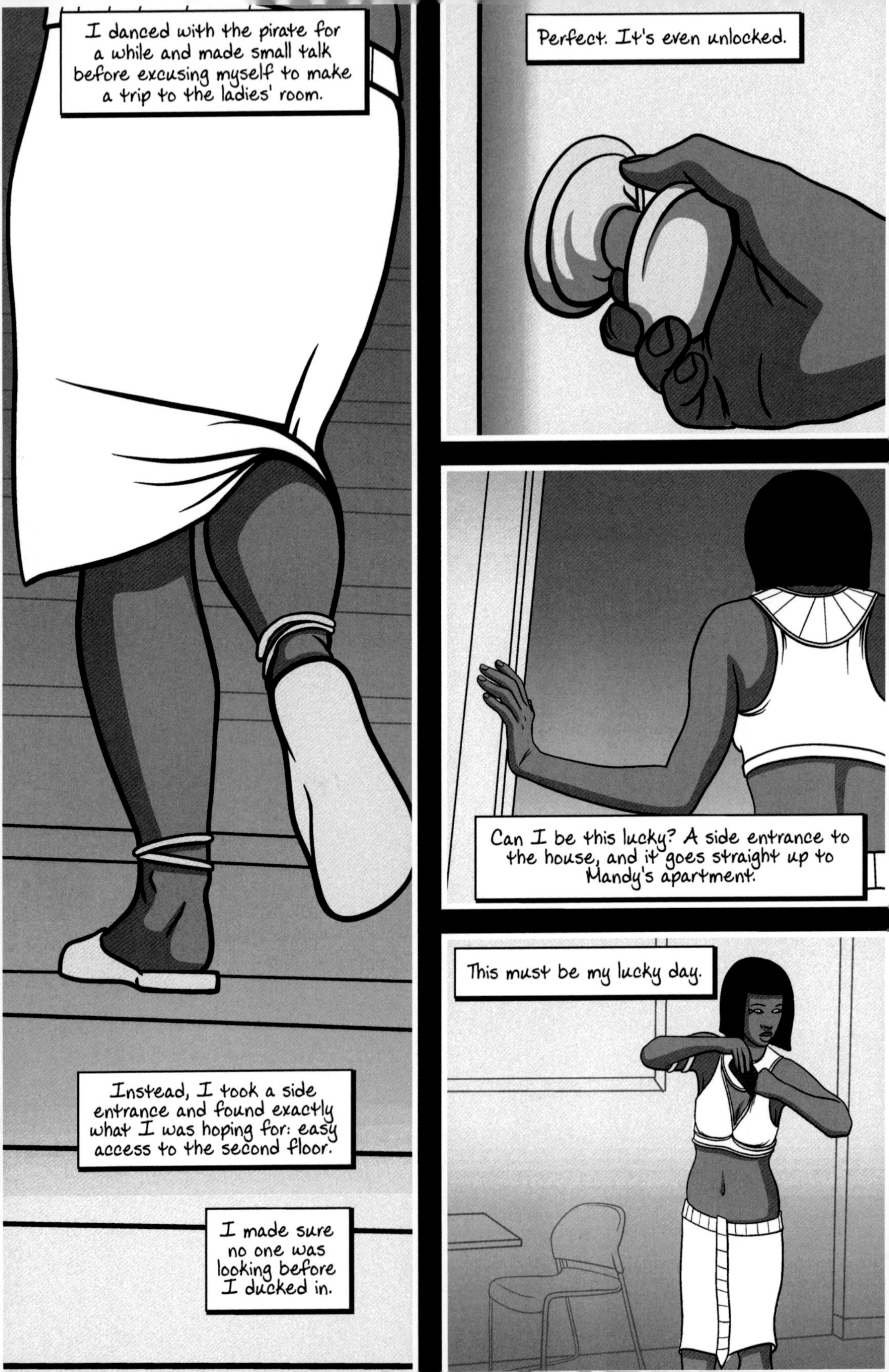

I danced with the pirate for a while and made small talk before excusing myself to make a trip to the ladies' room.
Instead, I took a side entrance and found exactly what I was hoping for: easy access to the second floor.
I made sure no one was looking before I ducked in.
Perfect. It's even unlocked.
Can I be this lucky? A side entrance to the house, and it goes straight up to Mandy's apartment.
This must be my lucky day.

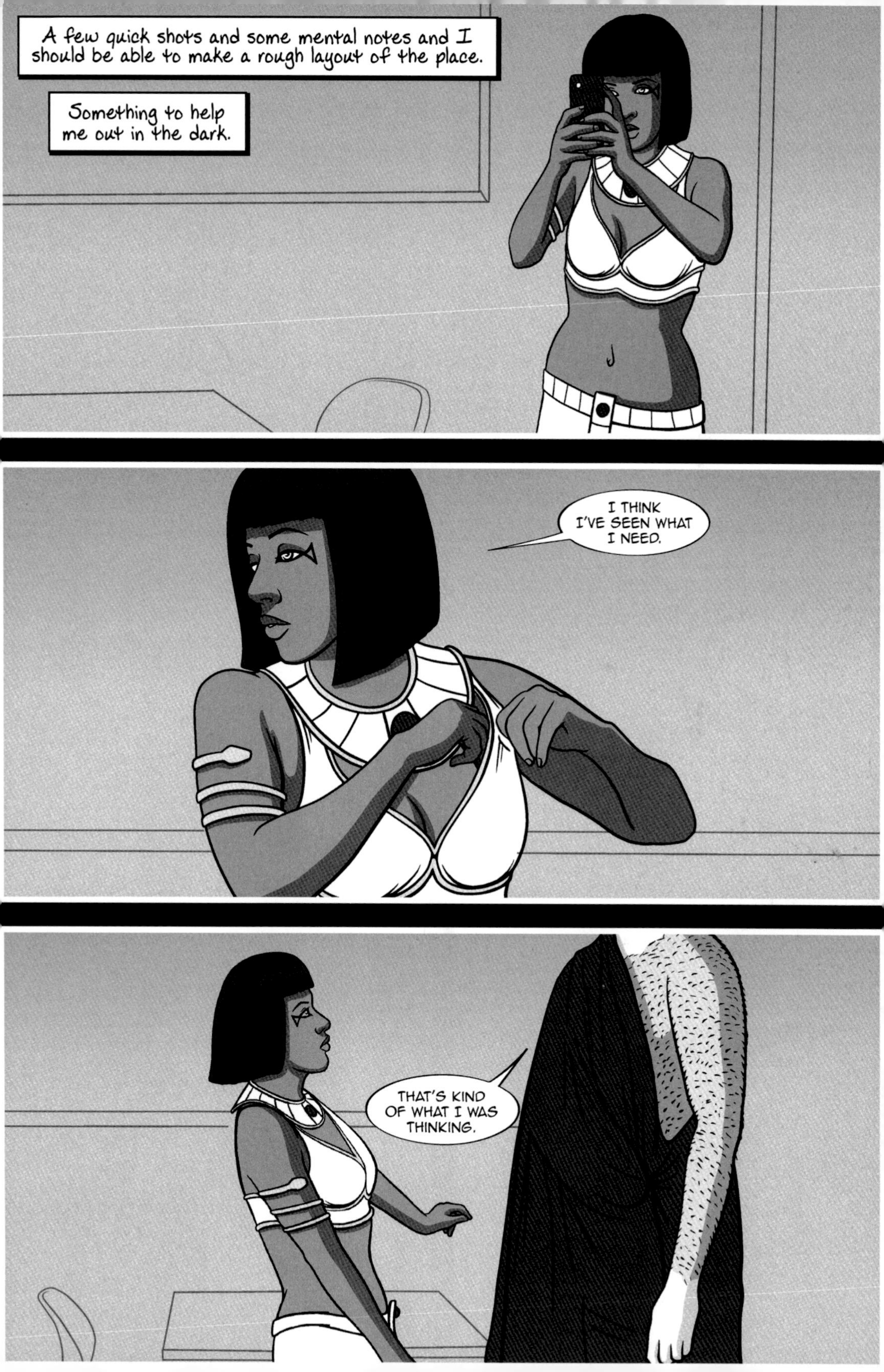
A few quick shots and some mental notes and I should be able to make a rough layout of the place.
Something to help me out in the dark.
I THINK I'VE SEEN WHAT I NEED.
THAT'S KIND OF WHAT I WAS THINKING.

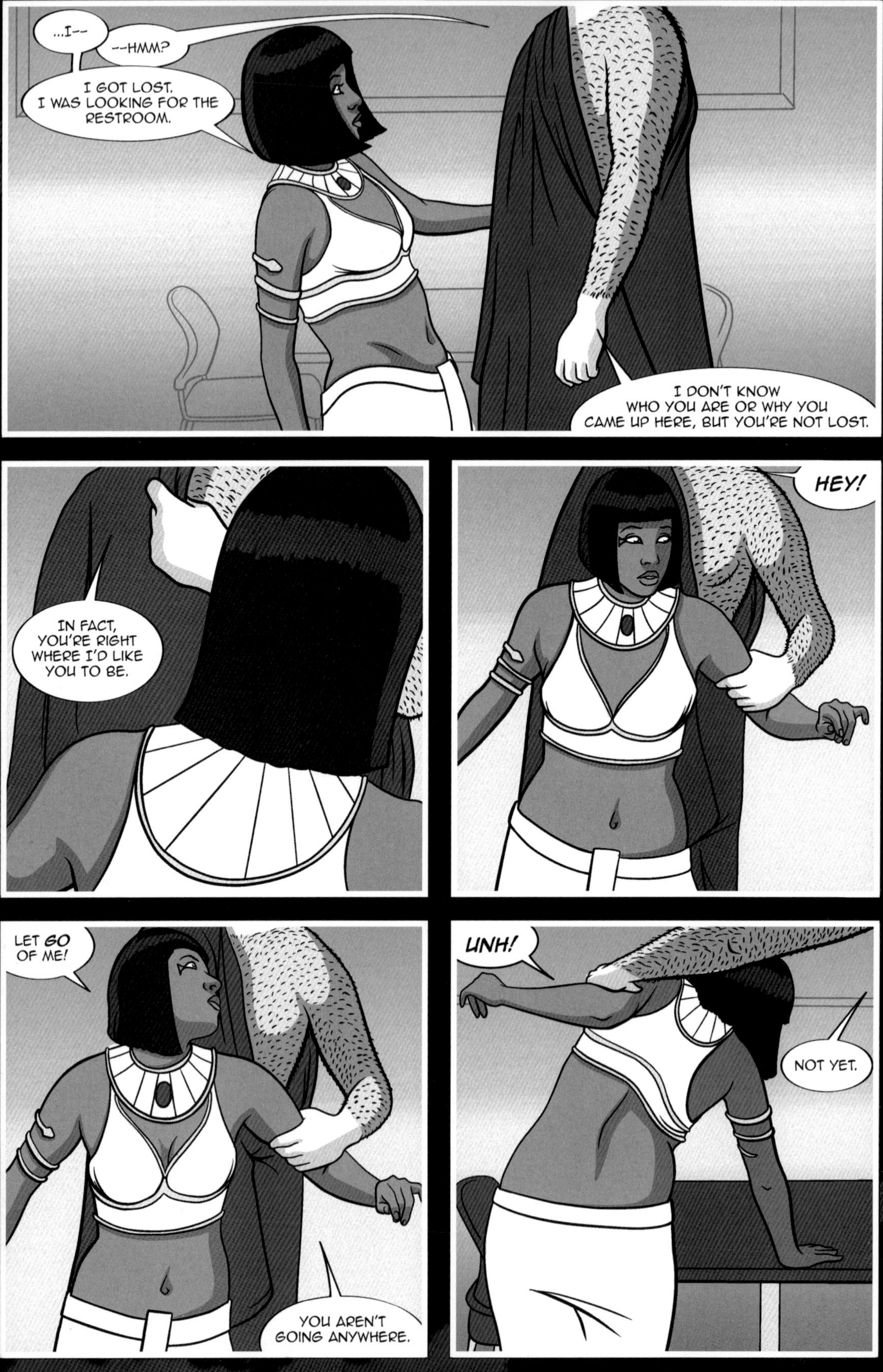
...I--
--HMM?
I GOT LOST. I WAS LOOKING FOR THE RESTROOM.
I DON'T KNOW WHO YOU ARE OR WHY YOU CAME UP HERE, BUT YOU'RE NOT LOST.
IN FACT, YOU'RE RIGHT WHERE I'D LIKE YOU TO BE.
HEY!
LET GO OF ME!
YOU AREN'T GOING ANYWHERE.
UNH!
NOT YET.

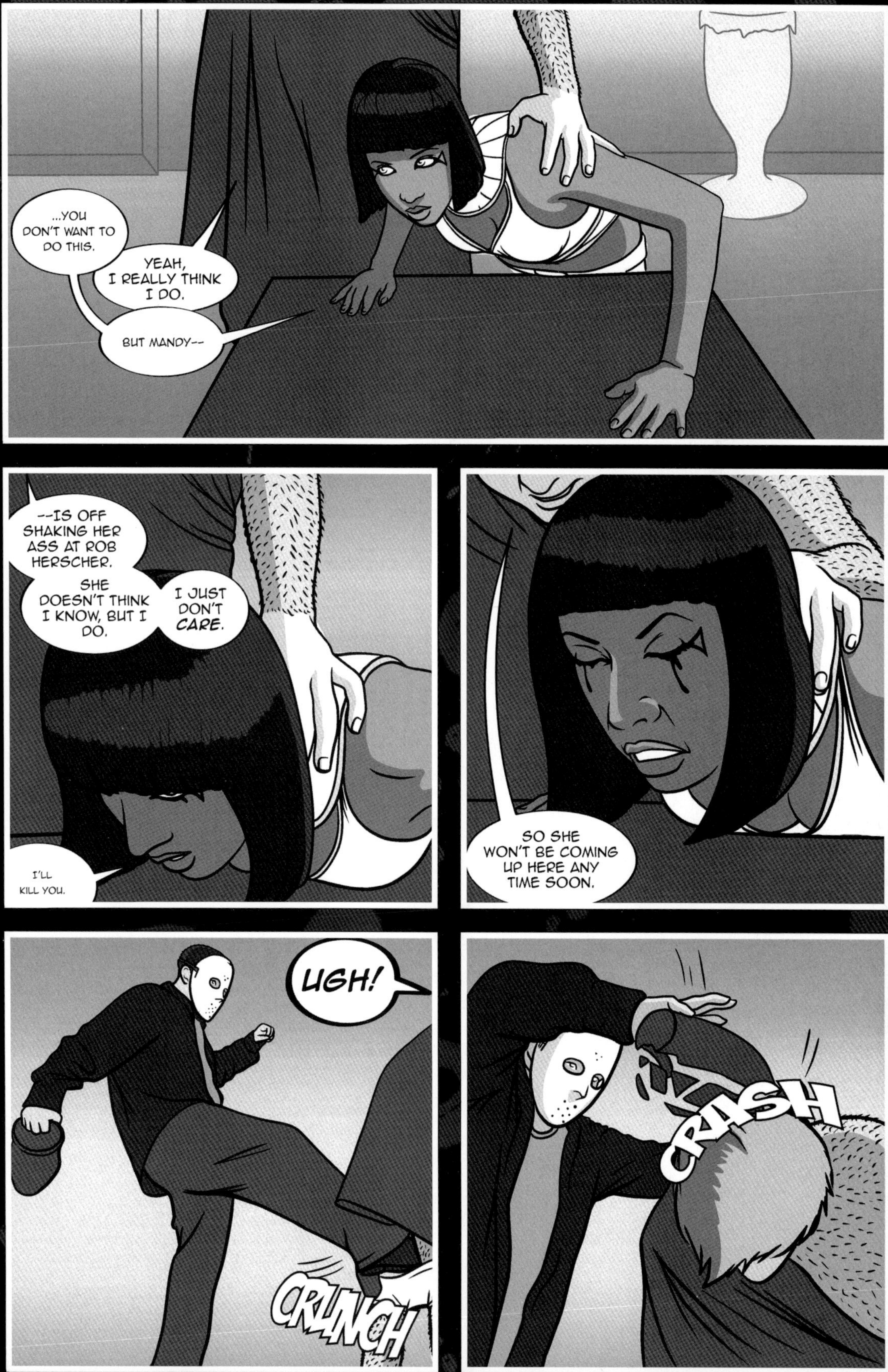
...YOU DON'T WANT TO DO THIS.
YEAH, I REALLY THINK I DO.
BUT MANDY--
--IS OFF SHAKING HER ASS AT ROB HERSCHER.
SHE DOESN'T THINK I KNOW, BUT I DO.
I JUST DON'T CARE.
I'LL KILL YOU.
SO SHE WON'T BE COMING UP HERE ANY TIME SOON.
UGH!
CRUNCH
CRASH

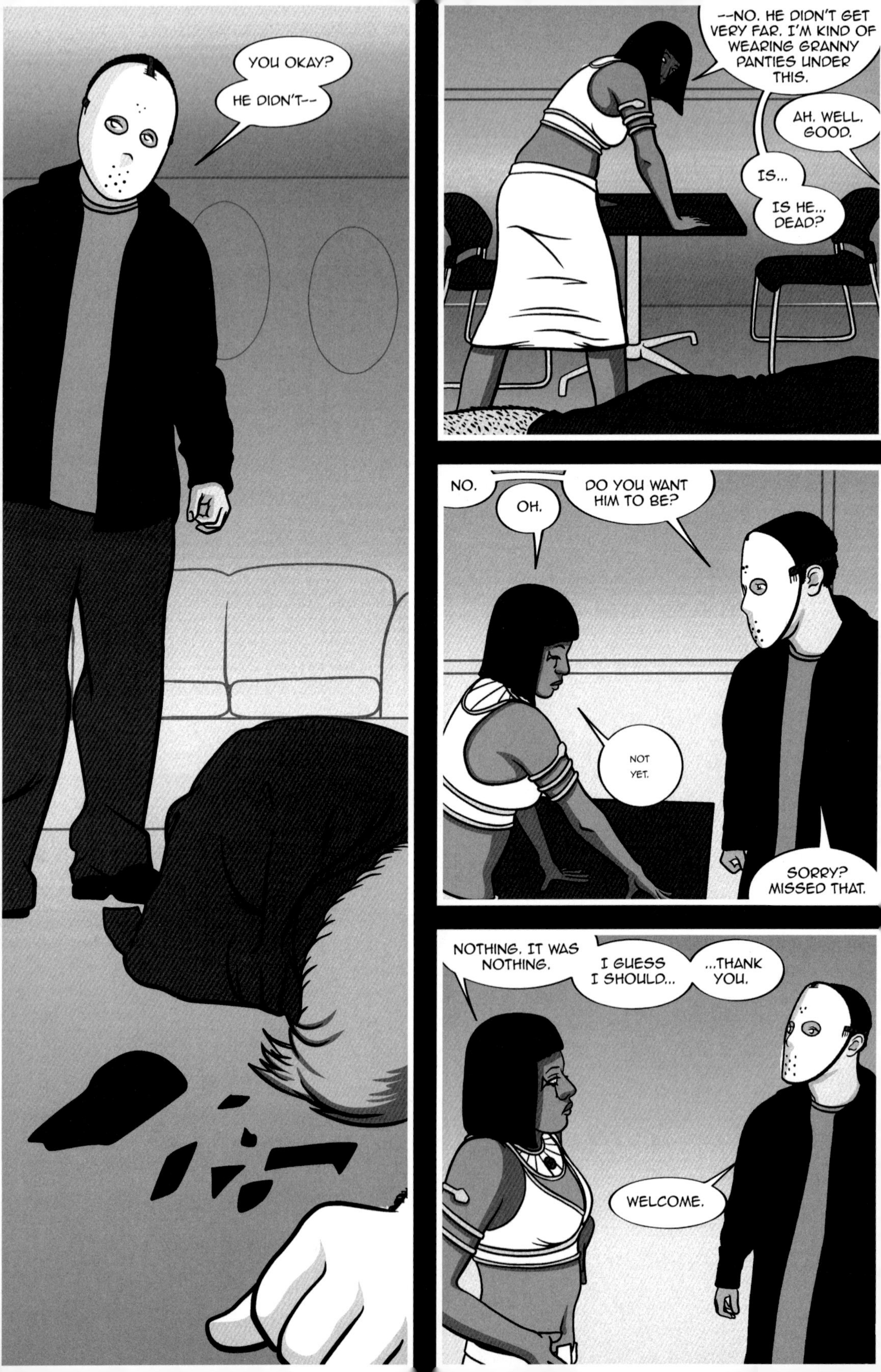
YOU OKAY?
HE DIDN'T--
--NO. HE DIDN'T GET VERY FAR. I'M KIND OF WEARING GRANNY PANTIES UNDER THIS.
AH. WELL. GOOD.
IS...
IS HE... DEAD?
NO.
OH.
DO YOU WANT HIM TO BE?
NOT YET.
SORRY? MISSED THAT.
NOTHING. IT WAS NOTHING.
I GUESS I SHOULD...
...THANK YOU.
WELCOME.

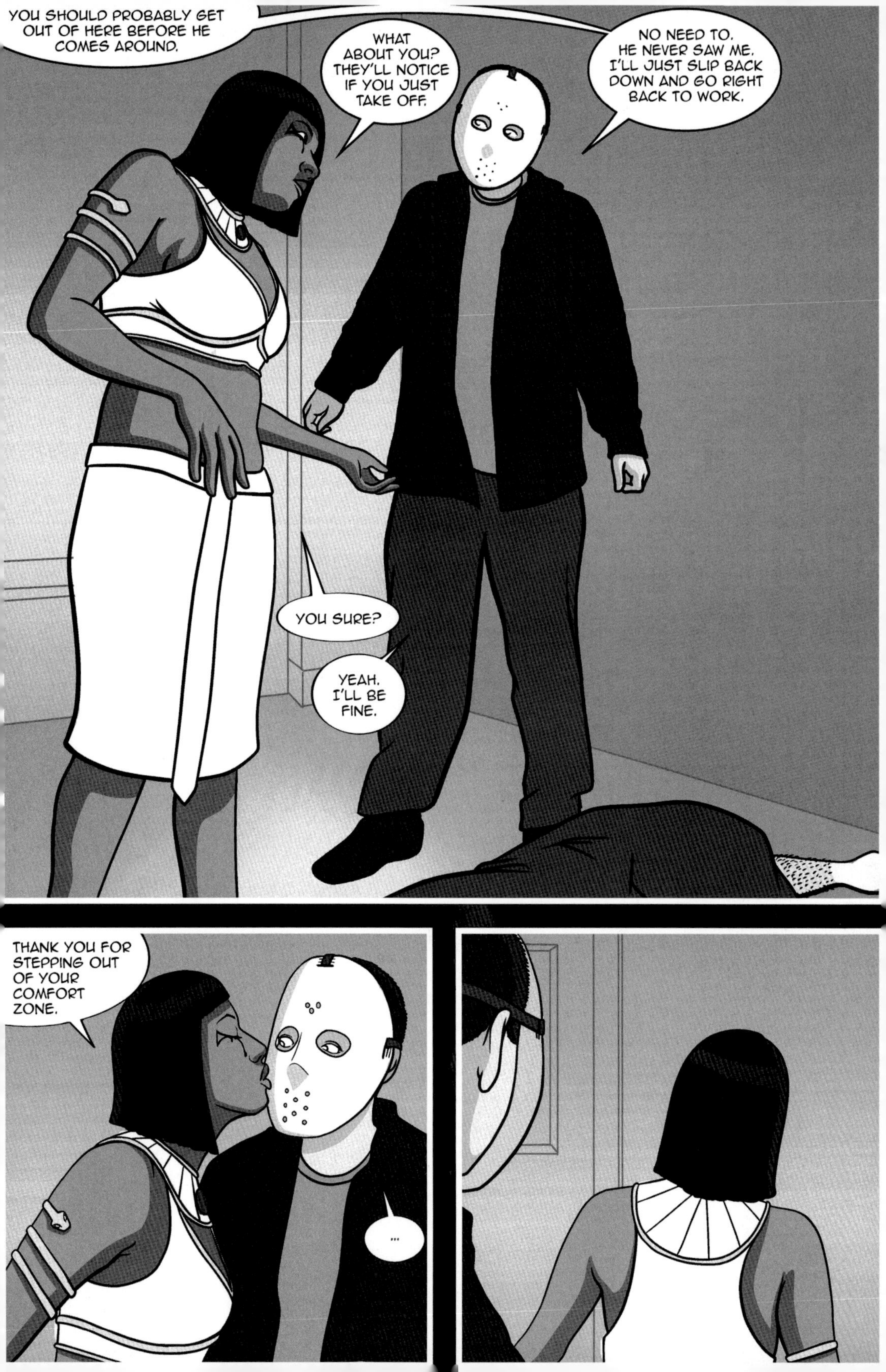
YOU SHOULD PROBABLY GET OUT OF HERE BEFORE HE COMES AROUND.
WHAT ABOUT YOU? THEY'LL NOTICE IF YOU JUST TAKE OFF.
NO NEED TO. HE NEVER SAW ME. I'LL JUST SLIP BACK DOWN AND GO RIGHT BACK TO WORK.
YOU SURE?
YEAH. I'LL BE FINE.
THANK YOU FOR STEPPING OUT OF YOUR COMFORT ZONE.
...

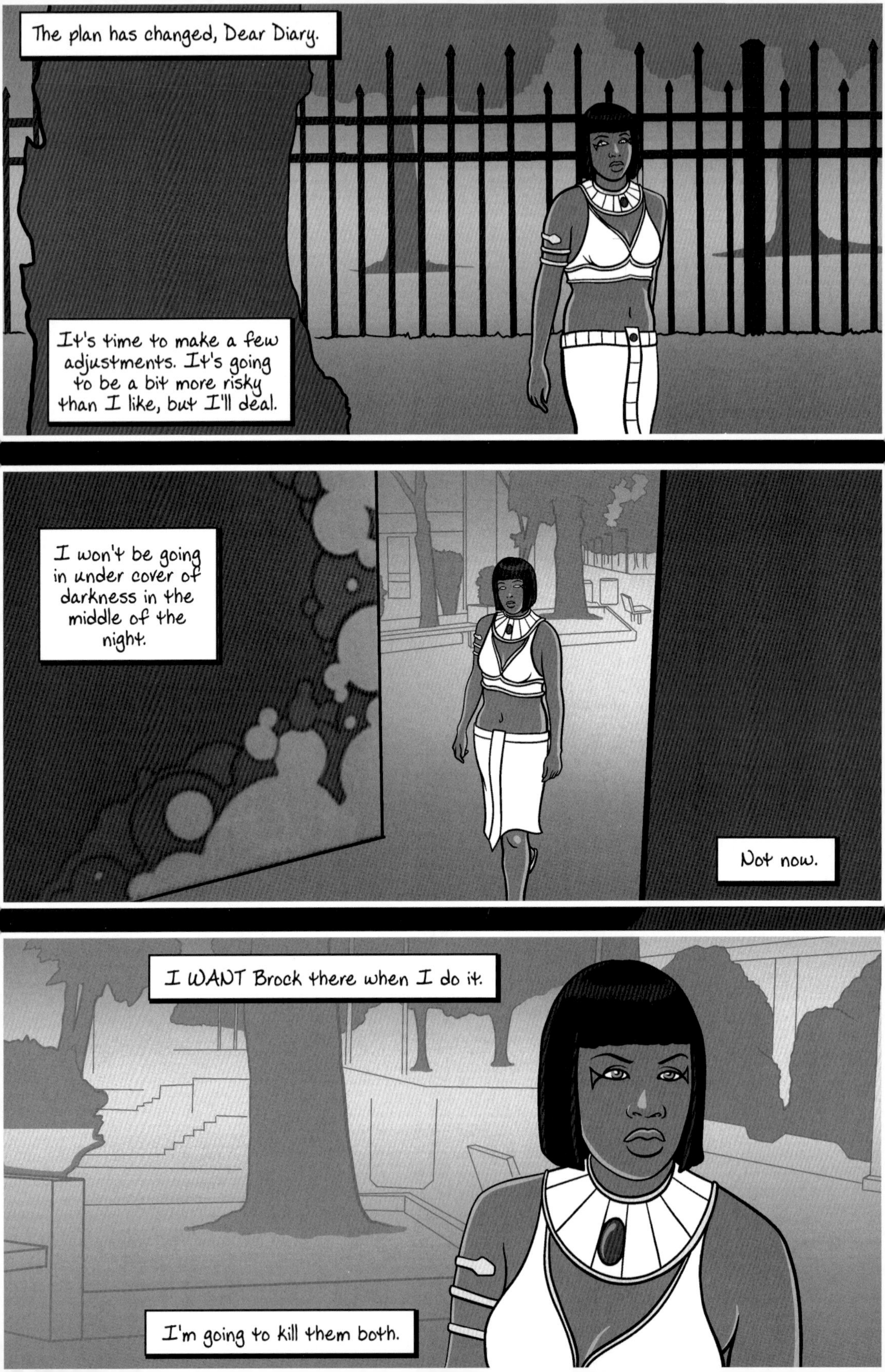
The plan has changed, Dear Diary.
It's time to make a few adjustments. It's going to be a bit more risky than I like, but I'll deal.
I won't be going in under cover of darkness in the middle of the night.
Not now.
I WANT Brock there when I do it.
I'm going to kill them both.

S**t**rikes Again.

Staff Writer | September 10, 2013 | 47 comments

CUTTER'S CIRCLE - A third young woman has been found dead, the victim of an assailant that local media have come to call the Trophy Hunter after his predilection for beautiful, wealthy young women. All three victims were attending Blair University.

The latest victim, identified as 20-year-old Tess Turner, was found in Memorial Park tied to a tree near the deactivated World War II tank. Once again police are withholding details, but they are confident that it is the work of the same person wanted for the murders of Katelyn Miller and Luna Weaks. She is the third victim in just two weeks.

"We're dealing with a clever and dangerous individual who is not slowing down and will not stop on his own," said Detective Sergeant Ezekiel Aarons of the CCPD. "Already he's a prolific killer, striking three times in less than three weeks. We need the community's help if we're going to find him before he kills again."

Anyone with information is encouraged to call the CCPD tip line at 555-8344. The victims' families are offering a $500k reward for information leading to a conviction.

Katelyn Miller (left), and Luna Weaks (right)

Trinna Goff
Out Of Coma

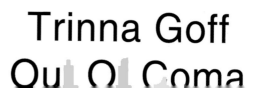

a VOICE in the DARK

"KILLING GAME, PT. 5"

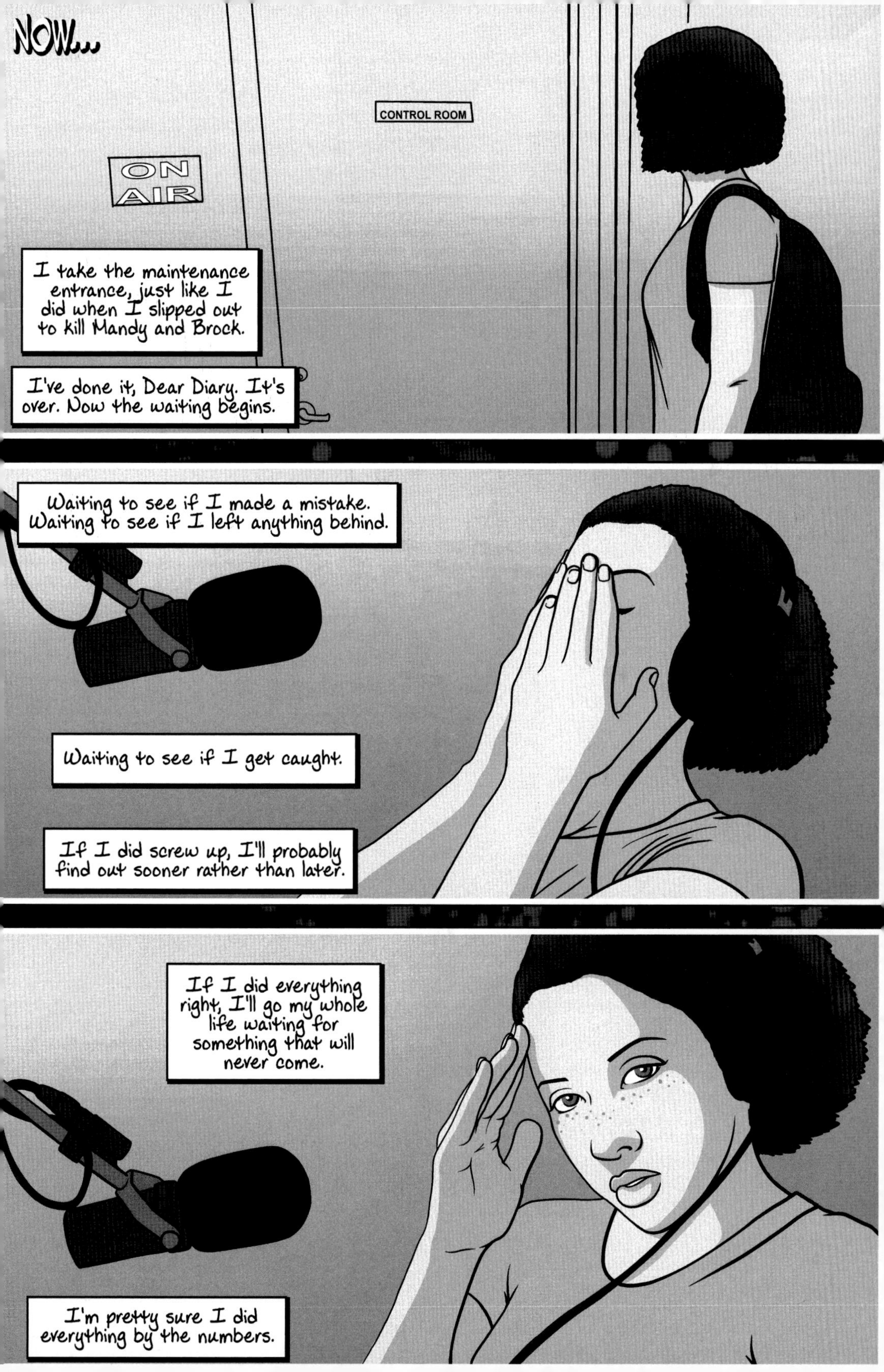
NOW...
CONTROL ROOM
ON AIR
I take the maintenance entrance, just like I did when I slipped out to kill Mandy and Brock.
I've done it, Dear Diary. It's over. Now the waiting begins.
Waiting to see if I made a mistake. Waiting to see if I left anything behind.
Waiting to see if I get caught.
If I did screw up, I'll probably find out sooner rather than later.
If I did everything right, I'll go my whole life waiting for something that will never come.
I'm pretty sure I did everything by the numbers.

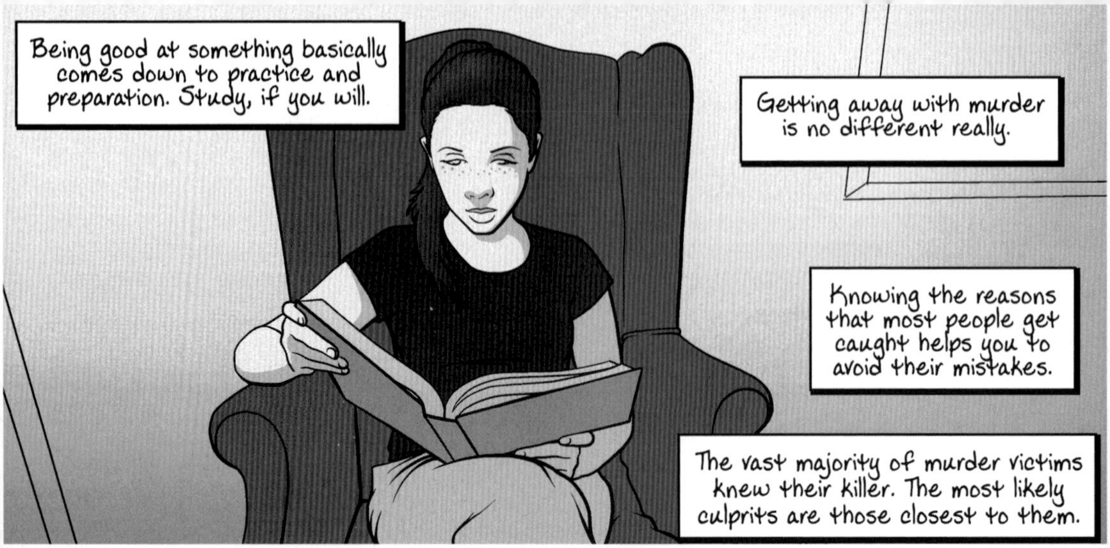
Being good at something basically comes down to practice and preparation. Study, if you will.
Getting away with murder is no different really.
Knowing the reasons that most people get caught helps you to avoid their mistakes.
The vast majority of murder victims knew their killer. The most likely culprits are those closest to them.

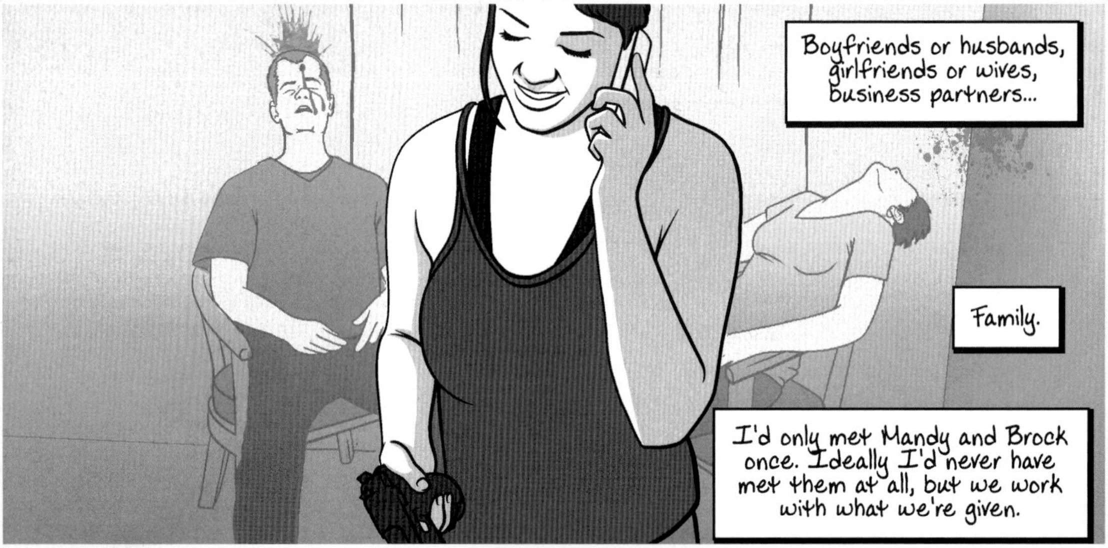
Boyfriends or husbands, girlfriends or wives, business partners...
Family.
I'd only met Mandy and Brock once. Ideally I'd never have met them at all, but we work with what we're given.

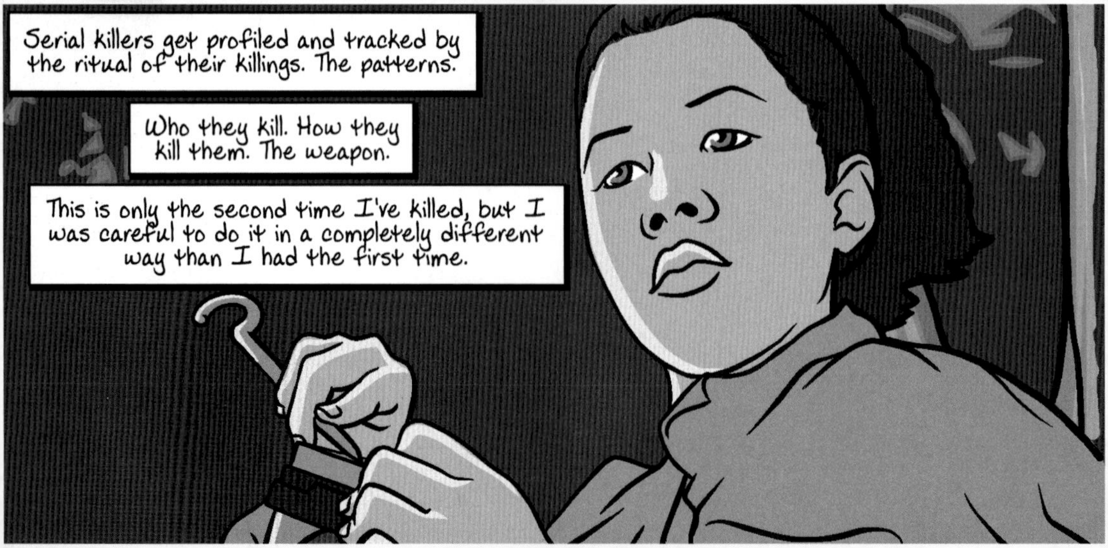
Serial killers get profiled and tracked by the ritual of their killings. The patterns.
Who they kill. How they kill them. The weapon.
This is only the second time I've killed, but I was careful to do it in a completely different way than I had the first time.

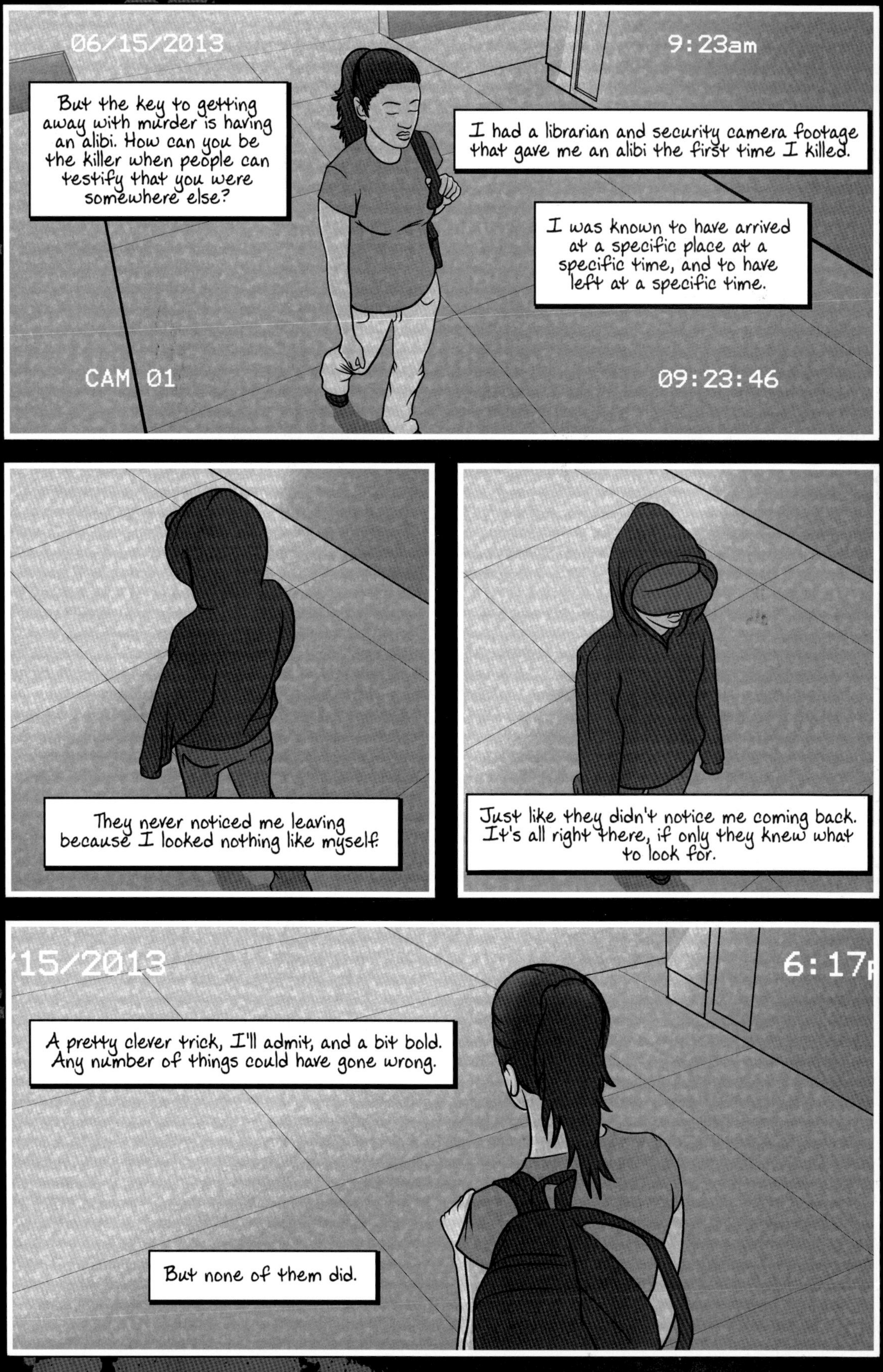
06/15/2013
9:23am
But the key to getting away with murder is having an alibi. How can you be the killer when people can testify that you were somewhere else?
I had a librarian and security camera footage that gave me an alibi the first time I killed.
I was known to have arrived at a specific place at a specific time, and to have left at a specific time.
CAM 01
09:23:46
They never noticed me leaving because I looked nothing like myself.
Just like they didn't notice me coming back. It's all right there, if only they knew what to look for.
/15/2013
6:17
A pretty clever trick, I'll admit, and a bit bold. Any number of things could have gone wrong.
But none of them did.

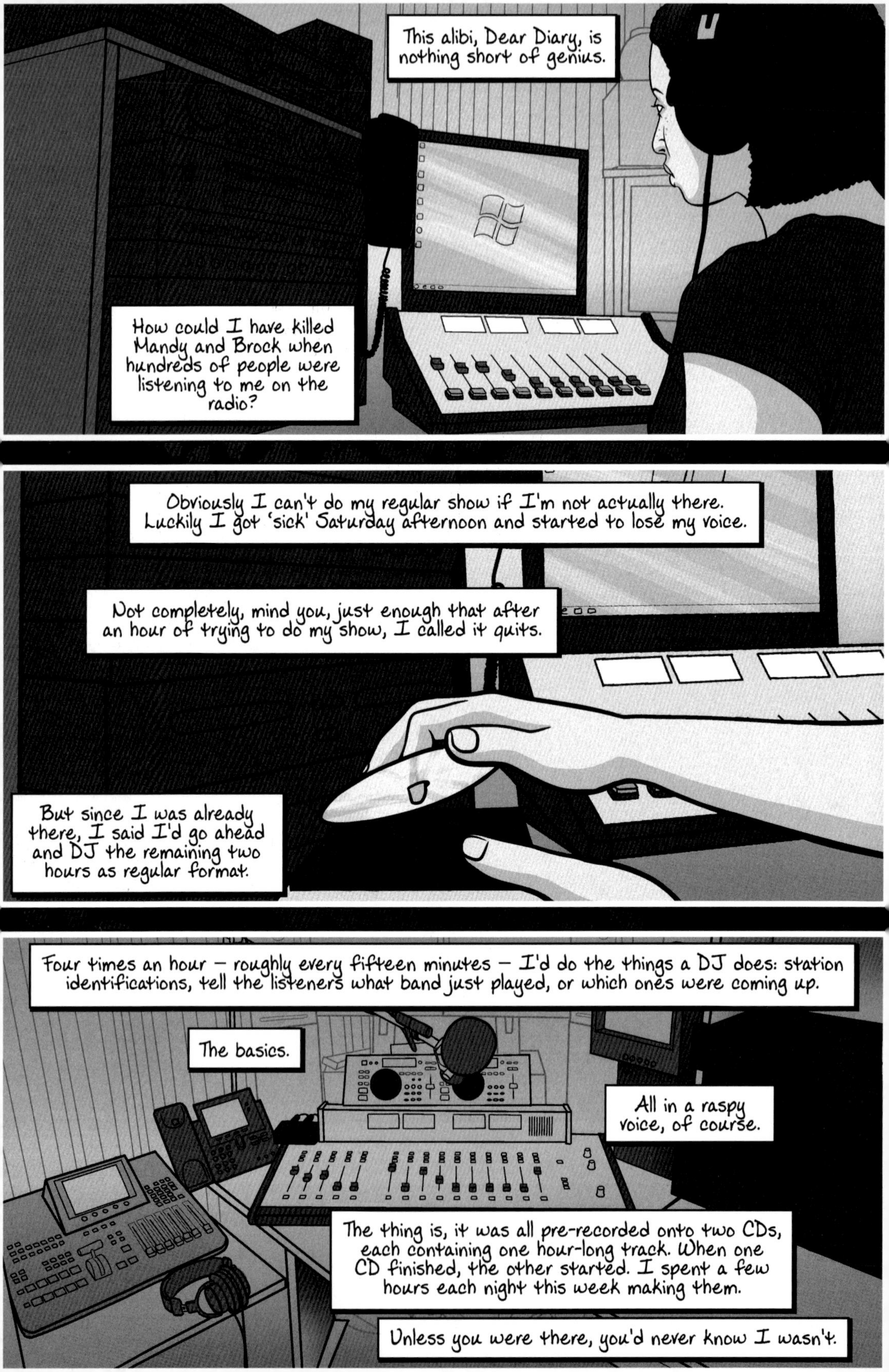
This alibi, Dear Diary, is nothing short of genius.
How could I have killed Mandy and Brock when hundreds of people were listening to me on the radio?
Obviously I can't do my regular show if I'm not actually there. Luckily I got 'sick' Saturday afternoon and started to lose my voice.
Not completely, mind you, just enough that after an hour of trying to do my show, I called it quits.
But since I was already there, I said I'd go ahead and DJ the remaining two hours as regular format.
Four times an hour – roughly every fifteen minutes – I'd do the things a DJ does: station identifications, tell the listeners what band just played, or which ones were coming up.
The basics.
All in a raspy voice, of course.
The thing is, it was all pre-recorded onto two CDs, each containing one hour-long track. When one CD finished, the other started. I spent a few hours each night this week making them.
Unless you were there, you'd never know I wasn't.

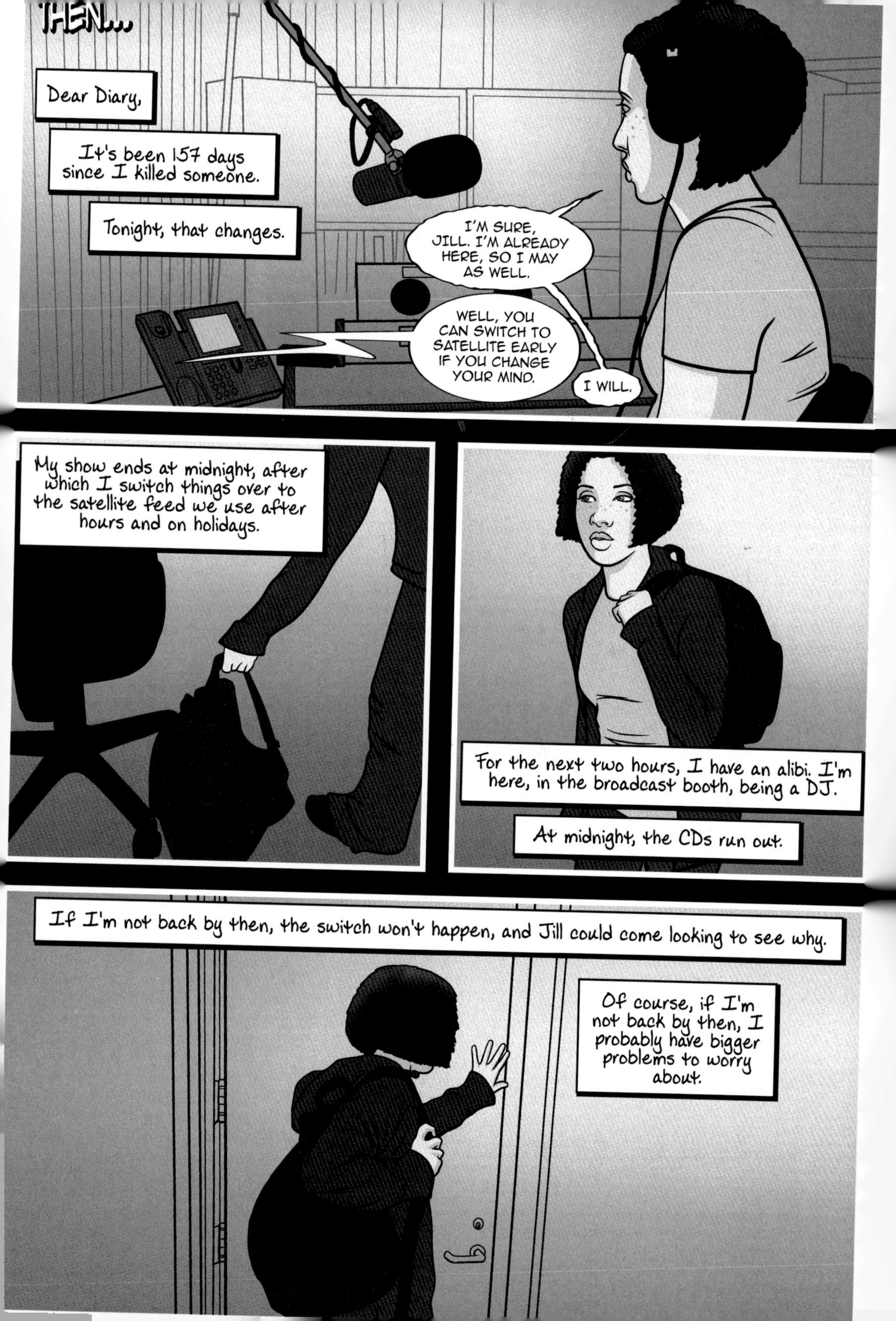
THEN...
Dear Diary,
It's been 157 days since I killed someone.
Tonight, that changes.
I'M SURE, JILL. I'M ALREADY HERE, SO I MAY AS WELL.
WELL, YOU CAN SWITCH TO SATELLITE EARLY IF YOU CHANGE YOUR MIND.
I WILL.
My show ends at midnight, after which I switch things over to the satellite feed we use after hours and on holidays.
For the next two hours, I have an alibi. I'm here, in the broadcast booth, being a DJ.
At midnight, the CDs run out.
If I'm not back by then, the switch won't happen, and Jill could come looking to see why.
Of course, if I'm not back by then, I probably have bigger problems to worry about.

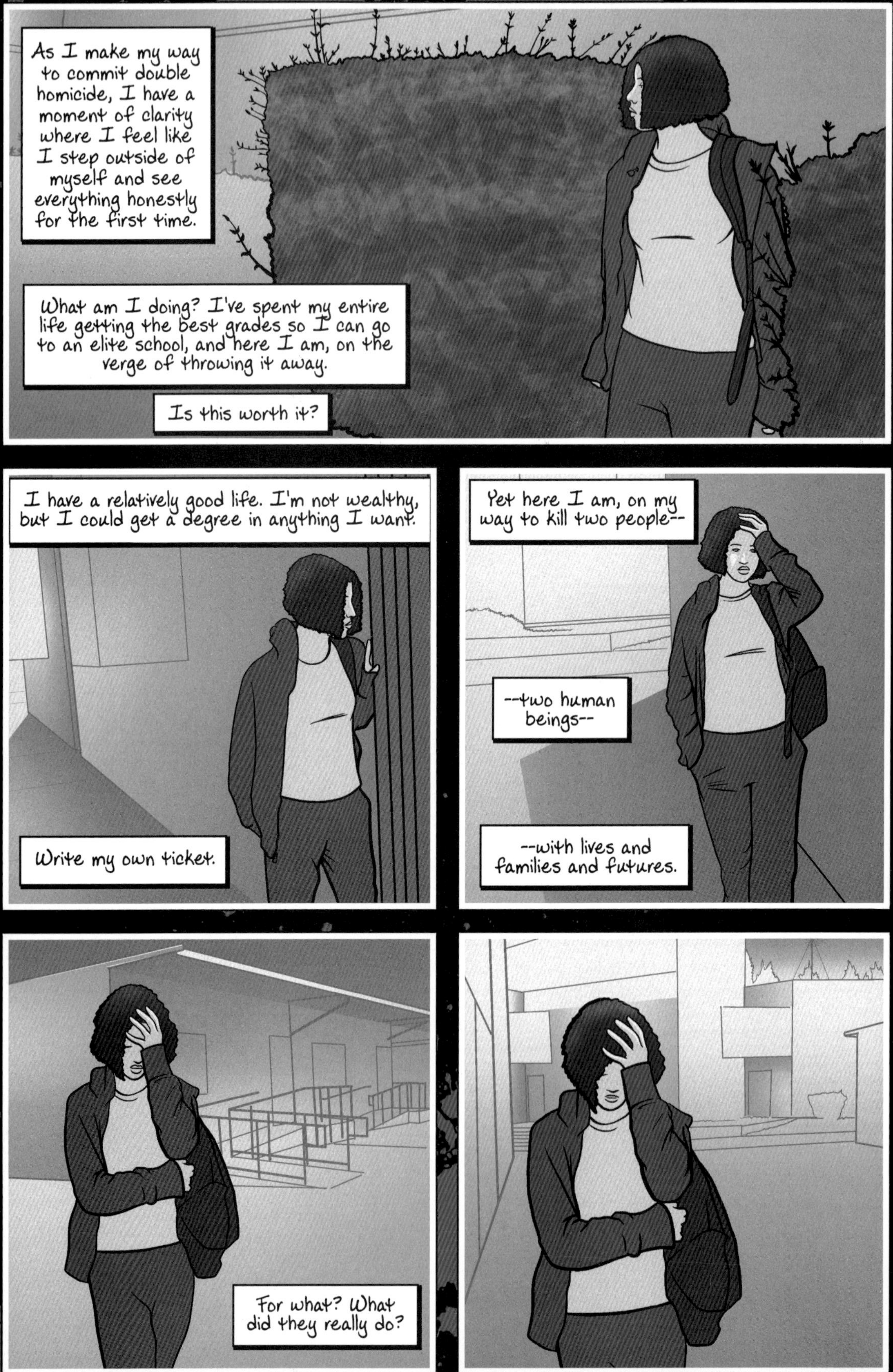
As I make my way to commit double homicide, I have a moment of clarity where I feel like I step outside of myself and see everything honestly for the first time.
What am I doing? I've spent my entire life getting the best grades so I can go to an elite school, and here I am, on the verge of throwing it away.
Is this worth it?
I have a relatively good life. I'm not wealthy, but I could get a degree in anything I want.
Write my own ticket.
Yet here I am, on my way to kill two people--
--two human beings--
--with lives and families and futures.
For what? What did they really do?

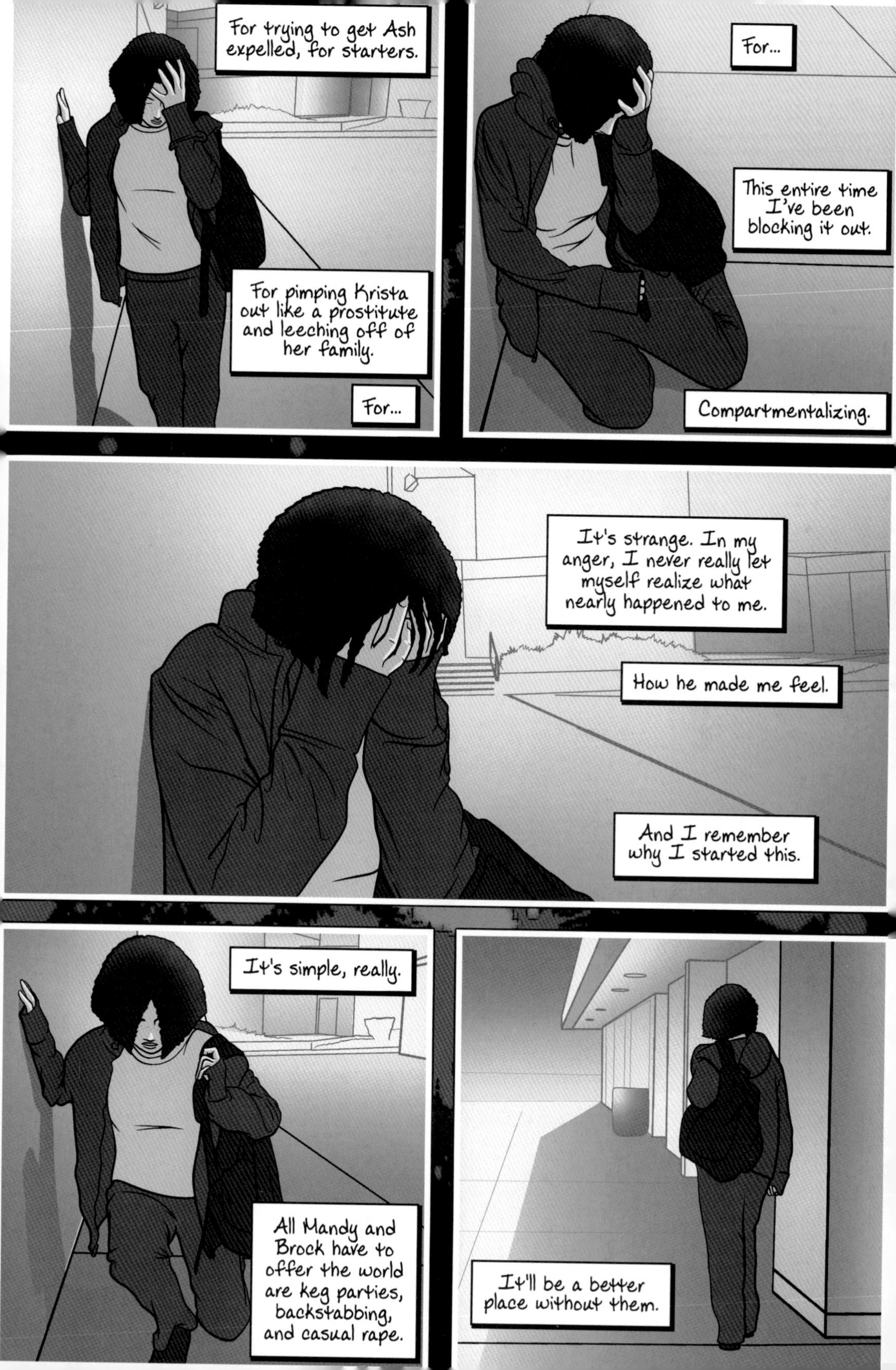
For trying to get Ash expelled, for starters.
For pimping Krista out like a prostitute and leeching off of her family.
For...
For...
This entire time I've been blocking it out.
Compartmentalizing.
It's strange. In my anger, I never really let myself realize what nearly happened to me.
How he made me feel.
And I remember why I started this.
It's simple, really.
All Mandy and Brock have to offer the world are keg parties, backstabbing, and casual rape.
It'll be a better place without them.

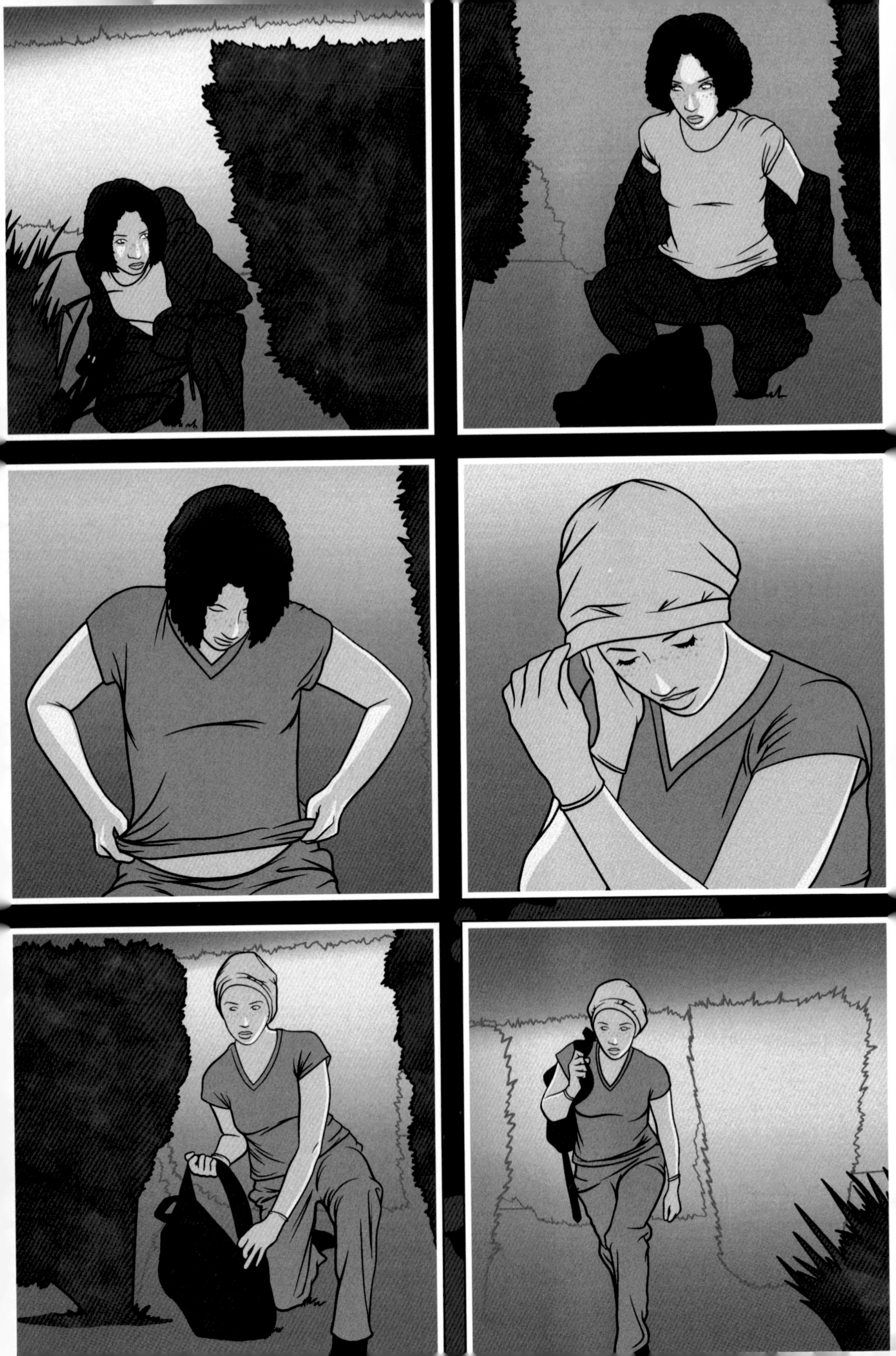

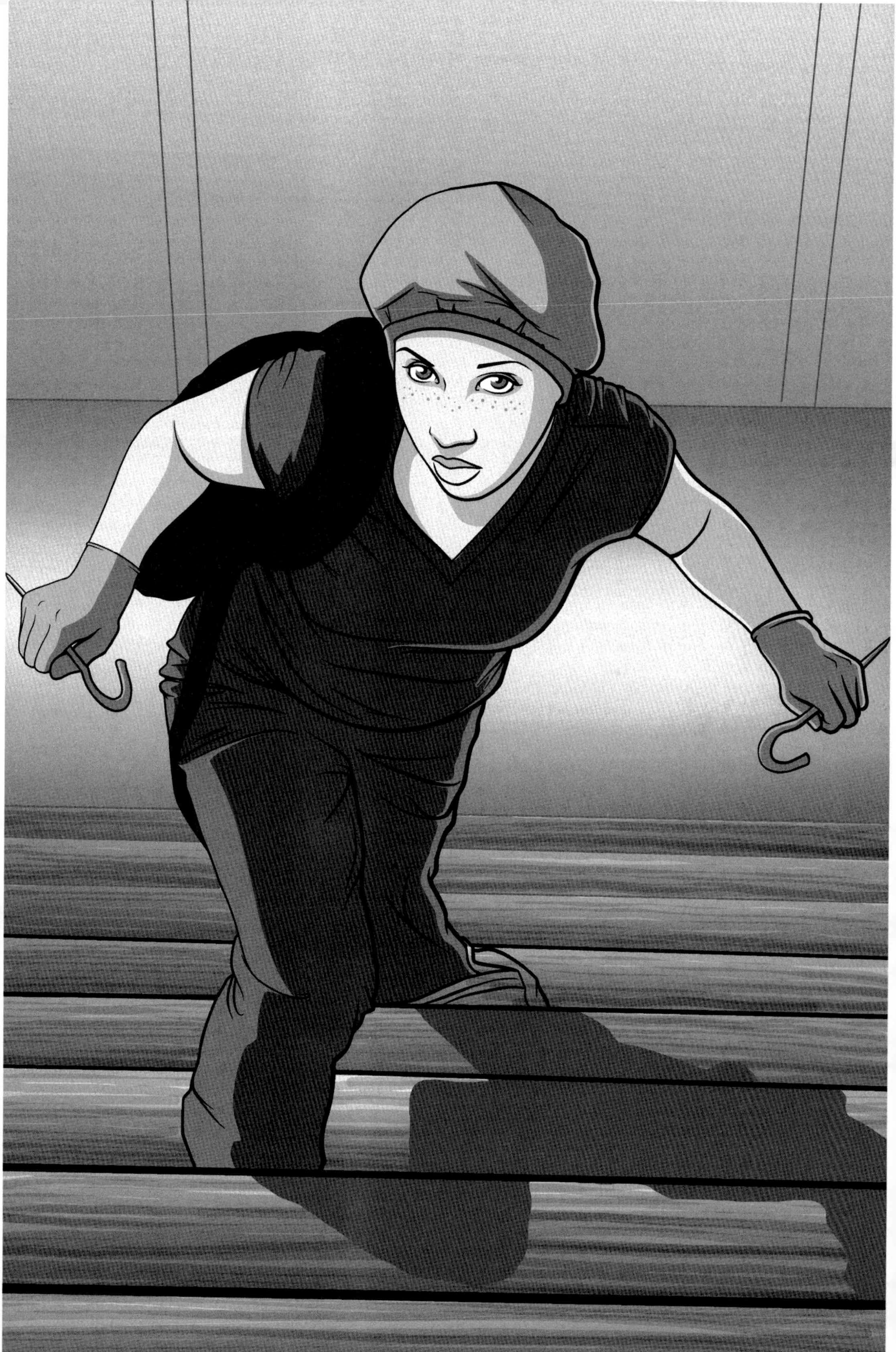

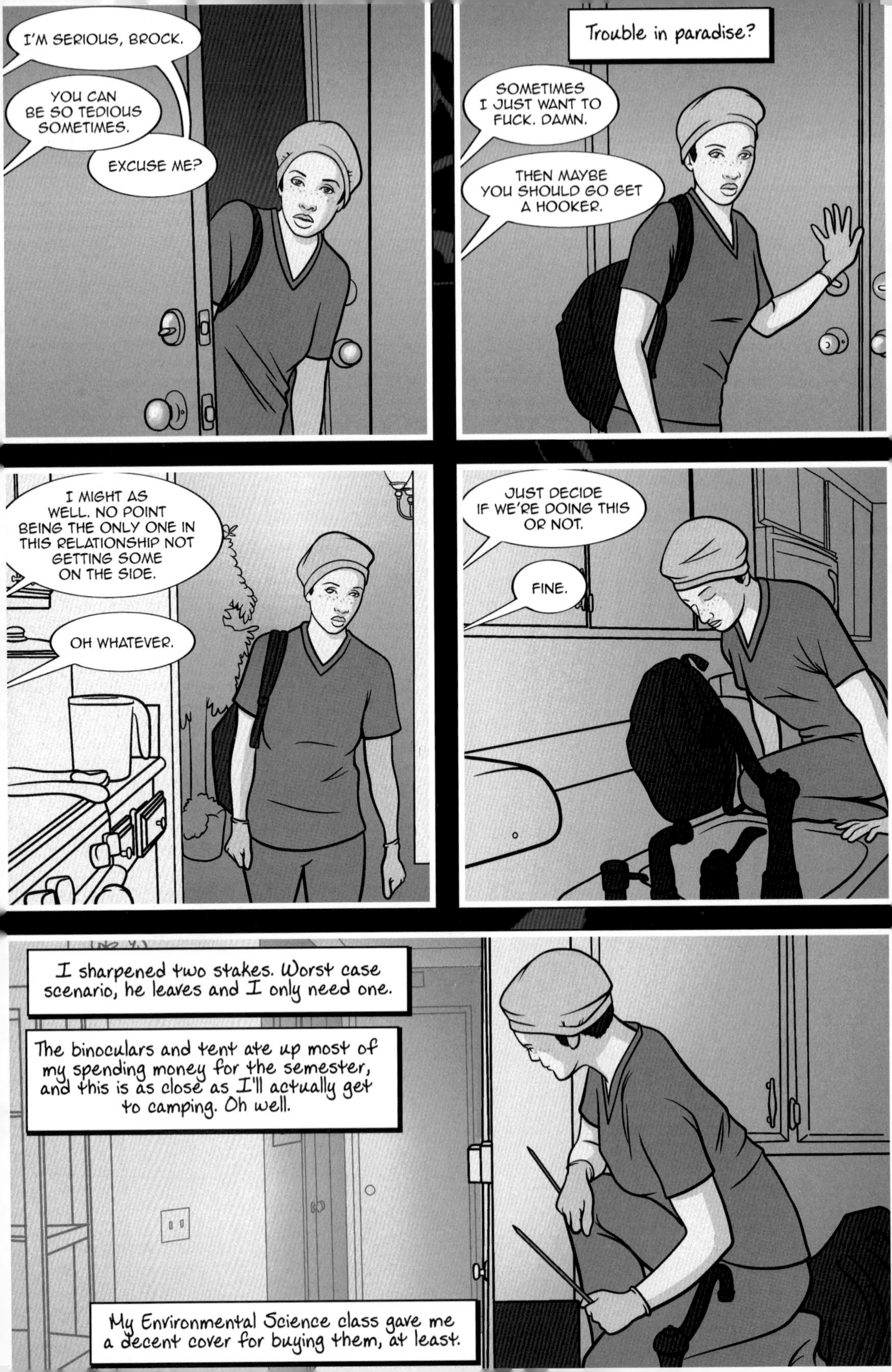
I'M SERIOUS, BROCK.
YOU CAN BE SO TEDIOUS SOMETIMES.
EXCUSE ME?
Trouble in paradise?
SOMETIMES I JUST WANT TO FUCK. DAMN.
THEN MAYBE YOU SHOULD GO GET A HOOKER.
I MIGHT AS WELL. NO POINT BEING THE ONLY ONE IN THIS RELATIONSHIP NOT GETTING SOME ON THE SIDE.
OH WHATEVER.
JUST DECIDE IF WE'RE DOING THIS OR NOT.
FINE.
I sharpened two stakes. Worst case scenario, he leaves and I only need one.
The binoculars and tent ate up most of my spending money for the semester, and this is as close as I'll actually get to camping. Oh well.
My Environmental Science class gave me a decent cover for buying them, at least.

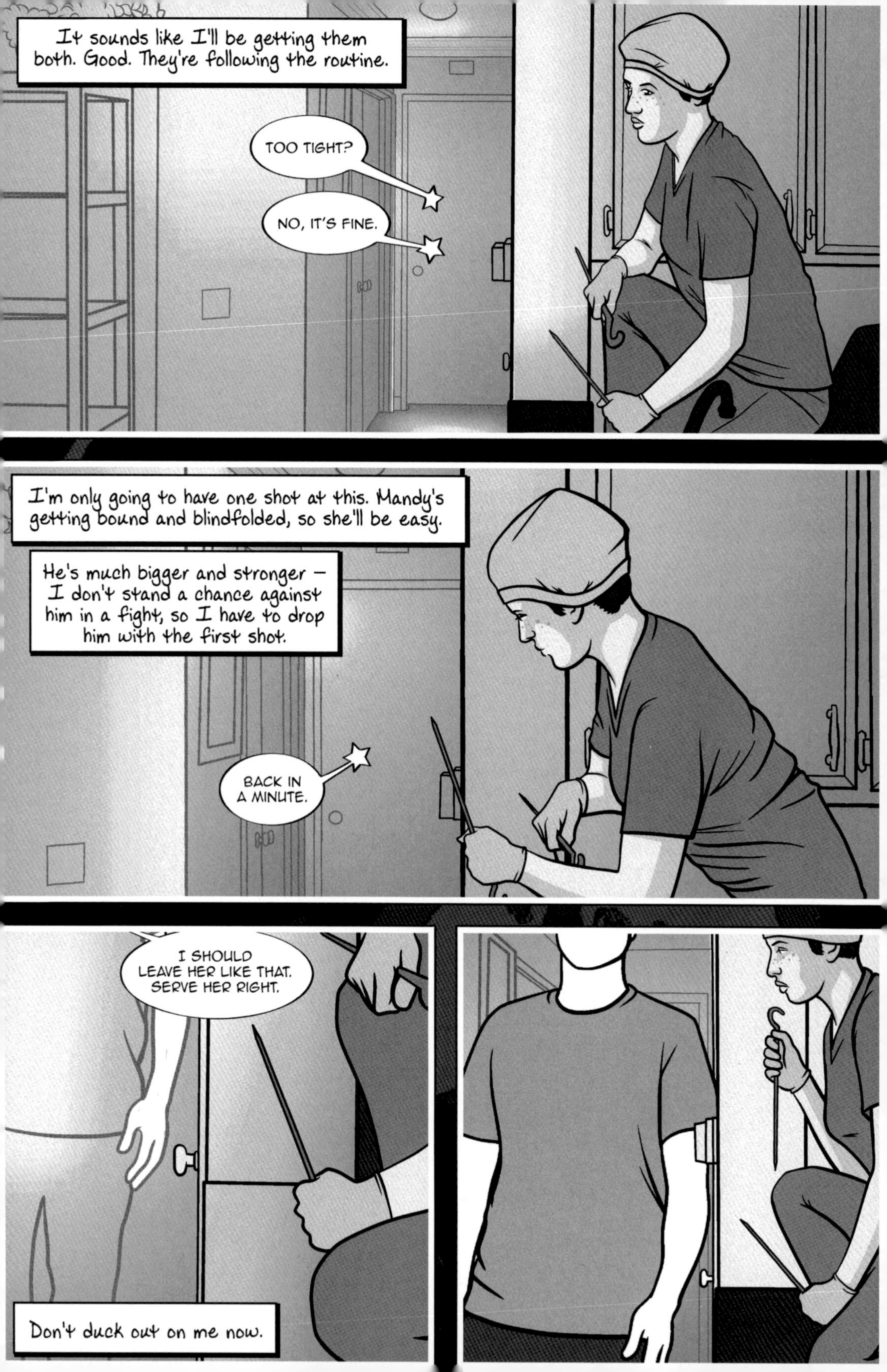
It sounds like I'll be getting them both. Good. They're following the routine.
TOO TIGHT?
NO, IT'S FINE.
I'm only going to have one shot at this. Mandy's getting bound and blindfolded, so she'll be easy.
He's much bigger and stronger — I don't stand a chance against him in a fight, so I have to drop him with the first shot.
BACK IN A MINUTE.
I SHOULD LEAVE HER LIKE THAT. SERVE HER RIGHT.
Don't duck out on me now.

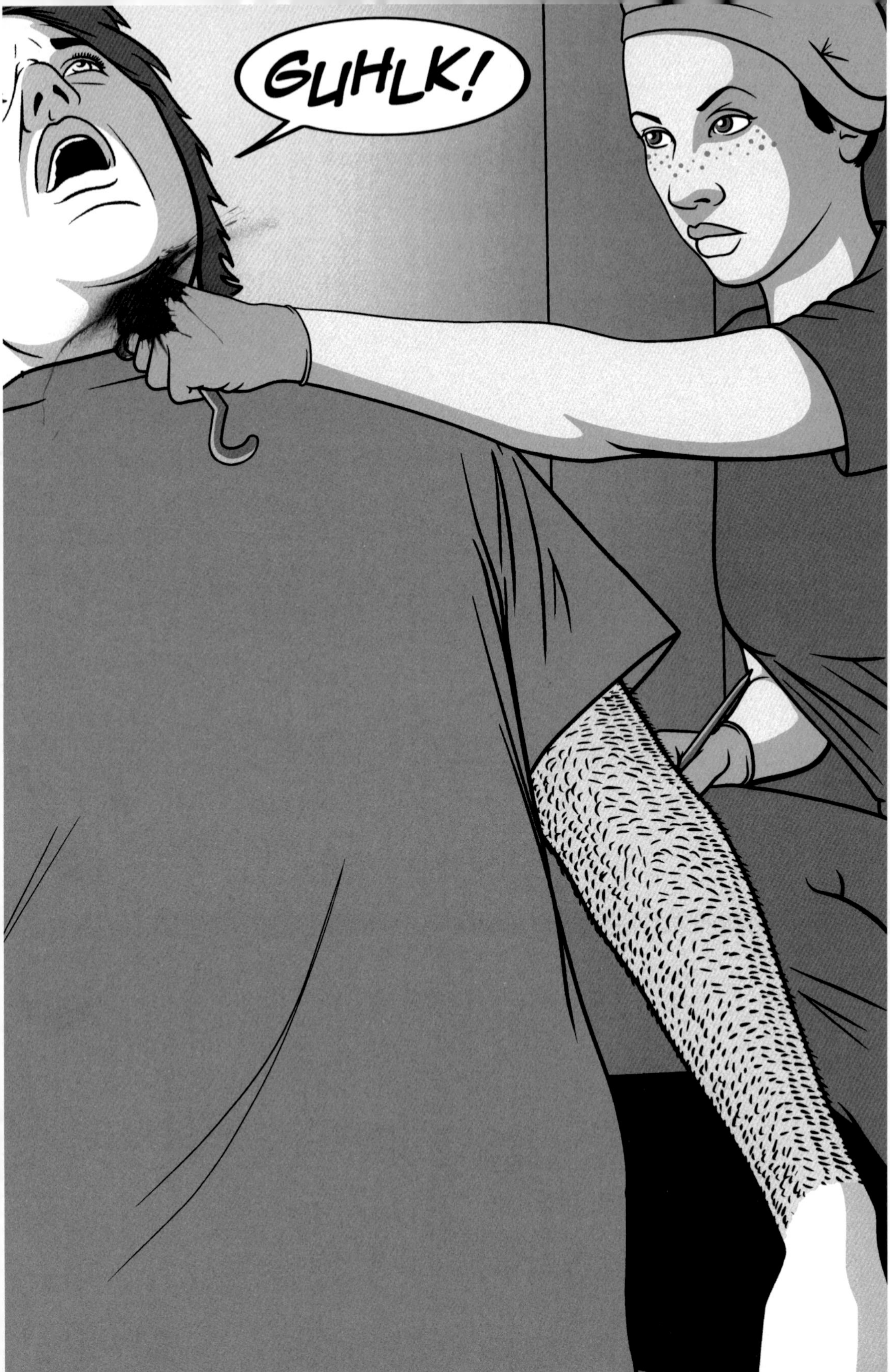
GUHLK!

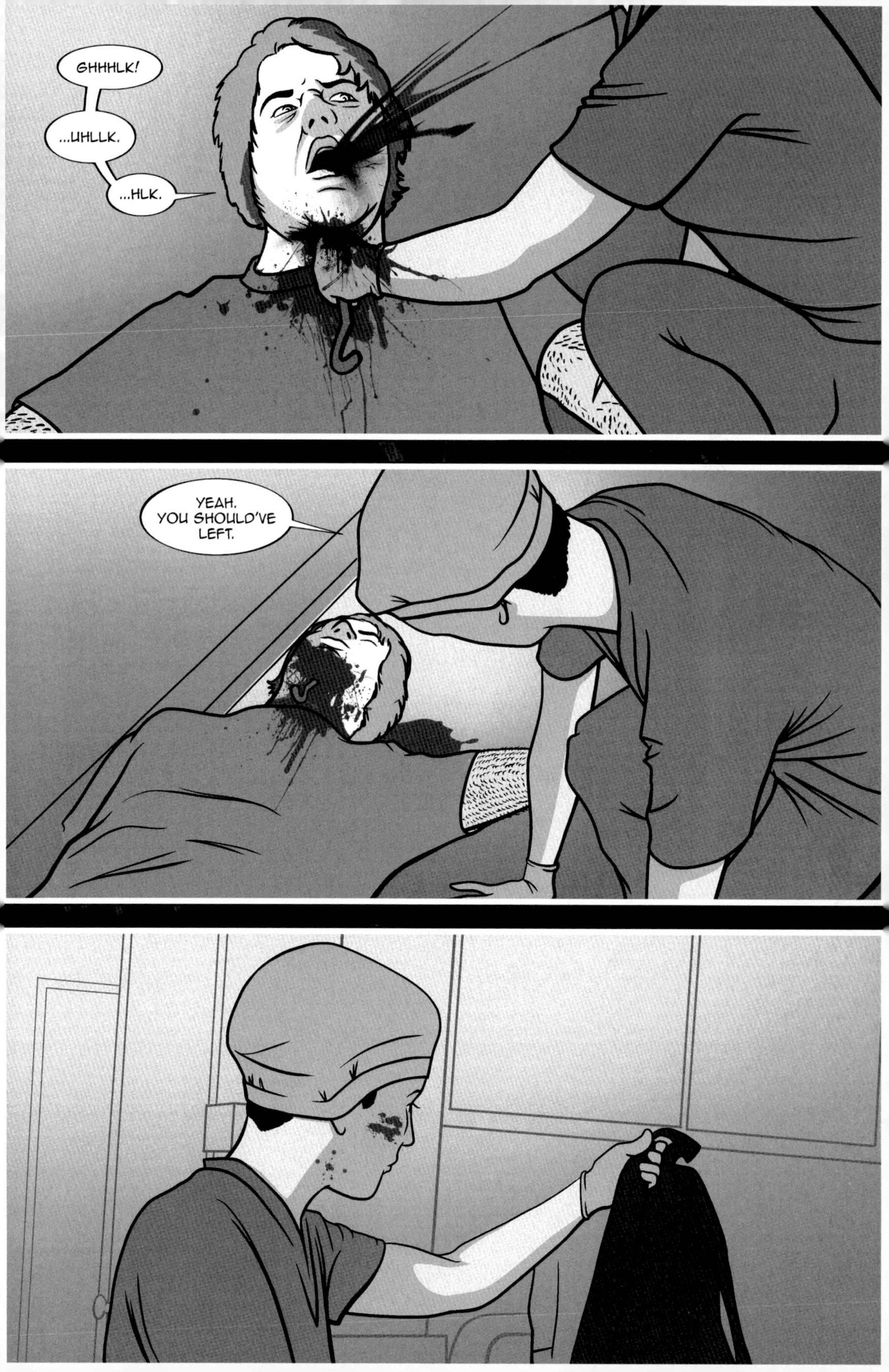
GHHHLK!
...UHLLK.
...HLK.
YEAH. YOU SHOULD'VE LEFT.

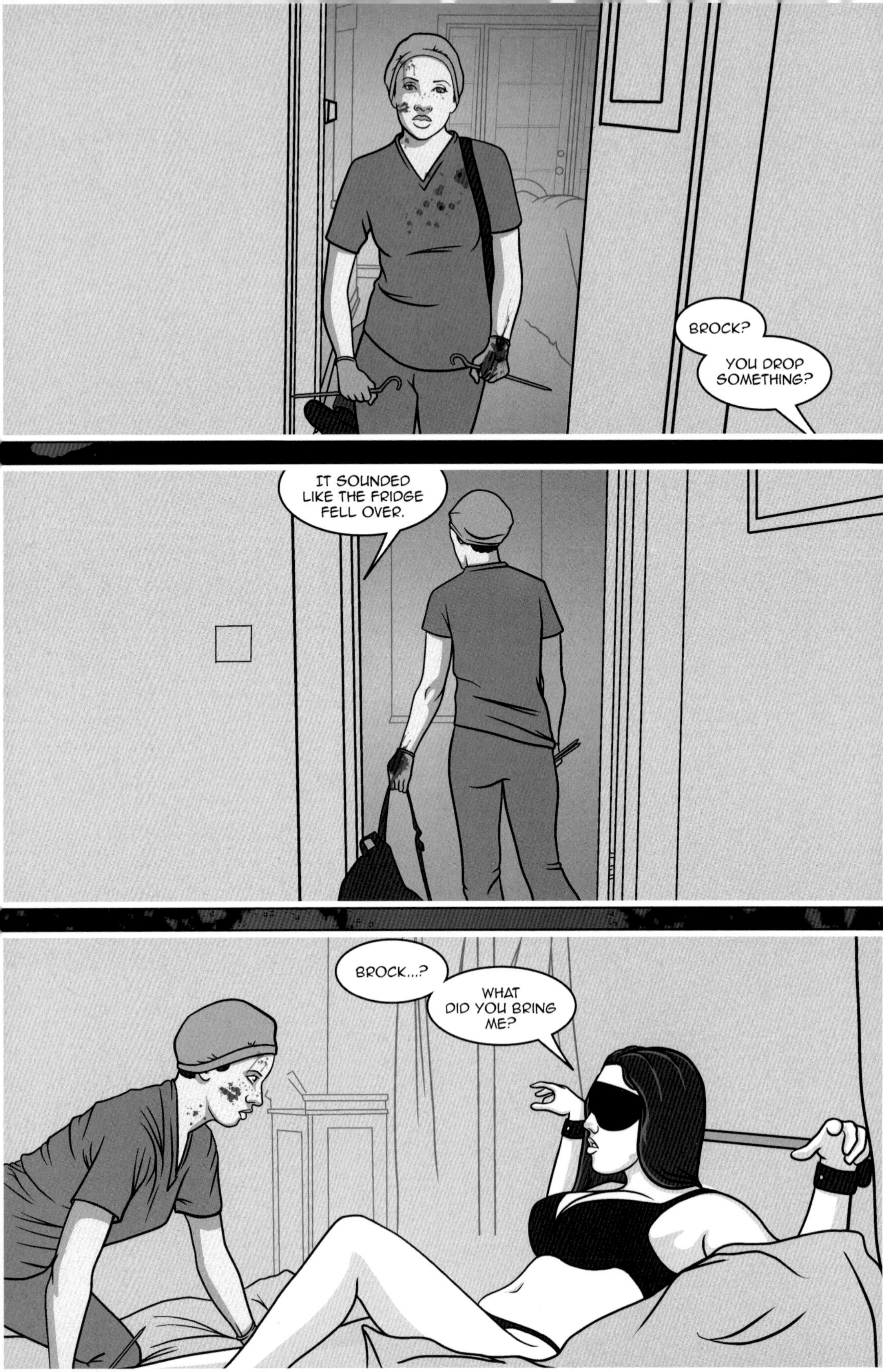
BROCK?
YOU DROP SOMETHING?
IT SOUNDED LIKE THE FRIDGE FELL OVER.
BROCK...?
WHAT DID YOU BRING ME?

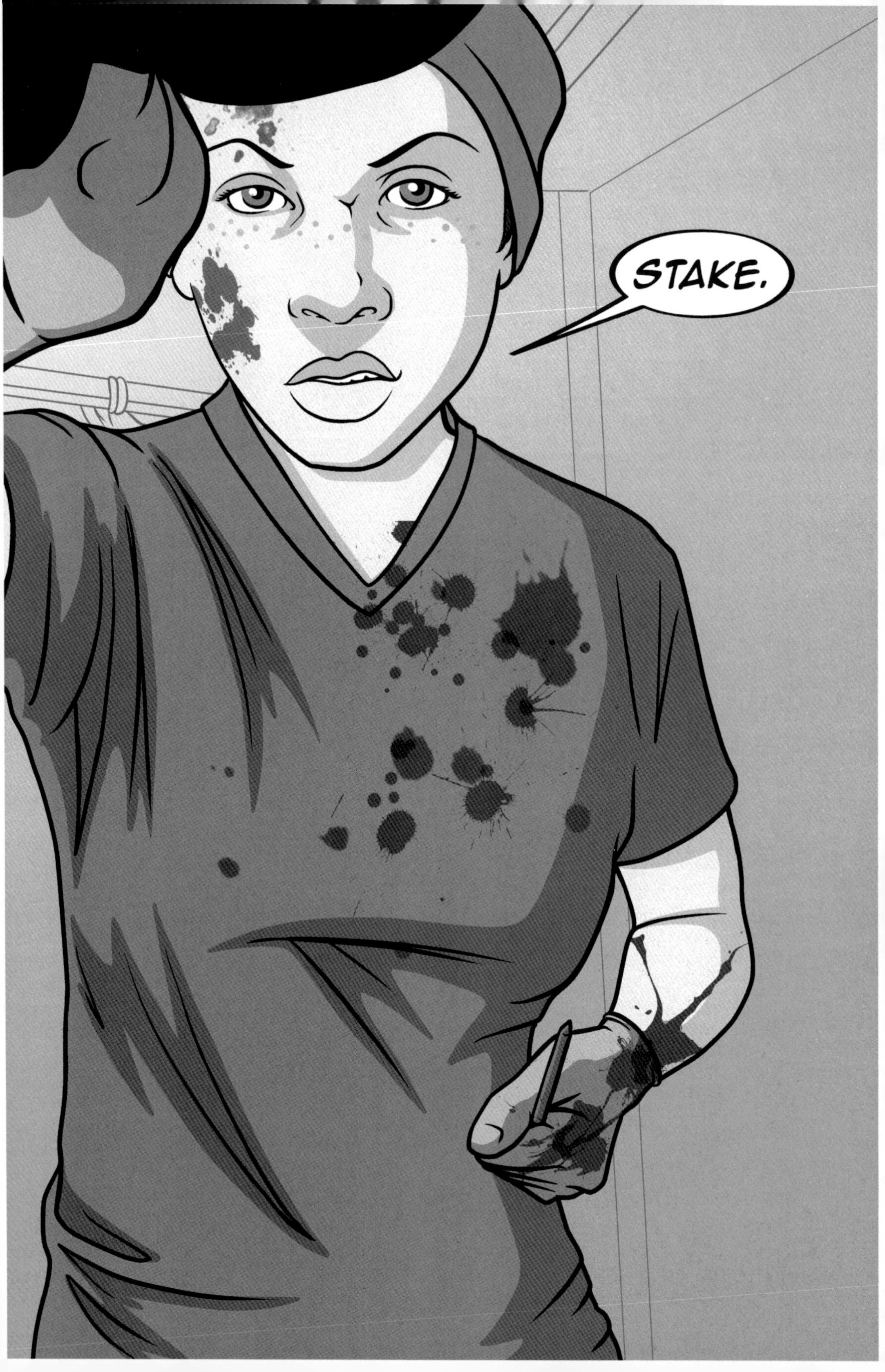
STAKE.

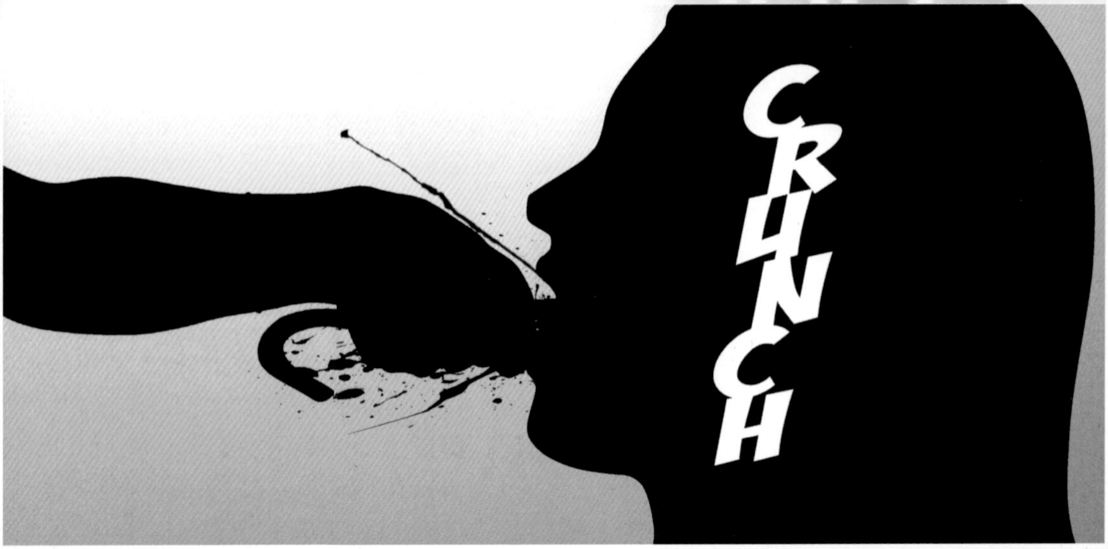
CRUNCH

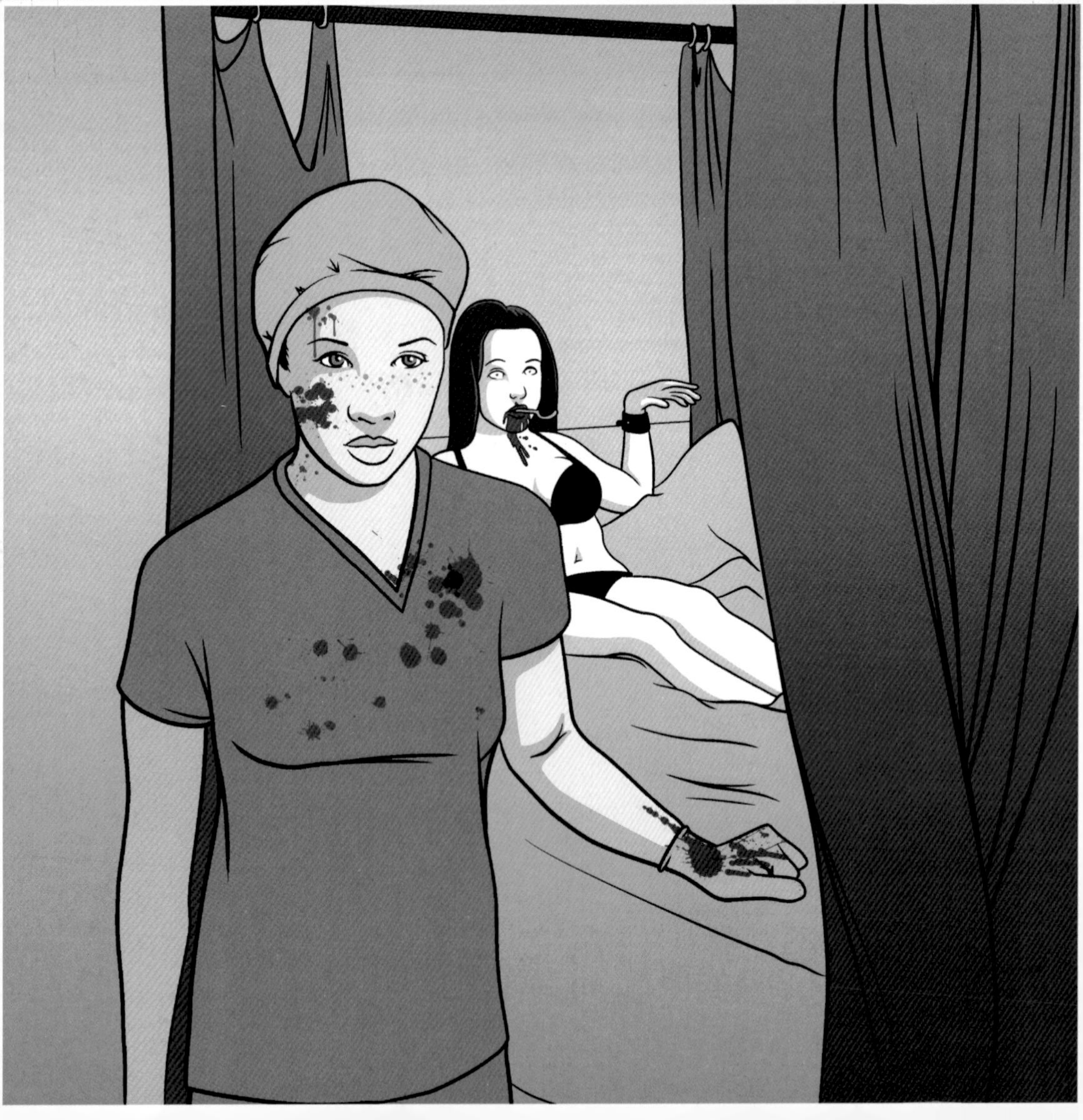

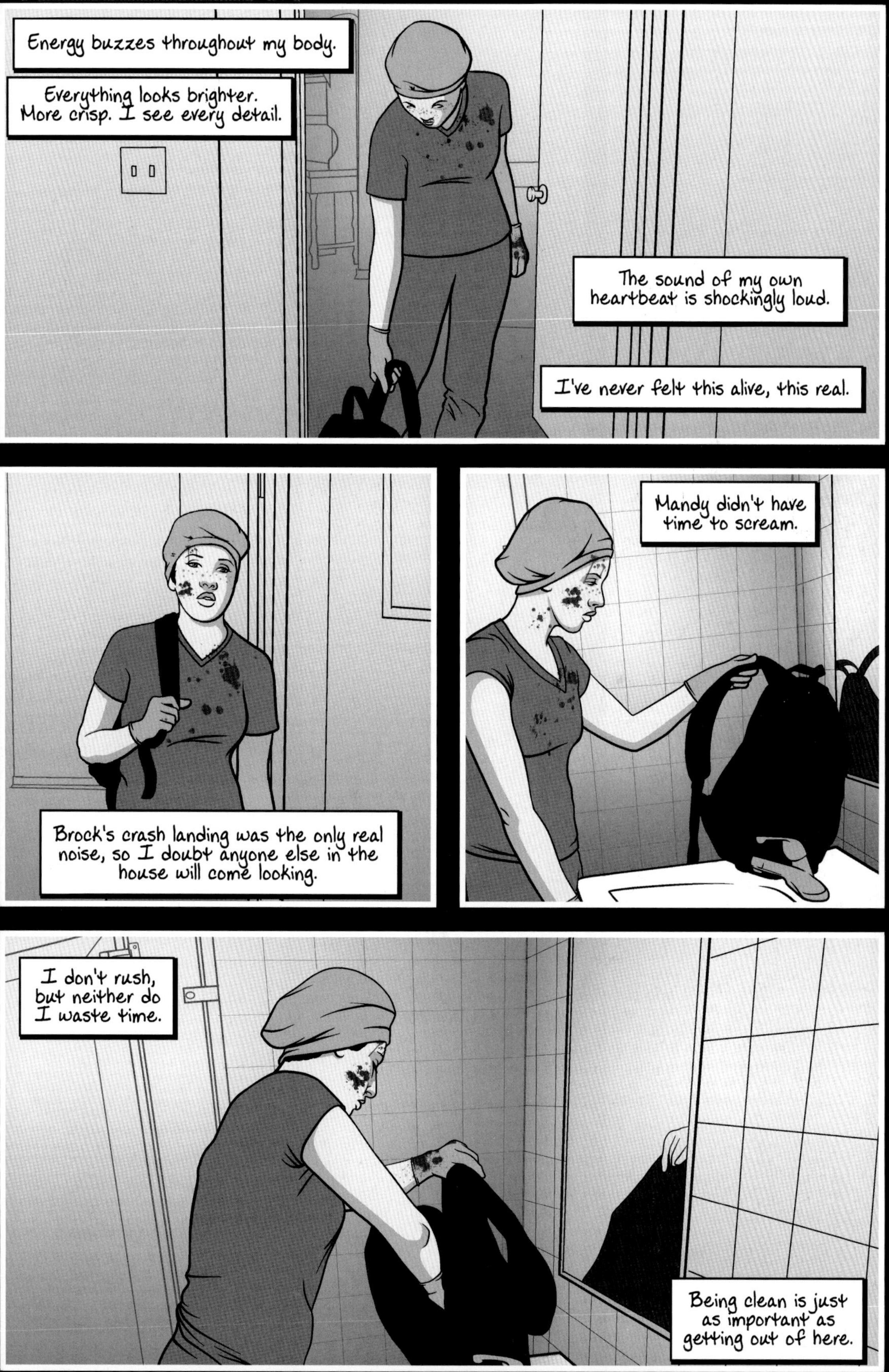
Energy buzzes throughout my body.
Everything looks brighter. More crisp. I see every detail.
The sound of my own heartbeat is shockingly loud.
I've never felt this alive, this real.
Brock's crash landing was the only real noise, so I doubt anyone else in the house will come looking.
Mandy didn't have time to scream.
I don't rush, but neither do I waste time.
Being clean is just as important as getting out of here.

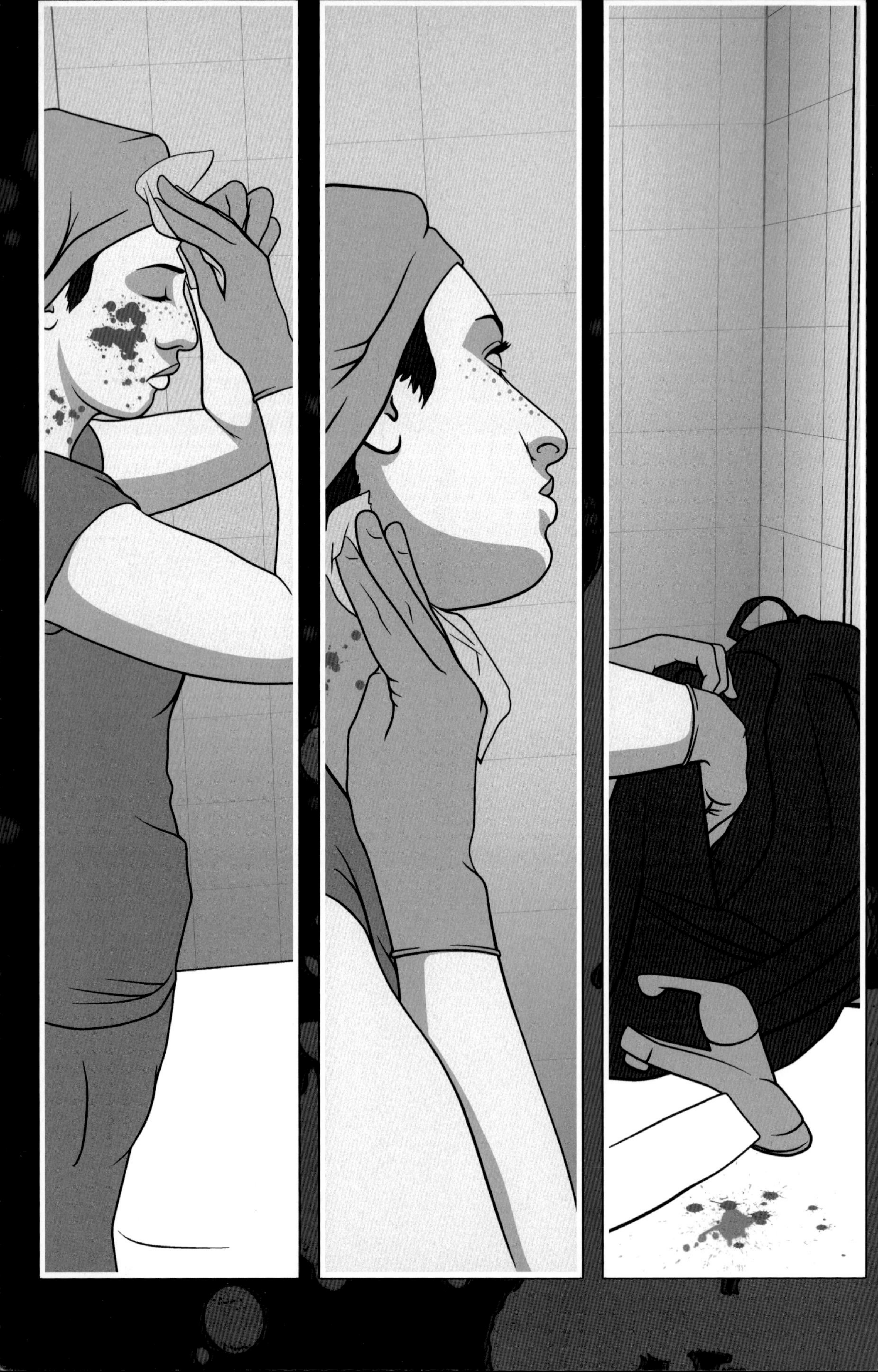

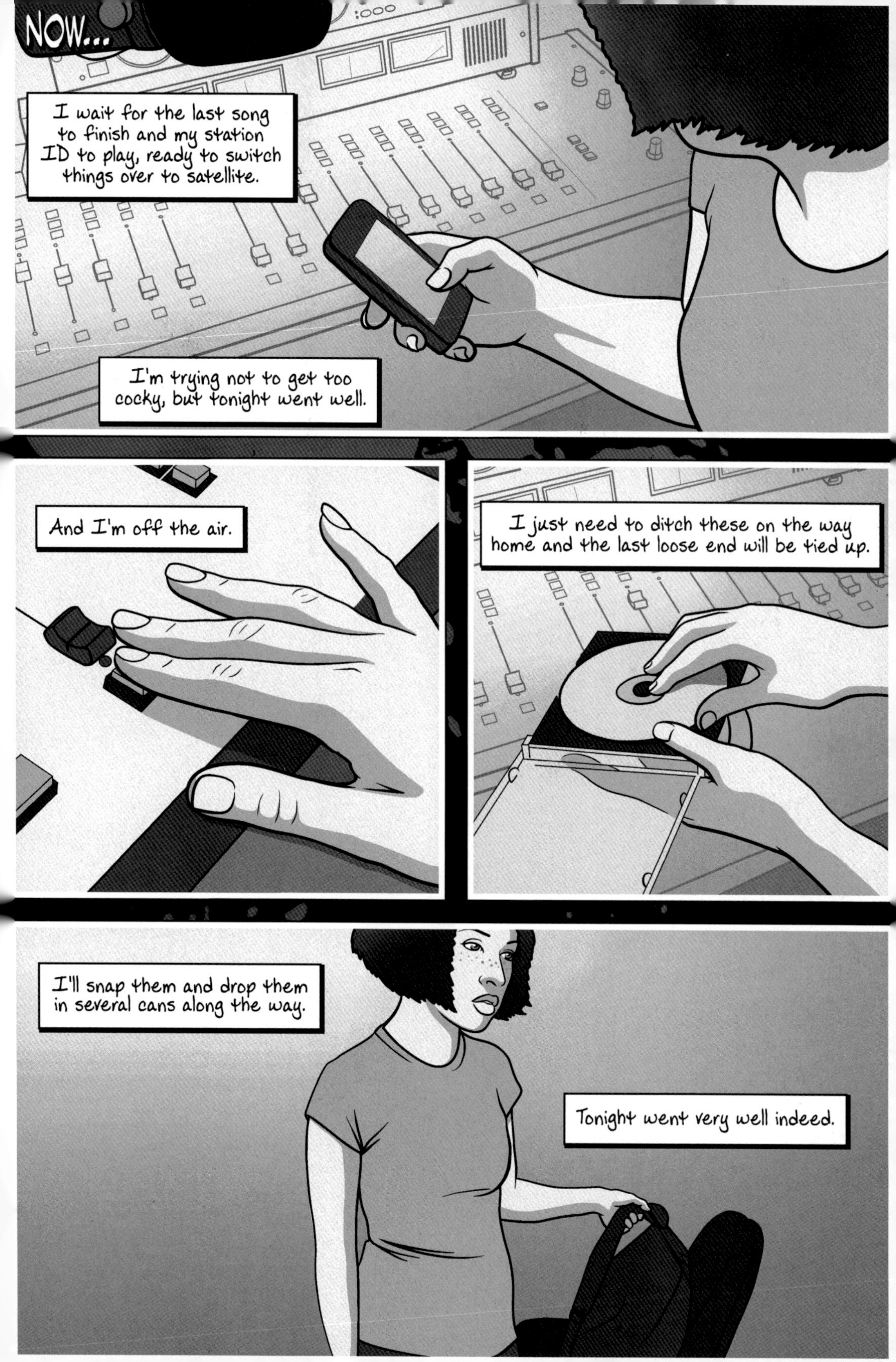
NOW...
I wait for the last song to finish and my station ID to play, ready to switch things over to satellite.
I'm trying not to get too cocky, but tonight went well.
And I'm off the air.
I just need to ditch these on the way home and the last loose end will be tied up.
I'll snap them and drop them in several cans along the way.
Tonight went very well indeed.

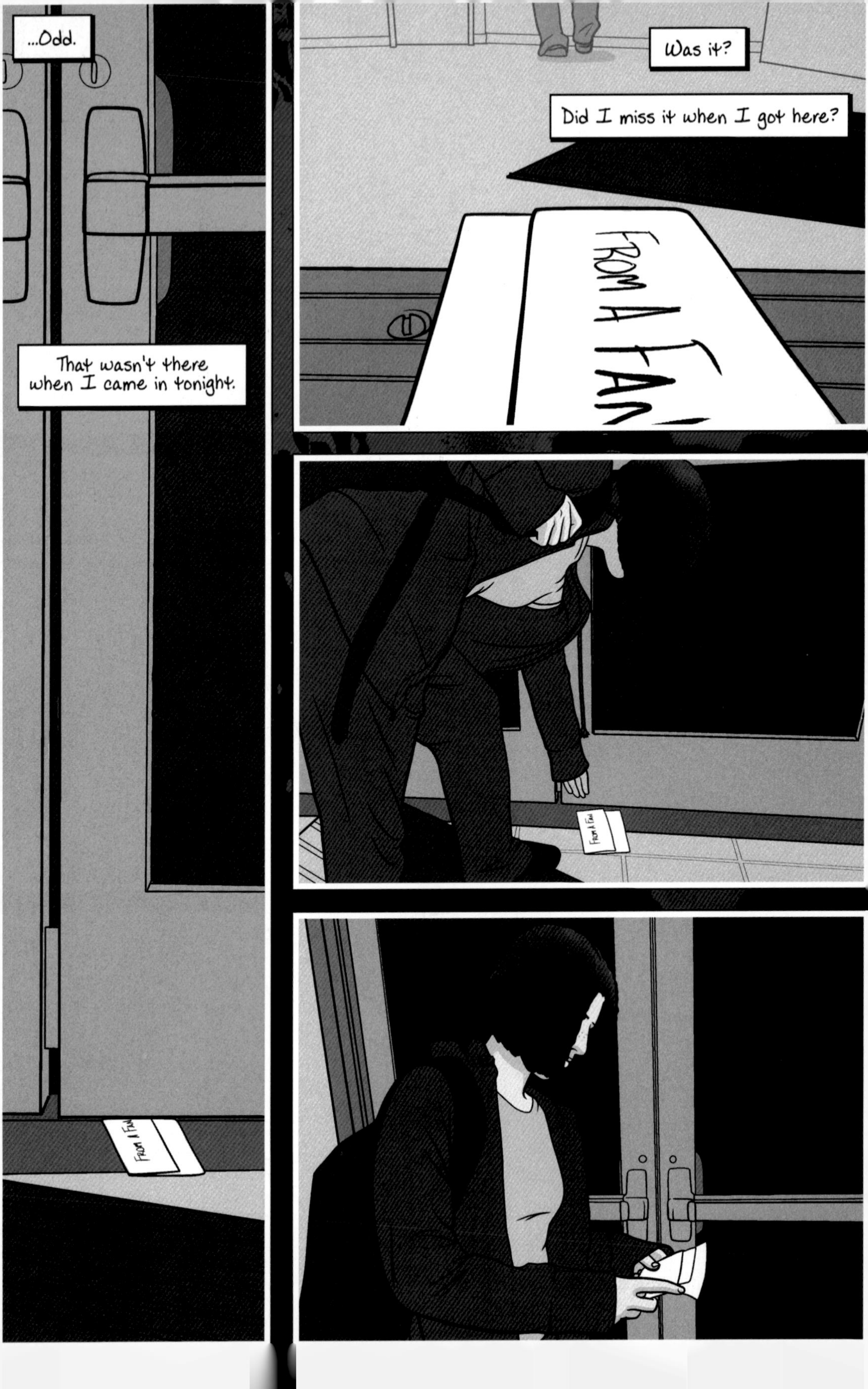
...Odd.
That wasn't there when I came in tonight.
Was it?
Did I miss it when I got here?
FROM A FAN

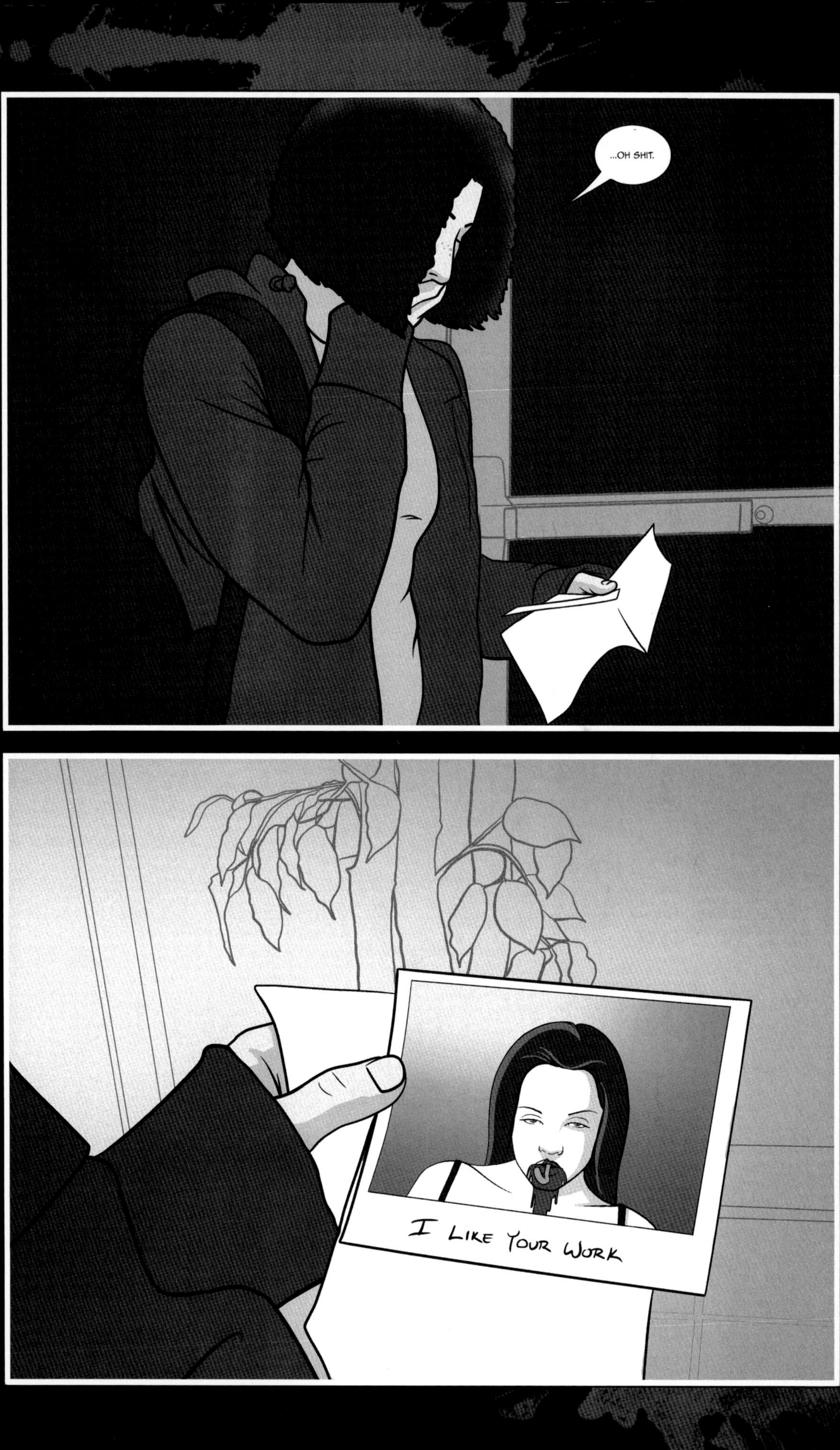
...OH SHIT.
I LIKE YOUR WORK

"Trophy Hunter" Still Silent

Staff Writer | October 12, 2013 | 21 comments

CUTTER'S CIRCLE - Over a month has passed since the killer known as the Trophy Hunter has killed, and police have no explanation as to why he stopped as suddenly as he started. After killing three young women in two weeks, fears were that his murder spree would only get worse in the days to come, but after the murder of Tess Turner there has not been another victim. Authorities say it is unlikely that he is hiding the bodies of new victims as all indications are that he wanted the attention that displaying them in public brought him. They also say it is unlikely that he quit of his own choice.

"Killers like this one, they don't just stop, not when they're getting the kind of attention he was getting," said Detective Sergeant Ezekiel Aarons of the CCPD. "They crave the spotlight. He was killing frequently. It doesn't make sense for him to just walk away now."

Possible theories include the chance that he was arrested on some other charge and is currently in custody without anyone knowing of the full extent of his crimes. No DNA has been left at the crime scenes, so even if he is in custody, there's no way to identify him at this time.

Anyone with information is encouraged to call the CCPD tip line at 555-8344. The victims' families are offering a $500k reward for information leading to a conviction.

Katelyn Miller (left), and Luna Weaks (center), and Tess Turner (right)

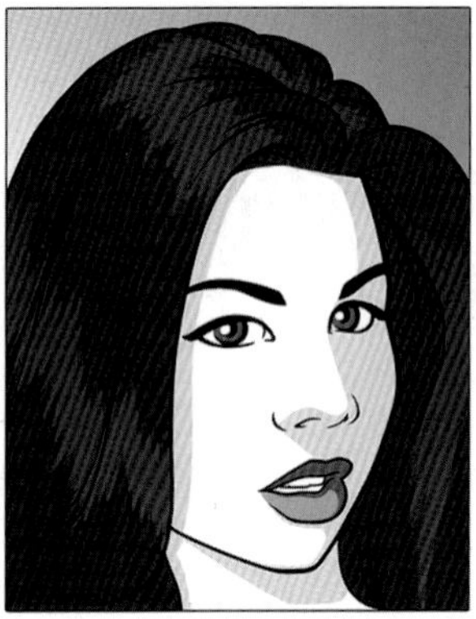
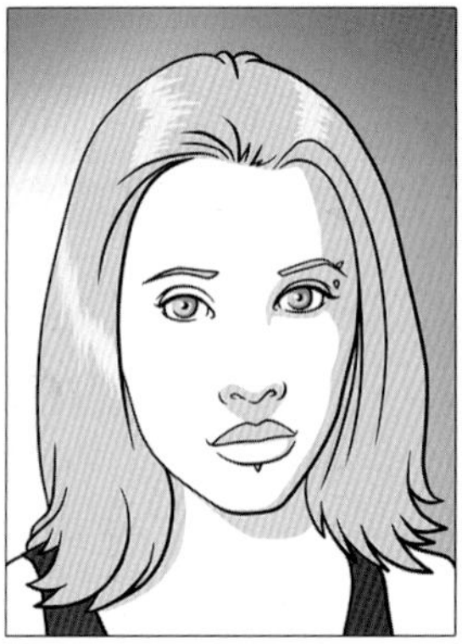
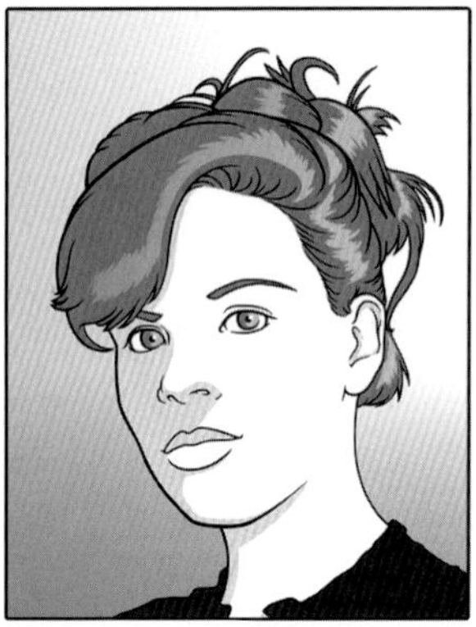

"Heather" Trial To Start In December

Staff Writer | October 12, 2013 | 87 comments

RIVERSIDE - Jessica Lindy, 18, the young woman accused of murdering her parents while on the phone with a local anonymous call-in show, is set to stand trial starting on November 20th in Riverside County Superior Court. The defense has indicated that they intend to establish a history of abuse that led Lindy to kill her parents in state of temporary insanity.

Mitchell "Mitch" Lindy, the accused's father, was a well-known local celebrity representing some of the biggest names in music. The murder sent shockwaves through the community, and is believed to be tied to the attempted suicide of Lindy's fellow Lakeside High classmate Trinna Goff.

a VOICE in the DARK

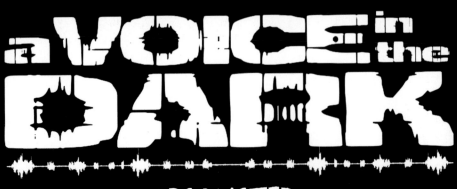

GRAY MATTER

ABOUT THE CREATOR

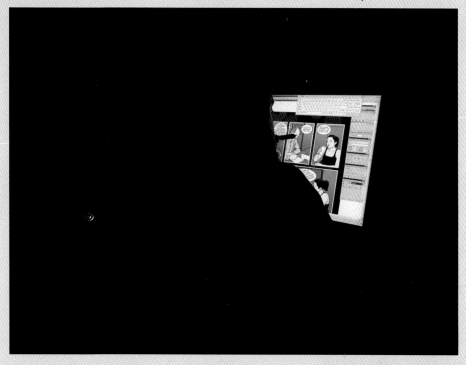

Creator Larime Taylor grew up on the deadpan humor of eighties cult classic *Heathers*, the quirky absurdism of *Edward Scissorhands*, and far too many bad slasher flicks. Mixing tongue-in-cheek black comedy with gritty drama and suspense, his resulting creation proudly wears its influences on its sleeve. He writes, draws, tones, and letters the book himself with his mouth.

Larime Taylor is a disabled mouth artist born with Arthrogryposis and lives in Las Vegas. Life on $750 a month from Social Security isn't easy, so he supplements his income with his art. Larime draws with his mouth on a Wacom Cintiq tablet generously provided by Wacom.

CHARACTER DESIGNS

In the early stages of development I did a number of pinups and templates for the characters to help me flesh out who they were. I thought you might like to see some of these early designs.

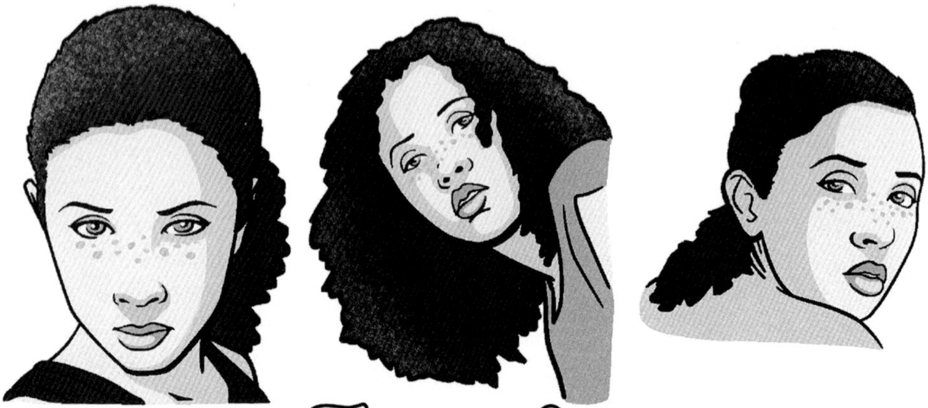

Zoey Aarons

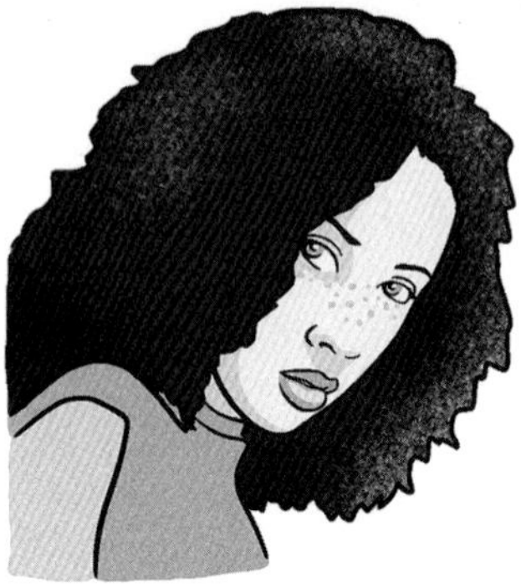

AGE: 18
HEIGHT: 5'9
HAIR: AUBURN
EYES: GREEN

DATE OF BIRTH: OCTOBER 14TH
BIRTHPLACE: SEATTLE, WA
YEAR: FRESHMAN
MAJOR: UNDECLARED

ZOEY IS YOUNGER THAN HER THREE QUADMATES AND THE ONLY FRESHMAN OF THE BUNCH. SHY, QUIET, AND SOMETIMES MOODY, SHE HAS SOME ADJUSTING TO DO, GROWING UP AS AN ONLY CHILD UNTIL HER FAMILY ADOPTED HER BEST AND ONLY REAL FRIEND, SEVEN, JUST OVER A YEAR AGO.

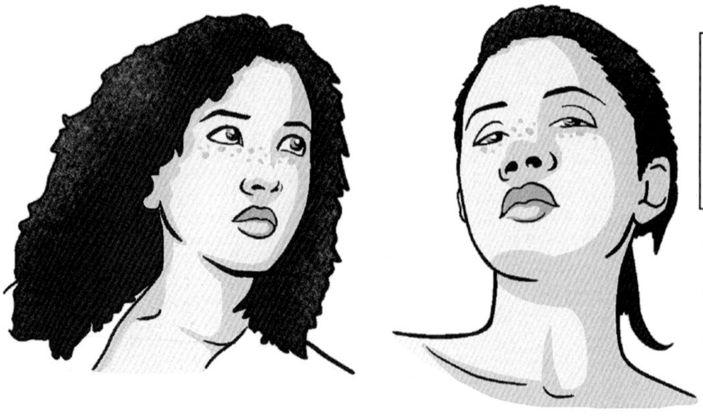

"THE SUMMER BEFORE I STARTED COLLEGE, I KILLED SOMEONE. IT WAS MY FIRST TIME."

"REAL-LIFE NEVER QUITE GOES LIKE PLAYTIME."

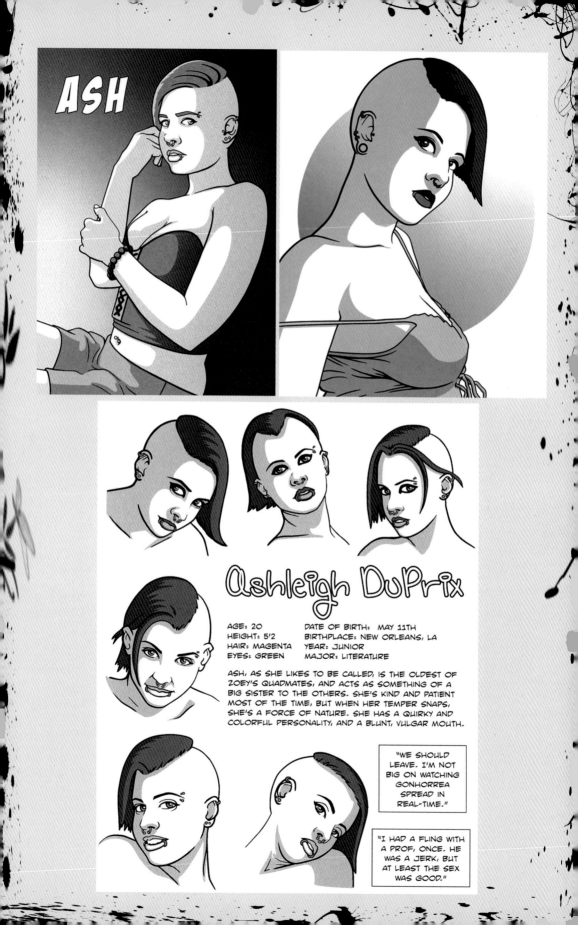

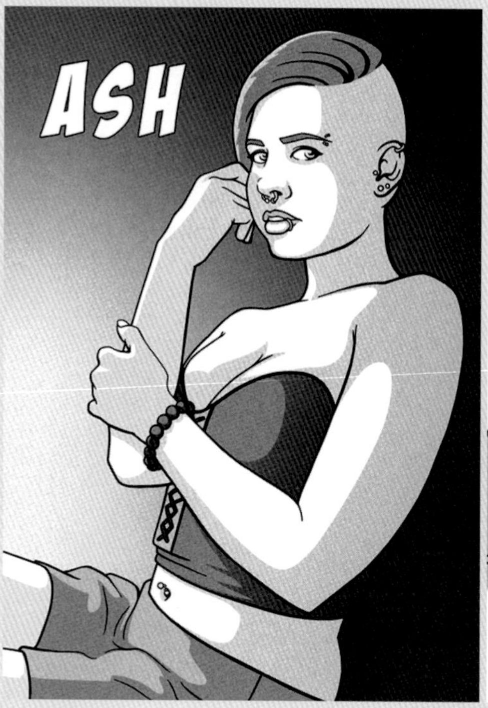
ASH

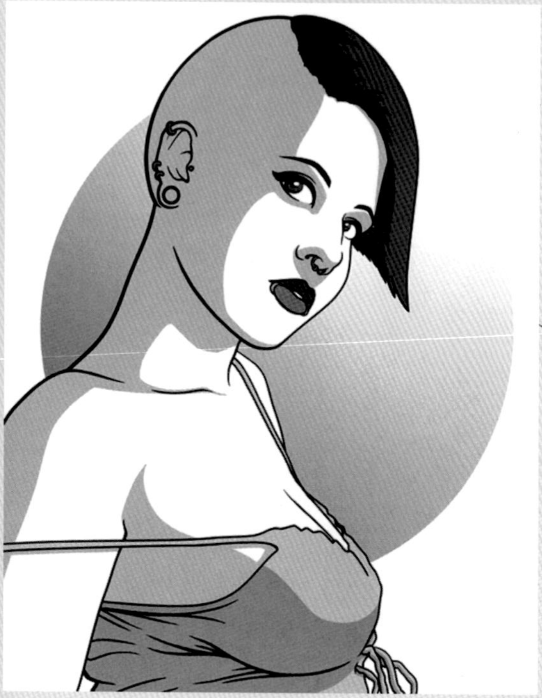

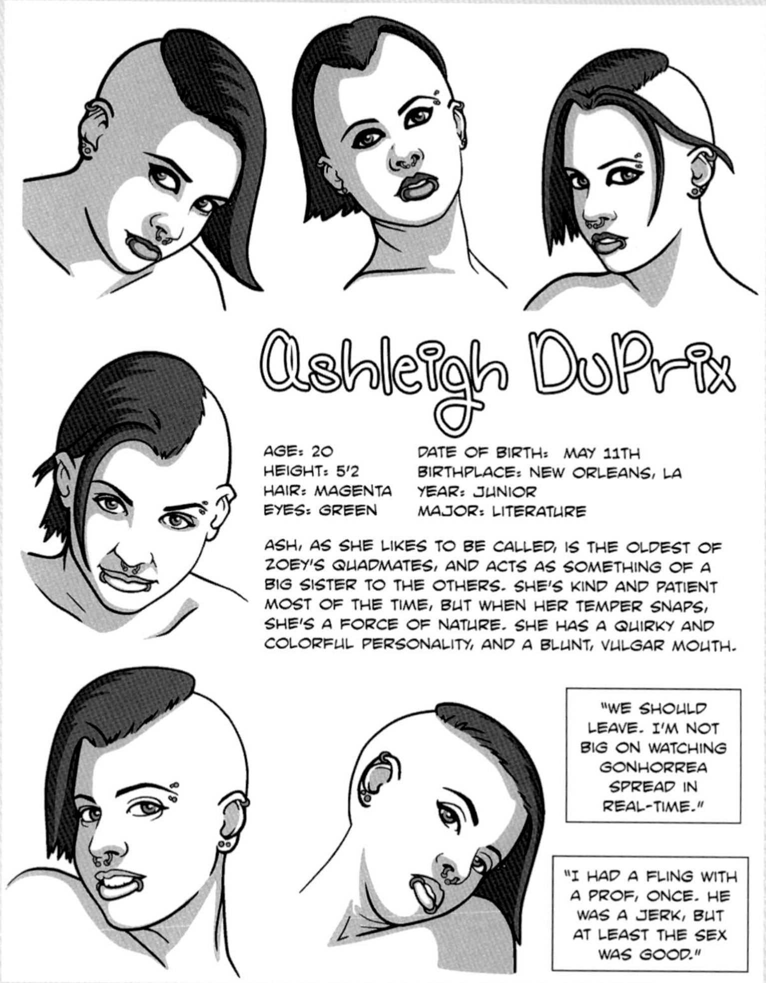
Ashleigh DuPrix
AGE: 20
HEIGHT: 5'2
HAIR: MAGENTA
EYES: GREEN
DATE OF BIRTH: MAY 11TH
BIRTHPLACE: NEW ORLEANS, LA
YEAR: JUNIOR
MAJOR: LITERATURE
ASH, AS SHE LIKES TO BE CALLED, IS THE OLDEST OF ZOEY'S QUADMATES, AND ACTS AS SOMETHING OF A BIG SISTER TO THE OTHERS. SHE'S KIND AND PATIENT MOST OF THE TIME, BUT WHEN HER TEMPER SNAPS, SHE'S A FORCE OF NATURE. SHE HAS A QUIRKY AND COLORFUL PERSONALITY, AND A BLUNT, VULGAR MOUTH.
"WE SHOULD LEAVE. I'M NOT BIG ON WATCHING GONHORREA SPREAD IN REAL-TIME."
"I HAD A FLING WITH A PROF, ONCE. HE WAS A JERK, BUT AT LEAST THE SEX WAS GOOD."

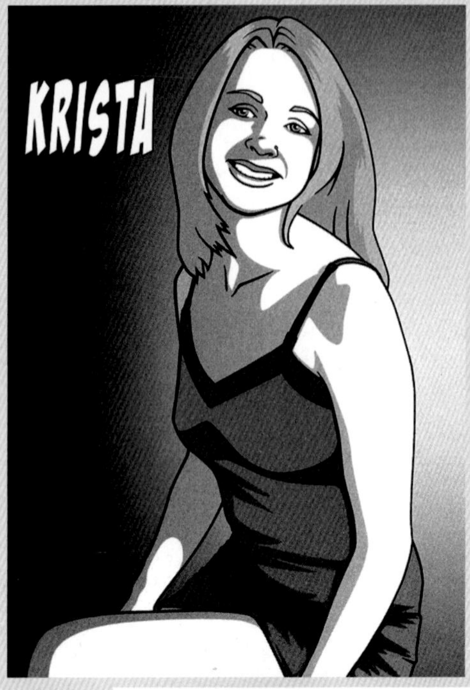
KRISTA

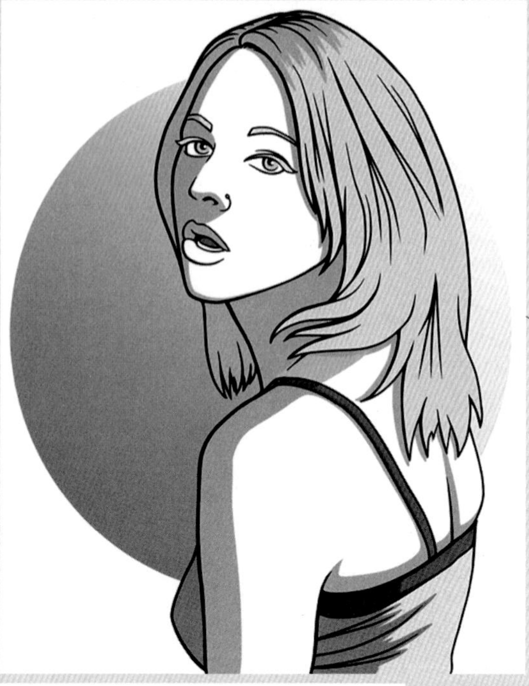

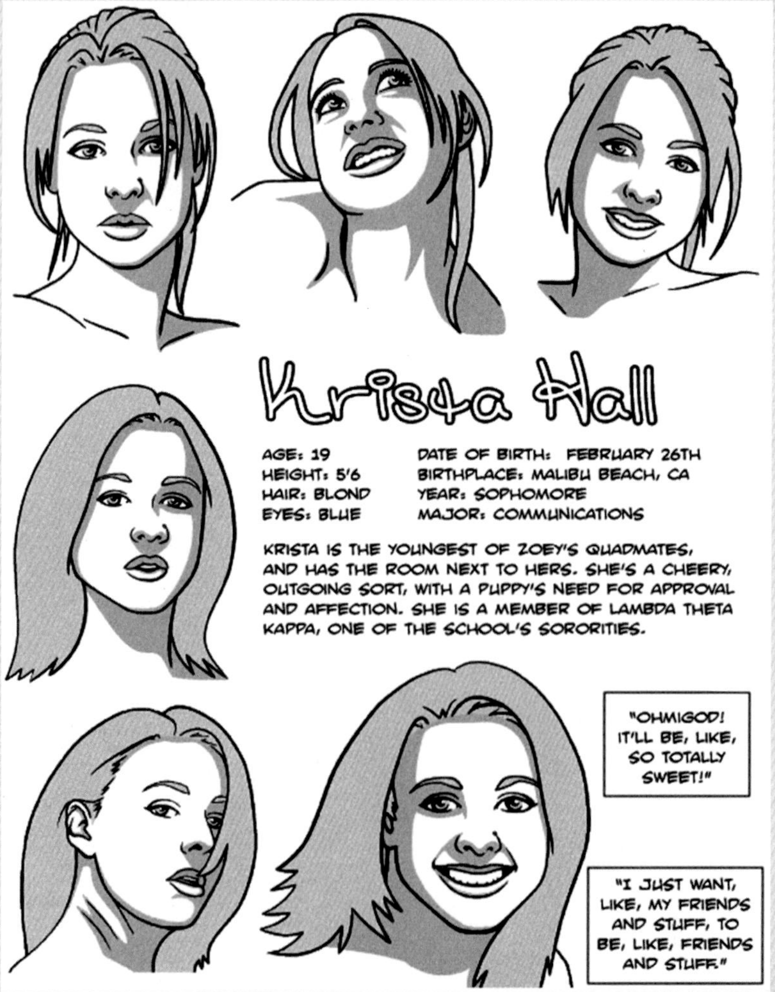
Krista Hall
AGE: 19
HEIGHT: 5'6
HAIR: BLOND
EYES: BLUE
DATE OF BIRTH: FEBRUARY 26TH
BIRTHPLACE: MALIBU BEACH, CA
YEAR: SOPHOMORE
MAJOR: COMMUNICATIONS
KRISTA IS THE YOUNGEST OF ZOEY'S QUADMATES, AND HAS THE ROOM NEXT TO HERS. SHE'S A CHEERY, OUTGOING SORT, WITH A PUPPY'S NEED FOR APPROVAL AND AFFECTION. SHE IS A MEMBER OF LAMBDA THETA KAPPA, ONE OF THE SCHOOL'S SORORITIES.
"OHMIGOD! IT'LL BE, LIKE, SO TOTALLY SWEET!"
"I JUST WANT, LIKE, MY FRIENDS AND STUFF, TO BE, LIKE, FRIENDS AND STUFF."

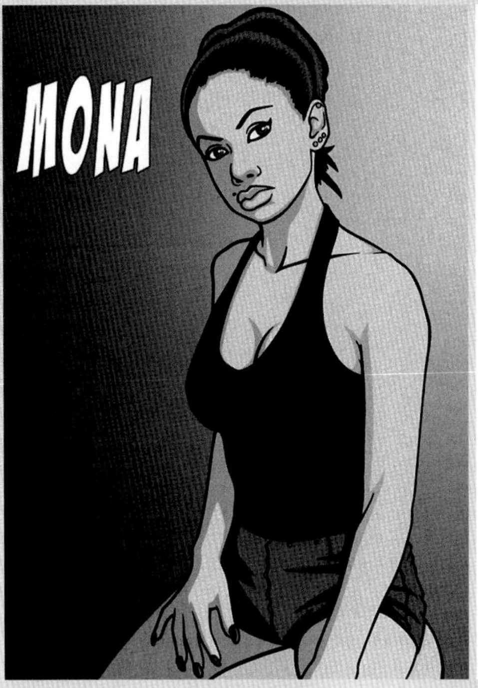
MONA

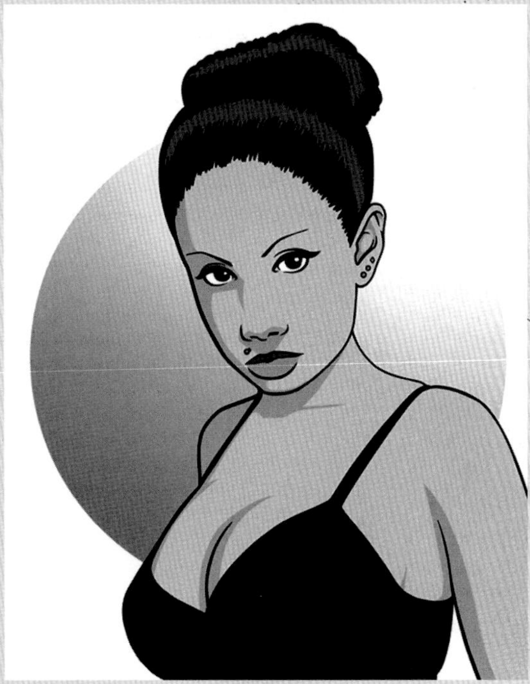

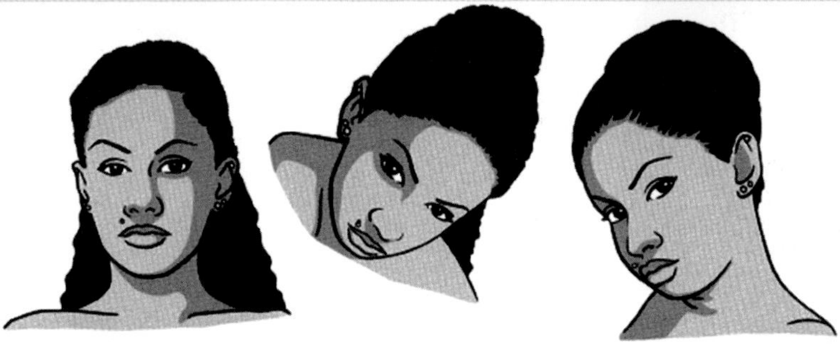

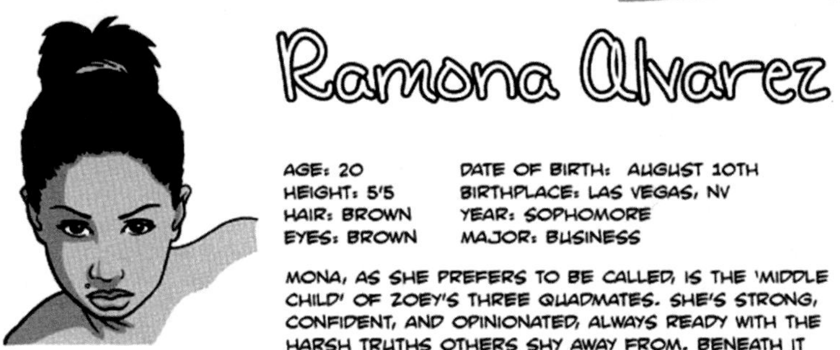

Ramona Alvarez

AGE: 20
HEIGHT: 5'5
HAIR: BROWN
EYES: BROWN

DATE OF BIRTH: AUGUST 10TH
BIRTHPLACE: LAS VEGAS, NV
YEAR: SOPHOMORE
MAJOR: BUSINESS

MONA, AS SHE PREFERS TO BE CALLED, IS THE 'MIDDLE CHILD' OF ZOEY'S THREE QUADMATES. SHE'S STRONG, CONFIDENT, AND OPINIONATED, ALWAYS READY WITH THE HARSH TRUTHS OTHERS SHY AWAY FROM. BENEATH IT SHE'S A GENTLE AND SUPPORTIVE FRIEND TO THOSE SHE LETS GET CLOSE TO HER.

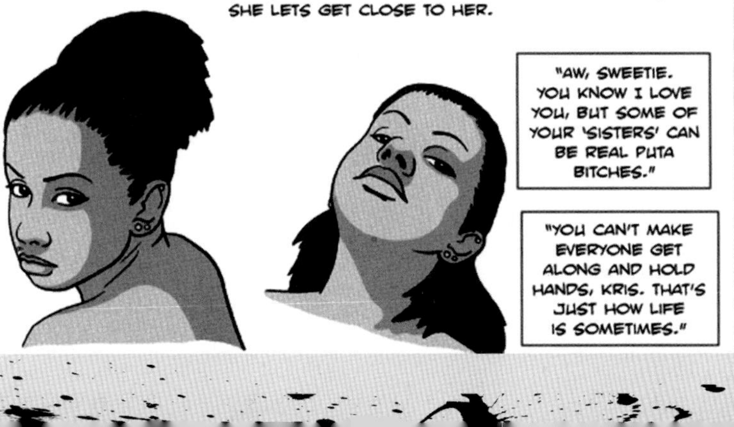

"AW, SWEETIE. YOU KNOW I LOVE YOU, BUT SOME OF YOUR 'SISTERS' CAN BE REAL PUTA BITCHES."

"YOU CAN'T MAKE EVERYONE GET ALONG AND HOLD HANDS, KRIS. THAT'S JUST HOW LIFE IS SOMETIMES."

SEVEN

Seven Aarons

AGE: 17
HEIGHT: 5'5
HAIR: BLACK
EYES: BROWN

DATE OF BIRTH: DECEMBER 20TH
BIRTHPLACE: SEATTLE, WA
YEAR: HIGHSCHOOL SENIOR
BORN: JAS SONG

SEVEN IS ZOEY'S BEST FRIEND AND ADOPTED KID SISTER. THE CHILD OF CAMBODIAN IMMIGRANTS, SHE WAS DISOWNED AFTER SHE WAS OUTED AT SCHOOL AS A LESBIAN. ZOEY'S FAMILY ADOPTED HER AND SHE CHANGED HER NAME TO DISTANCE HERSELF FROM HER PAST.

"I'VE NEVER EVEN SEEN YOU HAVE A CRUSH ON SOMEONE! YOU COULD BE A NUN!"

"...YOU AREN'T LEAVING BECAUSE OF ME, RIGHT?"

ZOEY'S EVOLUTION

A look at how I've drawn Zoey, from early designs through issue seven.

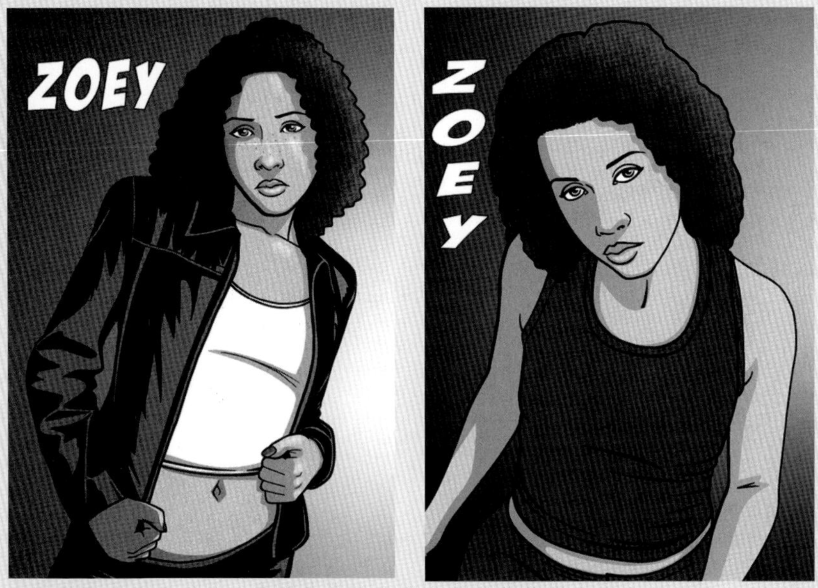
ZOEY
ZOEY

Original concept designs, 2012

Once I settled on the basic look, I did many drawings of her from many different angles to help me to become consistent at it.

The idea started as a parody of the 80s and 90s slasher film genre, and the big trope is that the ethnic girl always dies first, so in my story she would be the sole survivor.

Eventually I began to toy with the idea that she survives because she's the real killer. It all grew out of that flash of inspiration.

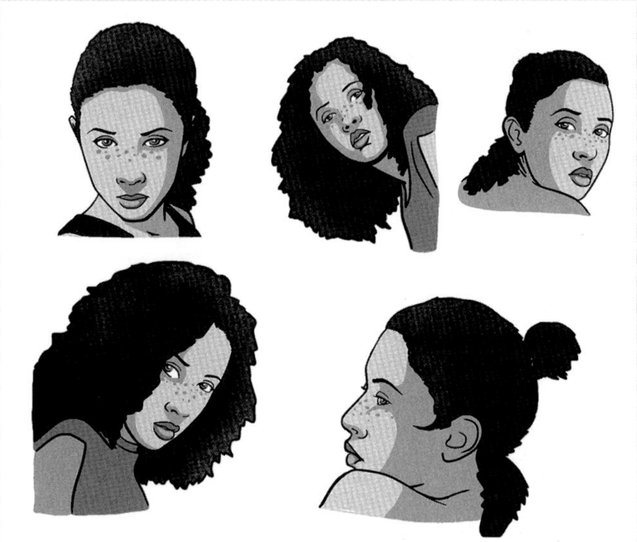

In the earliest pages, what was initially the Kickstarter material called *BLOOD MAKES NOISE*, I was drawing at 300dpi, which is fairly standard, though some artists like Colleen Doran draw at much higher resolution. I soon learned why as I was often frustrated with my line weighting and lack of fine detail.

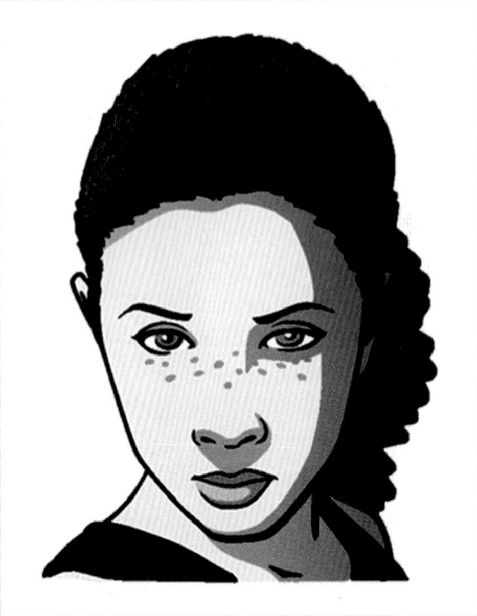

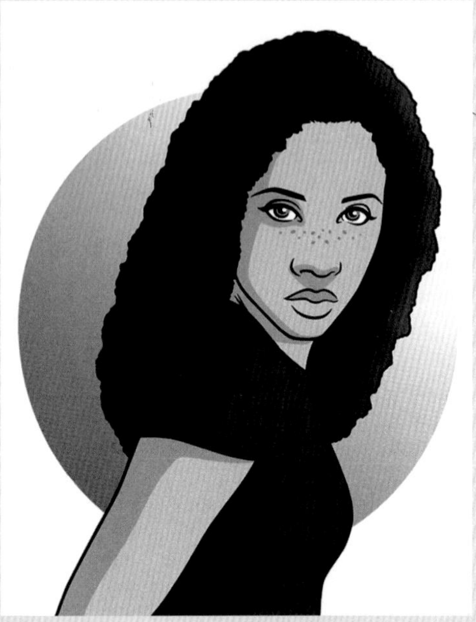

Zoey drawn at 300dpi (left) versus Zoey drawn at 600dpi (right).

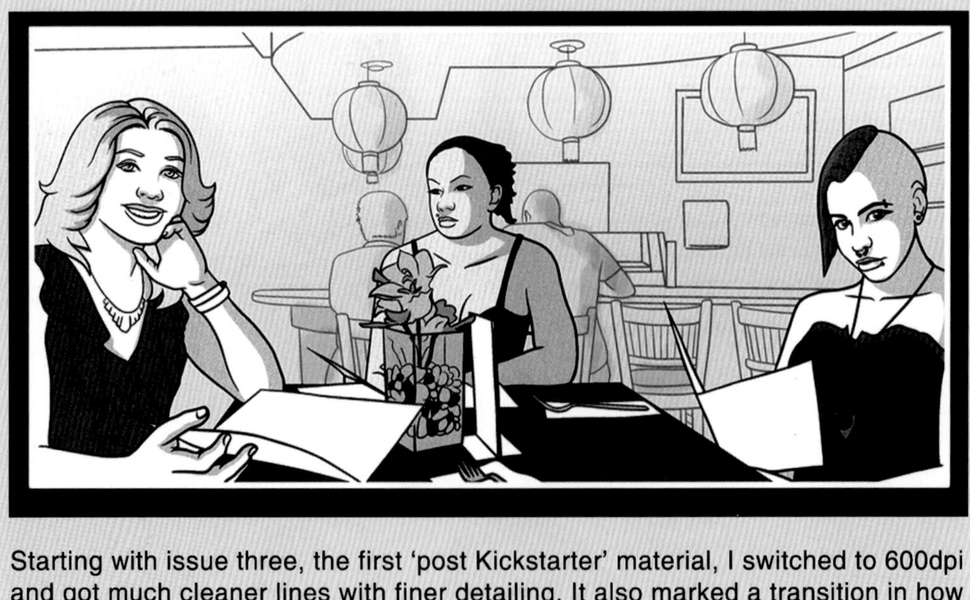

Starting with issue three, the first 'post Kickstarter' material, I switched to 600dpi and got much cleaner lines with finer detailing. It also marked a transition in how I drew the backgrounds, switching to lighter gray lines and a washed out style of shading. The above Hot Wok (a real restaurant!) panel was my first test of the new style. I felt that it gave greater depth and separation of foreground and background and made the figures pop more to the front.

In issue five I decided to give Zoey a haircut and new hairstyles, in part just to mix things up a bit, and in part to reflect Zoey starting to seek a sense of self and identity now that she's a young woman on her own in the wortld. Again I went through several versions to try and find the look I wanted.

My first few attempts were too far off in different directions, but the panels on the left are better. I finally found the look I was going for. I wanted to put more focus on her mixed ethnicity and find a look that complimented her face. Zoey should be pretty, but an unconventional pretty. She's exotic, not a supermodel. She tends to not bother with her hair or make-up because she doesn't think she's attractive, when in fact she is. She's more beautiful than she believes she is, and I like that. I like having a character that looks like a real and natural young woman. I take pride in the diversity of my characters and the real body types they all have.

I even let Zoey smile in a rare, fleeting moment.

By issue seven I had a pretty solid, consistent look for Zoey that I'll probably stick with for a while. Maybe she'll change more in future issues, still searching for her own identity in life. Maybe she'll get piercings or tattoos. Who knows?

MY PROCESS

By now most of you probably know that I'm disabled and draw with my mouth. I thought I'd share a few examples of how a page takes shape and explain a bit about my process. Because I can't do what most artists do and model myself, I take reference photos of friends and build my pages from there.

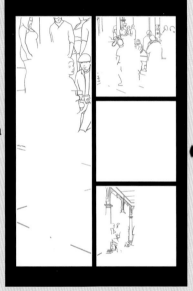

I tend to draw the backgrounds first as I find that the most boring. If I drew all the characters first I would never end up doing backgrounds if I'm honest! I do all the backgrounds in a lighter gray so it will fade to the back.

Next I do all of my figures in the foreground and any set pieces that are up close, like the wall that Ash and Zoey are hiding behind. By doing them in black, it makes them appear closer to us.

Lastly I do the tones. I used to hate this part most of all as it can be so tedious, but now I just zone out and play movies or TV shows while I work and kind of go on autopilot.

Last comes lettering, and then I do all the post-production and filter work.

THOSE PRETTY COVERS

The secret to those gorgeous covers you see on the monthlies pretty much comes down to my wife Sylv. She's legally blind, so she has to squint one eye and put her nose about two inches from the screen, and yet she creates magic from the very mediocre lines I give her to work with. She makes me look good, and you can rejoice in knowing that the next arc will be in color done by her. It's only black and white, but here are some before and after looks at the covers she's done.

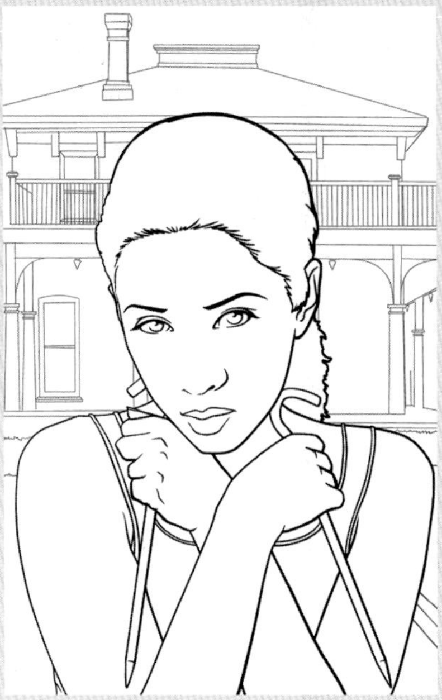

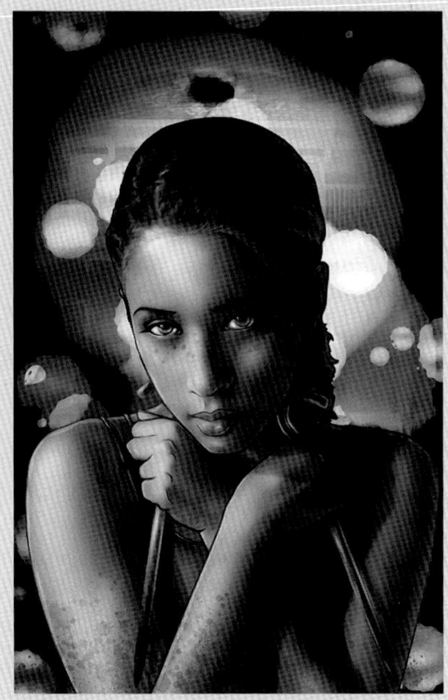

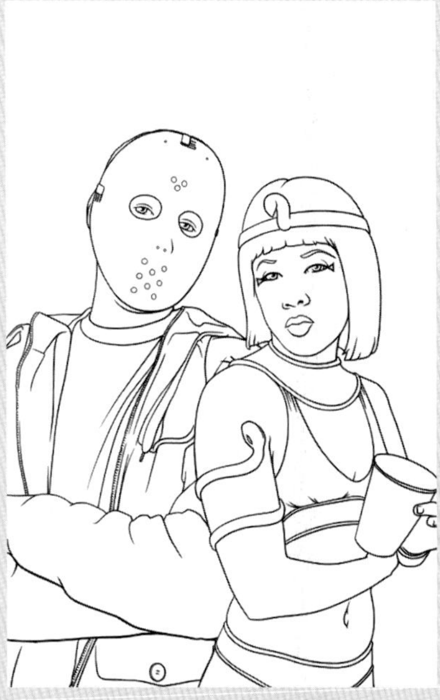

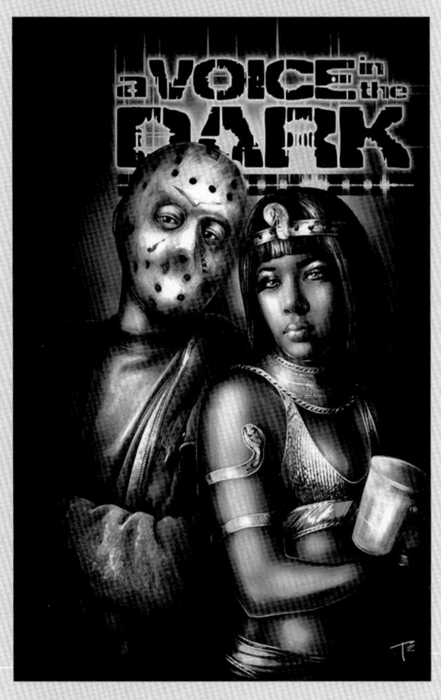
a VOICE in the DARK

a VOICE in the DARK

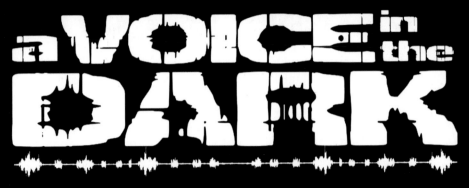

COVER GALLERY

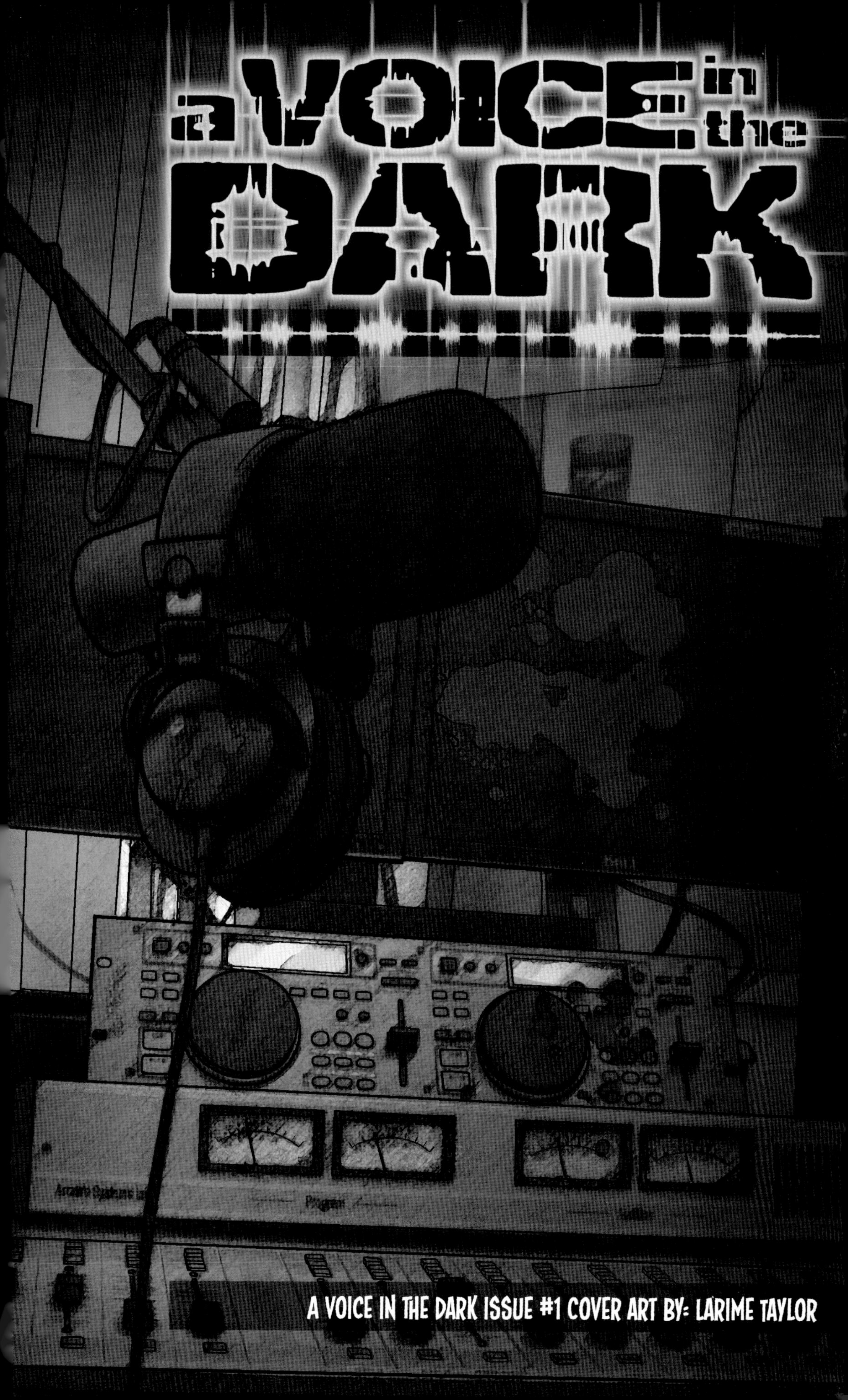
a VOICE in the DARK

A VOICE IN THE DARK ISSUE #1 COVER ART BY: LARIME TAYLOR

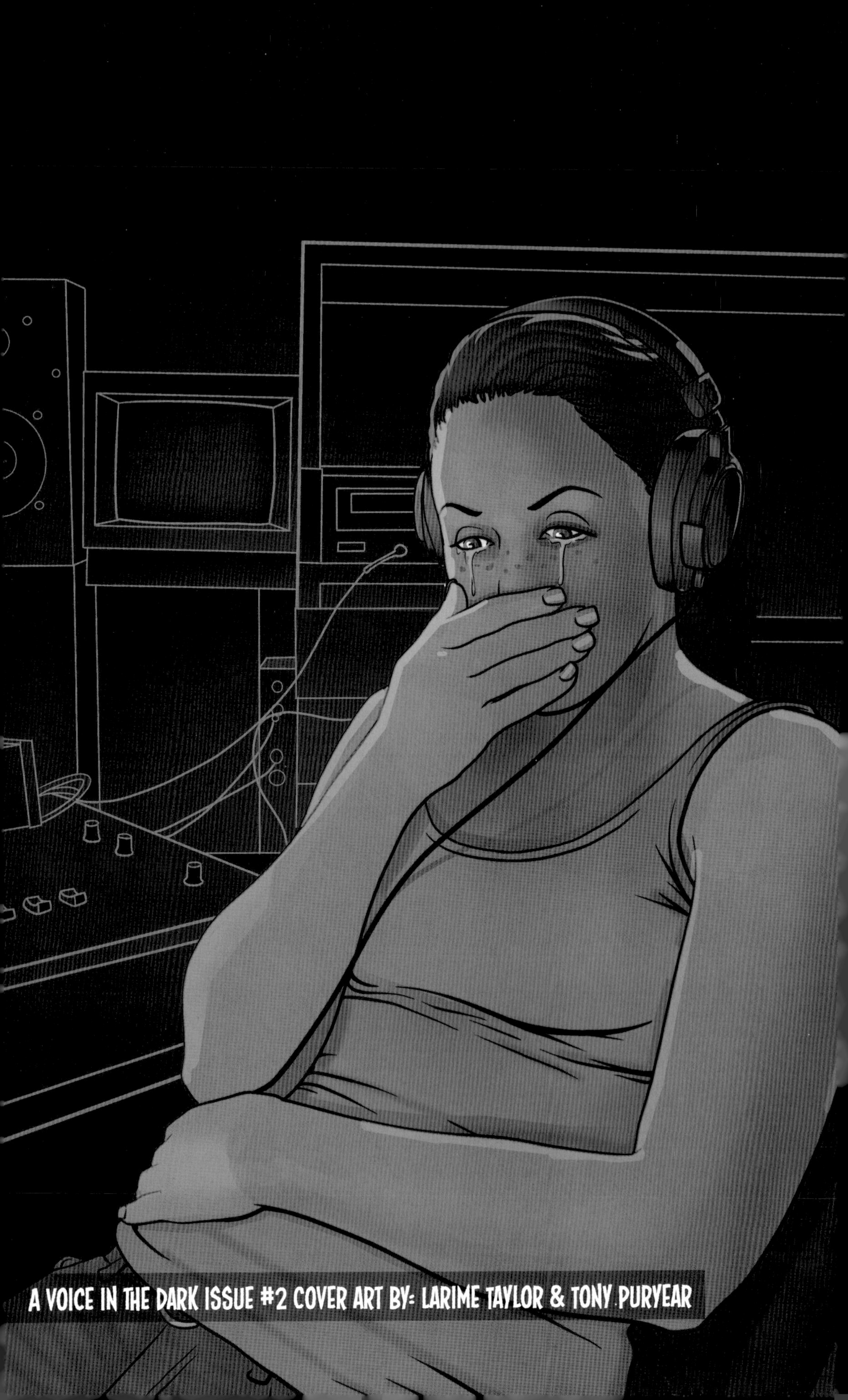

A VOICE IN THE DARK ISSUE #2 COVER ART BY: LARIME TAYLOR & TONY PURYEAR

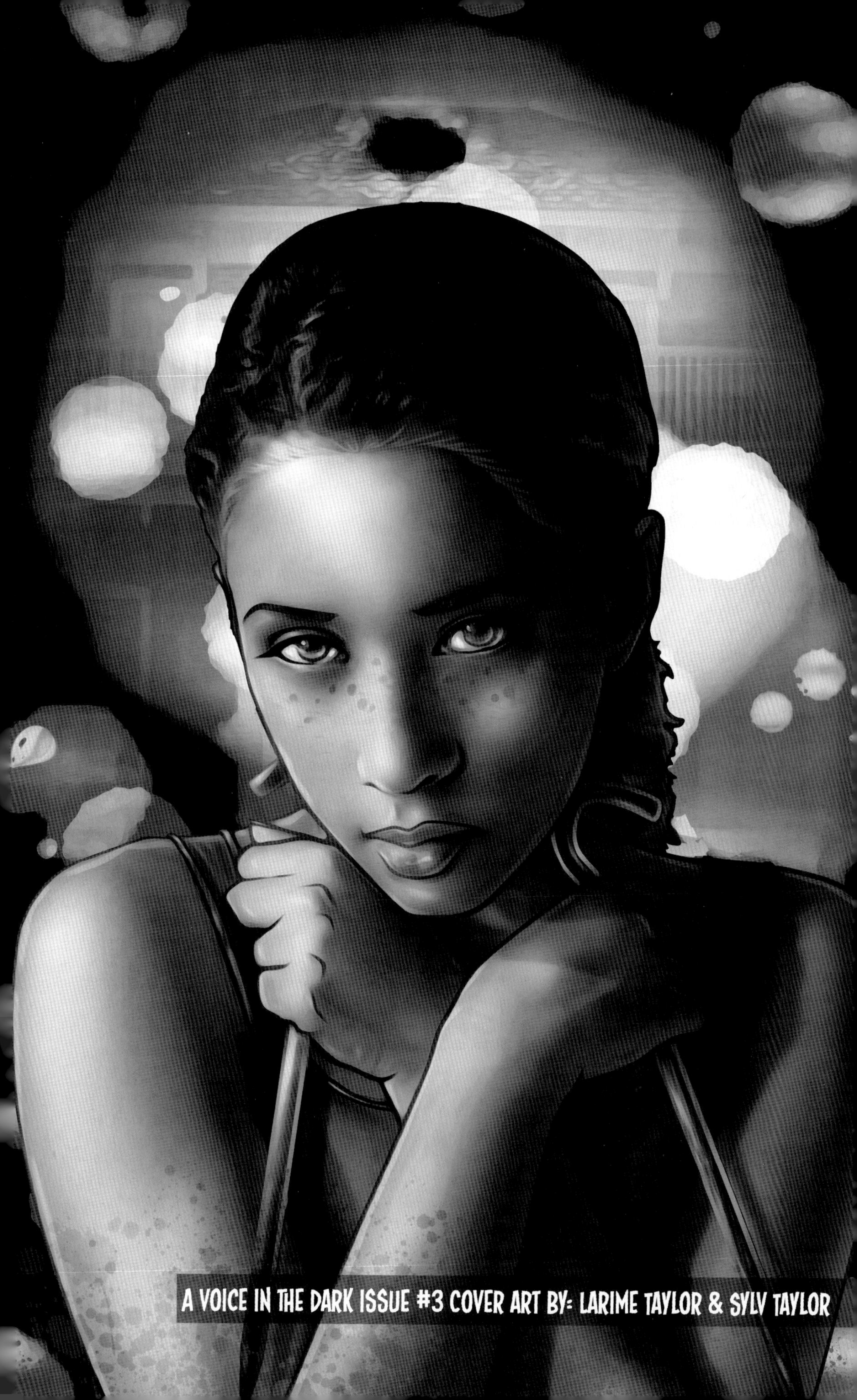

A VOICE IN THE DARK ISSUE #3 COVER ART BY: LARIME TAYLOR & SYLV TAYLOR

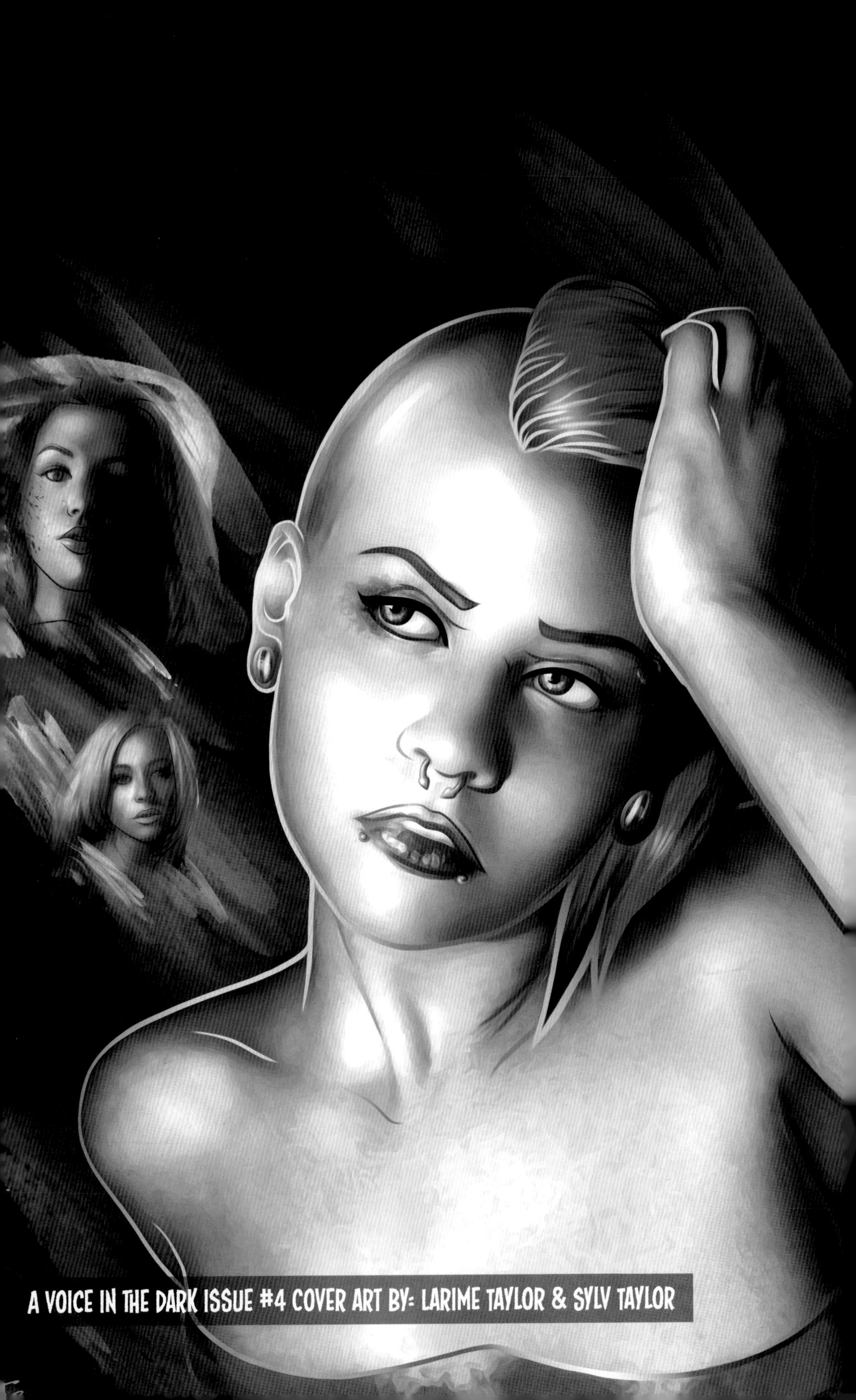

A VOICE IN THE DARK ISSUE #4 COVER ART BY: LARIME TAYLOR & SYLV TAYLOR

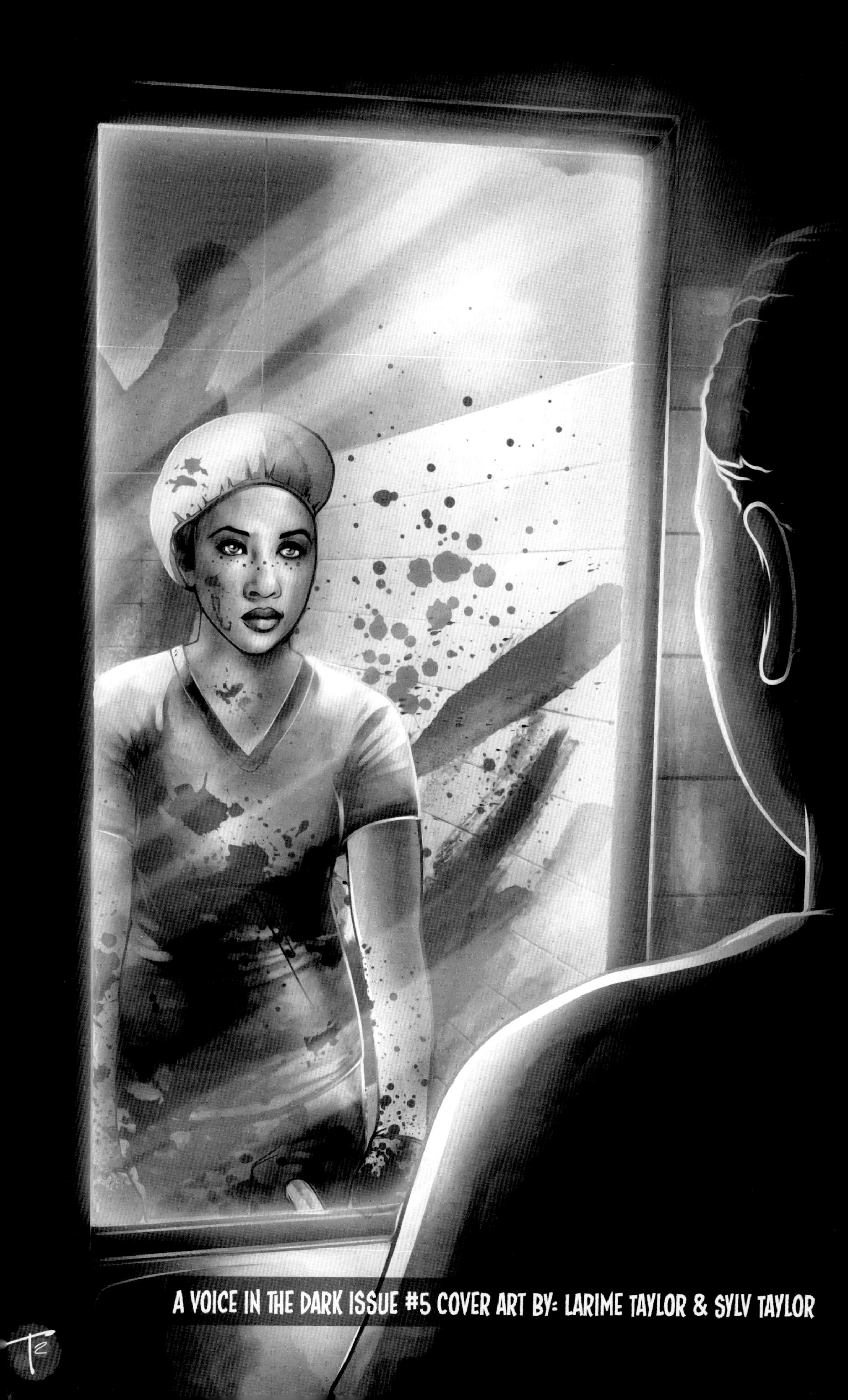
T2

A VOICE IN THE DARK ISSUE #5 COVER ART BY: LARIME TAYLOR & SYLV TAYLOR

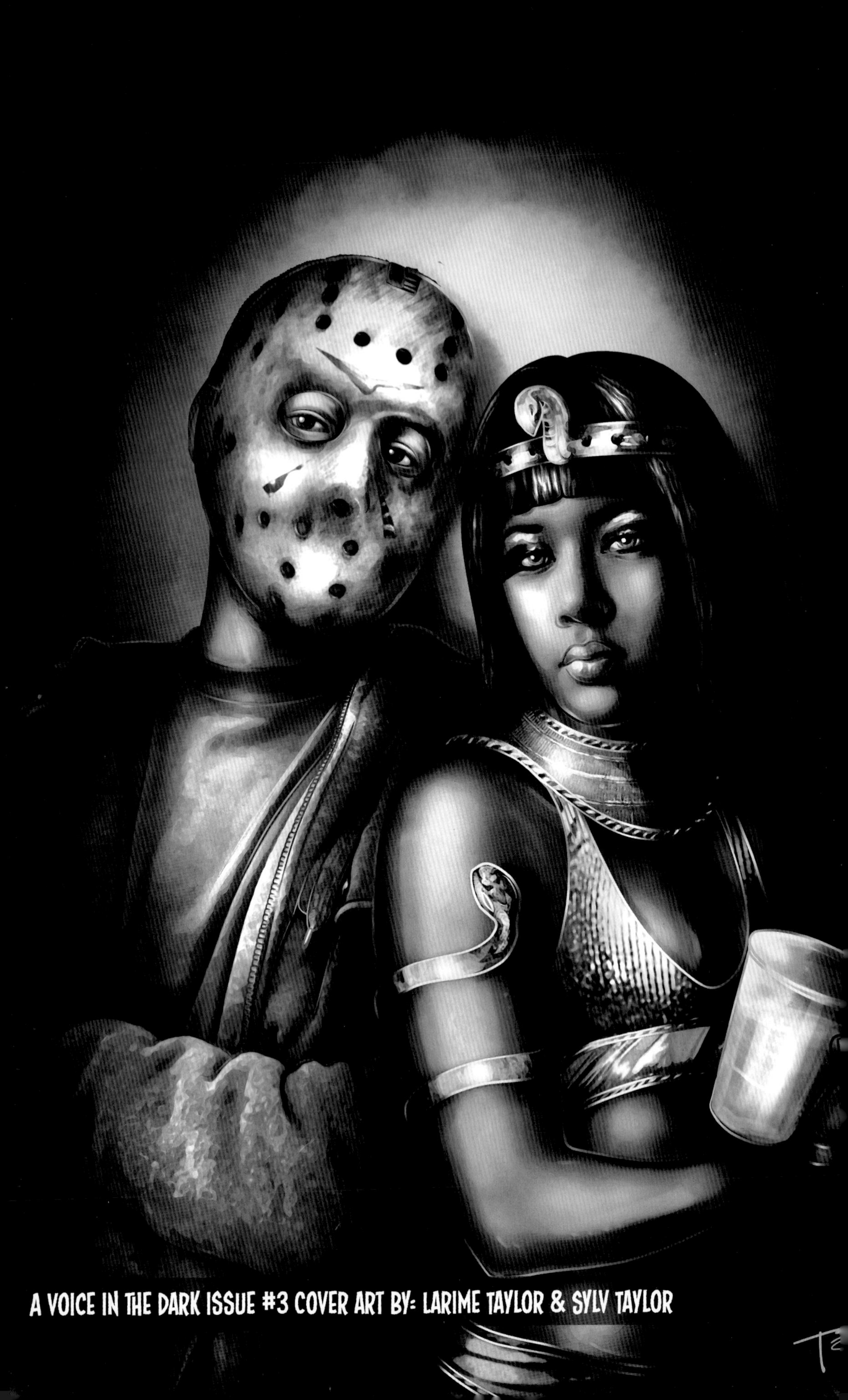

A VOICE IN THE DARK ISSUE #3 COVER ART BY: LARIME TAYLOR & SYLV TAYLOR

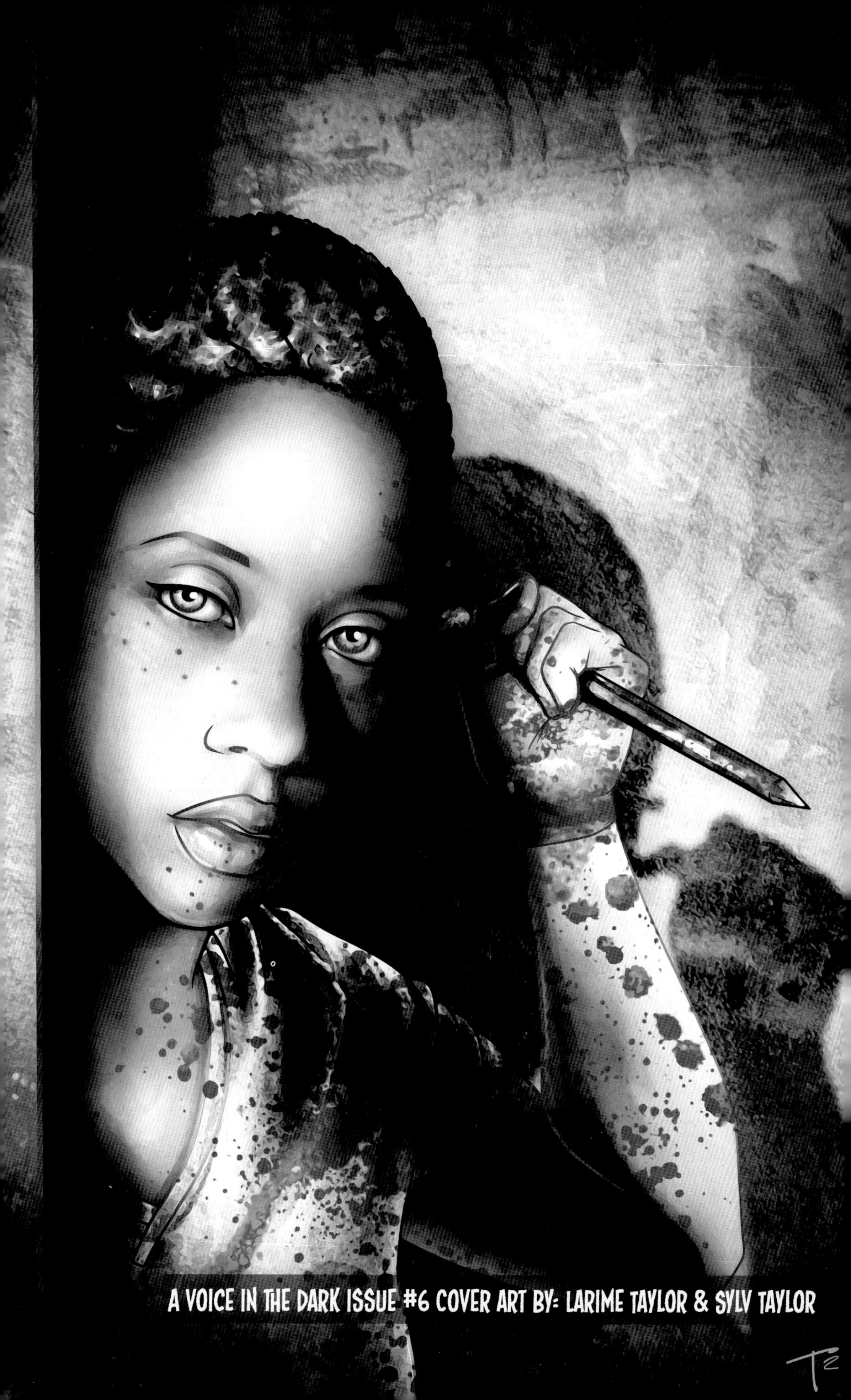

A VOICE IN THE DARK ISSUE #6 COVER ART BY: LARIME TAYLOR & SYLV TAYLOR

READ MORE TOP COW

INTRODUCTION BY STEVE NILES

ECHOES

Writer: Joshua Fialkov
Artist: Rahsan Ekedal

From acclaimed author JOSHUA HALE FIAKOV (Tumor, Pilot Season: Alibi) and rising artist RAHSAN EKEDAL (Creepy) a disturbing story of murder and mystery wrapped in questions of sanity. Minotaur Press premieres with a story of madness, family and death. Brian Cohn was learning to deal with the schizophrenia inherited from his father. Supportive wife, new baby on the way, drugs to control the voices. But, when at his father's deathbed, he learns that he also inherited the trophies of his father's career as a serial killer, his illness threatens to send him further down the path to madness?

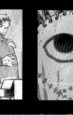

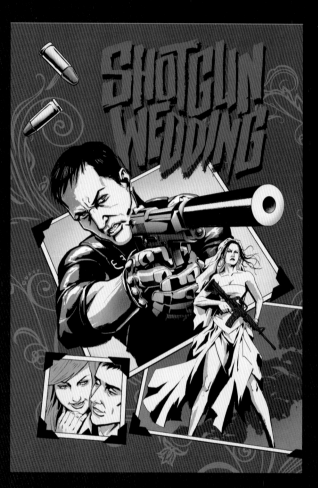

SHOTGUN WEDDING

Writer: William Harms
Artist: Edward Pun

Mike Stone wants nothing more than to marry the woman of his dreams. Denise is smart, sexy, teaches the second grade, and loves Mike more than anything in the world. What she doesn't know is that Mike is one of the world's top assassins and was once engaged to a fellow assassin named Chloe. And when Mike abandoned Chloe on their wedding day, she vowed revenge...

Collect all four issues of *Shotgun Wedding* to connect them to form one larger image.

READ MORE TOP CO

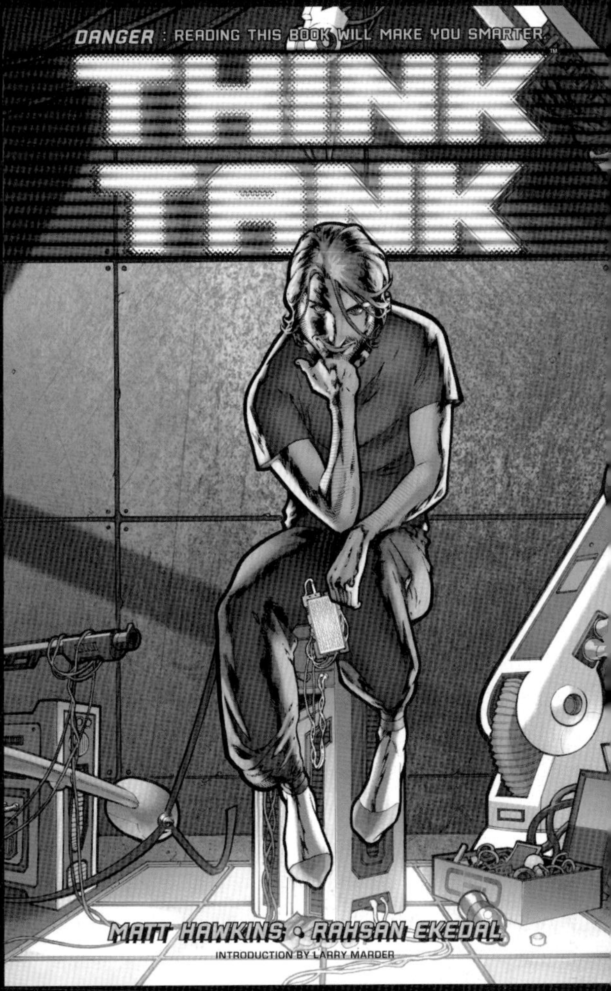
DANGER : READING THIS BOOK WILL MAKE YOU SMARTER
THINK TANK
MATT HAWKINS • RAHSAN EKEDAL
INTRODUCTION BY LARRY MARDER

THINK TANK

Writer: Matt Hawkins
Artist: Rahsan Ekedal
Cover: Rahsan Ekedal & Brian Reb

Dr. David Loren is many things: child prodigy, inven slacker... mass murderer. When a military think tank scientist decides he can no longer stomach creating destruction, will he be able to think his way out of h or find himself subject to the machinations of sm

Collecting the original series in its entirety, paperback also is jam packed with a complete co bonus articles behind-the-scenes sketches a

READ MORE TOP COW

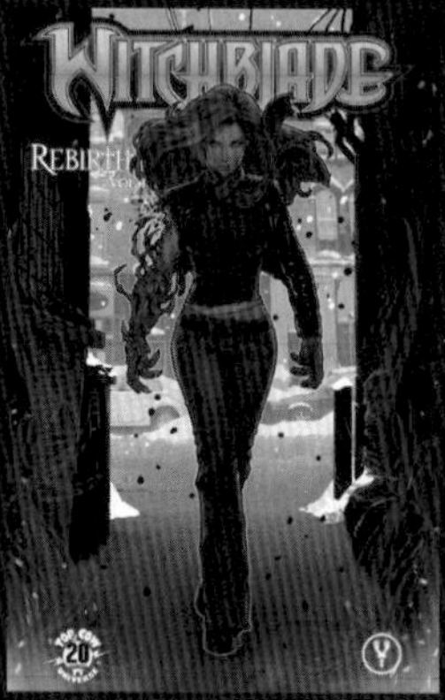
WITCHBLADE
REBIRTH

ISBN# 978-1-60706-532-6

WITCHBLADE REBIRTH VOLUME 1

Writer: Tim Seeley
Artists: Diego Bernard, Fred Benes, Arif Prianto

In the wake of Top Cow's REBIRTH, Sara Pezzini has relocated from New York to Chicago and struggles to adapt to being a private detective.

WITCHBLADE REBIRTH VOLUME 2

Writer: Tim Seeley
Artists: Diego Bernard, Fred Benes, Arif Prianto

This volume sees Sara Pezzini dealing with mercenary mana-hunters, spirit realms, fantastical steampunk warriors, and the most distilled embodiment of evil she's ever encountered.

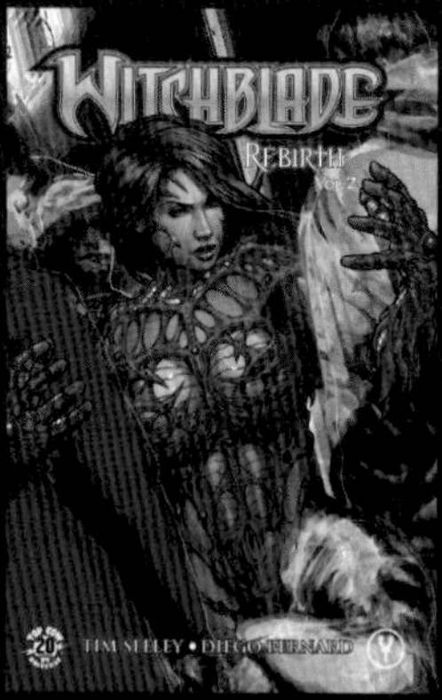
WITCHBLADE
REBIRTH

ISBN# 978-1-60706-637-8

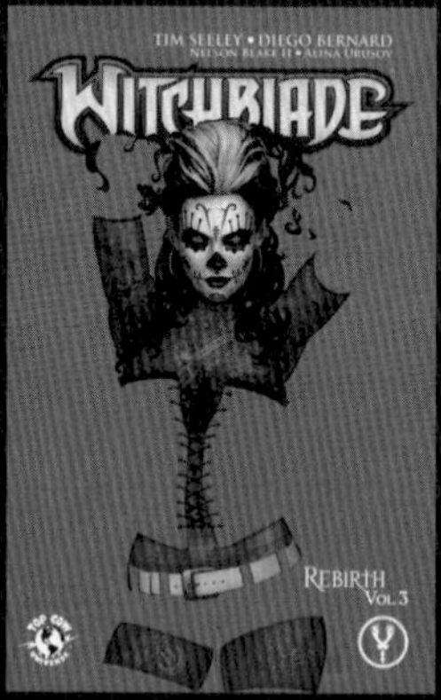
TIM SEELEY • DIEGO BERNARD
WITCHBLADE
REBIRTH
VOL. 3

ISBN# 978-1-60706-681-1

WITCHBLADE REBIRTH VOLUME 3

Writer: Tim Seeley
Artists: Diego Bernard, Fred Benes, Arif Prianto

Attempting to abandon her past and settle into a new life in Chicago, Sara Pezzini will have to contend against mercenaries, gangsters, and power hungry leprechauns, all while suffering the drudgeries of trying to stay profitable.

WITCHBLADE REBIRTH VOLUME 4

Writer: Tim Seeley
Artists: Diego Bernard, Fred Benes, Arif Prianto

It's all in a day's work for Sara Pezzini when Chicago is overrun with supernatural corruption and dark recreations of the Artifacts - including the devious "Anti-Magdalena" herself!

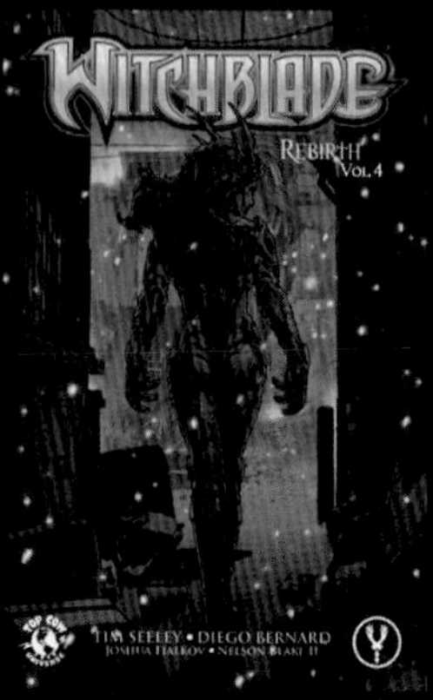
WITCHBLADE
REBIRTH
VOL. 4
TIM SEELEY • DIEGO BERNARD

ISBN# 978-1-60706-800-6

READ MORE TOP COW

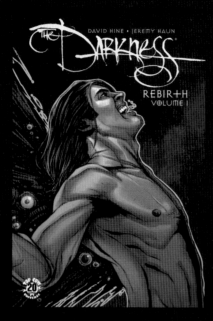

THE DARKNESS REBIRTH VOLUME 1

Writer: David Hine
Artists: Jeremy Haun, John Rauch

Hot on the heels of THE DARKNESS II video game release, this introductory-priced volume welcomes the new creative team of DAVID HINE (THE DARKNESS: FOUR HORSEMEN, THE BULLETPROOF COFFIN, Detective Comics) and JEREMY HAUN (ARTIFACTS, Detective Comics)! On the surface, Jackie Estacado has everything he ever wanted - control of the Darkness, a successful career, and happy family life. Only his desire to make his life truly perfect will be his undoing. What will Jackie do when everything begins to slip away?

THE DARKNESS REBIRTH VOLUME 2

Writer: David Hine
Artists: Jeremy Haun, John Rauch

Jackie Estacado had everything he ever wanted: riches, power, and a beautiful family. But Jackie relinquished his control of the Darkness. With his marriage crumbling and the encroachment of a rival gang on his turf, Jackie has failed to notice that there is something horribly, horribly wrong with his daughter, Hope. And Jackie will learn that there are things even the Darkness should fear.

READ MORE TOP C

Ron Marz • Michael Broussard
ARTIFACTS
volume 1
FEATURING AN INTRODUCTION BY
MARC SILVESTRI

ISBN# 978-1-60706-201-1

CATCH UP ON ARTIFACTS
VOLUME 1!

Writer: Ron Marz
Artists: Michael Broussard, Stjepan Sejic

Separately, thirteen mystical Artifacts will guide the fate
Together, thirteen Artifacts will end the Universe. When a my
kidnaps Hope, the daughter of Sara Pezzini and Jackie Esta
is put into motion. Starring virtually every character in the Top
is a series for diehard fans and new readers alike. Pick up Vol

Ron Marz • Whilce Portacio
ARTIFACTS
volume 2

ISBN# 978-1-60706-672-9

Ron Marz • Jeremy Haun • Dale Keown
ARTIFACTS
volume 3

ISBN# 978-1-60706-425-1

ARTIFACTS
volume 4
REBIRTH
Ron Marz • Stjepan Sejic

ISBN# 978-1-60706-562-3

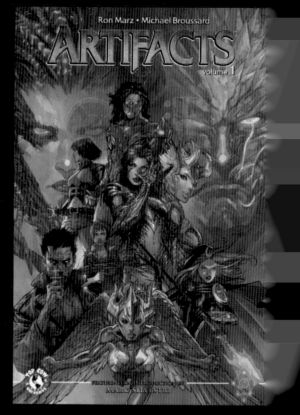